30-49

CASES IN INTERNATIONAL POLITICS

David V. Edwards, *General Editor*

ALLIANCES: LATENT WAR COMMUNITIES IN THE CONTEMPORARY WORLD

Edited by

Francis A. Beer
The University of Texas

HOLT, RINEHART AND WINSTON, INC.

New York Chicago San Francisco Atlanta
Dallas Montreal Toronto London Sydney

ALLIANCES: LATENT

WAR COMMUNITIES IN

THE CONTEMPORARY

WORLD

Alliances: Latent War Communities in the Contemporary World
Edited by Francis A. Beer

Copyright © 1970 by Holt, Rinehart and Winston, Inc.
Library of Congress Catalog Card Number: 70-111796
SBN: 03-076760-1
Printed in the United States of America
1 2 3 4 5 6 7 8 9

Preface

Alliances have been a part of international relations since the earliest recorded political and military relationships between complex communities. They remain important in the contemporary world, but two major characteristics are clearly new to the international scene. First, at least those alliances that include the largest nations have adapted to the changing technology of war by developing sophisticated strategies for the use of their members' nuclear capabilities. At the same time, in a world of proliferating international communities, alliances of more than two or three states have tended to generate complex standing bureaucracies.

This volume is intended as an introduction to contemporary alliances. Theoretically it focuses on two major aspects: conflict against external foes and cohesion among allies. It attempts to provide examples of analytical efforts that have appeared in the last several years, indicating the state of current theory and research; theoretical material is present in each essay. Substantively it presents materials that describe important alliances in three major international camps—West, East, and Third World—to give the reader a feel for concrete alliance processes. Additional descriptive materials appear in the appendixes, providing information for independent evaluation.

It is hoped that this book will be useful not only for generally interested readers, but also for teachers and students concerned with broad questions of international relations, national security, and international organization. It is among the first in a series of case materials in international politics under the general editorship of David V. Edwards. I would like to express my thanks for encouragement, criticism, and assistance both to him and to the members of the original seminar in which this book took form.

F.A.B.

Tunis, Tunisia
January 1970

Contents

ALLIANCES: LATENT WAR COMMUNITIES IN THE CONTEMPORARY WORLD

PART I

INTRODUCTION

After World War II the United States and the Soviet Union emerged as the dominant and competing poles of power in international politics. Each side constructed a series of alliances seeking to define its area of major security interest. The United States entered into agreements which did not irrevocably bind it to fight for its allies, but which indicated that American decision-makers, nevertheless, viewed this as a realistic possibility. In 1947, on the basis of a historical tradition of involvement in Latin America for over a century, the United States signed the Inter-American Treaty of Reciprocal Assistance (Rio Pact), undertaking to "assist in meeting [an] attack" against one of the other American states. Two years later it participated in the North Atlantic Treaty, which stated that the signer would take "individually and in concert with the other Parties, such action as it deems necessary, including the use of armed forces, to restore and maintain the security of the North Atlantic area." The United States was a party to the Australia-New Zealand-United States Security Treaty (ANZUS) in 1951, the Southeast Asia Collective Defense Treaty (SEATO) in 1954, and bilateral agreements with Iran, Pakistan, and Turkey in 1959, which brought it into relationship with the Central Treaty Organization (CENTO).

During this period the Soviet Union acted similarly. In 1950 it concluded a Treaty of Friendship, Alliance, and Mutual Assistance with the Chinese People's Republic, and in 1955 it joined with seven other Eastern European states in establishing the Warsaw Treaty Organization.

The nations of the third world also established international organi-

3

zations with alliance aspects. While security activities tended to be only one facet of these multipurpose institutions, and while the nations which composed them could not begin to match the sophistication in weapons technology of either of the superpowers, such groups remained significant as expressions of solidarity. They included the League of Arab States, which incorporated security tasks through the Joint Defense and Economic Cooperation Treaty of 1950, and the Organization of African Unity, established in 1963.

Over the years many of these bodies began to show signs of deterioration. Military cooperation between the Soviet Union and Communist China began to decline during the late 1950's, and the Albanian government had ceased full participation in the Warsaw Treaty Organization by 1961. During 1959 Iraq withdrew from the Baghdad Pact, which was subsequently redesignated as CENTO. In 1965 the French began a military withdrawal from SEATO and did the same in NATO the following year. In 1967 Pakistan started a progressive disengagement from SEATO, and in 1968 Prime Minister Harold Wilson stated that Great Britain would withdraw all military forces east of Suez by 1971.

※   ※   ※   ※   ※

Such alliances are the subject of this book.

An alliance, says Robert Osgood, reflects a "latent war community, based on general cooperation that goes beyond formal provisions and that the signatories must continually cultivate in order to preserve mutual confidence in each other's fidelity to specified obligations." [1] This formulation seems appropriate to designate alliances in the contemporary world, in spite of the fact that their war functions may be not only latent but also manifest and that they may obviously operate both in peacetime and wartime.[2]

Alliances have commonly been identified with aspects of international relations that could lead to conflicts, specifically in reference to the balance of power. At one level, alliances could be viewed as a natural mechanism of the international system. At another level, the formation of alliances appeared to be an appropriate strategy through which national decision-makers sought a pooling of resources, either to increase the

---

[1] Robert E. Osgood, *Alliances and American Foreign Policy* (Baltimore: Johns Hopkins Press, 1968), p. 19.

[2] To label alliances "latent war communities" is not to argue that alliances cause wars. In spite of research that has investigated the relationship between alliance aggregation and the onset of war, neither the generality nor the direction of this connection is sufficiently clear to draw firm conclusions. See J. D. Singer and M. Small, "Alliance Aggregation and the Onset of War, 1815–1945," in the text, pp. 62–67. See also J. D. Singer and M. Small, "Formal Alliances, 1815–1939: *A Quantitative Description,*" *Journal of Peace Research,* III (1966), 1–32; and "National Alliance Commitment and War Involvement, 1815–1945," *Peace Research Society* (International), V (1966), 109–140.

weight on their side of the scale or to move their own weight over to that side that would ultimately be heaviest.[3]

In specifying war-related activities, Osgood's definition appropriately includes organizations with core security activities, such as the North Atlantic Treaty Organization, the Western European Union, the Central Treaty Organization, the Southeast Asia Treaty Organization, the Australia-New Zealand-United States Alliance, and the Warsaw Treaty Organization. It also has room for other organizations with important, though less central, security concerns, such as the Organization of American States, the League of Arab States, and the Organization of African Unity. In addition, it encompasses less structured security arrangements, such as the Brussels Treaty, the series of agreements between France and the former French territories, analogous British agreements, the Balkan Pact, and a host of other bilateral arrangements. Finally it would appear proper to exclude forms of international cooperation with no relevance to security or defense.

Osgood's definition draws attention to the fact that alliances represent a special type of international cooperation, an aspect that has not only often been neglected, but that may also be particularly relevant in the contemporary world.[4] While implying that alliances are instruments of collective defense against external enemies, it does not rule out the possibility of collective security activities against internal disturbers of the peace and disrupters of the community.[5] Both formal treaty commitments and informal attentions by alliance partners are stressed. Within the framework of this definition an alliance may be more an ongoing process than a stable condition.

Even if one is primarily interested in international conflict, it remains important to consider cooperative aspects of an alliance in order to understand the dynamics of collective activity and in order to formu-

[3] See Quincy Wright, *A Study of War* (Chicago: University of Chicago Press, 1965), p. 131; Hans J. Morgenthau, *Politics Among Nations* (New York: Knopf, 1967), p. 175; and Frederick H. Hartmann, *The Relations of Nations* (New York: Macmillan, 1967), Chs. 16–19. Edwin H. Fedder also makes this point in "The Concept of Alliance," *International Studies Quarterly*, 12 (1968), 65–86. See also Herbert S. Dinerstein, "The Transformation of Alliance Systems," *American Political Science Review*, 59 (September, 1965), 589–601.
[4] George Liska has taken an initial step in combining conflicting and cooperative perspectives of alliance. According to Liska, alliance efficacy can by judged in terms of alliance functions that include, on the one hand, aggregation of power and interallied control and, on the other hand, international order or government. See Liska's *Nations in Alliance: The Limits of Interdependence* (Baltimore: Johns Hopkins Press, 1968), p. 116, and *Alliances and the Third World* (Baltimore: Johns Hopkins Press, 1968), p. 24. *See also* Osgood, *op. cit.*, p. 21.
[5] For different perspectives on complementaries, compatibilities, and conflicts between collective defense and collective security, see Arnold Wolfers, *Discord and Collaboration* (Baltimore: Johns Hopkins Press, 1962), Ch. 12, and Edward Vose Gulick, *Europe's Classical Balance of Power* (New York: Norton, 1955), Ch. 13.

late strategies for alliance construction and maintenance. If one is specifically concerned with forms of international cooperation, on the other hand, alliances may be seen as a species of international organization. As such, their military aspects may be relatively idiosyncratic, but their activities in other sectors—political, economic, scientific, cultural—may be relevant to the more general class to which they belong.

The selections in this book do not represent an attempt to evolve what might be considered a theory of alliance. Rather they aim to provide a sampler of a number of different alliance dimensions. Included are readings focusing on alliances and international conflict, specifically on the relationship of alliance formation to the onset of war and on the complexities of alliance war-fighting strategies, and essays on various facets of alliance cooperation, including analyses of alliances as self-contained systems and of the impact of different sectors of alliance activity, leadership, and crisis on cohesion. Several articles touch on patterns of coalitional division within alliances. The final section considers alliance disintegration.

There is a concern to describe the concrete workings of important contemporary alliances. Following a summary description of alliances between 1815 and 1939, four selections refer at some length to the North Atlantic Treaty Organization. Although the same coverage is not possible for NATO's companions, subsequent essays provide concise descriptions of the backgrounds, structures, and activities of the Organization of American States (OAS), the Warsaw Treaty Organization, Southeast Asia Treaty Organization (SEATO), the League of Arab States, the Organization of African Unity (OAU), and the Sino-Soviet alliance.[6]

The first two essays concentrate on the relationship between alliances and international conflict at two levels—that of the international system and that of the national decision-maker. J. David Singer and Melvin Small use the international system as a level of analysis, emphasizing the gross relationship between the onset of war and the occurrence of alliances. During the first part of the twentieth century, they find that a positive relationship between the alliance aggregation and the initiation of wars existed, but the relationship for the nineteenth century was negative. Even the twentieth-century data taken alone do not allow them to state with assurance whether wars tended to be caused by the formation of alliances, whether the formation of alliances came as a result of increasing war tensions, or whether both alliances and wars were the result of other external factors.[7] Carl H. Amme, Jr., stresses national per-

[6] The selections vary in their time of initial publication and also in the incidence of significant change in the particular alliance since that time. As a result, they are not all completely current. In particular, provisions for structural changes have been made in NATO, the OAS, and the OAU. For more current references, see the Selected Bibliography Appendix.

[7] See also William J. Horvath and Caxton C. Foster, "Stochastic Models of War Alliances," *Journal of Conflict Resolution*, 7 (June, 1963), 110–116, and Richard A.

spectives, concentrating on the connection between strategy and the perceptions of key decision-makers in the North Atlantic alliance. Depicting the existing policy consensus in the four major Allied nations— the United States, Great Britain, France, and Germany—he shows the differential effect of varying objectives and capabilities.

Subsequent articles focus on cooperative alliance processes. Elliott Vandevanter, Jr., considers NATO and the OAS as systems in themselves, paying special attention to the "most concrete structures and activities" of each organization in the military field. Looking at the two organizations as though they were "two engines," Vandevanter discusses "the inputs, the mechanisms, and the outputs." This essay is unusual in its conscious effort at systematic comparison. By treating NATO and the OAS in tandem, the author provides a broader perspective than would be possible in a case study of either alliance by itself.

Mancur Olson, Jr., and Richard Zeckhauser indicate the differential appeal of different kinds of alliance programs to member-nations. From their findings they conclude that allies tend to be less willing to contribute to programs in which all share an intangible common good than to activities in which each of them is able to see tangible private benefits. Thus, the smaller allies contribute proportionately less to general military forces—in which no one is quite certain how much individual defense is being created by his particular contribution—than to NATO infrastructure—that produces concrete military facilities on national territory and construction contracts for national industry.[8]

Two parts pay particular attention to national leadership in alliances. William T. R. Fox and Annette Fox define American perspectives on "seven distinctive roles for the United States in furthering the objectives sought through NATO": to make good the deficiencies of the alliance as a whole; to act as pilot in the strategic planning of the alliance; to guide the general policies of NATO; to induce, energize, and stimulate actions that its allies can only undertake by themselves; to fill the principal military commands in the alliance; to manage the nuclear deterrent for the alliance; and to demonstrate by example what other allies might also profitably do. Many of the same roles seem present in Richard F. Staar's description of the interaction between the Soviet Union and the other nations of the Warsaw Pact. Other Soviet leadership activities, however, such as the activities of the secret police and links between Communist parties, appear more idiosyncratic.[9]

Brody, "Some Systemic Effects of the Spread of Nuclear Weapons Technology: A Study through Simulation of a Multi-Nuclear Future," *Journal of Conflict Resolution,* 7 (December, 1963), 663–753.

[8] Their hypotheses have been further explored by Philip M. Burgess and James A. Robinson, "Alliances and the Theory of Collective Action," *Midwestern Journal of Political Science,* 13 (May, 1969).

[9] Space does not permit the inclusion of material on leadership activities of an alliance's international staff. Treatments of this theme appear in works on NATO

A distinction between routine and crisis cooperation in an alliance is developed in George Modelski's essay on SEATO. Routine activities include "diplomatic and political contacts . . . , generous assistance programs, and . . . the protection afforded by powerful armed forces in being." In crisis situations, however, SEATO is jolted by quantum increases in energy as "it helps to mobilize great power support for the states of South-East Asia." In spite of the fact that, in crises like Vietnam, much activity has occurred outside the boundaries of SEATO-proper, crises can be important vehicles for initiating and developing alliances. The Communist specter alone probably accounts in part not only for SEATO, but also for the whole ring of Western security arrangements including NATO, OAS, ANZUS, and CENTO. Its mirror image, the Western threat, is the explicit justification given by the Warsaw Pact nations for the creation of their alliance. Israel has played an important part in the cohesion of the Arab League. Such situations as the Congo have kept the African nations aware of the dangers of outside military intervention in their affairs.

Robert W. Macdonald's article about the League of Arab States considers in detail the dynamics of different sectors of activity and of coalition formation. Macdonald feels that some sectors have produced relatively integrative effects while others have led to division. Interestingly, there is a high overlap between Macdonald's "integrative activities" and those that he labels as "external" to the alliance, while similar ties appear to exist between "disintegrative" and "internal" activities. This runs counter to the implications of the hypothesis presented earlier by Olson and Zeckhauser, if one assumes that the production of "private" goods, which they found to be most integrative, is more likely in internal rather than external activities. While it is possible that the discrepancy is a result of different modes of analysis, it is also conceivable that different activities may be either integrative or disintegrative depending on variations in different environments and situations.

Macdonald also highlights the pattern of coalitional division within the League, between the supporters of Egypt and Iraq. Such group formation is paralleled by developments in other alliances as well. In NATO, for example, there has been an analogous, though more one-sided, struggle between the United States and France. The same process is indicated in the division of the Warsaw Pact nations between the nations of the so-called northern and southern tiers.

Similar coalitions are at work within the Organization of African Unity, as Nora McKeon's essay makes clear. Such divisions have contributed to the limited effectiveness of the OAU in alliance-related activities, such as the settlement of intra-African border disputes and the establish-

referred to in the Selected Bibliography Appendix and in Robert W. Macdonald, *The League of Arab States* (Princeton: Princeton University Press, 1965).

ment of common defenses against outside political, military, and economic intrusion into African territory.

The two final selections concentrate on the dynamics of disintegration. Raymond L. Garthoff's article on Sino-Soviet military relations between 1945 and 1966 is a study in the loosening of an alliance. Forged in the heat of the Chinese civil war and the Korean conflict, the ties between the two nations subsequently unravelled with the development of "politico-military rivalry and indirect conflict." Although this degree of estrangement has not yet been duplicated in other larger and more institutionalized alliances, recent tendencies toward fragmentation could conceivably follow similar patterns.

If alliances can be said to have a life cycle, William H. Riker presents one perspective on the prospects for their declining years. Alliances, Riker believes, are formed in order to multiply the resources available to achieve a particular aim. Through the workings of "the size principle," however, they tend toward the configuration of "minimal winning coalitions" with no more members than are absolutely necessary. In reality, the dynamics of alliance may be somewhat more complex; nevertheless, Riker's speculation on the future of international politics and on the break-up of "empires" seems relevant in the light of current strains on contemporary alliances.[10]

[10] Riker's work has been part of, and helped to create, a significant body of literature on the applications of coalition theory to politics. Such writing is extensive. Two articles of note that discuss Riker's size principle in terms directly relevant to alliances are Charles R. Adrian and Charles Press, "Decision Costs in Coalition Formation," *American Political Science Review,* 62 (June, 1968), 556–563, and Bruce M. Russett, "Components of an Operational Theory of Alliance Formation," *Journal of Conflict Resolution,* 12 (September, 1968), 285–301. Mathematical models relevant to the measurement of influence within alliances are discussed in Steven J. Brams, "Measuring the Concentration of Power in Political Systems," and Bruce M. Russett, "Probabilism and the Number of Units Affected: Measuring Influence Concentration," *American Political Science Review,* 62 (June, 1968), 461–475, 476–480, respectively.

PART **II**

ALLIANCES AND INTERNATIONAL CONFLICT

Alliance Aggregation and the Onset of War, 1815-1945

J. DAVID SINGER AND MELVIN SMALL

A Framework for Inquiry In any search for the "causes" of international war, there are at least four possible levels of analysis at which we might focus our attention: the individual, the sub-national interest group, the nation, and the international system. Furthermore, each of these four possible classes of empirical referent may be examined in terms of its *structural* attributes or in terms of its *behavior*. That is, the individual, the interest group, the nation, or the system is an object of analysis which reveals relatively *static* properties such as size, composition, organization, power, or capacity for change, and relatively *dynamic* properties such as activity level, aggressiveness, cooperativeness, responsiveness, initiative, or communicativeness. In addition to these two sets of attributes, an individual or a social organization will reveal *relationship* attributes vis-à-vis other actors at the same or other levels of organizational complexity. Nations, for ex-

Reprinted with permission of The Macmillan Company from *Quantitative International Politics* edited by J. David Singer. Copyright © 1968 by The Free Press, a division of The Macmillan Company.

This study is part of a larger project on the correlates of war, supported by the Carnegie Corporation of New York and the Center for Research on Conflict Resolution at the University of Michigan. We are also grateful to Anatol Rapoport and Keith Smith with whom we consulted often on conceptual as well as methodological problems. For his efficient aid in data analysis, our thanks go also to Wen Chao Hsieh.

Editor's note: For full references relating to this article, see Selected Bibliography Appendix.

13

ample, may be geographically near or distant, more or less interdependent economically, politically hostile or friendly, ethnically or industrially similar, and so forth. In sum, we may look for the causes of war in structure, behavior, or relationship at—or across—many levels of social organization. Combining these three classes of variables with the four suggested levels of analysis, we can postulate at least twelve different classes of information one might examine in any systematic search for those factors most often associated with war.

Of course, the moment these twelve categories are filled in with illustrative variables, it becomes evident that the structural-behavioral-relational trichotomization is not always clear-cut: one might argue, for example, that an individual personality attribute, such as rigidity, or a national one, such as autocracy, is more a behavioral than a structural property. At the least, we must recognize that we may have to infer one set of attributes from the observation of another set.

Regardless of the level of organization (or class of variable) at which we look, we must make at least two epistemological assumptions: (1) that explanatory variables will be found in more than one place, the exact number being a function of one's theoretical predilections; and (2) that the interaction of two or more such classes of variables will have more explanatory power than the mere correlation of any single class of variable with our dependent variable: the incidence of war. Which particular levels or classes one gives priority to is likewise a matter of individual judgment, with two considerations deserving attention in that selection. First, there is the question of parsimony, and this should lead to a preference for variables that are at the more general rather than the more idiosyncratic end of the continuum. Second, certain classes of possible predictors to events such as war seem to get considerable attention in the scholarly literature, at the expense of others of intuitively equal significance. On the basis of these considerations, and with the intention of turning later to other possible predictors (and combinations thereof) we focus here on one cluster of *structural* variables at the *systemic* level of analysis: alliance aggregation.

Alliance Without going into the quagmire of termino-
Aggregation as a logical and normative dispute which has char-
Predictor to War acterized much of the theoretical literature on
the balance of power, we can, nevertheless,
note that its defense or justification clearly rests on the assumption that the stability of the international system can be maintained without reliance on superordinate political institutions.[1] In the words of Kaplan (1957), it postulates a system which is "sub-system dominant"; that is,

[1] Almost all textbooks in the field devote some space to an effort to systematize balance-of-power concepts, with varying degrees of success. In addition, there are

one in which most authority is found at the national actor, or sub-systemic level, rather than at the supranational or systemic level. The same notion is conveyed by the international lawyers' distinction between a system in which most of the authority lines are horizontal and one in which they tend to be vertical in direction (Falk, 1959).

In the absence of significant legal or political institutions at the supranational level, the preservation of relative stability and the survival of the nations are seen as depending upon the presence or absence of one or more of the following phenomena, depending in turn upon the theoretical predilections or national outlook of the observer: For the nations themselves, the phenomena are their restraint and limit of ambition, their similarity of values, their approximate parity, the absence of permanent friendships and hostilities, or their willingness to coalesce against a challenger. For the system, these conditions might be the absence of alliances, the presence of a minimum number of alliance coalitions, the approximate parity of the coalitions, the fluidity and impermanence of these coalitions, or a high level of normative consensus. That some of these requirements are vague and that others are inconsistent seems not to discourage those who consider supranational institutions as unnecessary. In one fashion or another, they would rely upon what might be characterized as the diplomatic equivalent of Adam Smith's "invisible hand," a mechanism whereby the individual pursuit of individual interests redounds to the advantage and stability of the community as a whole.

Central to this notion is the understanding that the invisible or unseen hand will function only to the extent that all nations are free to deal and interact with all others as their national interests dictate. Thus, it is assumed that every dyadic relationship will be a mixture of the cooperative and the conflictful, with political, economic, ideological, and other issues all producing different interest configurations for each possible pair of nations. The net effect, it is believed, is such a welter of cross-cutting ties and such a shifting of friendships and hostilities that no single set of interests can create a self-aggravating and self-reinforcing division or cleavage among the nations; A and B may well have competitive economic interests in the Middle East, but harmonious strategic interests in the Caribbean, while B and C's political interests may coincide in regard to West Africa and clash in an international organization setting.

It follows from this sort of a model that anything which restrains or inhibits free or vigorous pursuit of the separate national interests will limit the efficacy of the stabilizing mechanism. And among those ar-

several theoretical efforts, among which are Claude (1962), Gareau (1962), Haas (1953), Kaplan (1957), Liska (1962), Deutsch and Singer (1964), and Waltz (1964). Three important efforts to examine the international system in the historical context are Gulick (1955), Langer (1931), and Rosecrance (1963).

rangements seen as most likely to so inhibit that pursuit are formal alliances. Nations in the same alliance are less free to compete with their allies in such spheres of incompatibility, and less free to cooperate with outsiders in areas of overlapping interests.[2] Just how *much* freedom to pursue normal interests is lost by an allied nation is, of course, most difficult to measure. Although some approximation of the degree of inhibition—or loss of interaction opportunity—can be gleaned from the text and associated documents of a given alliance treaty, a fuller appreciation would require a laborious examination of the treaty's context, and the motivations, relative power, and performance of the signatory nations. Despite the obvious simplifications, however, a differentiation based on the documents themselves is not without some merit, and we will, therefore, distinguish all the alliances examined as to whether they are military, neutrality, or entente commitments; the specific coding rules are outlined in a later section.

Be that as it may, if each alliance commitment reduces, to *some* degree, the normal interaction opportunities available to the total system, and the loss of such interaction opportunities is supposed to inhibit the efficacy of the balance-of-power mechanism, we should find that as the system's interaction opportunities diminish, war will increase in frequency, magnitude, or severity. Moreover, if the alliance configurations show less and less partial overlap, and they instead increasingly reinforce a tendency toward a very few (but large-sized) coalitions, the system's loss of interaction opportunities becomes even more severe. Carried to its extreme condition, this tendency culminates in a completely bipolarized system, with interaction opportunities reduced (theoretically, at least) to one; each nation would then have only friends or foes, and few relationships in between these two extremes. On the other hand, if there are no alliances in the system at all, these interaction opportunities will be equal to the total number of pairs or dyads possible with a given total number of nations in the system; this would be equal to $N(N-1)/2$.

There are, of course, several other lines of reasoning by which one might be led to predict that alliance commitments will negatively affect the stability of the international system, but they are largely variations on the present theme and several have been presented elsewhere (Deutsch and Singer, 1964). Thus, rather than dwell any longer here on the plausible reasons why alliance aggregation *should* correlate with the onset of war, it might be more useful to ascertain the extent to which it does. In order to put this proposition to the historical test, however, a number of preliminary steps are essential. These are the following:

[2] A recent statement which explicitly expresses these restraints is that by Secretary Rusk in regard to Soviet-American arms control negotiations: "Of course, anything that involves our NATO allies would have to be discussed fully with our NATO allies. We could not, for example, make arrangements ourselves, nor even could the four NATO members now sitting at Geneva be able to make arrangements on control posts throughout the NATO alliance without fullest consideration in NATO."

1. Articulate the hypothesis in the various forms it might reasonably take.
2. Delineate the empirical world in time and space from which the evidence will be gathered.
3. Describe the procedures by which the chaotic welter of historical fact is converted into data.
4. Present the raw data which emerge from the above operations.

Once those steps have been completed, we can move on to:

5. Ascertain the strength and direction of any correlations which would tend to confirm or disconfirm the various hypotheses.
6. Interpret the results of this search for correlations.

In the sections which follow, the above procedures will be described in appropriate detail.

The Basic Having articulated the reasons for examining *Hypotheses* the relationship between alliance aggregation and war, we can now spell out in more detail the hypotheses to be tested. In the next section, we can then move on to a specification of the procedures by which the key variables were converted from their widely scattered verbal state to collated and codified numerical form.

The hypotheses may be thought of as falling into two general classes, both of which belong to the systemic level of analysis. The first concerns alliance aggregation and the consequent loss of interaction opportunities in general; that is, it ignores the specific nature of the alliance configurations which are produced, and looks merely at the system's aggregate loss of such normal opportunities. The second of these is as concerned with the specific configurations as it is with the aggregate loss of normal dyadic interaction, and focuses on the extent to which the alliance commitments produce a bipolarized system. Bipolarization may thus be thought of as a special case of alliance aggregation.

ALLIANCE AGGREGATION AND THE MAGNITUDE OR SEVERITY OF WAR

Looking first at the matter of general alliance configurations, and the extent to which they reduce normal interaction opportunities, we may articulate the first basic hypothesis: *The greater the number of alliance commitments in the system, the more war the system will experience.* The second hypothesis pays more attention to specific alliance configurations, and thus reads: *The closer to pure bipolarity the system is, the more war it will experience.*

In order to put these propositions to the test, we must first identify the empirical world within which the postulated relationships are to be sought. Let us describe and justify the world which we have selected, but a preliminary indication of the basic procedure might best precede that. Basically, the method to be employed is a trend analysis. After developing several different measures of alliance aggregation and several measure of the onset of war, we will examine the extent to which the two sets of variables rise and fall together over time.

As to·the empirical domain in which the longitudinal data will be compared, the problem is to examine a span of time which is not restricted to the all-too-recent, and therefore most salient, period upon which much theorizing in international relations seems to be based. On the other hand, if we go too far back we may well find ourselves examining international environments of such disparity that generalizations embracing them become foolish and irrelevant. For the contemporary scholar, there does seem to be a chronological cutting point which provides a sufficiently extensive empirical world while, nevertheless, permitting a reasonable degree of comparability. We refer to the period opening with what we normally recognize as the beginning of the modern international system (the Congress of Vienna) and closing with the Japanese surrender in Tokyo Bay. Despite the many changes in the pattern and process of international relations during that 130-year period, we find a remarkable constancy. The national state was the dominant actor and the most relevant form of social organization; world politics were dominated by a handful of European powers; the Napoleonic reliance upon the citizen's army endured, with all of its implications for public involvement in diplomacy; the concept of state sovereignty remained relatively unchallenged; and while technological innovation went on apace, the period postdates the smoothbore and predates the nuclear-missile combination. In sum, it seems reasonable to conclude that this period provides an appropriate mixture of stability and transition from which generalization would be legitimate. As to whether such generalization might be extended beyond 1945 and into the present, we would be skeptical, but this is, of course, an empirical question, and one to which we will return in our conclusion.

Stated in the preceding rather general form, the hypotheses immediately raise a number of important conceptual and methodological problems. In addition to the procedures for operationalizing "number of alliance commitments" or "closer to pure bipolarity" (the independent variables) and "more war" (the dependent variable)—and these will be articulated in the next section—there are three relevant concerns of substance: (1) the time lag between the presence of a given number or percentage of alliance commitments and its effect in the form of international war; (2) the differentiation between separate regions of the world, especially between the "central" and the "peripheral" portions of the system; and (3) the differentiation between distinctive time periods in our 130 years, especially that between the nineteenth and twentieth centuries.

Let us look first at the matter of time lag. If, indeed, there *is* any relationship between the loss of interaction opportunities and war, that relationship must take a certain amount of time to make itself felt; the system certainly cannot be expected to respond immediately to a specific increase or decrease in interaction opportunities. Not only do we not find in the literature any compelling reason for assuming a given response time, but that response time might well differ for, let us say, different decades.[3] Consequently, each year's interaction opportunity measures have been correlated with the war indices for not only the following year $(Y+1)$, but for the following three $(Y+3)$ and five years $(Y+5)$ as well; for example, if a given alliance aggregation index for 1851 is relatively high, we want to know whether its effect is felt by 1852, by 1854, or by 1856. That is, our dependent variables for 1851 will reflect the amount of war which began in 1852, the amount which began between the beginning of 1852 and the end of 1854, and the amount which began between the beginning of 1852 and the end of 1856.

Two points of clarification are in order here. First, note that we are distinguishing between the amount of war which *began* in the specified time period, regardless of how long it endured, and the amount of war which the system experienced during that period. Second, we are looking at the amount of war which began at any time *within* three time periods of increasing length: within one, three, or five years, not during 1852, or 1854, or 1856 alone. Thus all forms of the basic hypothesis will be tested under three different chronological conditions.

Beyond the refinement of the hypothesis in order to account for varying time lags, we should also refine it to permit its testing within several different time- and space-bound worlds. That is, if we recognize the extent to which theorizing about diplomatic history has been dominated by European-centered scholars and practitioners from the Western world, it seems prudent to wonder whether a given relationship might be found in one region but not in another. Combining that awareness with a recognition that it was not until relatively recent times that the international system could be treated as a more or less single and interdependent one, it makes perfect sense to look for a point in time at which the non-European nations "joined" that central system. The most reasonable such point seems to be that which closed out World War I and marked the birth of the League of Nations; this organization, while its pretensions to universality were never fulfilled, quite explicitly included many non-European members and concerned itself with all continents. Thus, while treating the post-1920 system as a single one, we look upon the pre-1920 epoch as having both a central, Europe-oriented system and a peripheral one. Consequently, all sets of correlations will be examined in two systemic contexts. The first will be called the *total system* and will include all "independent" nations which existed during any part of the

[3] One admittedly intuitive analysis concludes, for example, that "the decision to wage war precedes by one to five years the outbreak of hostilities" (Abel, 1941).

entire 130-year period. The second context will be one in which we "shuck off" the peripheral nations prior to 1920, in order to eliminate the statistical "noise" generated by the less important and least active nations. This we will call the *central system,* and its composition is the same as the total system's for the final 25 years, but smaller for the first 105 years.

Further, we do not restrict attributed membership in the central system to European nations only, nor do all European nations fall into the central category for the pre-League period. In order to qualify for inclusion in the central system during that earlier period, a nation must either be located in Europe or deeply involved in relatively durable relationships with European nations. Given the difficulty of operationalizing this latter phenomenon and given the high degree of consensus among historians, we have adhered closely to that consensus.[4] To be more specific, we have *excluded* a number of European nations from our pre-League central system in line with the following criteria. Outside of Prussia and Austria, the German states are excluded because their 1815 treaty of confederation sharply restricts their diplomatic independence; for example, they are prohibited, formally and effectively, from alliances which might be directed at other members of the confederation. As for the Italian states, other than Sardinia, they, too, enjoy few of the perquisites of real independence prior to their unification in 1860. Modena, Parma, Tuscany, and the Two Sicilies are closely linked by dynastic ties to Austria and turn out to be little more than satellites of Vienna. As to the Papal States, the French and Austrian guarantees effectively preclude them from any significant degree of normal diplomatic interplay.[5]

Turning to the considerations which led us to *include* several non-European nations in (and exclude others from) the pre-League central system, only a few political entities even qualify (by population and recognition criteria) as independent nations at all (if we forget Latin America for the moment) and almost none of these are regularly involved in Continental diplomacy or with the Continental powers abroad. In Asia and Africa, for example, only China, Japan, Persia, Siam, Ethiopia, Korea, and Morocco meet the population and diplomatic recognition requirements between 1815 and 1920.[6] They are, of course, considerably

4 For a full description of the operations by which nations were coded and classified, see Singer and Small (1966).

5 There are, of course, a fair number of additional German and Italian states, but they fail to meet our population threshold of 500,000; the classification criteria are discussed below.

6 The population threshold of 500,000 was only established after a fairly exhaustive list of political entities was compiled and it then became evident that almost no nation of a lesser population revealed itself as an active participant. As to recognition, we found that Britain and France almost invariably led the way to recognition by a majority of members of the European state system. Thus, we get a parsimonious criterion which produces almost exactly the same results as would one requiring, let us say, 50 per cent of the major power members of the European system to serve as

more independent than the subordinate German and Italian states, and they do occasionally interact with the European powers (for example, Persia in the 1850's and Siam in the 1880's), but they remain largely unrelated to the wars and treaties of Continental diplomacy. China and Japan, however, are brought into our central system in 1895 as a consequence of the Sino-Japanese War. As to Western Hemisphere nations, the same considerations apply. Aside from the United States after the Spanish-American War, the Americas are even less involved in Continental affairs than the Asian and African nations. Between 1815 and our cutoff date of 1920 there are no alliance ties with a European power and there are only two international wars involving Europe in Latin America: that between France and Mexico in 1862–1867 and that involving Spain with Bolivia, Chile, and Peru in 1865–1866. And there are no cases of Latin American nations engaging in European wars.[7]

In sum, then, we treat the post-1920 international system as a relatively interdependent one, but divide the pre-League system into two parts: the central and the peripheral. The search for correlations between alliance aggregation and war is thus conducted in two somewhat different empirical worlds so that we may, in one, ignore those political entities which qualify as independent nations, but which may hardly be thought of as active participants in international politics. For the pre-League period, then, the following nations are treated as members of the *central system*, as of the year indicated; it should be noted that Sardinia, Prussia, and Serbia become, respectively, Italy in 1860, Germany in 1871, and Yugoslavia in 1919, and that Austria and Hungary are treated as a single nation until 1918. Those in the left-hand column are members throughout the entire period.

Austria-Hungary	Greece—1828
Denmark	Belgium—1830
England	Serbia—1878
France	Romania—1878
Holland	China—1895
Portugal	Japan—1895
Prussia	United States—1899
Russia	Norway—1905

legitimizers; actually these two constituted 40 per cent of that group until 1860 and from then until 1895 they constituted 33 per cent. Moreover, only Britain and France had sufficiently strong interest in Latin America to justify extending diplomatic recognition to nations in that area. By recognition we mean the accreditation of a representative at or above the rank of chargé d'affaires; neither the consul nor the diplomatic agent qualifies under this scheme.

[7] Moreover, there were only three Latin American alliances (Ecuador-Peru, 1860–1861; Colombia-Ecuador, 1864–1865; and Bolivia-Peru, 1873–1883) which met our criteria of formality, population of the signatories, and consummation in peacetime. In general, see Burr (1955).

Sardinia	Bulgaria—1908
Spain	Albania—1914
Sweden	Czechoslovakia—1919
Switzerland	Poland—1919
Turkey	Finland—1919

The following nations are excluded from the pre-1920 central system and treated as members of the *peripheral system* only, between the dates shown. The earlier date marks its qualification as a sovereign nation and the latter, if any, marks either its disqualification (via federation for the seven German and the five Italian states or annexation for Morocco and Siam) or its entry into the central system (marked by an asterisk); needless to say, the precise date at which the population criterion was met cannot always be shown, and others might select a year or two later or earlier.

Baden, 1815–1870	Brazil, 1826
Bavaria, 1815–1870	Colombia, 1831
Hanover, 1838–1870	Mexico, 1831
Hesse-Electoral, 1815–1866	Peru, 1837
Hesse-Grand Ducal, 1815–1867	Chile, 1839
Mecklenburg-Schwerin, 1843–1867	Argentina, 1841
Saxony, 1815–1867	Venezuela, 1841
Württemberg, 1815–1870	Bolivia, 1848
Modena, 1842–1860	Guatemala, 1849
Papal States, 1815–1860	Ecuador, 1854
Parma, 1851–1860	Haiti, 1859
Tuscany, 1815–1860	Salvador, 1875
Two Sicilies, 1815–1861	Uruguay, 1882
Morocco, 1847–1911	Santo Domingo, 1887
Korea, 1888–1905	Siam, 1887
Ethiopia, 1898	Paraguay, 1896
Persia, 1855	Honduras, 1899
United States, 1815–1899 *	Nicaragua, 1900
China, 1860–1895 *	
Japan, 1860–1895 *	

Turning to the post-1920 setting, in which we drop the distinction between central and peripheral systems, we find the following additional (not previously listed) nation members and their dates of qualification for entry into the total system:

Estonia, 1920	Afghanistan, 1920
Latvia, 1920	Nepal, 1920
Lithuania, 1920	Mongolia, 1921
Hungary, 1920	Costa Rica, 1920
Luxembourg, 1920	Panama, 1920
Liberia, 1920	Ireland, 1921

South Africa, 1920

Australia, 1920

New Zealand, 1920

Canada, 1920

Saudi Arabia, 1927

Iraq, 1932

Yemen, 1934

Cuba, 1934

Egypt, 1936

In addition to these spatial differentiations, a case can be made for an explicit chronological differentiation. Contemporary theoreticians are, all other things being approximately equal, more likely to argue from recent than from remote diplomatic events. Therefore, they may well be basing their postulated correlation between alliance aggregation and war on twentieth-century diplomatic history while tending to forget the nineteenth. To ascertain whether or not this has been the case, we have explicitly divided our 130-year epoch from Vienna to Tokyo Bay into two distinct periods, with the turn of the century marking the break. As to selecting this cutoff point rather than one closer to the midpoint, a number of considerations seemed relevant. First of all, there seemed to be an appreciable qualitative difference between World War I and the wars that preceded it. And bearing in mind the fact that time lags of up to five years are used, we must of necessity use a cutoff year no later than 1908. Secondly, the period *prior* to World War I is markedly different from that preceding most other wars, in that it produced a sharp and clear confrontation between the Central Powers and the Allies, and this bipolarization was well under way by 1902. To be sure, some of the alliances contracted before 1899 (Triple and Dual alliances) transcend both periods, but in order to evaluate their effects, we would have had to go back to 1879. Had we chosen this date, we would have eliminated from the nineteenth-century pattern those several interesting, though ephemeral, configurations of the 1879 to 1899 period which had little relationship to the post-1900 world. Moreover, only after 1900 does the rate of alliance activity show that marked increase which culminates in the grouping of France, England, Russia, and Japan into several interlocking alliances and ententes which by 1908 had resolved itself into the pre-World War I bipolarization.

Finally, there appears to be a marked difference in the amount and rate of diplomatic and military activity between the nineteenth and twentieth centuries; so that while 1899 does not represent an exact chronological midpoint, it is probable that the 85 years prior to 1900 represent an approximate equivalent of the 45 post-century years in terms of "diplomatic time."

To summarize this part of the discussion, then, our hypothesis will actually be put to the test in eighteen different forms, in order to differentiate among: (1) three different time lags, for (2) six different time-space systems. In matrix form, we would want to show the correlation between our several alliance indices and wars beginning for each of the spatial-temporal cells in the chart below:

Time Lags or Spans

Period	System	$Y+1$	$Y+3$	$Y+5$
1815–1945	Central only			
1815–1945	Total			
1815–1899	Central only			
1815–1899	Total			
1900–1945	Central only			
1900–1945	Total			

ALLIANCE AGGREGATION AND THE FREQUENCY OF WAR

Up to this point we have been discussing a relationship which, however interesting, may possibly not be getting at the basic theoretical proposition. That is, we have been assuming that any positive relationship existing between aggregate alliance commitments and war would be revealed in the correlation between our various alliance indices in a given year and certain indices of the *magnitude* or *severity* of war in certain years immediately following. It could be argued that the existence of a statistically significant correlation between interaction opportunity losses and the severity or magnitude of war is really, by indirection, a *dis*confirmation of the hypothesis. The reasoning might be that not only do magnitude or severity seldom covary with frequency, but that they are more likely to vary inversely. A glance at figures for sickness, auto, or industrial accidents or battle casualties, for example, would show that the *least* serious events occur most frequently and that in their most disastrous form these phenomena occur much less often. As a matter of fact, this is precisely what Richardson (1960) found in his *Statistics of Deadly Quarrels*. Classifying deaths on the basis of a $\log_{10}$ scale, he found that in 282 cases of mass violence between 1820 and 1945, deaths were distributed as follows:

$$3 \pm \tfrac{1}{2} - 188 \qquad 6 \pm \tfrac{1}{2} - 5$$
$$4 \pm \tfrac{1}{2} - 63 \qquad 7 \pm \tfrac{1}{2} - 2$$
$$5 \pm \tfrac{1}{2} - 24$$

Likewise, if we look at his observed frequency of ninety-one wars classified by the number of participants, a similar distribution holds:

2–42	7–3
3–24	8–2
4– 8	9–1
5– 7	10–0
6– 3	20–1

Our own results reveal the same pattern, even though our more stringent criteria for war produced a much smaller number of cases. Whether the seriousness of war is measured in terms of number of participants, duration, or battle-connected military deaths, the same inverse correlation between frequency and seriousness is found, as shown in Table 1.[8]

TABLE 1
*Frequency Distribution of all International Wars, 1815–1945,
by Size, Duration, Magnitude, and Severity (N = 41)*

	No. of Participants		Months Duration		Magnitude in Nation-Months		Severity: Battle Deaths in Thous.	
	Range	Freq.	Range	Freq.	Range	Freq.	Range	Freq.
High	21–26	1	61–84	2	750+	1	10,000+	1
Med.-High	16–20	0	46–60	4	151–750	3	1001–10,000	1
Medium	11–15	1	31–45	1	31–150	8	101–1000	7
Med.-Low	6–10	2	16–30	5	5–30	25	11–100	13
Low	1–5	37	0.5–15	29	1–5	4	1–10	19

Given this rather critical observation, it certainly behooves us to pay as much attention to the correlations between interaction opportunity and the *frequency* of war as to those between such phenomena and the *magnitude* or *severity* of war. This we shall do in the sections which follow.

*Operationalizing
the Variables*
In order to put any hypothesis to the empirical test, of course, one must at the very least demonstrate a correlation between the independent and dependent variables. Though a positive correlation between alliance aggregation and war, high enough not to have occurred by sheer chance, cannot be interpreted as a demonstration of any causal connection, the search for such a correlation is a necessary first step. That the presence or absence of covariation between alliances and war is not a mere artifact requires considerable subsequent analysis, but the first order of business, and that which concerns us here, is whether the hypothesized correlations are indeed borne out by the historical evidence.

This enterprise, in turn, cannot be launched until the constructs have been operationalized—until the researcher has converted the ambiguous verbal labels into variables whose shifting presence or absence

[8] This is a very simple and a-theoretical presentation of such distributions. For an indication of the theoretical implication of "mere" distributions, see Horvath and Foster (1963), Weiss (1963), Smoker (1964), and Denton (1966).

or strength can be repeatedly observed and recorded. That is, we must devise explicit and visible procedures by which the welter of events and conditions may be coded, sorted, and classified in so reliable a fashion that other scholars will, in applying the identical coding procedures to the same body of information, come up with almost exactly the same data. Whether these highly reliable procedures do, however, produce data which index the qualitative variables we seek is another matter. Whereas the relative *reliability* of our measures is easily established, their *validity* always remains a matter of some dispute. Recognizing, then, that the search for operational (or machine-readable) variables may well lead to the observation of phenomena quite remote from those about which we seek to generalize, let us turn to the procedures used here.

MAGNITUDE AND SEVERITY OF WAR:
THE DEPENDENT VARIABLES

Before examining the frequency and distribution of our *independent* variables, we had better know what it is they are supposed to be predicting to. In the overall project of which this study is a small part, war is one of the major dependent variables; the object is to ascertain which structural, relational, and behavioral phenomena at which levels of social organization most strongly correlate with war. War, however, means many things to many people, and as a consequence, some definition and operationalization are essential; a full and detailed treatment of the problem is presented elsewhere (Singer and Small, forthcoming), but a brief recapitulation is clearly in order here.

First of all, there are many deadly quarrels (to borrow Richardson's quaint phrase) which are not normally thought of as war: riots, murders, assassinations, pogroms, executions, duels, punitive expeditions, retaliatory strikes, and so on. Even when the deadly quarrel endures and involves nations, many ambiguities remain. How many nations must be involved, for how long, and with how many men or arms? And what is a nation? Secondly, even if we agree upon the meaning of war, there are several different classes of war, each having different relevance to the search for meaningful generalization about the international system.

In order to handle these ambiguities and inconsistencies, a two-step coding procedure was used. First, adapting from the schema found in *A Study of War* (Wright, 1942, App. 20) four classes of war were differentiated: international, imperial, colonial, and civil. The criterion here is strictly one of the political-legal status of the participants. Thus, an *international* war is one in which at least one participant on each side is an independent and sovereign member of the international system, with a population exceeding 500,000 and enjoying diplomatic recognition from our two legitimizers, Britain and France. If only *one* side includes one or more independent system members, then the war is classified as imperial or colonial, depending on the political status of the adversaries, as follows. When the dominant (and usually there is only one) adversary is a more or less independent political entity, but *not* a qualified system member by our criteria, the war is classified as *imperial;* examples might be Serbia before 1878, Persia before 1855, or a Pathan tribe. When the dominant adversary is an entity which not only fails to qualify as a system member but which is also an ethnically different people formerly or presently under the suzerainty of the system member(s) against which it is fighting, the war is seen as *colonial;* examples of such wars might be the Russo-Polish ones of 1831 and 1863 or the Spanish-Cuban of 1868–1878. Wars of this latter category would generally fall, in contemporary parlance, under the rubric of wars of national independence. Finally, a *civil* (or internal) war is one between a system member's government and such sub-national factions as are able to engage in armed resistance, insurgency, or revolution. Of course, any war may *become* an international war by the intervention of one or more independent members of the international system, and the classification of a war may, therefore, change between its onset and its termination.[9]

However, not all international wars are of equal interest to us here, nor is reliable information on all of them available. Thus, we exclude those wars in which the best estimate of total battle-connected deaths is less than 1,000.[10] Using these criteria of war type and casualty threshold, we find that there were forty-one international wars in the total international system between 1815 and 1945; if we ignore the pre-Versailles peripheral system, that number drops to twenty-four.

Having identified those international wars which interest the student of international relations as he examines the effects of alliance patterns, the next point to note is that these wars differ markedly in their duration, magnitude, and intensity. Thus, the correlation of alliance aggregation with mere war frequency would be of limited interest (if not downright misleading) and further gradation is clearly necessary. This gradation is achieved in the first instance by use of the nation–months-of-war measure, so that the simple *magnitude* of each war is the sum of the months which all nations individually experienced as participants in the war; other political entities, even though they participate in a qualifying war, do not contribute to that war's nation-months if they fail to

[9] There is a rapidly burgeoning literature on the subject, and it reminds us that very few civil wars remain purely internal for any length of time. See Rosenau (1964), Modelski (1961), and Eckstein (1963).

[10] This figure permits us to eliminate many border skirmishes, brief interventions, punitive expeditions, blockades, and bombardments of marginal interest to the international relations student, yet excludes no international war. Where our confidence levels were low and the deaths were estimated to be nearly 1,000, we did, however, include the wars. Three examples of such an occurrence were the French invasion of Spain in 1823, the conquest of the Papal States in 1860, and Spain versus Peru, Chile, and Ecuador in 1866.

meet the basic recognition and population criteria for system membership.

A second-order refinement is also necessary, on the recognition that a nineteenth- or twentieth-century British war-month holds rather different implications for this international system than, for example, a Bulgarian war-month. This differentiation could be recognized by introducing several different factors as modifiers. We might want to classify the nations by power, status, or size, and then weight their nation-months by the consequent absolute or relative score. But no such satisfactory index yet exists, especially when it must be applied not only to the early nineteenth century but to many non-European powers for which we have little accurate data at present. We have, therefore, resorted to the simple distinction between major and minor powers and calculated their wars and nation-months of war separately. Though the major-minor dichotomy may be too primitive for some theoretical purposes and not too readily operationalized, diplomatic historians have found it quite useful for centuries. Moreover, despite the invisibility of their criteria, they show near unanimity in the classification results.[11] Thus, our major powers and the dates during which they enjoyed that status are:

Austria-Hungary, 1815–1918
Prussia or Germany, 1815–1918, 1925–1945
Russia, 1815–1917, 1922–1945
France, 1815–1940
Britain, 1815–1945
Japan, 1895–1945
United States, 1899–1945
Italy, 1860–1943

A final point regarding our nation-months (magnitude) measure concerns the chronological placing of our forty-one wars. It should be reiterated here that our major concern must be not with the amount of war *going on* in the given year or years following each year's level of alliance aggregation in the system, but with the amount of war which *commenced* within that one-, three-, or five-year period. Our interest is in measures reflecting the *onset* of war. That most of the nation-months of World War II, for example, occurred during 1942 and 1943 is of much less interest in this study than the fact that they commenced in 1939.

In addition to nation-months as an index of the magnitude of war, at least one other factor seems to justify consideration. That factor we will call *severity* and it will be measured by the number of battle-connected deaths of military personnel sustained by all participants in any

[11] Some might quarrel with our use of the historians' consensus on the classification of nations into major and minor. One significant point of assurance is found in Morgenthau where approximately the same major-power listing as ours is used (1956, p. 324).

given war. As with the identification and classification of our wars, a full treatment of the problems encountered in locating, evaluating, and converting the casualty information into reliable data is provided in the aforementioned paper, and again only a brief summary is offered here. There have, of course, been several prior efforts to collect data on war casualties (Bodart, 1916; Dumas, 1923; Sorokin, 1937; Klingberg, 1945; Richardson, 1960; and Urlanis, 1960), but none provides a fully satisfactory compilation, even for the primitive statistical purposes encountered in this undertaking. All are partially guilty of employing either shifting or invisible criteria of classification, and as a consequence, several different sets of such figures were collected and then our own best estimates finally used. For each nation in each international war, we calculated (and estimated) two types of deaths: (1) military personnel who died, or were reported as permanently missing, as a consequence of malicious acts of the enemy; and (2) military personnel who died from accidents, wounds, disease, or exposure during the period of hostilities. Note that, in partial contradistinction to Richardson's criteria, we did *not* include: (1) civilians of participating nations who died as a result of enemy actions (and to have included this category in our World War II figures would not have changed appreciably the fact that almost half of all deaths in our forty-one wars were accounted for by this single holocaust); (2) such civilians who died from exposure or disease; (3) neutral civilians; and (4) those children who might have been born had there been no war. Battle-connected deaths of military personnel, thus, will provide our index of each war's severity.[12]

To summarize this section, then, our raw data are presented in Table 2. Note that *wars* are the items listed, and that in order to use these data for our purposes they must be transformed so as to show the magnitude and severity of all international wars which began in each of our 130 years. The results of that transformation as well as more detailed data and procedures are in a forthcoming statistical handbook.

ALLIANCE AGGREGATION: THE INDEPENDENT VARIABLE

Shifting our attention now from the outcome, or dependent variable, to the predictor, or independent variable, what procedures might be used to operationalize and quantify the extent to which alliance commitments reduced the interaction opportunities available to the international system? The problem here is somewhat more complex than that confronted in regard to the magnitude and severity of war, since a modest inferential leap is required. Referring back to the rationale behind our general hypotheses, we argued there that the effect of each alliance of

[12] As to civilian and military deaths from non-battlefield engagements, the major possible source is the siege. During the period under study, however, there were few sieges which led to an appreciable number of deaths; see Hargreaves (1948).

any type was to reduce the extent to which the pluralistic, self-regulating mechanism could operate effectively. And two different lines of reasoning were suggested, depending upon the intervening constructs selected. In one, we concentrated upon the loss of interaction opportunity due to aggregate alliance commitments of all nations in the system; this may be thought of as a simple subtractive procedure. In the other, we examined the loss of interaction opportunity due to the bipolarizing effect of these alliance commitments. To put it briefly, there should be a difference between the effects of a structure which reflects a crazy-quilt pattern of all sorts of overlapping alliance membership and one in which that membership approaches or reaches a state in which only a very few easily distinguishable coalitions merge. There may, of course, be a close interdependence between these two conceptually distinct conditions, since it is perfectly plausible to assume that alliance-building is by and large an activity directed *against* other nations and other existing or anticipated alliances. If such is the case, then, the mere aggregation of alliance commitments may well move the system in the direction of some minimum number of coalitions and hence *toward* bipolarity. We will revert to this matter when we present our data, and will then have some evidence for the extent to which these two conditions covary.

Returning, then, to our operationalizing procedures, let us look first at the aggregate measure of interaction opportunity loss, in its various forms. Perhaps the most orderly procedure would be to begin with an overview of the large number of alliance ties that interest us in an analysis such as this. The typology is based upon: (1) the nature of the obligation or commitment undertaken toward one ally by another; and (2) the nature of the signatories in terms of whether they are major or minor powers.

As to the first dimension, three classes of alliance commitment are considered. Class I, which will be called a *defense pact,* commits each signatory to intervene with military force on behalf of the other(s). Class II, which is called here a *neutrality or non-aggression pact,* commits each to refrain from military intervention against any of the other signatories in the event that they become engaged in war. Class III, labeled *entente,* merely requires that the signatories consult with one another in the contingent eventuality. It should be noted here that these classifications are based upon the treaty text itself and not upon the way in which the alliance was adhered to in actual practice.[13]

Perhaps a brief justification of our reliance on written alliances in general and their texts in particular is in order. Admittedly, other phenomena would reveal more fully the friendship-hostility, close-distant, or dependent-independent dimensions of international relationships, but

[13] Elsewhere, we not only spell out the coding rules in greater detail and with illustrations, but give the voluminous bibliography from which our basic information was drawn; see Singer and Small (1966).

TABLE 2

International Wars by Duration, Magnitude, and Severity: 1815–1945

Name of War and Participants	Dates	International System Duration (Months)	Nation Months	Battle Deaths (thousands)	Each Nation Duration (Months)	Battle Deaths (thousands)	National Dates (if different)
1. Franco-Spanish	4/7/23–11/13/23	7	14	1			
France					7	.4	
Spain					7	.6	
2. Russo-Turkish	4/26/28–9/14/29	16.5	33	130			
Russia					16.5	50	
Turkey					16.5	80	
3. Mexican	5/12/46–2/12/48	21	42	17			
Mexico *					21	6	
U.S.A. *					21	11	
4. Austro-Sardinian	3/24/48–8/9/48, 3/20/49–3/23/49	4.5	9	9			
Austria					4.5	5.6	
Sardinia (incl. Ital. rebels)					4.5	3.4	
5. Danish	4/10/48–8/26/48, 3/25/49–7/10/49	8	16	6			
Denmark					8	3.5	
Prussia					8	2.5	

TABLE 2—continued

Name of War and Participants	Dates	International System			Each Nation		National Dates (if different)
		Duration (Months)	Nation Months	Battle Deaths (thousands)	Duration (Months)	Battle Deaths (thousands)	
6. Roman	4/30/49, 5/8/49–7/1/49	2	7	2.2			
Austria					2	.1	5/8/49–7/1/49
France					1	.5	4/30/49, 6/3/49–7/1/49
Papal States *					2	1.5	
Two Sicilies *					2	.1	5/8/49–7/1/49
7. La Plata	7/19/51–2/3/52	6.5	13	1.3			
Argentina *					6.5	.8	
Brazil *					6.5	.5	
8. Crimean	10/23/53–3/1/56	28	115.5	264.2			
England					23	22	3/31/54–3/1/56
France					23	95	3/31/54–3/1/56
Russia					28	100	
Sardinia					13.5	2.2	1/10/55–3/1/56
Turkey					28	45	
9. Persian	10/25/56–3/14/57	4.5	9	2			
England					4.5	.5	
Persia *					4.5	1.5	
10. Italian	4/29/59–7/12/59	2.5	7	22.5			

Name	Dates					
Austria					2.5	12.5
France					2	7.5
Sardinia	5/3/59–7/12/59				2.5	2.5
11. Moroccan	10/22/59–3/26/60	5	10	10		
Morocco *					5	6
Spain					5	4
12. Roman	9/11/60–9/29/60	.5	1	1		
Italy					.5	.3
Papal States *					.5	.7
13. Sicilian	10/15/60–1/19/61	3	6	1		
Italy					3	.6
Two Sicilies *					3	.4
14. Mexican Expedition	4/16/62–2/5/67	57.5	115	20		
France					57.5	8
Mexico *					57.5	12
15. Colombian	11/22/63–12/6/63	.5	1	1		
Colombia *					.5	.3
Ecuador *					.5	.7
16. Schleswig-Holstein	2/1/64–4/25/64, 6/25/64–7/20/64	4	12	4.5		
Austria					4	.5
Denmark					4	3
Prussia					4	1
17. Spanish	10/25/65–5/9/66	6.5	17	1		
Chile *					6.5	.1
Peru *					4	.6
Spain	1/14/66–5/9/66				6.5	.3

TABLE 2—continued

Name of War and Participants	Dates	International System			Each Nation		National Dates (if different)
		Duration (Months)	Nation Months	Battle Deaths (thousands)	Duration (Months)	Battle Deaths (thousands)	
18. Austro-Prussian	6/15/66–7/26/66	1.5	15.5 [a] 4.5 [a]	36.1			
Austria					1.5	20	
Baden *					1.5	.1	
Bavaria *					1.5	.5	6/15/66–6/29/66
Hanover *					.5	.5	
Hesse-Electoral *					1.5	.1	
Hesse-Grand Ducal *					1.5	.1	
Italy					1.5	4	
Mecklenburg-Schwerin *					1.5	.1	
Prussia					1.5	10	
Saxony *					1.5	.6	
Württemberg *					1.5	.1	
19. Franco-Prussian	7/19/70–2/26/71	7	26.5 [a] 14 [a]	187.5			
Baden *					4	1	7/19/70–11/22/70
Bavaria *					4	5.5	7/19/70–11/15/70
France					7	140	
Prussia					7	40	
Württemberg *					4.5	1	7/19/70–11/25/70

20.	Russo-Turkish						
	Russia	4/12/77–1/3/78	8.5	17	285	8.5	120
	Turkey					8.5	165
21.	Pacific						
	Bolivia*	2/14/79–12/11/83	58	170.5	14	58	1	4/5/79–10/20/83
	Chile*					58	3
	Peru*					54.5	10
22.	Central American						
	Guatemala*	3/28/85–4/15/85	.5	1	1	.5	.8
	Salvador*					.5	.2
23.	Sino-Japanese						
	China*	8/1/94–3/30/95	8	16	15	8	10
	Japan*					8	5
24.	Greco-Turkish						
	Greece	2/15/97–5/19/97	3	6	2	3	6
	Turkey					3	1.4
25.	Spanish-American						
	Spain	4/2/98–8/12/98	4	8	10	4	5
	U.S.A.*					4	5
26.	Boxer						
	China	6/17/00–8/25/00	2	18	2	2	1.5 [b]
	Austria					2	
	England					2	
	France					2	
	Germany					2	
	Italy					2	
	Japan					2	

TABLE 2—continued

Name of War and Participants	Dates	International System			Each Nation		National Dates (if different)
		Duration (Months)	Nation Months	Battle Deaths (thousands)	Duration (Months)	Battle Deaths (thousands)	
Russia					2		
U.S.A.					2		
27. Russo-Japanese	2/8/04–9/15/05	19	38	130			
Japan					19	85	
Russia					19	45	
28. Central American	5/27/06–7/20/06	2	6	1			
Guatemala *					2	.4	
Honduras *					2	.3	
Salvador *					2	.3	
29. Central American	2/19/07–4/23/07	2	6	1			
Honduras *					2	.3	
Nicaragua *					2	.4	
Salvador *					2	.3	
30. Moroccan	7/7/09–3/23/10	8.5	17	10			
Morocco *					8.5	8	
Spain					8.5	2	
31. Italo-Turkish	9/29/11–10/18/12	12.5	25	20			
Italy					12.5	6	
Turkey					12.5	14	

#	Name / Belligerent	War dates						Participation dates
32.	1st Balkan	10/17/12–4/19/13	6	20	82			
	Bulgaria					4	32	10/17/12–12/3/12, 2/3/13–4/19/13
	Serbia (& Montenegro)					4	15	
	Greece					6	5	
	Turkey					6	30	
33.	2nd Balkan	6/30/13–7/30/13	1	4	61			
	Bulgaria					1	18	
	Greece					1	2.5	
	Romania					.5	1.5	7/11/13–7/30/13
	Serbia					1	18.5	
	Turkey					.5	20	7/15/13–7/30/13
34.	World War I	7/29/14–11/11/18	51.5	606.5	10,000			
	Austria					51	1,200	7/29/14–11/3/18
	Belgium					51	87.5	8/4/14–11/11/18
	Bulgaria					35.5	14	10/12/15–9/29/18
	England					51	908	8/5/14–11/11/18
	France					51	1,350	8/3/14–11/11/18
	Germany					51.5	1,800	8/1/14–11/11/18
	Greece					16.5	5	6/29/17–11/11/18
	Italy					41.5	650	5/23/15–11/11/18
	Japan					50.5	.3	8/23/14–11/11/18
	Portugal					32.5	7	3/1/16–11/11/18
	Romania					15.5	335	8/27/16–12/9/17
	Russia					40	1,700	8/1/14–12/5/17
	Serbia					51.5	48	
	Turkey					48.5	325	10/28/14–11/11/18
	U.S.A.					19	126	4/17/17–11/11/18

TABLE 2—*continued*

Name of War and Participants	Dates	International System			Each Nation		National Dates (if different)
		Duration (Months)	Nation Months	Battle Deaths (thousands)	Duration (Months)	Battle Deaths (thousands)	
35. Greco-Turkish	5/5/19–10/11/22	41	82	50			
Greece					41	30	
Turkey					41	20	
36. Chaco	5/12/28–12/19/33,	84	168	130			
	1/8/34–6/12/35						
Bolivia					84	80	
Paraguay					84	50	
37. Sino-Japanese	12/19/31–5/6/33	16.5	33	60			
China					16.5	50	
Japan					16.5	10	
38. Italo-Ethiopian	10/3/35–5/9/36	7	14	20			
Ethiopia					7	16	
Italy					7	4	
39. Sino-Japanese	7/7/37–12/7/41	53	106	1,000			
China					53	750	
Japan					53	250	
40. Russo-Finnish	11/30/39–3/12/40	3.5	7	90			
Finland					3.5	40	
Russia					3.5	50	

41. World War II

	9/1/39–8/14/45	71.5	910	16,000	
Australia		71.5	23		9/3/39–8/14/45
Belgium		.5	7.8		5/10/40–5/28/40
Brazil		10	.1		7/6/44–5/7/45
Bulgaria		34.5	10		12/8/41–10/28/44
Canada		71	37.5		9/10/39–8/14/45
China		44	1,350		12/7/41–8/14/45
England		71.5	270		9/3/39–8/14/45
Ethiopia		5.5	5		1/24/41–7/3/41
Finland		39	42		6/25/41–9/19/44
France		19.5	210		9/3/39–6/22/40, 10/23/44–8/14/45 [c]
Germany		68	3,500		9/1/39–5/7/45
Greece		6	25		10/25/40–4/23/41
Holland		.5	6.2		5/10/40–5/14/40
Hungary		43	40		6/27/41–1/20/45
Italy		57	77		6/10/40–9/2/43, 10/18/43–5/7/45
Japan		44	1,000		12/7/41–8/14/45
Mexico		3.5	.1		5/1/45–8/14/45
New Zealand		71.5	10		9/3/39–8/14/45
Norway		2	1		4/9/40–6/9/40
Poland		1	320		9/1/39–9/27/39
Romania		39	300		6/22/41–9/13/44
Russia		47	7,500		6/22/41–5/7/45, 8/8/45–8/14/45
South Africa		71	6.8		9/6/39–8/14/45

TABLE 2—continued

Name of War and Participants	Dates	International System			Each Nation		National Dates (if different)
		Duration (Months)	Nation (Months)	Battle Deaths (thousands)	Duration (Months)	Battle Deaths (thousands)	
Thailand					45	.1	11/30/40–1/31/41, 1/25/42–8/14/45
U.S.A.					44	292	12/7/41–8/14/45
Yugoslavia					.5	410	4/6/41–4/17/41

* Indicates peripheral system nation.
a Number includes central system nation-months only in Austro-Prussian and Franco-Prussian Wars.
b All foreign losses insignificant in Boxer Rebellion.
c Vichy 11/30/40–1/31/41, 11/8/42–11/11/42.

two considerations are relevant here. First, it seems perfectly reasonable to assume that the decision to undertake such an alliance commitment does indeed reflect and respond to many of these more specific, prior relationships. Moreover, one cannot argue that the commitments are undertaken in a frivolous manner, with little awareness of the implications or little intent to honor them. On the basis of our earlier analysis of such commitments, we found, for example, a significant positive correlation between alliance membership and war involvement on the side of the alliance partner. Second, there are some serious obstacles to getting at the more complex phenomena surrounding alliance formation. For example, much of this could be ascertained via content analysis of diplomatic communications, yet the availability of all, or a representative sample of, such documents is problematical; and that method is still a costly and time-consuming one. Moreover, other research groups are moving ahead on the "automation" of content analysis, and there is little point in duplicating that important pioneering venture at this juncture (Holsti, *et al.*, 1964).

Turning to the second dimension, there is the matter of the signatories' power status. Here our interest is in whether a given alliance tie— and every multilateral alliance is treated, for analytical purposes, as if it were a number of separate bilateral ones—is between two major powers or between two minors, or between a major and a minor. Combining the two sets of dimensions, then, we see that nine types of bilateral alliance commitment are possible.[14]

As should be quite evident by now, it is no simple matter to identify all alliances of all relevant types for 130 years and ascertain their scope, membership, and duration. For a study of this type, based as it is on what aims to be the complete population of events rather than a sample thereof, this requirement is mandatory. Let us summarize, therefore, the coding rules which are developed in greater detail in the above-cited paper. First, only those alliance commitments embodied in a formal, written treaty, convention, or executive agreement were included, whether or not it was secret at the time. Among those which were excluded were (1) collective security agreements, such as the League Covenant and the United Nations Charter; (2) charters and constitutions of international organizations, such as those of the Universal Postal Union, International Labor Organization, or the Danube River Commission; (3) treaties of guarantee to which all relevant powers registered their assent, such as the Belgian Neutrality Agreement of 1839, the Washington Conference Treaties of 1921–1922, and the Locarno Pacts of 1925; (4)

---

14 Though some scholars tend to differentiate between an alliance and a coalition, the distinction seems unimportant. Gulick, for example, defines an alliance as a "bilateral or trilateral agreement for offensive or defensive purposes," and then defines a coalition as "a similar agreement signed by four or more powers or a conjunction of several alliances directed toward the same end" (1955, p. 78). He alludes to other distinctions, but they make the difference no clearer.

agreements limited to general rules of behavior, such as the Kellogg-Briand Pact and the Geneva Conventions; (5) alliances which were consummated during, or less than three months before, a war in which any of the signatories participated, unless the alliance endured beyond the formal treaty of peace; (6) any alliances contracted during the two world wars, whether or not the signatories were belligerents; and (7) any alliance which did not include at least two members of our system.

In addition to these problems of ambiguity regarding inclusion or exclusion, there was the matter of chronological coverage. The effective inception date is almost always stipulated in the text or associated documents; if not, the date of ratification was used. In those few cases for which formal termination is not clear, we have relied upon a consensus of the historical monographs available. Finally, renewals were not counted as separate treaties unless the specific commitments were changed, as from entente to defensive alliance. The hundred and twelve alliances which met our criteria are shown in Table 3, along with the effective dates and the class of commitment undertaken by the signatories.

Once all of the relevant alliances were discovered, classified, and counted, it was a simple matter to complete the operationalization of our aggregate interaction opportunity indices. For each year, we merely converted the raw numbers of each type of alliance into a percentage figure, so that we ended up with a list of the five following independent variables.

1. Percentage of all nations having at least one alliance *of any class* with any type of nation, major or minor.
2. Percentage of all nations having at least one *defensive* pact with any type of nation.
3. Percentage of *major* powers having at least one alliance *of any class* with another major power.
4. Percentage of major powers having at least one *defensive* pact with another major.
5. Percentage of major powers having at least one alliance *of any class* with any *minor* power.

In addition to these five measures of aggregate interaction opportunity loss [15] we also sought a measure of the extent to which the various alliances created a degree of bipolarity in the system for each year. Here the procedure was a bit more complicated, and to balance off manageability with relevance, the computations were only made for *defensive* pacts among *major* powers. The first step was to calculate the maximum

---

[15] We also gathered data for neutrality pacts and ententes, but further refinements of those measures is called for in order to handle the problem of which alliance commitment takes precedence when a nation belongs to alliances of different classes. Findings based on those measures will be reported subsequently.

TABLE 3

Inter-Nation Alliances, 1815–1939, with Commitment Class and Dates

Members	Incept.	Termin.	Class	Members	Incept.	Termin.	Class
Austria Baden * Bavaria * Hesse-Electoral * Hesse-Grand Ducal * Prussia Saxony * Württemberg * Hanover * Mecklenburg-Schwerin *	6/1815–1848, 1850 1838 ** 1843 **	1866	1	Austria Parma *	1851	1859	1
				France Sardinia	1/1859	1859	1
Austria England Prussia Russia France	11/1815 11/1818	1823	1	Modena * Parma * Tuscany *	?/1859	1860	1
				Ecuador * Peru *	1/1860	1861 (?)	1
England France	7/1827	1830	3	England France Spain	10/1861	1862	3
				Prussia Russia	2/1863	1864	1
Russia	7/1833	1840	1	Colombia * Ecuador *	1/1864	1865 (?)	1

TABLE 3—continued

Members	Incept.	Termin.	Class	Members	Incept.	Termin.	Class
Turkey				Baden * Prussia	8/1866	1870	1
Austria Prussia Russia	10/1833–1848, 1850	1854	3	Prussia Württemberg *	8/1866	1870	1
England France Portugal Spain	4/1834–1840, 1841	1846	1	Bavaria * Prussia	8/1866	1870	1
Austria England Prussia Russia Turkey	7/1840	1840	1	Bolivia * Peru *	2/1873	1883	1
England Russia	6/1844	1846 (1853?)	3	Austria Germany Russia	10/1873	1878	3
Austria Modena *	12/1847	1859	1	Austria Russia	1/1877	1878	2
Austria Germany	10/1879	1914	1	England Turkey	6/1878	1880	1
				France Spain	10/1904	1914	3

Parties	Concluded	Renewed	Parties	No.	Concluded	Terminated	No.
Italy	5/1882		England, Spain	2	5/1907	1914	3
Austria, Germany, Russia	6/1881	1887	France, Japan		6/1907	1914	3
Austria, Serbia	6/1881, 1889 ***	1889, 1895	Japan, Russia	2, 1	7/1907	1914	3
Austria, Germany, Romania, Italy	10/1883	1914	England, Russia	1	8/1907	1914	3
Germany, Russia	5/1888		Japan, U.S.A.	2	10/1908	1909	3
Austria, England, Italy	6/1887	1890	Italy, Russia	3	10/1909	1914	3
Austria, Italy, Spain	2/1887	1895 (1897?)	Bulgaria, Serbia	2	3/1912	1913	1
France, Russia	5/1887	1895	Bulgaria, Greece		5/1912	1913	1
	8/1891, 1894 ***	1894, 1914	Greece, Serbia	3, 1	6/1913	1914	1

TABLE 3—continued

Members	Incept.	Termin.	Class	Members	Incept.	Termin.	Class
China Russia	5/1896	1902(?)	1	Czechoslovakia Yugoslavia	8/1920	1933	1
Japan Russia	6/1896	1903	3	Czechoslov. Romania	4/1921	1933	1
Austria Russia	5/1897	1908	3	Romania Yugoslavia	6/1921	1933	1
England Portugal	10/1899	1914	1	Czechoslov. Romania Yugoslavia	2/1933	1939	1
France Italy	12/1900, 7/1902 ***	1902 1914	3 2	Belgium France	9/1920	1936	1
England Japan	1/1902	1921	1	France Poland	2/1921	1939 (1934?)	1
England France	4/1904	1914	3	Poland Romania	3/1921	1939	1

Countries				Partners			
Afghanistan Turkey	3/1921	1939	1	Persia Russia	1	10/1927	1939	2
Persia Turkey	4/1926	1937	2	Greece Romania	2	3/1928	1934	2
Afghanistan Persia	11/1927	1937	2	Greece Turkey	2	10/1930	1934	2
Afghanistan Iraq Persia Turkey	9/1937	1939	2	Romania Turkey Turkey Yugoslavia	2	10/1933 11/1933	1934 1934	2 2
Austria Czechoslovakia	12/1921	1927	2	Greece	2	2/1934	1939	1
Estonia Latvia	11/1923	1939	1	Romania Turkey Yugoslavia				
Czechoslovakia France	1/1924, 1925 ***	1924 1939	3 1	Greece Italy	3 1	2/1928	1938	2
Italy Yugoslavia	1/1924	1927	2	Italy Turkey	2	5/1928	1938	2

TABLE 3—continued

Members	Incept.	Termin.	Class	Members	Incept.	Termin.	Class
Czechoslovakia Italy	7/1924	1930	3	Hungary Turkey	1/1929	1939	2
Russia Turkey	12/1925	1939	2	Bulgaria Turkey	3/1929	1938	2
Germany Russia	4/1926	1936	2	Bulgaria Greece Romania	7/1938	1939	2
France Romania	6/1926	1939	2	Turkey Yugoslavia			
Afghanistan Russia	8/1926	1939	2	France Turkey	2/1930	1939	2
Lithuania Russia	9/1926	1939	2	England Iraq	1932	1939	1
Italy Romania	9/1926	1930	3	Finland Russia	1/1932	1939	2
Albania Italy	11/1926, 1927 ***	1927 1939	3 1	Latvia Russia	2/1932	1939	2
France Yugoslavia	1/1927	1939	2	Estonia Russia	5/1932	1939	2

Signatories	Date	Date	Date	Date	Signatories	
Hungary Italy	4/1921	1939	1/1932	1939	Poland Russia	2
France Russia	11/1932, 1935 ***	1935 1939	12/1936	1939	Argentina Bolivia Brazil	2 1
England France Germany Italy	6/1933	1936(?)			Chile Colombia Costa Rica Cuba Dominican Republic	3
Italy Russia	9/1933	1939			Ecuador Guatemala Haiti	2
Argentina Brazil Chile Mexico Paraguay Uruguay Colombia Panama Finland	10/1933 4/1934 11/1936 2/1938	1939			Honduras Mexico Nicaragua Panama Paraguay Peru Salvador U.S.A. Uruguay Venezuela	2
Germany Poland	1/1934	1939	3/1937	1939	Italy Yugoslavia	2
Austria Hungary Italy	3/1934	1938	4/1937	1939	Arabia Yemen	3 1

TABLE 3—*continued*

Members	Incept.	Termin.	Class	Members	Incept.	Termin.	Class
Estonia Latvia Lithuania	8/1934	1939	3	China Russia	8/1937	1939	2
France Italy	4/1935	1938	3	France Germany	12/1938	1939	3
Czechoslovakia Russia	5/1935	1939	1	Portugal Spain	3/1939	1939	2
Mongolia Russia	3/1936	1939	1	Germany Italy	5/1939	1939	1
Egypt England	10/1936	1939	1	Denmark Germany	5/1939	1939	2
Germany Japan Italy	11/1936 11/1937	1939	3	Estonia Germany	6/1939	1939	2
				Germany Latvia	6/1939	1939	2

Classes of alliance are:: 1-Defense Pact; 2-Neutrality or Nonaggression Pact; 3-Entente.

Inception dates show month and year, but termination dates cannot be ascertained with the same precision; where n sensus exists for that date, an alternate year (?) is also shown.

Comma between dates indicates temporary break in the alliance.

Brackets indicate that one or more bilateral alliances were merged in a new and larger grouping.

* Indicates that nation belongs to peripheral system only.

** Indicates that nation qualified for system membership *after* joining alliance, i.e, this date,

number of dyads that could be formed from among the population of major powers, using the formula $\dfrac{N(N-1)}{2}$. Then we calculated the percentage of these which had been exhausted, via the following steps. All defensive pact links were counted and the target(s), if any, of each identified; either a single nation or all members of a given alliance can be classified as targets. Next, we eliminated all linkages that were no longer possible: (1) those between members within each alliance; (2) those between members of opposing alliances; and (3) those between a target nation and all members of the alliance directed against that target nation. For any nation which was neither a target nor an alliance member, the maximum number of linkages still open was then counted, using the rule that it might contract an alliance with other non-allied or non-target nations, plus either all members of the largest alliance, or all the non-allied target(s), whichever was the larger number. Once the number of feasible remaining defensive alliance links was ascertained, that number was divided into the original number that would have been possible in the absence of any such alliances, to give the percentage of major power defensive alliance ties exhausted.

One problem that confronted us was the occasional ambiguity regarding the target nation of a given alliance. That is, in 48 of our 130 years, there was sufficient disagreement among historians as to whether or not there is any target at all. In those cases, we computed an alternative bipolarity index. As in other places where professional consensus was used in place of a costly and complex operationalizing procedure, our authorities are identified in the basic descriptive article (Singer and Small, 1966). In the tables, therefore, two sets of bipolarity indices and two sets of correlations are shown, and in the next section the intercorrelations between them are also shown. Let us illustrate (Figure 1) this procedure by reference to the alliance configuration of 1913; in that year, there were eight major powers, offering a maximum of twenty-eight possible linkages.

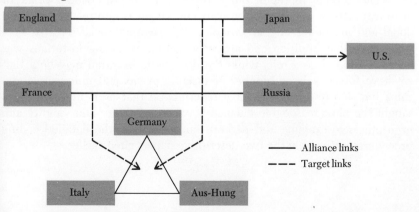

Fig. 1. Major Power Alliance Configurations, 1913.

In Figure 1 we see that twenty-one (or 75 percent) of those twenty-eight possible linkages were exhausted by alliances or by the logic of the targets as follows:

By Alliance (5)	(*By Target* (14)	
England-Japan	England-Italy	England-United States
France-Russia	England-Germany	France-Germany
Austria-Germany	England-Austria	France-Austria
Austria-Italy	Japan-Italy	Russia-Italy
Germany-Italy	Japan-Germany	Russia-Germany
	Japan-Austria	Russia-Austria
	France-Italy	Japan-United States

Two (2) more linkages are exhausted because if the United States allied with Germany, Austria-Hungary, and Italy, it obviously could no longer ally with France and Russia.

Before leaving this section, one more procedure needs to be described. Just as we ran correlations for three different time lags during which the onset of war could be measured, we felt that there was no a priori justification for assuming that our alliance data for a single year gave us the best independent variable. It could just as readily be argued that the sytem's alliance patterns are best reflected in their average magnitude over a longer period of time; for example, the duration of a given configuration might be as important as its magnitude. Therefore, three separate indices for each year and each independent variable were computed, showing that year's index, an average for that year plus the two preceding years, and an average for that year plus the four preceding years. Thus, for 1908 we have indicators on the independent variable side for 1908, the 1906–1908 average, and the 1904–1908 average. While all correlations have been run, only the three-year average is reported. (The remaining figures may be requested from the authors.)

These, then, represent our effort to convert the chaotic welter of historical facts or impressions on wars and alliances into relatively operational and machine-readable variables. The rigorous social scientist may well argue that intuition and apparent consensus among historians was permitted too large a role, while the diplomatic historian may hold that we have forced a large number of discrete events and unique relationships into too few Procrustean categories. Be that as it may, we have sought the most reasonable balance between reliability and validity and urge others to examine and perhaps improve upon, the detailed coding procedures outlined in the two descriptive papers cited earlier.

Observed With our operationalizing procedures out of
Correlations the way, and our raw data's legitimacy more or
less established, we can now turn to the many
alternative correlations which were sought and/or found. Because of our
uncertainty as to which represented the best measure and because of the
low marginal cost of the additional measures, we developed and gathered
data on a multiplicity of indices for both the dependent and the independent variables. Therefore, prior to an examination of the correlations
between our independent and dependent variables, it might be helpful
to look *within* each of these groups, summarize their intercorrelations,
and ascertain the extent to which each of our seven independent variables
and our five dependent ones seem to be measuring the same phenomena.

COMPARING THE DEPENDENT VARIABLES

It will be recalled that we collected our data in such form as to
permit the measurement of both the amount of war *underway* in any
given year and the amount which *began* in any given year. In this study,
however, concerned as we are with the extent to which alliance aggregation predicts to the *onset* of war, we will only present the data showing
the number, magnitude, and severity of wars *beginning* in a given year.
For a number of theoretical and methodological reasons, the underway
data will be reserved for a separate and later paper.

The reader will also recall that the exploratory nature of the study
demanded that we allow three different time lags during which a given
alliance pattern's "effects" could be measured. That is, uncertain as to
how long it took for the hypothesized consequences of alliances to be
felt, we gathered data to show the effects within one year, within three
years, and within five years following each years's alliance configuration.
Thus, if we are looking, for example, at the alliance data for 1868, those
various indices were all correlated with the data for wars which began in
1869, which began between January 1869 and December 1871, and those
which began between January 1869 and December 1873. Once these
data were in, however, it became clear that, if any alliance effects were
to be found, they had largely made themselves felt within three years, especially in the twentieth century.[16] Thus, only the $Y + 3$ correlations
will be shown in the tables here.

[16] An interesting point emerges when these various time lags are examined carefully.
In the nineteenth century the effects are seldom fully evident until five years have
elapsed, whereas three years suffice in the twentieth century. This pattern strongly
suggests that, in contrast to "real" time, "diplomatic" time has indeed speeded up
in more recent years. In a subsequent paper, we will report a number of other indications of this time compression tendency. A suggestive treatment of this problem in
social science is Moore (1963).

TABLE 4
Correlations Among Dependent Variables: The Onset of War Within Three Years of Each Year's Alliance Aggregations, 1815–1945

	Total System						Central System					
	N-M War Begun—All	N-M War Begun—Majors	Battle Deaths—All	Battle Deaths—Majors			N-M War Begun—All	N-M War Begun—Majors	Battle Deaths—All	Battle Deaths—Majors		
N-M War Begun—All												
N-M War Begun—Majors	95						96					
Battle Deaths—All	97	96					98	97				
Battle Deaths—Majors	97	97	99				98	98	99			
No. Wars Begun	34	35	28	27			52	54	49	47		

As Table 4 reveals, whether we look at the total international system or the central system alone, there is indeed an impressively high correlation among most of these dependent variable indicators.[17] It is patently evident that we were overly concerned. That is, whether we look at the total system or the central system, and whether we look at all nations or major ones only, the correlation coefficient between nation-months and battle deaths is only a shade less than one. (Unity, of course, would show that the indices were all measuring precisely the same thing.) The only low, but nevertheless still significant, correlations are between the magnitude and severity measures on one hand and the frequency ones on

[17] A statistical note is in order here. We recognize that our observations do not satisfy the requirements which most statisticians would demand in order to speak of levels of significance. First, we are not sampling here, but are observing the entire population of events. Second our indices—annual readings of alliance aggregation and war onset—obviously are not independent of one another from year to year. Third, the distributions are not "normally" distributed, and any normalizing transformation would have distorted a perfectly satisfactory scale. However, one must use some objective and quantitative benchmark by which "strong" relationships may be differentiated from "weak" ones, and by which one may classify these observed relationships as compelling or not. Thus, we have used the Pearson product-moment correlation as our measure of the strength of the observed relationships and gone on to scrutinize each such correlation value (r) to ascertain whether or not we might call it strong or weak. For that purpose, we use Fisher's exact test of statistical significance (two-tailed to allow for negative correlations) and treat all r's that exceed the requirements for an .01 level of significance with a given N as strong. For the nineteenth century and an N of 85, that threshold is .25, and for the twentieth and an N of only 45, the threshold requirement goes up to a coincidental .45; values meeting these levels are italicized. Note that r's are rounded off to only two places and that the decimal point is omitted.

the other. Given the distributions described earlier, this was to be expected.

COMPARING THE INDEPENDENT VARIABLES

Comparing the alliance aggregation figures to one another is a somewhat more complex matter than that involving the war data. Here, we have not only the standard spatial and chronological subsets, but the various combinations of signatory status and alliance class. Further, there is the distinction between aggregate commitments and those which generate our two alternative indices of bipolarity. In addition to these latter, which, as indicated earlier, are based solely on the polarization among the major powers, there are (1) all classes of alliance among all nations; (2) all classes of alliance among major powers; (3) defense pacts among all; (4) defense pacts among majors; and (5) all alliances between majors and minors. As noted earlier, we are not examining here the extent to which neutrality pacts and ententes "predict to" war, inasmuch as the count on these is somewhat misleading; that is, neutrality or entente commitments were counted only when no defense pact existed between the nations in any dyad. In other words, only the highest class of commitment between each pair was counted.

As Table 5 reveals, there exists a very impressive intercorrelation among these several alliance measures. In the central system, every indicator correlates strongly with every other, and in the total system, the only absence of correlation is that between the initial and the alternative bipolarity figures on the one hand, and the all-allied and all-in-defense-pact figures, on the other. This lack of significant correlation need not surprise us, given the fact that the bipolarity measures reflect major power cleavages only. Again, but to a considerably lesser extent than with war, we are tapping approximately the same structural phenomena.

Having digressed for the important purpose of ascertaining the extent to which our many different measures tend to tap the same phenomena, we may now move on to the primary concern of the study: the extent to which alliance aggregation in its various forms predicts to war.

TOTAL SYSTEM, 1815–1945

In order to make more comprehensible the many pairs of correlations within our six different systematic settings, a brief recapitulation would seem to be in order. The correlations will be so presented in the separate tables as to identify: (1) the international system or portion thereof which is under examination; (2) the time period for which it is being examined; (3) the specific independent variables being used; and (4) the specific dependent variables. As we indicated earlier, a great many more correlations were run than are reported here; among those

TABLE 5

Correlations Among Independent Variables:
Annual Alliance Aggregations, 1815–1839

	Total System						Central System Only					
	% Nations in Alliance	% Nations in Defense Pact	% Majors in Alliance	% Majors in Defense Pact	% Majors Allied with Minors	Major Bilateral Defense Exhausted—a	% Nations in Alliance	% Nations in Defense Pact	% Majors in Alliance	% Majors in Defense Pact	% Majors Allied with Minors	Major Bilateral Defense Exhausted—a
% Nations in Defense Pact	74						80					
% Majors in Alliance	50	53					77	74				
% Majors in Defense Pact	32	60	81				58	83	81			
% Majors Allied with Minors	64	61	64	59			80	70	42	33		
Major Bilateral Defense Exhausted—a	00	–01	47	57	26		54	53	47	57	51	
Major Bilateral Defense Exhausted—b	45	50	60	68	67	58	57	70	60	68	48	58

not shown here are (1) eight of the nine *r* values for each cross-correlation, with only the three-year average for alliance indices and the three-year lag for war indices correlated in the text and accompanying tables; (2) all neutrality pact and entente data, with only the defense pact and all alliance class categories shown in the text; and (3) all data dealing with war actually underway, with only the data on *onset* of war shown in the text. Contrary to some practice, we will include all *r* values in each table, even those which are not equivalent to statistically significant levels; those which equal or exceed the .01 level requirement will be italicized. As to sequence, we begin with the total system for the entire 1815–1945 period, and then drop the peripheral nations and concentrate on the central system only for the same full period. Next we look at the total system in the nineteenth century, and then move on to the central system only for that eighty-five year period. Finally, we examine the twentieth-century total system and central system in that order.

Turning, then, to our first and most comprehensive empirical world —that of the total international system for the entire 1815–1945 period (shown in Table 6)—we find one set of consistently high correlations. That is, the grossest of the independent variables—percentage of *all* nations in at least one alliance of *any* class—shows significant correlations with all four of the magnitude and severity indicators, but not with the number of wars beginning within three years. On the major power side, however, no such findings emerge. As a matter of fact, there are no other sufficiently high *r* values at all for this total-system–entire-period setting, although the major with minor correlation approaches that level.

TABLE 6

Total System, 1815–1945: Correlations Between Alliance Indicators and Magnitude, Severity, and Frequency of War Beginning Within Three Years

	% of All in Any Alliance	% of All in Defense Pact	% of Majors in Any Alliance	% of Majors in Defense Pact	% of Majors with Minor	Bipo-larity Initial	Bipo-larity Alternate
Nation-Months War—All	30	–05	05	06	17	08	13
Nation-Months War—Majors	28	–01	10	04	22	14	18
Battle Deaths for All	34	–01	11	01	21	15	19
Battle Deaths for Majors	31	–01	12	04	21	17	21
Number of Wars	07	–01	06	04	18	–03	01

CENTRAL SYSTEM, 1815–1945

Let us now take the first of several steps in the direction of increasingly restrictive empirical worlds, and shuck off all the peripheral system nations, leaving the central system only, but still for the entire time period. The picture is pretty much the same, as we see in Table 7; that is, the percentage of all nations in any class of alliance correlates strongly with all four magnitude (nation-months of war) and severity (battle deaths) indices. Again, defense pacts among all, or among majors only, do not show a high covariation; but in this more restrictive setting, the percentage of majors having at least one alliance of any kind with a minor power does predict significantly to all the war measures. Note that even the frequency measure correlates, albeit modestly, with the major-minor measure, but not with any of the other alliance indicators.

TABLE 7

*Central System, 1815–1945: Correlations Between Alliance Indicators and
Magnitude, Severity, and Frequency of War
Beginning Within Three Years*

	% of All in Any Alliance	% of All in Defense Pact	% of Majors in Any Alliance	% of Majors in Defense Pact	% of Majors with Minor	Bipolarity Initial	Bipolarity Alternate
Nation-Months War—All	33	11	06	–02	34	12	16
Nation-Months War—Majors	34	14	11	03	34	15	13
Battle Deaths for All	35	12	11	01	34	15	18
Battle Deaths for Majors	35	14	12	04	34	17	20
Number of Wars	19	07	05	–03	28	–07	16

TABLE 8

*Total System, 1815–1899: Correlations Between Alliance Indicators and
Magnitude, Severity and Frequency of War
Beginning Within Three Years*

	% of All in Any Alliance	% of All in Defense Pact	% of Majors in Any Alliance	% of Majors in Defense Pact	% of Majors with Minor	Bipolarity Initial	Bipolarity Alternate
Nation-Months War—All	–16	–16	–23	–34	–21	–32	–23
Nation-Months War—Majors	–04	01	–26	–14	–01	–23	–19
Battle Deaths for All	–27	–23	–38	–42	–33	–33	–28
Battle Deaths for Majors	–26	–19	–41	–38	–27	–30	–25
Number of Wars	–00	01	–10	–05	05	–21	–12

TOTAL SYSTEM, 1815–1899

As suggested in a previous section, it seemed useful to inquire as to whether the relationship between alliance commitments and war might be stronger or weaker in different epochs; thus we have not only divided our total population into central and total systems, but have also divided it into nineteenth- and twentieth-century systems. Let us therefore shift from the full population (that is, total system, entire 130-year period) and examine the total system up through 1899 only. A brief glance at Table 8 indicates that this concentration upon the nineteenth-century total system exercises a striking effect on our correlations. That is, we no longer find alliance aggregation in general predicting to war, and those *r*'s that are close to significant are all in the *negative* direction. And when we move over to include major powers only, their general alliance involvement does indeed show a strong—but negative—correlation with both the severity measures; the same holds for major-minor alliances vis-à-vis battle deaths for all. As to our initial bipolarity measure, we find relatively strong correlations vis-à-vis one of the magnitude measures and both of the severity measures.

Although the statistically alert reader may already anticipate what our *post*-1900 correlations will look like, it would be premature either to present them next or to offer an interpretation of the above rather consistent negative correlations. Rather, let us stay in the same nineteenth-century time frame, but again shuck off the nations of the peripheral system and look exclusively at the nineteenth-century central, or European, state system.

CENTRAL SYSTEM, 1815–1899

Here, as Table 9 makes evident, the same nineteenth-century pattern continues. That is, all of the strong correlations are in the negative direction, with the severity indices again most sensitive to alliance aggregation. Worth observing is that every one of the alliance indicators correlates strongly and inversely with all battle deaths and with major-power battle deaths arising from war beginning within three years of the alliance condition.

TOTAL SYSTEM, 1900–1945

We can now look at some of the evidence that should have been anticipated once the nineteenth-century data were contrasted to data for the entire period. That is, if alliances and war show some modest positive correlations for the entire 130 years and somewhat stronger, but *negative* correlations for the first 85 years, we may logically expect positive and somewhat stronger *r*'s for the twentieth-century data. This indeed is

TABLE 9

Central System, 1815–1899: Correlations Between Alliance Indicators and Magnitude, Severity and Frequency of War Beginning Within Three Years

	% of All in Any Alliance	% of All in Defense Pact	% of Majors in Any Alliance	% of Majors in Defense Pact	% of Majors with Minor	Bipo-larity Initial	Bipo-larity Alternate
Nation-Months War—All	−19	−14	−15	−08	−16	−19	−14
Nation-Months War—Majors	−20	−14	−19	−09	−13	−17	−16
Battle Deaths for All	−45	−45	−44	−45	−33	−34	−30
Battle Deaths for Majors	−46	−41	−48	−42	−30	−32	−28
Number of Wars	−05	−02	−03	07	−04	−20	−06

TABLE 10

Total System, 1900–1945: Correlations Between Alliance Indicators and Magnitude, Severity, and Frequency of War Beginning Within Three Years

	% of All in Any Alliance	% of All in Defense Pact	% of Majors in Any Alliance	% of Majors in Defense Pact	% of Majors with Minor	Bipo-larity Initial	Bipo-larity Alternate
Nation-Months War—All	53	43	24	05	43	15	28
Nation-Months War—Majors	46	48	35	16	47	24	36
Battle Deaths for All	56	48	29	08	46	19	31
Battle Deaths for Majors	51	48	31	13	45	23	36
Number of Wars	18	29	50	26	54	27	26

what we find, despite the fact that our N of only 45 years raises the *r*-value requirement to a coincidental .45. Thus, the percentage of all nations in any class of alliance, as well as in defense facts, correlates highly with all four magnitude and severity measures in every case but one (.43 with nation-months of war for all). Likewise, the major-minor figure predicts well to three of these four dependent variables. On the bipolarity side, however, none of the correlations are high enough to be interesting.

CENTRAL SYSTEM, 1900–1945

Turning to the last of our empirical worlds, the pattern is essentially the same for the central as for the total twentieth-century system. Though defense pacts among all do not predict to war compellingly in this case, alliances in general among all do, as do major-minor alliances in three of the four cases. Again, the bipolarity correlations are all moderately in this direction, but as in the total system, they still fail to satisfy the .01 requirements.

TABLE 11

Central System, 1900–1945: Correlations Between Alliance Indicators and Magnitude, Severity, and Frequency of War Beginning Within Three Years

	% of All in Any Alliance	% of All in Defense Pact	% of Majors in Any Alliance	% of Majors in Defense Pact	% of Majors with Minor	Bipolarity Initial	Bipolarity Alternate
Nation-Months War—All	45	04	23	05	42	14	27
Nation-Months War—Majors	49	17	35	18	47	24	36
Battle Deaths for All	50	09	29	09	46	19	32
Battle Deaths for Majors	50	13	31	14	45	23	36
Number of Wars	25	–02	24	–05	40	–05	02

Summary and Interpretation Given the material with which we worked, the data-making operations, and the observed correlations between and among our many variables, what can we now say regarding the basic hypothesis? Do alliance aggregations in general, or bipolarity tendencies in particular, correlate in any meaningful way with the onset of international war in the nineteenth and twentieth centuries?

Assuming that our measures are as valid and reliable as claimed, the evidence seems to be relatively unambiguous. We say relatively because there are two quite distinct and incompatible patterns, but the incompatibility is easily resolved by dividing the entire historical epoch into two periods. That is, if we look at the twentieth-century segment only, the hypothesis is rather strongly confirmed. (Taking the seven independent variable indicators and the four measures of war magnitude and war severity, for both the central and the total systems, we have fifty-six opportunities for a strong positive correlation to appear. Our results show such a correlation on seventeen of these occasions.) Looking first at the alliance aggregation measures, for both the central and the total systems, we find that the percentage of all nations in the system having at least one alliance with any other nation predicts to the amount of war on all eight of the possible occasions. And the percentage of major powers having at least one alliance with a minor does likewise on six of the eight possible occasions. Defense pact aggregation does so on three of the eight possible occasions. Combining this powerful tendency with the fact that there are quite a few more correlations that are only slightly weaker and that not a single negative correlation appears, we may only conclude that the well-accepted hypothesis has indeed been borne out by our historical evidence.

Does the hypothesis do as well in an earlier epoch? Clearly not. To the contrary, on all eight of the possible occasions for a positive correlation to turn up between gross alliance aggregation and the magnitude or severity of war in the nineteenth century, the correlation was negative. And if the same matrix were constructed for defense pacts, seven of the eight turn out to be negative. Furthermore, if we look at all classes of alliance among major powers only for the nineteenth century, all eight correlations are again negative, four of them strongly so. Even if we focus on major-power defense pacts for both of these nineteenth-century systems, five of the eight negative correlations meet our rather stringent threshold criteria. Finally, all eight of the war correlations with major-minor alliance percentages are negative, three at the .01 equivalent level. The observed relationship between alliance aggregation and the onset of war in the nineteenth century, then, is clearly a negative one, and shows a distribution which is diametrically opposed to, and almost as strong as, that found for the twentieth century.

To what extent is the alliance aggregation pattern repeated when we try to predict to war from *bipolarity?* In general, the same tendencies appear, but with somewhat lower coefficient values. That is, if we look at both the initial and the alternative indices of major-power bipolarization, and correlate them with our four magnitude and severity indices in both forms (central and total) of the twentieth-century system, all sixteen r's are positive, but only twelve of these are in significance ranges better than .1 (not .01). Any doubt as to the general tendency is dispelled, however, when we examine the nineteenth-century total and central systems. As with alliance aggregation, every one of the *r* values is negative, with eight of the sixteen meeting the .01-level requirement.

Given the extraordinarily low probability of such correlations occurring in such consistent form by sheer chance, we have no choice but to conclude that alliance aggregation and bipolarization do indeed have a meaningful relation to the onset of war. But it is important to note the theoretical implications of these relationships. It is certainly clear that formal alliance patterns do not exercise a uniform impact over time. To the contrary, both alliance aggregation and bipolarity covary strongly with the amount of war that follows within three years during the twentieth century, and correlate *inversely* to almost the same degree during the nineteenth century.

Regardless of the war-onset measure we use, the pattern is similar. Whether it is nation-months of war or battle-connected deaths, whether the data are for the total system or the central one only, and whether they reflect all members of the system or major powers only, when alliance aggregation or bipolarity in the nineteenth century increases, the amount of war experienced by the system goes down, and vice versa. And in the twentieth century the greater the alliance aggregation or bipolarity in the system, the more war it experiences.

Now the cautious or skeptical reader may say that "it depends" upon what we mean by "amount of war," and ask whether the same picture emerges when we look at the sheer *number* of wars. As a matter of fact, it does, but not quite as impressively. That is, almost all of our independent variables correlate negatively with the number of wars beginning within the $Y + 3$ period during the nineteenth century, and positively during the twentieth century. And the five exceptions out of the fourteen opportunities are barely perceptible: we find r's of .01, .05, and .07 for the nineteenth, and −.02 and −.05 for the twentieth. Moreover, if there were any concern that it is the sheer magnitude and severity of the two world wars that accounts for the twentieth-century positive correlation, it should be noted that when the *number* of wars begun is used as the dependent variable, the *r* values for percentage of all nations in alliances of any class are .18 and .25. For all major-power alliances, these are .50 and .24, and for major-minor alliances, they are .54 and .40, for the total and central systems respectively.[18] In sum, whether we measure amount by number of wars, the nation-months involved, or battle deaths incurred, alliance aggregation and bipolarity predict strongly away from war in the nineteenth century and even more strongly toward it in the twentieth. One might say that those who generalize about the effects of alliance activity—and most postulate a destabilizing effect, es-

[18] To be doubly sure, we also ran these correlations *without* the world war years, with only a minor reduction in the coefficients resulting.

pecially in regard to bipolarity—have been so preoccupied with more recent history that they have neglected the patterns which obtained in an earlier, but by no means incomparable, period; one recent exception is Waltz (1964).

It is obvious that correlation and causality are rather different things, and that correlation at a high level is *necessary* to the establishment of a casual relationship, but not at all *sufficient*. Unless a logically tight and empirically correct linkage between the independent variables and the dependent ones can be presented, and competing explanations can be disconfirmed, we have established something less than causality. Thus, it seems appropriate to conclude on a cautious note, by indicating the sorts of substantive and methodological questions which remain.

For example, are we able to demonstrate a close empirical and chronological connection between specific alliances and specific wars? At this juncture, our data are not in the form which would permit a direct answer, but we do have some results of a tangential nature. That is, if we look at the frequency with which a given nation belongs to any alliance within three years prior to any war, and compare that figure to the frequency with which it participates in any war, we find that for all 82 of our nations over the 130 year period, the correlation is .60; and for the 67 central-system members, the figure is a very high .72. But this still does not establish a casual connection. Again, there is the simple, but not unreasonable, argument that national decision-makers will tend to step up their alliance-building activities as they perceive the probability of war to be rising. This might well account for our twentieth-century correlations, and we have, as yet, produced no evidence to contravene the hypothesis.

Beyond this, even though we have uncovered a compelling relationship between alliances and the onset of war, the magnitude of that relation still remains an empirical question, and it may well be that other factors will account for much more of the variance than these two sets of variables. As a matter of fact, if we use the statistical rule of thumb which permits us to say that the amount of variance accounted for by a given independent variable—the coefficient of determination—is approximately the square of the product-moment correlation, we see how limited the alliance effect may be. With the twentieth-century (positive) correlations averaging out at .29 and the nineteenth-century (negative) ones averaging out at .26, these alliance factors may be interpreted as accounting for somewhere between 8.4 and 6.8 percent of the variance.[19]

Furthermore, a number of qualifications and caveats regarding some of our independent variables come to mind. As to the five different alliance-aggregation indices, we did indeed cover a wide range of possi-

---

[19] Another way of saying this is to reiterate that bivariate analyses can seldom explain (account for) highly complex and obviously multivariate social phenomena.

bilities, using all classes of alliance, as well as defense pacts alone, using all nations as well as major powers alone, using six different spatio-temporal forms of the international system, and using nine different lead and lag combinations, but the exploration, nevertheless, remains incomplete. Again, though we have gathered data on neutrality pacts and on ententes, data on these classes of alliance have not been processed for use here, and it may well be that their presence and absence might shed further light on the alliance-war relationship. Another possibility worth examining might be that of *changes* in alliance aggregation; that is, each year's increments or decrements vis-à-vis the previous year or years might reveal a discernible pattern that either strengthens or challenges the tendency discovered in this study. Likewise, an investigation into the *rates* of change might produce some valuable results. Finally, a closely related systemic property is that of the number of individual alliance changes and shifts made in a given year or more by all nations in the system. This measure we call lateral mobility, and some preliminary work on it is already underway.

Similar thoughts occur when our bipolarity measures are considered. First of all, the measure itself reflects the degree of cleavage among major powers only, and while one would intuitively expect the total system to partially parallel the major power sub-system, we have no hard evidence that it does. Moreover, the measure is by no means as compelling an indicator of bipolarization as it might be. Since embarking on this project we have discovered in the sociometry and graph-theory literature some promising alternative operations by which such cleavage might be measured; some of these operations require that we first develop a better procedure for identifying alliance targets, while others do not.[20] In the same vein, it immediately occurs to us that bipolarity by itself may not be as interesting or compelling a predictor as when it is combined with one or more additional variables. For example, it might well pay to examine the joint effects of polarity and parity: is high bipolarity more likely to precede the onset of war when the two coalitions are approximately equal in power and capability or when a clear disparity exists?

Or, it might well be that the traditional theory overlooks a simple but crucial element: can the invisible hand ever function within so small a population? Certainly a large numerical discrepancy exists between the thousands of buyers and sellers in an economic marketplace and the 82 actors in our pre-1945 total system or the 120-odd ones in the postwar system. It might turn out that hypotheses generated from models of oligopoly or duopoly will stand the empirical test more successfully than those generated by a free and open market model.

[20] See, for example, Harary (1961), Coleman (1964), Rapoport (1963), Rapoport and Horvath (1961), Berge (1962), and Flament (1963).

Then, again, there is the matter of structural or cultural context. Is it not possible that the structural variable utilized here—alliance aggregation—is in turn responsive to other systemic properties, and that its predictive power is a function of its interaction with such variables? To put it another way, are nations as likely to respond to short- and middle-range security requirements and make alliances on that basis alone, when the diplomatic culture is increasingly ideological or less homogeneous, or when the structure of the system is more rigid or its supra-national aspects are increasing? Similarly, it can be argued that our approach is entirely too formal, and that emphasis might better be placed on other indices of international relationship: diplomatic communication, trade, tourism, or less formal and perhaps unwritten indicators of reciprocal commitment. Though these suggestions would carry us beyond our immediate concern here, they are certainly well taken.

A final concern is that raised in a thoughtful critique (Zinnes, 1966) regarding the extent to which this analysis really "tested the balance-of-power theory." As the title of this paper and its specific sections makes clear, we are not testing *the theory*, but only one basic proposition which we believe can be deduced from it; moreover, to grace the conceptual and empirical chaos of the balance-of-power literature with the label "theory" is much too generous. Within that critique, however, a specific problem of considerable importance *is* raised, and it merits a brief discussion. As we understand the criticism, it concerns the validity of our independent variable, and questions whether our alliance aggregation and alliance involvement indicators really reflect the diminution of cross-pressures as implied in our theoretical argument. Our argument, it will be recalled, is that each alliance commitment undertaken by a nation reduces its interaction opportunities, and thus the interaction opportunities available to the entire system; as these diminish, we reason that the allied nation is now "less free to compete with its new allies and less free to cooperate with non-allies." The randomized cross-pressures on it give way, to some extent, to pressures that are likely to be more discriminatory and systematic. That is, the nation is now less likely to treat all others in a neutral fashion, but will tend to remove some of them from the neutral category and treat them more nearly as friends or as opponents. Given what we know about reciprocity in diplomatic behavior, it follows that those nations which are now treated in a non-random fashion will respond more or less in kind. The original randomized pressures (impinging on it from many directions) will now come in upon the newly allied nation from more parallel or polarized directions, with a net loss of pluralistic cross-pressures in the system as a whole.

The criticism is that this model, while a reasonable interpretation of the classical formulation, ignores the fact that cross-pressures are *not* reduced unless the "nations belong to one and only one alliance." (Zinnes, 1966, p. 7). It goes on further to contend that in only 22 of our

130 years does that condition hold, and that our various indicators are therefore not theoretically valid. The assertion here, as we understand it, is that multiple alliance commitments do not necessarily diminish the cross-pressures, and may, under some conditions, even increase them. While the question is an empirical one, neither we nor others have yet sought to test it against evidence, and we must, therefore, fall back on logical analysis. In principle we would expect the assertion to hold in only an extremely limited set of cases: those in which a nation belongs to two alliances which are clearly *directed against one another*. And the only case in our population which clearly satisfies this unlikely condition is that of Italy, which belonged to both the Triple Alliance and the Entente (in a fragile sort of way) during the period leading up to World War I.

Even if there were other cases of such multiple membership in conflicting alliance groupings, however, the criticism would not hold. That is, it would only hold if the international system were composed solely of those two alliance memberships; as long as the system is larger than the five nations hypothesized in the critique, the assertion fails to stand. This is so because the allied nation, in its dealings with nations outside the two conflicting alliances, will not be as free as a non-allied nation would be in dealing with these more remote system members. In sum, we consider our independent and our intervening variables to be valid, and, therefore, remain satisfied that we have indeed examined a proposition which is central to the classical balance of power paradigm.[21]

These considerations bring us, therefore, back to the points raised at the outset of the paper. In any search for the "causes" of war, the quest for correlates may lead us not only into attributes of the international system, but into attributes of the more war-prone nations, their pre-conflict and pre-war relationships, and their pre-war behavior and interaction. It is our working assumption that any theory of the causes of war will include all four sets of independent variables. But we urge that considerable exploration of systemic properties be given high priority. Unless we understand the environment within which inter-nation conflict occurs, and can ascertain the approximate effect of that environment, there is no meaningful way of establishing the controls which are essential to any experimental inquiry. And if we look upon this quantitative approach to diplomatic history as a sequence of ex post facto, natural world experiment, the importance of such controls cannot be exaggerated.

[21] Furthermore, even though our alliance aggregation index is not responsive to multiple memberships, the alliance *involvement* index presented in an earlier paper *is*, and the correlations between the two indicators when applied to all nations in any alliances and to all in defense pacts are .90 and .87, respectively (Singer and Small, 1966, p. 20).

NATO Strategy
and Flexible Response

CARL H. AMME, JR.

Essential Differences The security of European NATO nations is no longer completely dependent upon the United States as it was immediately following World War II and the fall of Czechoslovakia to the Communists. The perception of a diminished Soviet military threat, the growing strength of the European nations, and the vulnerability of the United States to Soviet nuclear attacks have all had an influence in the evolving strategic differences in the Atlantic Alliance. The improved stability of the military confrontation now permits the nations of Europe to attempt to shape their own individual destinies.

Because each nation sees its destiny in different terms, each also conceives of different means or strategy to achieve its objectives. Although there are limited alternatives, the basic strategy of each sovereign nation is largely determined by considerations of national self-interest, the nation's primary values and objectives, and the means or capabilities it possesses. Thus attempts to arrive at an enduring agreement on an Alliance strategic concept in peacetime can result, at best, only in compromises.

In each dimension of warfare there are differences among the four major nations in the Atlantic Alliance. Table 1 highlights in simplified form the salient features of the different strategic concepts for the de-

Reprinted from Amme, Carl H., Jr., *NATO Without France: A Strategic Appraisal,* with the permission of the Hoover Institution on War, Revolution and Peace, Stanford University. © 1967 by the Board of Trustees of the Leland Stanford Junior University.

TABLE 1
Salient Features of Strategic Concepts
for Defense of Western Europe

Country	Conventional Warfare	Tactical Nuclear Warfare
United States	Prolongation of conventional defense as long as possible	Employment of tactical weapons in a selective manner
Great Britain	Short conventional defense to ascertain Soviet intentions	Employment of tactical weapons in demonstration of resolve and then in conjunction with strategic force
France	No conventional defense except for border incidents	Immediate nuclear retaliation on Russia
Germany	Short conventional defense at border to ascertain Soviet intentions, but with a very low nuclear threshold	Almost immediate use of battlefield nuclear weapons in zone of conflict, with possible demonstration strikes on Soviet territory

fense of Western Europe. Despite these differences, the views of Britain, France, and Germany on nuclear policy have a common theme: every country is more concerned with deterrence than with defense.

The West European nations are mistrustful of American attempts to build up military forces in Europe sufficient to defend their borders against major attack with conventional means. They see this action as degrading the credibility of deterrence, and they fear the consequences of a large-scale conventional war in Europe, an implication of the United States concept of flexible response. As Professor Henry Kissinger points out, a Soviet penetration of even a hundred miles in the fluctuations of conventional combat is a vital matter in which the national existence of a state is at stake.[1] Europeans, viewing the success of the NATO deterrent posture in the last seventeen years, are reluctant to change from a strategy that threatens an aggressor with massive destruction to one that reduces losses for a defender. They want the continuance of a nuclear deterrent that is reliable and credible. To some, the presence of American forces assures reliability and credibility, and the buildup of conventional strength is either unnecessary or harmful in its effects. To others, such as France, credibility rests on the direct control of nuclear forces by the country whose vital interests are at stake.

Deterrence, in the final analysis, is a psychological and political

[1] Henry A. Kissinger, "NATO's Nuclear Dilemma," *The Reporter*, XXVIII, 7 (28 March 1963), 27–28.

posture. The means may be fixed but the deterrent effect is relative. As Bernard Brodie stated, it must be measured ". . . not only by the amount of power that it holds in check, but also by the incentives to aggression residing behind that power." [2] In the French view, the fact that the United States has sufficient strategic nuclear arms to destroy the Soviet Union several times over does not of itself invalidate the deterrent effect of the fifty or so nuclear-equipped Mirage IV aircraft and the planned interim missile sites, even if they are vulnerable to a Soviet preemptive strike. Certainly, the existence of these forces will weigh on Soviet calculations, and the Kremlin must also consider the possibility of United States retaliation in the event the French *force de frappe* were struck first. This French force, as well as the NATO-committed British nuclear force, which is ultimately under the orders of its own government, would simply erect new disincentives to counteract whatever incentives the Soviets may have to attack.

Since deterrence is the key problem in European eyes, strategic concepts revolve around this issue and the strategic nuclear forces that provide the means to deter. In regard to tactical nuclear weapons in Europe, no country other than France questions the arrangements whereby these weapons are under sole American control to be released to our allies in the event they are needed in time of war. As has been pointed out, Great Britain and Germany regard tactical nuclear weapons mainly as a direct but intermediate step in deterrence. But when it comes to the final arbiter—". . . the credibility of a nation's will to confront an adversary with a war that no one can win"—each of the major allies wants to have its own voice in the control of strategic nuclear weapons. In such considerations Professor Robert E. Osgood points out ". . . national views on military logic are bound to be heavily infused with the logic of politics and psychology." [3]

France has chosen the way of an independent nuclear force. Great Britain, under the Conservatives, has regarded its V-Bomber forces as an ". . . independent contribution to the long-range strategic forces of the Western Alliance." Under Labor, Great Britain seeks to exercise more influence on United States control and all that it implies. Mr. Harold Wilson, the Prime Minister, has called for ". . . much closer cooperation in NATO for deciding not only questions of targeting, guidelines, and the rest, but deciding . . . the consensus, the circumstances in which the bomb should be dropped." [4] The position of Germany on strategic forces is clearly in the formative stages. There are conflicting political forces

[2] Bernard Brodie, "Anatomy of Deterrence," *World Politics*, II (January 1959), 177.
[3] Robert E. Osgood, *The Case for the MLF* (Washington Center of Foreign Policy Research, 1964).
[4] Prime Minister Harold Wilson, *Parliamentary Debates* (Hansard). Fifth series, Vol. 687, House of Commons Official Report: Session 1963–64 (London: Her Majesty's Stationery Office, Col. 445).

operating upon the government. On one side, there are the pressures from President de Gaulle and some politicians of the right wing of the Christian Democrats to choose a continental coalition. On the other side, there are pressures from the United States, Great Britain, and some of the smaller European nations to choose a wider basis of collaboration within the Atlantic Alliance. There is very little articulated demand from the German people for Germany to become an independent nuclear power. But the government leaders are keenly aware of the dangers of an incipient trend that might develop in this direction.

On the whole, Germany recognizes that the United States is the only country with the strength and will to protect German vital interests. Consequently, the German position is to seek closer collaboration with the United States on strategic nuclear forces and thereby exercise more influence on United States strategy. At the same time, the Germans will try to avoid alienating France in order not to jeopardize the possibility of reunification of Germany and closer political integration in Europe.

There is a clear incompatibility between the American concept for the defense of Western Europe and the strategic concepts of the European nations that put more emphasis on deterrence. Europeans would prefer to alter our strategic concept for Europe, which stresses deterrence through defense (denial), to one similar to our stragetic concept for the United States, which stresses deterrence through punishment.[5] Although we proclaim that our strategy is indivisible and that we have ". . . undertaken the nuclear defense of NATO on a global basis," some of our pronouncements and actions to create a strong conventional defense in Europe, or even to increase the number of tactical nuclear weapons (as was advertised by Secretary of Defense McNamara[6]), are viewed by Europeans as an effort to confine the fighting to Europe and to leave the United States untouched. The American argument for adopting a common strategy of flexible response based initially on conventional defense is seen by many Europeans as a desire to raise the nuclear threshold on issues that may be vital to the Europeans but not vital to the United States. Even when faced with a bona fide threat in the 1961 Berlin Crisis, the proposed American strategy which incorporated a conventional probe along the autobahn was not wholly subscribed to by the other NATO nations involved. West Germany, in particular, wanted to preserve Berlin as the future capital of a reunited Germany and stressed the importance of preserving the quadripartite status of East Berlin. Bonn wanted no diminution of resolve on that score. In the end, this quadripartite status was lost by allowing the Berlin Wall to be built.

[5] Glenn H. Snyder, *Deterrence and Defense* (Princeton: Princeton University Press, 1961), pp. 8–9. Snyder makes the distinction between deterrence by *denial* and deterrence by *punishment*. The "capacity to deny territory to the enemy, or otherwise to block his aims, may be a very efficient deterrent."
[6] *New York Times*, 2 June 1965.

As long as European national interests and objectives vary from this, the attainment of a common strategy is hardly likely. One only has to recall the Suez crisis to bring home this point. There should, however, be opportunities for clarifying and coordinating arms and strategies for the crises that arise.

Deterrence and   The American strategy for limited war is a
Defense in   war-fighting strategy in the traditional sense.
Central Europe   It has the objective of defense, and a successful
defense implies victory, or at least stalemate, on the battlefield. How well the American concept of flexible response can stand up to enemy attack in practice and achieve victory—a stand-off, a restoration of the *status quo ante*, or even positive political goals —depends to a large extent on the military force postures of both sides. The presence of sufficient well-deployed military forces is essential to provide a successful defense; what constitutes sufficiency, however, depends on the kinds of action the enemy might undertake. A range of contingencies and alternative courses of actions must be examined. Timothy W. Stanley has pointed out that some of the ". . . most disastrous military mistakes in history have resulted from trying to make a choice of terrain, tactics, timing, and weapons for the enemy. One has to assume not one or two possibilities, but a full range of actions of which the enemy is capable." [7] On the other hand, one does not have to emulate Lewis Carroll's "White Knight" by trying to anticipate every conceivable contingency.[8] There is a limit to the range of actions that are remotely plausible in the European context. In the first place, any outbreak of conflict in Europe would take place under the umbrella of strategic deterrence. Before various conflict contingencies can be examined, it is necessary to ask why any conflict—aside from a border incident—should take place at all.

In the overall context, stable nuclear confrontation is generally assumed to exist—at least insofar as a nuclear exchange between the two superpowers. This stability is based on the firm conviction, verging on certainty, that nuclear retaliation would result in such unprecedented

---

[7] T. W. Stanley, *NATO in Transition* (New York: Praeger, 1965), p. 246.
[8] Lewis Carroll, "The White Knight" in *Through the Looking Glass*, Chapter VIII.
"I was wondering what the mouse-trap was for," said Alice. "It isn't very likely there would be any mice on the horse's back."
"Not very likely, perhaps," said the Knight; "but, if they *do* come, I don't choose to have them running all about."
"You see," he went on after a pause, "it's as well to be provided for *everything*. That's the reason the horse has all those anklets round his feet."
"But what are they for?" Alice asked in a tone of great curiosity.
"To guard against the bites of sharks," the Knight replied. "It's an invention of my own."

death and destruction to the attacker that no nation would initiate the first strike. Such stability depends on (1) a redundant supply of strategic missiles which are highly invulnerable to enemy attack and which possess the assured capability of overcoming enemy defenses and (2) the continuing assessment that there will be no technological advance which will radically change the vulnerability of either side to the nuclear attack of the other.

But nuclear deterrence may be used for other things such as deterring a nonnuclear attack. Here the element of uncertainty creeps in. Such a deterrent strategy can still be successful so long as the threat is made to appear to the opponent as commensurate with the vital interests of the nation making the threat, and so long as the strategy raises doubts in the mind of the opponent as to whether the objectives he seeks are worth the risk. If the stakes seem at the time to be relatively minor or peripheral, it will be difficult to make the threat of nuclear retaliation credible. The enemy may then take the chance of achieving certain modest goals (e.g., the Berlin blockade of 1948 and building the Berlin Wall in 1961), particularly if the means available to the other side appear insufficient to deny him success.

Uncertainty in the effectiveness of nuclear deterrence to cover every kind of threat has impelled the United States to seek a range of options between what is clearly vital to United States national interests in the true meaning of the word and what is not. For what threatens our vital interests, nuclear deterrence is based on certainty of retaliation; for what threatens national interests that are not considered vital, nuclear deterrence has an element of uncertainty about it. In an attempt to remove the uncertainty from the latter category, the United States has attempted to structure a careful series of graduated threats and commitments that would be more credible than the threat of nuclear retaliation alone. The measures structured consist of a mixture of (1) attempts to convince the enemy that the United States national interests are vital, (2) not-so-credible threats of nuclear retaliation, (3) more credible threats of conventional defense backed by the postponed threat of using tactical nuclear weapons, (4) the actual commitment of conventional force to battle in the event that the first three fail to deter, and (5) the ever-present articulated or tacit threat of escalation that accompanies any armed conflict.

These measures may not, however, remove the uncertainty. The argument can be made that the United States would not intervene with nuclear weapons in Europe because of the risk that the continental United States might be attacked. The implied threat that France might use her *force de frappe* to trigger an American nuclear response can similarly be discounted. These are legitimate arguments. At the same time, the credibility of the threat of a Soviet invasion of Western Europe must be taken into account. The two sides of the credibility equation must be considered together. In other words, how plausible or credible would be a major Soviet invasion of Western Europe coupled with American and French abstention in the use of nuclear weapons? The record over the last twenty years and the force deployments in Western Europe would suggest that the combination of these two credibility factors balances out. Stated differently, the probability that the Soviet Union would refrain from an attack in the face of American and French threats to use nuclear weapons is exceedingly high. The probability that the Soviet Union has no intention to attack is also high. This indicates that deterrence is credible or that the Soviet Union has had no intention of attacking Western Europe, or both.

The prevalent view that a Soviet military threat in Central Europe has receded (if it has not disappeared entirely) appears to be based on evidence and logic. The historical evidence is a record of manifest caution by the Soviet Union in any military confrontation with the United States—particularly in the face of the strong United States commitment of the Seventh United States Army, Third and Seventeenth United States Air Forces, thousands of tactical nuclear weapons, the implied threat of the United States strategic nuclear forces, and the support of the not inconsiderable European NATO forces in West Germany. The logic of this United States commitment would indicate to both sides that the decision in fact has actually been made to defend West Europe with all means necessary. This decision immediately places the onus on the Soviet Union to decide whether acquiring all or part of Europe is worth the cost. This is different from the arguments on relative military capabilities that deal only with the comparative cost of defense versus offense. The value of the objective to be gained must be judged, and this is almost always more valuable to the side in possession.

Surely it must be clear that the leaders of the Soviet Union must calculate beforehand the cost of military action in terms of nuclear destruction and lives to be lost. It is generally conceded that the NATO military forces cannot defend against a major conventional invasion without resort to nuclear weapons. Should it be otherwise, the Soviets would be unable to achieve the military objective desired without resort to nuclear armaments.

Assuming the Soviets place a high value on a particular objective, high enough to command acceptance of the cost of aggressive military action against Western Europe, the question must be asked—what objective and at what cost? For instance, should the high-value Soviet objective be seizure of Western Germany in order to prevent the Federal Republic from acquiring an independent nuclear force, the almost-certain cost would be a nuclear war. This war might be initiated by the Soviet Union (in accordance with its preconceived military strategies), or—as the Western forces are overrun—by either the NATO Alliance or the United States.

Now, if the above reasoning holds true, why should the Soviets not use nuclear weapons immediately and benefit from the tremendous advantage of surprise? Further, can it be imagined that the Soviet Union would plan a deliberate invasion to seize Western Germany—without significantly reinforcing its forces or without having the satellite states mobilized? Would the Rumanian, Polish, Czech, and Hungarian Communist political and military leaders help plan, or even agree after-the-fact, to a deliberate unprovoked military aggression? And can anyone doubt that the reinforcement would be immediately noticed by NATO, which would in turn alert and mobilize its military elements?

It has been suggested that the Soviet Union might seek a more limited objective, such as a probe, e.g., the seizure of a border town such as Lübeck or even Hamburg. The idea would be to achieve a *fait accompli* quickly and place the burden of escalation upon the West. It is conceivable that such a surprise military operation could be successful in the initial action, provided it were mounted as a Blitzkrieg with a substantial force of at least three or four assault divisions. But it is difficult to conceive that the Soviet Union would undertake major aggression for such limited objectives. First, such purposeful, large-scale conventional attacks are not consistent with Soviet war doctrine, which stresses combined nuclear and conventional attacks in an attempt to seize the strategic initiative. Neither are they consistent with Communist doctrine of peaceful coexistence and the avoidance of "adventurism." Second, such adventuristic moves clearly place Soviet core interests in jeopardy. The Kremlin leaders could hardly be certain that the thermonuclear standoff would prevent the United States from launching a strategic strike against the USSR, or from even using tactical nuclear weapons on the battlefield to prevent the seizure. In any event the Soviets still would realize that the West could not accept such a sacrifice without taking immediate military steps to restore the *status quo ante* or at least to exact a comparable loss from the Soviet Union. Third, once committed to the defense of so vital an area with the NATO military forces at hand, the war would rapidly expand to a full-scale European war and the pressures for nuclear escalation would be almost irresistible. This would hardly be an acceptable price for the Soviets to pay for a limited objective. A limited Soviet military aggression of the size of a probe seems on the face of it even more implausible than an all-out invasion. Yet since it has been suggested as possible by responsible spokesmen on both sides of the Atlantic, it should be examined as a contingency.

The third and final contingency is the conflict that might arise out of a crisis or a miscalculation of NATO resolve. Such a conflict is considered by most military analysts as the most likely contingency. The crisis might be an uprising in East Germany, the attempted seizure of power in West Germany by a resurgent nationalist group, the hemming-in of an important military convoy on the East German autobahn in connection with a crisis at Berlin, or even a serious riot and storming of the Berlin Wall. A crisis might be managed or exploited by the Soviets to achieve what they consider minor or peripheral gains—gains that might be achieved by deterring NATO's military opposition with the threat of escalation. (The burden would then be on NATO.) This type of limited engagement would be in keeping with the Soviet strategic concept and with the Communist doctrine of eschewing adventurism. If effectively opposed by NATO, and an armed conflict results, the Soviet Union would have the option of backing down, of holding to the gains so far established, or of pushing further. The last option represents the greatest chance of miscalculation and the greatest danger that the conflict would spread.

Coordinating Arms and Strategies Crucial to the task of coordinating arms and strategies in an alliance for dealing with these contingencies is a definition of common political goals in the event of conflict. In the Atlantic Alliance these have not been defined beyond the commitment of collective defense against an unidentified aggression laid down in the treaty itself. It is fashionable to say that, in Europe at least, nuclear weapons have made war obsolete as a means of achieving political objectives. The truth of this assertion depends on the objective sought and the military means employed for achieving the objective. Certainly, armed conflict cannot be ruled out entirely in Europe. Long before writers began to quote Clausewitz, it had been recognized as axiomatic that the political aim of war should be within the military means. It never is as far as the defeated nation is concerned. The political objectives of Japan in World War II proved in the end to be beyond her military means. The political objectives of the United States, however, were well within her military means, and peace was restored with Japan on reasonably satisfactory terms. On the victorious side, there is always the strong temptation to expand the limited political aims to conform with the full extent of the military capacity. This is dangerous; for example, when the United Nations changed their political objective of merely repelling the North Korean invasion to the complete military defeat of that country, it brought on a quite unexpected war with Communist China. On the other hand, the vague political objectives that accompanied the policy of "unconditional surrender" in World War II caused the Western allies to lose opportunities to achieve political goals well within their military capabilities. In Europe, nuclear weapons afford both sides the means to expand the military action up to general war— a result that neither side would deliberately seek. Therefore, the ability to exercise restraints on the use of force in Europe is just as important as to expand the use of force to achieve the objective sought.

If conflict breaks out in Europe, for whatever reason, the Alliance should at least have an agreed purpose in mind and certain clear political objectives. Yet each local conflict situation will vary according to the circumstances surrounding the initial crisis, the value of the objectives, and the conscious decisions of the two sides to commit armed forces in battle to achieve a local victory. For when military forces do battle there is only one purpose: victory. It is extremely difficult to conceive of circumstances where one side or the other would deliberately decide to resort to force to attain an objective, and to then refrain from throwing the necessary resources into battle to achieve the objective and to avoid defeat. It is not impossible, however, to imagine that limitations and constraints would be imposed by both sides on the objectives to be sought and on the use of nuclear weapons in battle to prevent the conflict from escalating to general war. Too much is at stake. From 122 to 149 million fatalities could result from a Soviet strike against United States cities and military targets.[9] There is no doubt that the Soviet leaders understand well that Russia could expect carnage of similar monstrous proportions; but still, exercising constraints on force implies a limited political objective. The only sensible objective for the types of conflicts examined would be the minimum objective of restoring the territorial *status quo ante bellum* on the least disadvantageous or unsatisfactory terms.

There are some practical problems that must be dealt with. The question is not the abstract one of whether we can restore the *status quo* with the military means at our disposal. The question rather is whether we can defeat the enemy's armed forces in a specific locale over a particular issue. Once armed conflict takes place, the tendency on both sides is to take additional measures necessary to achieve a favorable outcome —but not measures that would worsen the outcome. To suggest, however, that both sides would be mutually deterred from using nuclear weapons out of fear of a worsened outcome suggests also that a conventional defeat is a more acceptable outcome. This may well be true, provided the conventional defeat is not one of *vital* proportions—or perceived as vital. But then the question should be asked if there are any conceivable conventional victory-defeat outcomes of armed conflict in Europe that would not be considered vital by one side or the other.

The record would indicate that whereas the Soviets have made threats, they have committed no acts of aggression against the Alliance.

[9] Secretary of Defense McNamara before the House Armed Services Committee on the FY 1966–70 Defense Program and 1966 Defense Budget (18 February 1965), p. 47. There is something inherently inconsistent with these figures. They represent an inability to be accurate except within a range of twenty-seven million yet they suggest that one can be precise within one or two million on the upper and lower figures. Perhaps "over 100 million" would be a more general and representative figure. Mr. McNamara goes on to suggest that these figures could be reduced by about one-half with adequate fallout shelters.

True, the Berlin blockade on the autobahn and railroads in 1948, the construction of the Berlin Wall in 1961, and a number of lesser infringements on what the United States regarded as rights of access were accepted by the United States without recourse to force. None of these issues were vital, however. Whereas they could all be regarded as infringements of rights, they could hardly be classed as acts of aggression. The United States, on the other hand, has taken special pains to create in Berlin a symbol of vital interests, if not an American vital interest per se. The United States and the other occupying allied powers have made the freedom of West Berlin an unambiguous symbol of the West's determination to resist further Soviet encroachment. To acquiesce to the loss of Berlin's independence (no longer a marginal matter) would cause such a serious blow to the West, that it is hardly conceivable that the Atlantic Alliance could survive. It is even less conceivable that the city's absorption by the Communists could be carried out without a fight. Finally, considering the absolute commitments made by the United States and its allies to Berlin and the impossibility of mounting an adequate conventional defense, there can be little question that the United States would respond elsewhere at places of its own choice, as well as at Berlin itself, and that we would use nuclear weapons if needed. In fact, this was made clear during the Berlin crisis of 1961. The Soviet threat of signing a peace treaty with East Germany and of creating a "free city" of West Berlin was resisted firmly by the United States. It could hardly be asserted that United States vital interests were involved at this stage. But President Kennedy saw larger political effects in the move and stated:

> If we do not meet our commitments in Berlin, it will mean the destruction of NATO and a dangerous situation for the whole world. All Europe is at stake in West Berlin.[10]

He reinforced the Seventh United States Army, called up certain units of the reserves and National Guard and resolved that the United States would go to war, even to nuclear war, if the Soviet Union took action aimed at destroying the freedom of West Berlin.[11]

Three factors would indicate that nuclear weapons would be used under important circumstances. First, McNamara's idea that the European nations would come up with the additional forces to make a forward conventional defense-deterrence successful ". . . for dealing with even larger Soviet attacks" has been dashed. The Alliance can no longer even reckon on the French divisions and aircraft. The war in Vietnam is placing a strain on United States resources and already 15,000 special American troop ratings have been withdrawn from Europe. Britain

[10] Arthur M. Schlesinger, Jr., *A Thousand Days*, pp. 379–80.
[11] *Ibid.*, p. 391.

is also suffering from a chronic financial drain, and there are pressures to reduce the British Army of the Rhine even further. Secondly, the very existence of nuclear arsenals and elaborate plans for their use on both sides would indicate that any large conflict, which cannot be terminated early enough, would in all probability escalate to nuclear conflict. A third factor is the continuing nature of deterrence. Deterrence—whether it relies on conventional forces, nuclear forces, or a composite mixture—does not fail once and for all. The effectiveness of deterrence depends on the opponent's belief that the necessary military action would be taken to match the value of the objective sought. Each deliberate step in escalation would signify a higher value placed on the objective. For example, if it were possible for one side to use nuclear weapons in a distinct, obvious, and discriminate way on the battlefield to prevent the loss of a vital objective, that side would do so rather than surrender. The burden of expanding the nuclear war beyond the battlefield would then be placed on the other side. Since each step in the escalation ladder brings the contestants nearer to general war—an outcome that neither side would want—it would appear that at some point along the line graduated deterrence would work, and restraint would be exercised by each side from the very start to keep the issue from becoming vital to either. Therefore, in pursuing the minimum objective of restoring the *status quo,* NATO must have a force posture that permits it to react quickly to oppose any enemy move and to prevent the move from developing into a vital issue.

It is strongly suggested that the most likely issue would be small at the start and would arise from a crisis or a miscalculation of resolve. Since the most likely locale would be along the border partitioning Germany or at Berlin, strategic concepts should be examined in these contexts. Certainly, a response to low-level conflicts in line with the French strategic concept that hurls nuclear destruction upon the Soviet Union can hardly be considered a rational response, since it fails to consider that deterrence is a continuing phenomenon. If conflict starts by miscalculation, the proper response would be to take the necessary steps to prevent the conflict from continuing or from enlarging. Whether one accepts the American concept of a conventional response with a high threshold or the German concept of battlefield nuclear and atomic demolition mine (ADM) responses at a much lower threshold, one can certainly rule out the French concept of massive retaliation as a sensible way to defend Western Europe or to keep the lid on the fighting.

If France is serious about her strategic concept of "massive retaliation" for everything but border incidents, one can only wonder why she desires to keep her two divisions in Germany. Their location in Germany is much too far from the Iron Curtain to be useful in a border incident, and anything larger than a border incident is theoretically ruled out under her concept. But France may perhaps plan on using these forces to block on German territory a larger "probe" or incursion before it threatens France.[12] France's true reason for wanting to keep her forces in Germany is more than likely political: to influence Germany's action by retaining rights stemming from the Occupation that relate to the stationing of armed forces in Germany until a peace treaty is signed for all of Germany. This would give France increased weight vis-à-vis the Soviet Union: Russia stations troops in East Germany and France stations troops in West Germany.

De Gaulle's calculated move to get American forces out of France will have a serious effect on the operation of the American strategic concept of flexible response in the case of any sizeable penetration. The idea of depending on a conventional defense until the ground forces are in danger of being overrun before employing tactical nuclear weapons is unrealistic, at least in terms of the logistic difficulties and the lack of strategic depth. Preoccupied as we have been with the central sector and the Thuringian gap, we nevertheless have recognized the possibility of being outflanked through the north German plain where the much weaker British Army of the Rhine is on guard. Theoretically, we could always have fallen back to a defense line along the Rhine and Weser—perhaps comforted by the thought that we still had some strategic depth in France and our logistic lines behind us. If the scenario just described ever had any relevance to reality, it has all been changed with de Gaulle's unilateral action. The one thing de Gaulle has done is to force us to re-examine our strategic concept for limited war—especially as it relates to the defense of West Germany.

However, too much importance should not be attached to erecting the straw man of a sizeable Soviet penetration for the purpose of downgrading the American limited war concept. Clearly a conventional defense in such a case would be the worst possible application. Yet for the more likely contingencies mentioned—a border or a Berlin crisis—an initial conventional response could very well be the only sensible one to employ. The chances are, both sides would act to snuff out the conflict as quickly as possible with the minimum of violence. But if the conflict gets out of hand and conventional defense/deterrence proves inadequate, then the problem would be when and how to initiate the use of nuclear weapons—keeping in mind the assumed minimum objective of restoring

---

[12] It is suggested that the geographical position of France permits her to entertain the concept of nuclear retaliation even for a "probe," since a probe must first strike Western Germany, and by the time it threatens France it is no longer a probe. General Pierre Gallois, a French strategic theorist, in discussion with the author, suggested that if the enemy threatened France from "outside the gates of Strasbourg," the appropriate reply would be to strike Russia with nuclear weapons. This viewpoint indicates the kind of situation in which the French might regard nuclear retaliation as an appropriate response. Unanswered is the question of how the Soviets achieved this position "outside the gates of Strasbourg" without "bloodying" quite a few American and German allies in the process.

the *status quo ante bellum*—with the least possible devastation and the maximum possible control to prevent escalation to a Europe-wide or a general nuclear war.

A *Conceptual* This brings us face to face with the problem
Variation of of escalation and the idea of a firebreak or
Flexible Response distinguishable threshold of violence. The two
are intimately related. The clear distinction between the nonuse and the use of nuclear weapons is considered by many as a threshold of violence or firebreak that, once crossed, would quickly cause the conflict to escalate to general war. Leading defense spokesmen of the major NATO nations have expressed this belief. The difference is that the American concept calls for maintaining this firebreak at a high level of violence and provocation whereas the European members would establish it at a low level to enhance deterrence.

That the so-called nuclear threshold, or firebreak, is clearly distinguishable is widely accepted. Hardly anyone subscribes to the view that a tactical nuclear weapon is just another weapon, as was advocated by some enthusiasts in the early 1950's. Furthermore, the nuclear firebreak is the kind of unambiguous distinction which facilitates tacit agreement on constraints that prevail in war. History has shown that constraints defined in such clear-cut categories are more reliable than those defined in quantitative degrees within categories. Thus, "no gas" in World War II was an easier limit to accept than "a little gas" or just one type of gas. Tacit acceptance in Korea of "no atomic bombs" was easier to understand than "small atomic bombs" on certain kinds of targets.[13]

Admitting that a distinguishable firebreak exists, however, does not support the belief that crossing the firebreak would inevitably result in uncontrolled escalation to general nuclear war. The danger of escalation exists, of course, but establishing a firm ceiling on the conflict by adopting a policy of postponing the use of nuclear weapons until allied territory and ground forces are in danger of being overrun is not the answer. For then the issue becomes vital and demands for tactical nuclear weapons to stem the invasion would be quite large and the unprecedented combat losses on both sides would exert pressures on the political leaders to expand the aims to something greater than the restoration of the *status quo*.

There exist two possible alternatives to this dilemma. First, the United States could adopt a strategic concept more in line with German desires. Such a concept would call for lowering the violence threshold or firebreak and giving an unambiguous commitment to West Germany that tactical nuclear weapons would be used much earlier than is now con-

[13] For a more detailed discussion of this point see the author's "Psychological Effects of Nuclear Weapons," U.S. Naval Institute *Proceedings*, April 1960, p. 34.

templated. There are dangers to this approach. A miscalculation of enemy intentions might be made, and nuclear weapons might be used when none are needed—thus precipitating a nuclear battle that no one wants. There are also practical difficulties in establishing an arrangement for giving an unambiguous nuclear commitment to West Germany, difficulties that go beyond the obvious political problems involved. It is basically a matter of credibility. All the assurances in the world won't convince the Germans or the Soviets that the United States would not use nuclear weapons unless it were clearly perceived that United States vital interests are threatened. As Secretary of Defense McNamara put it, ". . . a credible deterrent cannot be based on an incredible act." [14]

Deterrence is, in effect, a psychological posture. We attempt to create in the mind of a potential enemy a fear or a belief in our willingness to act. Certainly no rational enemy would deny that we would have the will to employ nuclear weapons if the stakes are vital. On the other hand, he would hardly conceive that we would be irrational enough to use these weapons if the stakes are minute. In the final analysis, the problem is a matter of making the perception of the United States commitment to West Germany "vital" enough to risk a thermonuclear exchange.

The second alternative rests on the same psychological premise. It seeks to improve the credibility of deterrence not by enhancing the "vitalness" of our commitment but by making the consequences of using nuclear weapons less horrendous and by establishing other firebreaks or thresholds of violence at an intermediate level between the first use of nuclear weapons and general nuclear war. The problem here is making the threshold distinguishable. As pointed out earlier, making a distinction between nuclear weapons during war by judging their yield (except in the most general sort of way), by estimating the range and point of origin of the delivery vehicle, or by divining whether the collateral population damage was intentional or not, is for all practical purposes impossible in the confusion of battle. About the only hope of establishing a difference between nuclear weapons in time of war is to base the distinction on the use to which the weapons are put. For example, nuclear weapons with impact only in a certain area and in no other may be distinguishable provided the accompanying dialogue is made explicit and unambiguous in both words and actions. Also, atomic demolition weapons (ADM's) can be very distinguishable as battlefield weapons because of their emplacement on defended territory and their immobility. However, there are three objections to their use. They must be prepositioned before hostilities to be of much use in fast moving actions, and this prepositioning seems to be presently politically unacceptable. Present defensive concepts call for attempts to stop incursions conventionally before using nuclear weapons. If ADM's are placed near the violated borders, they are likely to be overrun before decisions to use them can be made.

[14] Quoted in Schlesinger, op. cit., p. 853.

Finally, there is the dangerous and unmanageable problem of radioactive fall-out.

Nevertheless, it may be possible to distinguish "battlefield" nuclear weapons from other tactical nuclear weapons used for purposes of interdiction and penetration attacks on military bases deep in enemy territory—not only by their smaller yield and lesser range but mainly by the fact that their bursts are confined to the immediate battle area. If the other side did not perceive the limitation, it would be because it did not want to perceive it. The precedence already has been established in Korea and Vietnam that certain targets could be treated as sanctuaries—as long as it appeared advantageous to do so. If one side struck at airfields and other military bases outside of the battle zone, the action would be deliberate. Such an act could hardly be considered an unintentional violation of a limitation that the leaders had failed to perceive. Whether such a distinction can be made in practice or not, efforts to do so by peacetime and wartime actions and pronouncements would at least create a presumption in the mind of the enemy, and among our allies, that the United States would be less reluctant to cross the first: use nuclear firebreak in certain circumstances. This could only have the effect of reinforcing graduated deterrence. This conclusion is supported by the expressions of concern by Soviet leaders over the United States concept for limited war and for the use of tactical nuclear weapons to keep a European war limited.

The logic of the American strategic concept of flexible response is judged by United States national security and the geographical position of the United States. But the same considerations of national security apply to other nations within the Alliance whose territories are not geographically separated from the scene of potential battle. The obligation of a state to protect its citizens and its territory is conditioned by the understanding that threat to any part is subordinate to the preservation of the state as a whole. The state may be forced to sacrifice part to preserve the whole, but the obligation is compelling for a state to protect its security and to devote whatever resources are needed to preserve the harmony of the whole without destroying the vitality of the parts.

The same obligations in theory apply to an alliance; in practice, however, the obligation is not as strong. History is full of broken treaties, abandonment of allies, and reversals of alliances. The Europeans are conscious of this, and they are determined not to subordinate thier own national security to preserve the alliance. They have no intention of permitting their homelands to be regarded as a part that might be sacrified in time of war to preserve the vitality of a so-called indivisible alliance, the core of which is the United States. The Atlantic Alliance is to them, as it is to the United States, an instrument to preserve their own security. Alliances are made for national purposes, not the reverse. Thus European fears center around the flexible American strategic concept for a limited war in Europe that might be limited or terminated at the expense of the allies. That the American concept has wide acceptance among Americans is quite natural. The point of this discussion is that it does not enjoy wide acceptance among Europeans.

European leaders recognize that the United States depends on a general war strategy for its own survival. They also understand that the limited war concept of flexible response—as it serves to protect the allies —is based on the logic of United States national self-interests. They see nothing wrong in having a choice of conventional as well as nuclear options to deal with various contingencies. What they do object to is not having the same choice of options for their nations. They mark well the United States priorities that emphasize nuclear options as the most vital for survival. From Secretary McNamara's Ann Arbor speech, they are aware that the United States reserves to itself the choice of at least two strategic options—striking enemy cities or striking missile sites and airfields; perhaps they suspect there are more. Many of the European nations do not have nuclear options—nor the early commitment of the United States to use nuclear weapons when their vital interests are at stake. It is hardly any wonder that these European nations are reluctant to expend their resources on additional conventional forces before a nuclear option, vital to their ultimate survival, is provided.

This is an important point. Some of our European allies accept without question our commitment to come to their defense. For the smaller nations, it is practically the only alternative available to them. They have neither the incentive nor the resources to become nuclear powers. The problem is mainly with Germany—for France and Great Britain have at least one nuclear option. Since the interlocking legal, political, and institutional restraints prevent Germany from becoming a nuclear power, how does one provide an unambiguous commitment to use nuclear weapons? And how do we create other nuclear firebreaks which will prevent uncontrollable escalation to general nuclear war? Official pronouncements and assurances will not do it alone. Practical and credible military arrangements may.

In a real world, however, things do not happen exactly as they are conceived in the abstract. The debate over conflicting strategic concepts by its very nature is largely a dialectic for political discussion. In a real crisis, a series of actions would very likely take place that would reveal how vital the issues are and the governments would act accordingly. The logic of the situation—even to the French—would indicate that certain intermediate steps would be taken before inviting holocaust. The problem then is to provide a force posture that will allow these intermediate steps to be taken and if nuclear weapons are needed, to permit their use in such a controlled and discriminate manner that holocaust does not result.

PART III

ALLIANCE COOPERATION

NATO and the OAS

ELLIOTT VANDEVANTER, JR.

I. Concerning a There are several ways of conducting generic
Method of studies. One is to analyze individual members
Analyzing Alliances in great detail; another is to look at two or
more members of the same species to compare
similarities and differences. Most of the investigations of international
alliances to date have concentrated on the former method. Even the few
comparisons that have been made *between* alliances have dealt only with
their formal structures—not with the ways they perform.

This paper will compare—functionally as well as structurally—
America's two foremost alliances: NATO and the OAS. The dual purpose
is: (1) to learn more about alliances in general, and (2) to consider possible changes in one organization in light of the experiences of the other.
By comparing two organizations as disparate as NATO and the Organization of American States (OAS) one may derive new insights about the
nature of alliances, just as the sociologist taught us more about political
systems by relating primitive and advanced models.

Acknowledging that a comparative analysis of alliances is desirable
does not get us very far on the road, however. We have already alluded
to the inadequacy of mere structural comparisons. If alliances are organ-
ic—if they are made up of a series of elements so interdependent that a
change in one will necessitate a readjustment in another—we must study

From P-3832, *A Further Inquiry into the Nature of Alliances: NATO and the
OAS,* by E. Vandevanter, Jr., The Rand Corporation, April 1968. Reprinted by
permission.

these systems in their evolutionary milieu. We must probe the interrelationship of structures and activities, problems and procedures, purposes and environments.

The term usually applied to this type of examination is "functional analysis." Unfortunately, the technique has not yet been highly developed, even for *national* political systems. To extend it to the *international* realm involves pioneering to a degree which might discourage the experienced political scientist. With the temerity of novices, let us expropriate the tools of the structural analysts and adapt them to our needs.

Frank G. Goodnow laid a foundation many years back when he divided the functions of government in two: politics and administration.[1]

A half century later David Easton increased the number by half, arguing that any polity involves three functions: "inputs"—which he subclassifies as demands and supports—and "outputs."[2] Others, following "separation-of-power" distinctions, consider legislative, executive, and judicial activities as the three functions of government.[3]

Talcott Parsons maintains that a social system must perform four functions: adaptation, goal achievement, integration, and latency.[4] Harold Lasswell identifies seven categories of functions, which we need not enumerate here.[5] This number may be approaching the upper limit of modern development, for Gabriel Almond also settles for seven functions. Although his nomenclature differs substantially from Lasswell's, he subdivided all seven, *à la* Easton, into inputs and outputs.[6]

To add to the uncertainty, many authors use the term "functional" to refer to an agency which deals in a single area of technical activity, such as the International Postal Union. David Mitrany and Ernst B. Haas have written widely on the subject of international functional organizations. Thus we can recognize that Amitai Etzioni is not intending to telescope the categories of Almond, Lasswell, *et al.*, when he speaks of "monofunctional" international organization.[7]

It would be presumptuous of us to attempt to synthesize the work of these outstanding scholars. Nonetheless, if we are to attempt to use any of their concepts, we must either accept one theorist's set or develop

---

[1] Frank J. Goodnow, *Politics and Administration*, New York, 1900.
[2] *World Politics*, Vol. IX, No. 3, April 1957.
[3] Lawrence Scheinman, "Euratom: Nuclear Integration in Europe," *International Conciliation*, May 1967.
[4] Peter M. Blau and Richard Scott, *Formal Organizations*, Chandler Publishing Company, San Francisco, 1962, p. 38.
[5] Harold Lasswell, *The Decision Process*, University of Maryland, 1956.
[6] Gabriel Almond, "A Functional Approach to Comparative Politics," Almond and Coleman (eds.), *The Politics of Developing Areas*, Princeton University Press, 1966, p. 15.
[7] Amitai Etzioni, *Political Unification*, Holt, Rinehart and Winston, New York, 1965, p. 7.

a new one of our own. We will, in this piece, avoid using "functional" in the Mitrany-Haas sense of an organization confined to a technical field. In looking at the breakdown of functions suggested by the authors who have divided them into categories, we can notice that, despite the quantitative and terminological differences, all of them conform in one way or another to the "engine" concept of a social system. That is to say, they all visualize (1) something going into one end of a machine, (2) being blended, integrated, allocated, or changed by the machine, and (3) emerging from the other end in altered form. They designate the inputs variously as supports, demands, politics, aspirations, interests, etc. They refer to the outputs as laws, actions, prescriptions, imperatives, regulations, judgments, or what have you—but the idea is the same.

The theorists deviate from a purely mechanical concept in one respect, more explicitly recognized by Almond and Easton than the others: They conceive of the engine not as a rigid machine but rather as a flexible device that assumes different configurations to suit the environment, to accommodate to changes in inputs, or to adjust to the effects of the outputs.[8]

The engine model suits our purposes for another reason: An engine can be considered as more or less efficient in terms of the amount of energy it requires to produce an end item. It is high time that political scientists moved beyond the "traditional" image of an alliance as an altruistic "one-for-all-and-all-for-one" proposition. The more modern replacement theory will be developed around the idea that alliances are calculated ventures in which each partner expects certain returns for his investment. The coalition must appear to the individual member as "efficient"—that is, it must offer him more in return than what he has to put in—or he will not join or continue as a member. (The same applies to specific projects within a working alliance: If a proposal would bring returns less valuable than its cost to the nation, that nation will vote against it.)

For this first rough cut, then, we will look at these two alliances as we would two engines; we will study the inputs, the mechanisms, and the outputs. To make the task more manageable, and to focus on the most concrete structures and activities, we will confine the comparisons to the military field.

II. Input Functions For our purposes Easton's separation of input functions into "demands" and "supports" seems to introduce a necessary distinction which is missing in some other categorizations. It comes closer to dealing with the question of "why" nations

[8] *Viz.*, David Easton, "The Analysis of Political Systems," in *Comparative Politics*, Roy C. Macridis and Bernard E. Brown (eds.), Dorsey Press, Homewood, Ill., 1964, p. 91.

join together in these coalitions. In a sense, the "demands" that a member makes on an alliance, and the "supports" he is willing to give it, are but another way of measuring its utility to him. We could also speak of weighing benefits and costs, or—in still different terms—of sensing the "pleasure-pain" relationship.

Under this concept, the first step in our analysis of input functions would be to study the individual members of NATO and the OAS to see why each has joined the coalition. Since there are now fourteen members of NATO and twenty members of the OAS (the United States being the only nation with membership in both), the task of studying individual motivations would be almost unmanageable. We will, therefore, investigate demands and supports under three subgroupings: (1) the membership as a whole; (2) the non-American members; and (3) the United States. We will also attempt to differentiate where possible between "declaratory" policy and the real intent of nations.

THE MEMBERSHIP AS A WHOLE

Why have the two sets of allies gathered together in the two coalitions? What did they expect to achieve by this collective action? Although it is sometimes overlooked, the two alliances differ in their constitutional purposes. NATO is primarily a military venture; the OAS is designed to operate in the political, economic, and cultural fields, as well as the military. NATO is a collective "defense" pact; the OAS is a collective "security" arrangement. A few discriminating political scientists have noted the difference and clarified the distinction; other authors use the terms interchangeably.[9] One student of alliancemanship, Arnold Wolfers, has stated the case for precise terminology and provided us with definitions. According to his description, a collective "defense" arrangement is aimed at a particular known party *outside* the association. A collective "security" arrangement is designed to oppose any aggressor, known or unknown, *within or without* the association.[10]

NATO unquestionably belongs in the first category. The preamble of the treaty announces that the members resolve to "unite their efforts for collective defense." NATO leaders have never attempted to disguise the fact that the purpose of the alliance is to oppose Soviet aggression in Europe. Clearly, the potential military adversary of the alliance lies outside its boundaries and has been identified.

It could be argued that in several places the NATO Treaty pledges the members to subscribe to the principles of the United Nations, which would tend to make it a collective security organ. While acknowledging

---

[9] For example, the title itself of the article, "Denmark and NATO: The Problems of a Small State in a Collective Security System," would be a contradiction under the purest terminology. Joe R. Wilkinson, *International Organization*, Vol. X, No. 3.

[10] Arnold Wolfers, *Alliance Policy in the Cold War*, Johns Hopkins Press, 1959.

the primacy of the world organization, NATO has never considered itself to be or labeled itself as a subordinate arm of the United Nations. Furthermore, NATO has never contemplated using all or part of its military establishment against a member state.

The OAS, on the other hand, meets all the qualifications of a collective "security" arrangement. The Act of Bogota, which embodies the Charter of the OAS, defines the organization as a "regional agency" of the United Nations, which is clearly a collective security system.[11]

It might be assumed at first glance that a collective defense arrangement could be considered as merely a lesser included component of a collective security arrangement. When it operated against one of its own members, an association would be acting in the larger sense; when it took up arms against an outsider, it would become an alliance. But some commentators believe that the purposes of the two types of arrangement are so antithetic that they cannot coexist. Jerome Slater, citing Arnold Wolfers, says, "An Alliance is often thought of as the opposite of a collective security system." [12] If this is so, the OAS is clearly an anomaly, for not only its declaratory policy but its actions as well have established it as both a collective security and a collective defense organization. On the one hand, the bulk of its planning and preparatory actions have been designed against external aggression—presumably these plans identify the probable aggressor. The Inter-American Defense Board (IADB), the only existing military agency associated with the OAS, has concentrated in its General Military plan exclusively on those threats emanating from outside the Hemisphere. On the other hand, the *actions* of the OAS have been primarily devoted to resolving disputes between members of the organization. Since we will be referring frequently to the past experience of the OAS, it may be appropriate at this time to take a quick look at what their activities have involved. Table 1 gives a thumbnail sketch of the 18 occasions on which the OAS has been requested by a member to take action in accordance with the Rio Pact in a situation involving actual or imminent armed conflict. A complete discussion of each of these incidents may be found in the semi-official OAS biography.[13] This book also includes a detailed chronology of the Cuban situation and full coverage of OAS action in the Dominican Republic crisis (which was handled under Article 39 of the OAS Charter).

[11] The most scholarly of the OAS biographers argues that this description is too strong because it exaggerates the degree of subordination which has been assumed by the OAS. Nonetheless, the self-classification as an arm of the United Nations sets the OAS apart from NATO, which has assumed no formal obligations in this respect. See Charles G. Fenwick, *The Organization of American States*, Kaufmann Printing, Washington, D.C., 1966, p. 80.

[12] Jerome Slater, *A Revaluation of Collective Security*, Ohio State University Press, 1965, p. 47.

[13] Inter-American Institute of International Legal Studies, *The Inter-American System*, Oceana Publications, Dobbs Ferry, N.Y., 1966.

TABLE 1

OAS Activities in Support of Rio Treaty

I Case Number	II Complainant	III Accused	IV Date	V Organ of Consultation Called/Met	VI Action
1.	Costa Rica	Nicaragua	1948–1949	Yes/Council acted provisionally	Sent Investigating Committee of Military Experts. Amity Pact signed.
2.	Haiti	Dominican Republic	1949	No	Nations appeared ready to reach accommodation.
3.	Haiti/Dominican Republic	Dominican Republic (Haiti)	1950	Yes/Council acted provisionally	Requested countries to moderate their action and mediate. Appointed committee to monitor action.
4.	Ten Countries	Guatemala	1954	Yes/No	Offending government of Guatemala was overthrown before Foreign Ministers could assemble.
5.	Ecuador	Peru	1955	No	Other nations mediated.
6.	Costa Rica	Nicaragua	1955–1956	Yes/Council acted provisionally	(a) Investigation committee appointed and report prepared. (b) Nicaragua declared aggressor. (c) Other nations asked to expedite sale of military equip-

No.	Complainant	Respondent	Year	Council Action	Remarks
7.	Honduras	Nicaragua	1957	Yes/Council acted provisionally	ment to Costa Rica. (d) Agreement between contestants signed. (a) Investigation committee reported. (b) Agreement signed between parties transferring case to International Court of Justice.
8.	Dominican Republic	Cuba/Venezuela	1959	No	Fifth Meeting of Consultation of Foreign Ministers called.
9.	Nicaragua	Costa Rica/ Honduras	1959	Yes/Council acted provisionally	Investigating committee reported. Costa Rica and Honduras agreed to suppress would-be invaders of Nicaragua.
10.	Peru	Cuba	1961	No	Action transferred to Inter-American Peace Committee.
11.	Venezuela	Dominican Republic	1960–1962	Yes/Yes	(a) Investigating committee report. (b) Sixth Meeting of Consultation of F.M. (c) Condemned Dominican Republic, and (d) ordered breaking of diplomatic relations and economic sanctions.
12.	Bolivia	Chile	1962	No	Offered good offices to facilitate pacific settlement.

TABLE 1—*continued*

I Case Number	II Complainant	III Accused	IV Date	V Organ of Consultation Called/Met	VI Action
13.	Dominican Republic/ Haiti	Haiti/Dominican Republic	1963–1965	Yes/Council acted provisionally	(a) Appointed committee. (b) Parties finally agreed to mediation.
14.	Panama	United States	1964	Yes/Council acted provisionally	(a) Investigating committee appointed. (b) Parties reached settlement. (c) Panama appealed to United Nations.
15.	Panama	Cuba	1959	Yes/Council acted provisionally	(a) Investigating committee reports. (b) Invaders surrender. (c) Cuba cited as allowing invaders to use her ports.
16.	Peru/Colombia	Cuba	1961–1962	Yes/Yes	(a) Eighth Meeting of Consultation of F.M. (b) Expelled Cuba from Inter-American system. (c) Ordered trade embargo against Cuba.
17.	United States	Cuba	1962	Yes/Council acted provisionally	Council "recommended" that nations take action to seal off Cuba. (It did not "agree" to take action.)
18.	Venezuela	Cuba	1963–1964	Yes/Yes	(a) Ninth Meeting of Consultation. (b) Condemned Cuba

For the most part, the information in Table 1 is self-explanatory. Column V will be better understood by the reader after we have explained in Chapter III the responsibilities and prerogatives of the various organs of the OAS. In five instances (Cases 2, 5, 8, 10, and 12) some development, such as the willingness of the contending nations to accept outside mediation, made it unnecessary to convoke the supreme decision-making body, known as the Organ of Consultation.

We will refer back to Table 1 from time to time. At present, however, we are interested primarily in knowing who was the recipient of action taken under the Charter. Only in case number 17, where the Council acted in the Cuban missile crisis of 1962, was military action recommended against a nation outside of the hemisphere. Even in this case, the effects of the action recommended by the Council had an impact on a member of the organization as well.

Let us look again in a slightly different manner at the reason why these two sets of allies gather together to form these coalitions. NATO leaders have frequently asserted its dual mission of: (1) deterring external aggression and (2) combatting external aggression if it should occur. Although NATO leaders have sometimes followed the courses that would minimize the possibility of active conflict *between* NATO members, neither this goal nor the suppression of internal unrest is ever publicly mentioned as a NATO mission. Thus, judging from both declaratory statements and from actions, we may conclude that settlement of internal arguments is not one of the activities expected from the North Atlantic Treaty Organization.

The missions of the OAS are more comprehensive and more difficult to summarize. Article 4-C of the Charter lists one purpose: "to provide for common action . . . in the event of aggression."[14] This would place the OAS in a similar category with NATO as a defensive alliance. Article 4-D adds, however, a purpose not found in the NATO Charter: "to prevent possible causes of difficulties and to insure the pacific settlement of disputes that may arise among the member states." In short, the two groups of nations had some similar, but—more importantly—some different reasons for getting together.

OBJECTIVES OF NON-AMERICAN MEMBERS

Most observers seem relatively certain that the European nations sought above all else in the North Atlantic Treaty to create ties that would bind the United States to their protection and thus extend the nuclear umbrella across the Atlantic. They also expected to receive significant assistance in the form of economic aid and military equipment.

The reasons why the Latin American countries formed the OAS do not stand out in such sharp relief. Historians of the OAS universally

[14] *Ibid.*, p. 332.

point to the long history of attempts at hemispheric confederation stretching back to the days of Simon Bolivar's Panama Conference of 1826. Several analysts have suggested that the primary reason the Latin Americans joined the OAS was to form an entangling association which would protect them against the United States rather than from external aggression.[15] Certainly Latin American countries do not fear the Soviet Union as the Europeans do—or as Europeans did when NATO was formed. Nor does it appear from their actions, since the organization was put together in 1945, that the majority of Latin American countries want to set up procedures or military formations to stamp out insurrection at home or in neighboring states. They have also shied away from making standing provisions to intervene in conflicts between states. Some attribute this to a fear that the United States would use any permanent military establishment—which it could dominate—as a tool to coerce Latin American governments to do its bidding. Others read it as a concern by democratic governments that an international military structure might be used to subvert civilian control. Still others ascribe it to a willingness to refrain from meddling in others' business in return for being left alone oneself.

On the other hand, most Latin American members have, on numerous occasions, joined in community efforts to terminate or moderate disputes between partners.

Thus, it appears that Latin American nations conceive of the OAS more as a means of preserving peace in the hemisphere than as a defensive association against outside armed attack. The techniques of Communist aggression have introduced a new element, however: the strategy of internal insurrection sponsored by outside sources. Latin American nations have not yet developed a consensus on how to face up to this menace. Some advocate strenuous alliance activity in support of the status quo. Others resist any measure that smacks of intervention in internal national affairs. Triumph of one attitude or the other will probably depend on whether more countries are sucked into the Communist orbit in the next few years.

UNITED STATES OBJECTIVES IN NATO AND THE OAS

The reason behind American sponsorship of the North Atlantic Treaty needs no elaboration here. It does serve a purpose to recall, however, that, initially, the task of preventing further Soviet takeovers in Europe was almost exclusively an American one. The peacetime preparations involved high proportions of United States men, money, and materials. The deterrent was the Strategic Air Command. And if war had come, the allies hopes of victory would have hinged on SAC too.

[15] Ernst B. Haas, "The Challenge of Regionalism," *International Organization,* Autumn 1958.

In time this situation changed, at least to the extent that the United States now expects a much greater relative contribution from Europeans to the fighting capacity of the alliance. Though the strategic nuclear forces may still represent the critical factor in both deterrence and war, the United States is unwilling to rely on them to the extent it once did. Since the American homeland is now vulnerable to direct attack in a thermonuclear engagement—a situation that did not exist when NATO was formed—the United States has a greater stake in keeping wars limited than it did initially. Limited war in Europe represents one more dike—however small and unpretentious it might be—that must be breached before the Western Hemisphere would be engulfed in nuclear war. Understandably, the United States aim in NATO has changed from a negative one of denying territory to the opposition to an active expectation of help from a strong and healthy set of allies. Now, more than ever, the United States objective in NATO is to build up a strong local defense posture in Europe.

The evolution illustrates the dynamic aspect of the system. The results that have come from the "outputs" of the machine (European prosperity and strength may, of course, be attributed to other influences besides NATO) have altered the input relationship. These consequences have affected American demands and supports. Quite properly, the United States expects its support contributions to go down in proportion to those of its allies; which they have, at least in terms of its pro rata share of community expenses.

The goals which the United States has aimed at in the OAS, being more diffuse from the beginning, have held constant in the aggregate but have changed in priority. The OAS in its present configuration was an outgrowth of World War II. The Inter-American system coalesced during the war in response to the external threat, which while never severe was quite evident (particularly when it looked as though England would fall). The IADB was established in 1942 as an agency for drafting plans for protection of shipping, surveillance of sea lanes, allocation of strategic materials, establishment of air ferry routes to Europe, and other tasks. After the war the United States wanted to continue this collaboration.[16]

In the back of their minds United States planners of the immediate postwar period undoubtedly gave some thought to the maintenance of peace *between* countries. Americans also recognized that the United Nations, in the absence of an active regional organization, would be encouraged to dabble in Latin American affairs in a way that might run counter to United States interests. But intra-hemispheric squabbles or diplomatic maneuvers in the United Nations were secondary considera-

---

[16] Hanley tells us that during World War II the State Department wanted a permanent multilateral body but the Army and Navy preferred bilateral arrangements. Hanley, *op. cit.*, p. 36. Apparently these positions are virtually reversed today.

tions in the early postwar years. The predominant concern was an armed attack from overseas. The Guatemalan experience and Castro's alignment with the Communist camp brought home to Americans the dangers of subversion. Given Castro's avowed intention to export communism to other Latin American countries, and the evidence that he is trying to carry out that threat, United States planners now view subversion and Communist-inspired revolution as the number one problem in the area. President Johnson made this clear in his TV address on May 2, 1965, on the Dominican Republic situation when he said the United States could not permit establishment of another Castro-type government in the Western Hemisphere. Congress echoed his sentiments.

This question of priority makes a considerable difference in American attitudes toward the alliance. If the prime concern is external armed attack, the American objective would be, as it is in NATO, to build up hearty local defense capabilities. However, if the main purpose is to prevent conflicts between nations, the United States aim could well be just the opposite: to keep local forces weak and to limit their capacities to the defense role. If the greatest danger is visualized as coming from internal insurrectionists or guerrillas supported by neighboring states, the United States would attempt to persuade Latin Americans to develop internal economic, social, and military conditions that would militate against revolutions occurring, gaining popular support, or becoming militarily successful.

Clearly the priorities have changed. Defense against external armed attack is now of least concern; prevention or suppression of insurrection is top-drawer. This makes the planner's task difficult because anti-revolutionary measures require a mixture of political, social, economic, and military measures that often run counter to each other. For example, strengthening the military establishment may actually impede progress toward stable democracy.

In short, the purposes which the United States pursues in NATO and the OAS differ substantially, at least in the importance to be placed on the build-up of local forces.

OPPOSITION TO NATO AND THE OAS

While the official policies of the United States, the European nations, and the Latin American allies have all been favorable toward the two alliances, there also exist a number of vocal opinion groups who maintain that the allies individually or collectively would fare better if they dispensed with the formal coalitions. It is not the purpose of this study to evaluate the worth of the alliances; we assume that both NATO and the OAS are desirable. Nonetheless, anyone interested in alliance functioning should have some idea of the objections that have been raised to them. We will dismiss out of hand the Communist opposition, which constitutes, in actuality, a testimonial to their effectiveness. Several non-Communist writers who lean toward the World Government or internationalist frame of mind have objected to the organizations because they feel these regional coalitions undercut the United Nations. Other observers see the possibility of *détente* between the Soviet Union and the United States imperiled by the machinations of the European partners.[17] Still others believe that German reunification is the key to a peaceful Europe; NATO, they feel, stands in the way of such a development.[18]

Critics of the military aspects of the OAS argue more passionately but with a degree of logic as well. Antagonism is based on the belief that, with a few exceptions, Latin American nations are held in the grip of selfish and corrupt oligarchies. Thus, military support of a weak regime perpetuates oligarchical rule and merely postpones the achievement of true democracy. The extreme polemicists, like Victor Alba, are more opposed to what are normally considered progressive regimes because they believe they have not and will not accomplish the required reforms, and yet they will outlive the oppressive governments.[19] Others, more moderate, contend that collective security associations are incompatible with peaceful change.[20] Some moderate observers tend to feel that the dismal record of the Alliance for Progress shows that the privileged classes will not give up their perquisites voluntarily. Hans Morgenthau suggests for a remedy that the United States, instead of suppressing insurrection, compete with the Communists in stimulating revolutions.[21] Such a course would, naturally, be almost the direct opposite of what the United States and the OAS is trying to do today. In evaluating the commitments inherent in different types of organization, we should bear in mind the possibility that the United States might someday want to vary its tactics or at least employ them selectively.

SUPPORTS

The price that a nation must pay in return for the benefits of collective action can be segregated into several categories. First, each

[17] Walter Lippmann said: "*Détente* and a strong Atlantic alliance are incompatible." He chose *détente*. *The Washington Post*, April 4, 1967.
[18] Ronald Steel, *The End of Alliance*, Viking Press, New York, 1964, and Robert Kleiman, *Atlantic Crisis*, W. W. Norton, New York, 1964. Both appraise NATO unfavorably for a combination of the last two reasons.
[19] He particularly condemns the Frei regime in Chile, which many observers hold as a model of progress, because he maintains it is duped by a clever oligarchy which uses it as a reform facade while retaining backstage control. Victor Alba, *Alliance Without Allies*, Frederick A. Praeger, New York, 1965, p. 28.
[20] Kenneth Thompson, "Collective Security Reexamined," *American Political Science Review*, September 1953.
[21] Hans Morgenthau, *Foreign Affairs*, April 1967.

member sacrifices some freedom of action to the extent that it is committed by the actions of one partner or by the will of the others. This cost varies with the type of alliance. It depends upon the *casus foederis*—the conditions under which the agreement will take effect—and upon the obligations which each member assumes if the agreement should become effective. Both NATO and the OAS represent departures from the traditional pattern in that they apply in peacetime as well as in war—although the commitments are far less binding in peace.

These commitment costs are difficult to quantify and would, in any case, be evaluated differently by the actors and observers.[22] Potential payments are represented by the positive possibility of being forced to do something the nation does not wish to do, and by the negative aspect of being inhibited from taking certain action by the objection of the others. One of the reasons given by President de Gaulle for the disengagement of France from the NATO organization was the likelihood of being drawn into a war against her will. On the other side of the coin, the United States frequently is constrained to consult with or seek approval from other allies before taking action which it has the physical power to carry out on its own.

Alliances often bring concrete costs, as well, in the form of contributions necessary to carry out community programs. The extent of the obligation varies widely. The basic moral commitment calls for a nation to maintain forces which will be able to help its neighbor in case he is attacked. In some cases, the determination of the size and composition of military forces is based largely on individual national judgment; in NATO, the central alliance agencies issue guidance, but there is some doubt about how much these recommendations are conditioned by the known willingness of nations to produce forces. Country contributions to other collective programs, such as the NATO infrastructure and the funds for operating the international headquarters, are determined in committee negotiations. In a perceptive study, two economists have theorized that negotiated programs (of the type used in NATO but barely tested in the OAS) bring forth much greater effort, relatively speaking, from the smaller countries.[23]

For our purposes, at this time supports can be summarized as follows:

1. Both abstract and concrete costs are important to the member nations and each partner continually evaluates utility in terms of changing costs and benefits. This process causes countries occasionally to

---

[22] Historians now generally derogate Bismarck, the master alliance-maker, on the grounds that his free-wheeling policy saddled imperial Germany with commitments which ultimately led to her downfall. *Viz.*, A. J. P. Taylor, *The Struggle for Mastery in Europe, 1848–1918*, Oxford, New York, 1954, pp. 260–266.

[23] Mancur Olson, Jr., and Richard Zeckhauser, *An Economic Theory of Alliances*, The RAND Corporation, Santa Monica, Calif., RM-4297-ISA.

change attitudes about the alliance in general (as France and Mexico have done). It also causes them to favor certain projects or activities and to disapprove of others.

2. Abstract costs vary with the type of decision-making process and the extent of the obligation that applies when the commitment goes into effect. The NATO decision-making procedure is less binding than the OAS, but the obligations, once community action has been prescribed, are more entangling.

3. There are various ways of enticing members to accept concrete costs and these inducements should be studied more thoroughly if comprehensive programs are desirable.

III. The Machinery　The machinery of international government can be diagrammed with relative simplicity in comparison to national structures. The separation-of-power principle, which establishes checks and balances between elements in national governments, necessitates a careful delineation of authority. This requirement scarcely exists in alliance organization. Single agencies frequently act in the triple role of legislature, executive, and judiciary. Moreover, the interest groups whose activities so complicate national political scenes play an insignificant part in most international polities. In the military sphere the only transnational influences that one can detect are the intermittent service affinities which occasionally cause the United States Navy, say, to champion a viewpoint closer to the British Navy than to the United States Air Force.

Although this study will focus on the military aspects of the two alliances, we must begin with an investigation of alliance structure by looking at the top governing bodies whose responsibilities cut across political, economic, and military fields. Figure 1 contains simplified schematic diagrams of the two alliance structures placed side by side. Let us begin with the top directing agencies. Both are committees made up of one delegate from every member nation, each with a single equal vote. The routine activities are conducted by permanent representatives who comprise, on the one hand, the North Atlantic Council and, on the other hand, the Council of the OAS. On special occasions the national delegates can be Heads of Government, Foreign Ministers, or, in the NATO case, Defense Ministers.

Both of the permanent organizations—the two Councils—habitually meet once a week, although they often meet on call in emergencies. The North Atlantic Council has recently moved from Paris to Brussels; the OAS Council resides in Washington. Each of the so-called "Permanent Representatives" to the North Atlantic Council is a national ambassador in his own right. The Permanent Representatives on the OAS Council, however, are normally ambassadors from their country to the United States who take on the OAS assignment as an additional duty.

This variation helps to explain why the OAS Council has been given less authority than the NAC. Some Latin American countries felt that a regular ambassador to the United States might be subjected to unilateral pressure and thus too easily persuaded to go along with Yankee schemes. Therefore, the OAS Charter stipulates that, in any situation in which collective sanctions or military action is contemplated, a special gathering known as an Organ of Consultation (made up of the foreign ministers of each nation) will be convened as the action body. Much as an afterthought, it appears, the permanent OAS Council was authorized to act "provisionally" until the Organ of Consultation is actually in session.

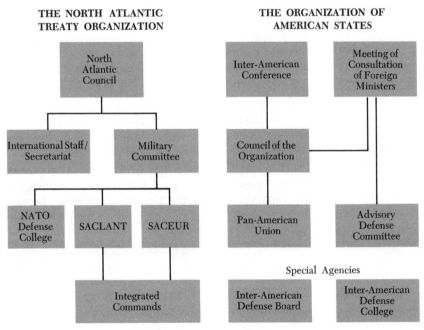

Figure 1.

Schematically this difference between NATO and the OAS need concern us little. Nor has it appeared to have much practical effect. On occasions when action has been required—and when the Organ of Consultation has not been called or has not had time to convene—the Council of the OAS has been able to act as decisively as one would expect the superior agency to behave.

Each organization has a Secretary General without voting privileges who acts as chairman and administrative expediter. Much of the work is done in subcommittees made up of national representatives who are normally working members of the national delegations. The Secretary General is also head of the international secretariat and the international staff.

The two Councils present a striking contrast in their methods of making decisions. NATO operates on a unanimity system which, in effect, allows a single dissenting nation a veto over the combined activities of the remainder. In the OAS, however, a majority vote on routine matters, and a two-thirds majority on important issues, commits the organization and its members. (Of course, both treaties recognize that a nation cannot be compelled to go to war against its wishes. The NATO Charter explicitly states that a refusal of one nation to take up arms will not restrict the actions of the remainder.) The Councils are the heart of the governing system of the two alliances; they carry out the legislative role and act as the apex of the executive hierarchy. (There is no judiciary as such.)

Some non-policy executive actions are carried out by the international staff and secretariats. The system requires the preparatory and follow-up action of these community agencies because, while most of the decision-making and policy work is performed by the committees of national representatives, these representatives are mainly concerned with protecting the interests of their country. Someone has to act for the corporate entity. The NATO secretariat and staff far outnumber the Pan-American Union, which acts in the same capacity for the OAS even though the latter has burgeoned in the last ten years.[24] The OAS contingent numbers approximately 600 personnel.[25] NATO has more than 2,000 personnel in its international secretariat and staff, while there are more than 20,000 personnel involved in the military complex of international headquarters and combined agencies.[26] Budgetwise the OAS now requires operating funds on the order of $16 million a year to support all of the communal activities undertaken by the organization.[27] NATO's operational expenses are running more than $100 million a year for the civilian secretariat, the military staffs, and the other integrated systems.

A number of authors have analyzed the weaknesses that are inherent in the position of Secretary General and which account for the ineffectual leadership which has been the trademark of the international sections of both NATO and the OAS. All three former Secretaries General of NATO—Lord Ismay, Paul Henri Spaak, and Dirk U. Stikker—have written of the problems they encountered and of the deficiencies of the system in which they had to work. A former official in the OAS system, William Manger, laments that the Secretary General's office of that organization has degenerated into a bureau for furnishing secretarial help

[24] John C. Dreier, *The Organization of American States and the Hemisphere Crisis,* Harper & Row, New York, 1962, p. 116.
[25] William Manger, *Pan America in Crisis,* Public Affairs Press, Washington, D.C., 1961, p. 80.
[26] *The Times,* London, December 17, 1966; Edward Lanchbery, *NATO's Fifteen Nations,* June–July 1967.
[27] *International Organization,* Winter 1967, p. 212.

to the committees. He feels that this condition resulted from the chastening experience of an early Secretary General who tried to propose a substantive improvement program and was rebuffed by the national delegates.[28]

Other commentators have pointed to the relative impotence of the Secretaries General of NATO and the OAS as compared to the same office in the United Nations. They observe that the United Nations leader has been able to deploy military peacekeeping forces to the Suez, the Congo, and Cyprus, whereas neither the NATO nor OAS Secretary General has been able to act so independently or energetically. The comparison is not quite relevant. The United Nations Secretary General has been able to act because he can project himself into the power of vacuum created by the rival interest of the major powers. This contest means that the Security Council cannot act positively to direct action—nor can it act negatively to prevent action. This condition, plus the desire of most of the nations of the General Assembly to have some action taken, has provided the United Nations Secretary General with maneuver room which he has often exploited. In NATO or the OAS the nations themselves control the action. When they cannot agree in NATO, the system operates in a sort of "fail safe" manner to prevent the international structure from taking any action at all. In the OAS, although a decision for action is much more likely to be forthcoming, the Secretary General is likewise powerless to act if he cannot coalesce a qualified majority.

The weakness of the position of Secretary General stands out most clearly in NATO, where in spite of the dynamic personality of some of the occupants, they have been out-performed by a nominally subordinate officer, SACEUR, who has wielded more influence and been able to accomplish more in the way of combined action. For one thing, of course, the Secretary General deals with political issues, which are far more difficult to resolve than military questions; but from the organizational standpoint, it seems, paradoxically, that the proximity of the Secretary General to the decision makers has handicapped him. An official further down in the hierarchy, such as SACEUR, has the privilege of issuing provisional directives on his own initiative. He operates with a wide degree of autonomy on technical matters. He can also draft plans which may be accepted or rejected in their entirety by higher authority, but which are not subject to amendment without his concurrence. Thus, he is able to build up an aura of "command" even though his mandatory authority is severely limited. The Secretary General, working directly under the thumb of the Council, does not have this freedom of action. Sitting so close to the Council members, and having them readily available for consultation, he is obliged to clear even minor matters with them before issuing instructions.

Next in the chain of defense organization in NATO is the agency known as the Military Committee. It is composed of the Chairman of the

28 Manger, *op. cit.*, p. 80.

Joint Chiefs of Staff, in the case of the United States, and his counterparts abroad. Each representative has one vote and, again, decisions must be taken unanimously.

The Military Committee has never provided forceful leadership. Unanimity among fifteen members is just too hard to come by in cases of importance. Therefore, when full agreement is achieved, it is usually acquired by compromise or ambiguous wording, which reduces the effectiveness of decisions made. Nonetheless, the Military Committee does perform a useful function by getting the military leaders together periodically and by having them discuss the important military issues. Non-controversial matters are handled with reasonable dispatch and, over a period of years, slow progress has been made on the more divisive questions.

Until two years ago the Military Committee functioned as a collection of independent national delegations. Since no representative at that level was charged with considering problems from an over-all alliance standpoint, the only integrated planning was done at a lower level. In 1963 the Military Committee created an international section, with a director and a small staff, to study problems from a community angle. The importance of the internationalized section was enhanced in 1966 when the next subordinate agency, the Standing Group, was abolished. Many believe that the director will take over much of the work formerly performed by SACEUR, who had stepped into the breach and become the "Chief of Staff for the Alliance." [29] It remains to be seen, however, whether the director will have the freedom of action to develop cohesive and complete plans on his own like SACEUR or whether he will be hamstrung as the Secretary General has been by having to clear each step in a planning operation with the thirteen different national representatives.

Turning now to the OAS, one is surprised to learn that it has no counterpart to the Military Committee. In the schematic diagram we note the names of two agencies which might serve in this capacity. The first one, called the Advisory Defense Committee, is a bona-fide arm of the OAS—but it has never held a meeting. The Advisory Defense Committee would be similar in composition to the NATO Military Committee —that is, it would be made up of the military heads of the armed services of each country. The OAS charter specifies, however, that this committee will serve only in those extraordinary situations when an Organ of Consultation has been convened and requested its advice. When such meetings have been held in the past, the members of the Organ of Consultation have not seen fit to ask for military assistance. One expert observer doubts that they ever will.[30] The other agency which might fill the

[29] In the words of Alastair Buchan, "The Reform of NATO," *Foreign Affairs*, January 1962.
[30] Paul T. Hanley, *The Inter-American Defense Board*, unpublished doctoral thesis submitted to Stanford University, May 1964, p. 88.

role of the Military Committee in the OAS is the Inter-American Defense Board (IADB). The IADB, however, is not a regular component of the OAS system, although funds to operate it are provided by the OAS through the Pan-American Union. The IADB has occupied a peculiar status since it was first established in 1942 as a consultative organ to co-ordinate the wartime activities of the Western Hemisphere nations.[31] As things stand today the IADB does not even have permanent tenure for the life of the OAS. It is authorized to continue in existence, however, until such time as two-thirds of the members decide it should be dis-banded. This means that the likelihood of its continuing for a long time is pretty good.

At first glance it may not strike one as very important whether the IADB is an internal agency of the OAS or not. Actually this seemingly innocuous issue lies at the heart of the question of how much weight the decisions of the IADB carry. With the IADB a separate consultative agency, as it is today, the nations can take its recommendations or leave them. If the board were to become an arm of the OAS, its resolutions would either become effective immediately or they would be processed through the hierarchy until they were either accepted or rejected at the appropriate level. When promulgated, they would be binding on the na-tions—even on those nations who objected to the proposal—as are other decisions in the OAS structure.

It might be possible, of course, to so restrict the duties and privi-leges of a permanent military body so as to avoid this situation. A cur-tailment of that type would involve primarily taking away its privileges of initiation. It could be allowed to deal *only* with those tasks assigned specifically to it by the Council, and it could be required to respond only in the explicit terms passed on to it by the Council. Restrictions of this type, however, would curtail its effectiveness and would certainly make it a less broad-gauge agency than it is today. As a comparison, only a minute part of the work of NATO's Military Committee is done in re-sponse to specific directives from the North Atlantic Council.

Neither side in the long-running official debate over the status of the IADB has addressed the problem in these terms. The advocates of "institutionalizing" the IADB have steadfastly maintained that such a step would not change either its responsibility or its advisory functions. Let us look at this question in some detail.

At the Third Special Inter-American Conference at Buenos Aires on February 15, 1967, the Argentine delegation proposed a modification to the OAS Charter which would, in essence, convert the present IADB to a permanent Advisory Defense Committee to advise the Organ of Consultation and to act as a preparatory organ for collective self-

---

[31] Several monographs have been written about the IADB. The best and most thorough which has come to my attention is the Hanley manuscript mentioned above. I have used it as a basis of much of the description presented here.

defense.[32] Representatives of the IADB concluded that this proposal would assign to the new Advisory Defense Committee the "same responsibility now given to the Inter-American Defense Board." [33]

Several delegates at Buenos Aires spoke in opposition to the Argentine proposal. As is normal in debates of this kind, the arguments ranged over a wide spectrum and some of them were clearly emotional rather than logical. The main objection derived from a concern that this step would convert the OAS into a military alliance. Some delegates were worried that the measure would legitimatize community intervention in the internal affairs of the member states. There was also the unjustified criticism that it portended the establishment of a permanent inter-American peace force.[34]

Some of the complaints, however, dealt with the problem we were discussing above in a way that demonstrates a vague uneasiness combined with an uncertainty of how to state the problem. One delegate claimed the new arrangement would establish a "kind of inter-American peace force staff"—seemingly a legitimate complaint unless the Advisory Defense Committee was specifically prohibited from this role. One of the tasks of the permanent organization would be to deal with plans for assembling collective forces and their possible employment. Another objector put his finger closer to the visceral issue when he said that the present work of the IADB furnished satisfactory guidance for defense against external armed attack, but he continued:

> . . . the IADB at present is studying hypotheses for what has actually been called subversion. Plans will surely emerge from these hypotheses which will be directly transmitted to each government, *and which can be accepted or not.*[35]

Oddly enough, the speaker did not pursue the point which seems to flow logically from this statement: that nations would *not* have the freedom to reject proposals emanating from an internal OAS agency if they met the approval of the majority. Other opposition spokesmen, however, worried about delegation of authority to a "supranational entity." [36] Another critic noted specifically:

> . . . if the advisory defense committee is created with the powers provided for in the draft, we should ask ourselves whether, in such a committee, decisions could be made by a majority of votes.[37]

[32] *Minutes*, Inter-American Defense Board, Council of Delegates, Session 480, Appendix II, March 30, 1967, p. 3.

[33] *Ibid.*, Session 478, Appendix III, March 9, 1967, p. 2.

[34] These unattributed statements are extracted from the *Minutes* of Session 480 cited above.

[35] *Ibid.*, p. 15, italics added.

[36] *Ibid.*, p. 16.

[37] *Ibid.*, p. 17.

One delegate went back to the original intentions of the states when they first framed the OAS. He quoted the words of Dr. Alberto Lleras Camargo, former Secretary General, to the effect that the founding fathers had deliberately made the Advisory Defense Committee a *non-permanent* advisory organ so that

> . . . the committee will not meet to undertake studies on its own account or to submit reports that have not been entrusted to it and whose nature has not been previously defined by the governments, the Meeting of Consultation, or the Conference. Hence, it does not enjoy the scope for its deliberation that is allowed the other technical organs, which are dependents of the council . . . .[38]

Clearly, many delegates shared a concern that an unrestricted permanent military organ within the OAS could take the bit in its teeth and ram through, with majority support, plans and programs which might be objectionable to a few members. In this manner, they visualized a gradual shift of active direction from the political to the military authorities. It strikes the casual observer that, if this were not a legitimate concern, someone should have taken pains to show the skeptics why this could not occur. So far as is detectable from the public record no such attempt was made. The proponents of the change returned repeatedly to the argument that nothing in the proposal would create a permanent collective force—which is true. But they avoided any assurance that the staff would not work on plans which would enable the rapid assembly and use of a collective force. One advocate of the change guaranteed the members that there would be created no force "whose command would operate independently of the respective governments or that could take action without directives from the governments."[39] This approach, too, neglects the point that a staff or a collective force could take action without directives from *some* of the governments—in fact, it could and probably would have to take action against the interests of a minority. The same delegate argued that "the powers of the Advisory Defense Committee would be no different from those of the IADB," but he failed to allay the fears of some that the change to a permanent component would give added authority to its recommendations.

Members of the Inter-American Defense Board themselves appear also to be oblivious to these objections. The Chairman, in reporting to the delegates of the IADB what he had witnessed at Buenos Aires, observed that the effect of the Argentine proposal would have been to "correct the abnormality of organization" which now exists. He appeared to feel that the opposition was focusing on a bogey-man, and he dismissed their fears in these terms:

---

[38] These unattributed statements are extracted from the *Minutes* of Session 480, p. 12.
[39] *Ibid.*, p. 7.

There is no explicit connection between the proposed Advisory Defense Committee and the concept of an inter-American force. There is no endorsement of or suggestion of intervention or encroachment on the sovereignty of any member state.

Yet, in the discussion of the Argentine proposal those in opposition dwelt mainly on their unwillingness to endorse an inter-American military force, intervention and the creation of a *supranational* military organization which would usurp the authority of the head of state over military forces of that state.[40]

We must dwell for a moment longer on the principle that is involved here by scrutinizing a hypothetical case. The mission of the IADB, as paraphrased in its official pamphlet, is to conduct "the military planning and preparation of recommendations to the American states for the collective self-defense of the hemisphere." [41] If carried to its logical conclusion, this type of planning would certainly involve recommendations on the size and composition of collective military forces to be used in potential emergency situations. It is said that the IADB has never interpreted its mission in a way that would authorize it to deal with the question of size of forces to be maintained or equipment to be used by the member nations. Nonetheless, positive planning for hemispheric defense or collective intervention would certainly lead it into this realm of activity. In the NATO procedure, if Norway, for example, did not like the force commitments levied on it by SACEUR or the tasks assigned to its forces, it could turn thumbs down on the plans he submitted to the Military Committee and its single negative vote would nullify collective approval. If, however, the IADB, as an arm of the OAS, submitted similar plans to its superior agency, an affirmative vote of 14 out of 20 of the nations could saddle the dissenters with programs not to their liking. The distinction seems critical; no nation wishes to place itself in a position in which other nations could dictate the size, composition, or use of its armed forces.

Apparently there was substance behind the rhetoric of objection at Buenos Aires. When the Argentine proposition was brought to a vote, it was defeated, 11 to 6, with three countries abstaining. The United States, which was rumored to be actively soliciting support for the proposal backstage, was one of those nations which abstained. This rather lopsided expression of opinion will probably lay to rest for some time to come any official attempt to insert a permanent military element in the OAS machinery; but it also discouraged those who are closely connected with the IADB from seeking the maximum use of the tool they already have at their disposal.

---

[40] *Minutes,* Session 478, *op. cit.,* p. 2. I have italicized "supranational" because we will return later in the discussion to this point.
[41] Yellow handout, *Inter-American Defense Board,* Washington, D.C., undated, p. 12.

So much for the IADB and the Military Committee, which are the top military echelons in our two partnerships. It is impossible to show on a small diagram the extensive military command network that fans out below the Military Committee on the NATO side of the chart. This structure has been the means by which NATO has brought its program of collaboration and coordinated effort to fruition. Success has been possible, many believe, largely because officials in this international structure have been able to put aside national affiliations in the interests of the community. Whereas committees (like the two Councils, the Military Committee, or the IADB) can argue over and make modifications to a plan drawn up elsewhere, they are generally unable to provide the homogeneity in outlook that is necessary to *draft* plans for dealing with complex problems. Nor are they able to exert executive direction that is necessary to keep an organization operating efficiently once it has been established.

We need not go into detail to contrast the NATO and OAS configuration below the Military Committee and the IADB. In NATO, as we have mentioned, there exists an extensive international command and planning network which consists of some 31 headquarters and more than 20,000 people. They operate such integrated activities as the ACE-HIGH communication system, the Early Warning network, the SHAPE Technical Center at The Hague, etc. Alongside these agencies are numerous *ad hoc* collaboration arrangements such as NADGE, NAMSO, the Starfighter production organization, etc.[42]

The OAS for its part has only one appendage that resembles the combined activity in NATO. That is the Inter-American Defense College, a half-scale replica of the NATO Defense College. The scope of the Inter-American Defense College would hardly justify its mention here, compared to the across-the-board NATO effort, if it did not represent a prototype. Its existence demonstrates that common ventures can be conducted in the Western Hemisphere, even under the present IADB system, if nations can be persuaded that they are worthwhile.

This completes the brief inventory of the formal structure of the two organizations. In a more comprehensive study it might be desirable to investigate the activities of other bodies, such as the yearly meeting of the chiefs of military services of the Western Hemisphere countries. That effort does not appear warranted here, however, in order to answer the questions we are investigating in this paper.

IV. The Outputs The outputs of the NATO and OAS systems can be subdivided into two major classifications, depending on whether they directly affect major purposes of the alliance or whether they have only an indirect bearing on the accomplishment of goals.

[42] See my RM-5282-PR, *Common Funding in NATO,* The RAND Corporation, Santa Monica, Calif., for an explanation of these programs.

GOAL ACHIEVEMENT OUTPUTS

In Chapter II we identified the primary military goals of the two alliances. For NATO, they are: (1) to deter external aggression, and (2) to combat external aggression if it should occur. Judging by these criteria alone, NATO would be rated a success. Although it is impossible to assign it full credit for dissuading the Soviets from further takeovers in Europe, one would have difficulty in ascribing this result to any other organization. As a consequence of success in the deterrent mission, NATO has not yet been tested in its ability to combat aggression. The general opinion exists, however, that if it were put to the test, it would have a difficult time combatting aggression by any means short of all-out nuclear conflict.

The OAS experience provides more material for quantitative evaluation. It has also established two goals: (1) to provide for common action in event of aggression and (2) to settle peacefully disputes among member states. Performance in response to Goal 1 was tested to some extent in the Cuban missile crisis of 1962. The Council responded to the challenge by recommending that member states "take all measures, individually and collectively, including the use of armed force, which they may deem necessary to insure that the government of Cuba cannot continue to receive from the Sino-Soviet powers military matériel and related supplies which may threaten the peace and security of the Continent. . . ." [43] Of course, the only important implementing action was taken by the United States.[44] But that is immaterial, for the United States possessed sufficient power and was content to carry the burden of action. Response by a combined force would have been more difficult to initiate and to control. The important fact is that the alliance did make a collective decision in a crisis and, in doing so, provided Washington with moral support and legal justification for taking an action which would have been riskier and more vulnerable to outside opposition if done unilaterally.

OAS performance in regard to its second purpose can be judged by referring to the material in Table 1 [page 94]. Complaints of one member state against another have been registered on eighteen occasions. In no instance have prolonged conflicts broken out. Some of the solutions were only temporary, as is evidenced by the recurring friction between the perennial trouble-makers (Nicaragua, Dominican Republic, Cuba) and the other members. But even temporary solutions serve a purpose. Nicaragua is now a member of the close-knit Organization of Central American States, whose common army should make intra-organizational

---

[43] *The Inter-American System, op. cit.,* p. 165.
[44] Twelve other countries offered military assistance and port facilities. Frank R. Pancake, *The Latin American Military and Inter-American Security,* unpublished term paper, University of Virginia, May 1, 1967, p. 31.

disputes less warlike. In the case of the Dominican Republic, the OAS by mediation, investigation, and sanctions postponed active hostilities until the demise of Trujillo made aggression against its neighbors less likely. The Cuban defection was handled more effectively through the OAS than would have been possible otherwise.[45]

In only one instance—the Dominican Republic expedition of 1965—has the OAS undertaken a combined military action or intervened in the internal affairs of a member state. In a previous case—the Nicaraguan attack on Costa Rica (Number 6 in Table 1)—the Council branded one side the aggressor and called upon nations to take military measures. Apparently the four fighter planes delivered immediately by the United States to the aggrieved nation, Costa Rica, reversed the power balance and allowed her to repel the attackers. Informed observers have asserted that the United States refused to act without the sponsorship of the OAS.[46]

In another instance, the OAS came close to establishing a combined operational force. During the Cuban missile crisis of 1962, after the OAS recommended that all members take action to see that no further military supplies entered Cuba, two other nations—Argentina and the Dominican Republic—offered to blend their ships with the United States Navy to form a composite command.[47] The speedy resolution of the crisis made this step unnecessary.

The Dominican Republic expedition—the first Inter-American Peace Force—involved more than 11,000 Americans, 1,000 Brazilians, and small contingents from Honduras, Costa Rica, and Nicaragua. A full account of this operation is contained in Chapter IX of the *Inter-American System* (cited above). We are concerned at this point with the process through which the OAS was able to come to an agreement to take action. Surprisingly, this semi-official biography fails to mention the opposition to OAS intervention. One has to look elsewhere to find that the motion to send a task force was adopted only by a bare two-thirds majority of fourteen, with Mexico, Uruguay, Chile, Ecuador, and Peru voting for noninvolvement and Venezuela abstaining.[48] This omission is too important to be an oversight. It appears to be part of a deliberate effort by some associated with the OAS to play down the understandable fact that blissful harmony does not reign throughout the organization on all issues. Actually, the cardinal strength of the OAS may lie in the fact that it can act over the objection of a few members.

[45] For a well-documented argument that the OAS has served as a useful collective security instrument, see Jerome Slater, *A Revaluation of Collective Security*, Ohio State University Press, 1965.

[46] John D. Dreier, *The Organization of the American States and the Hemisphere Crisis*, Harper & Row, New York, 1962, p. 64.

[47] Pancake, *op. cit.*, p. 31.

[48] *International Organization*, Winter 1967, p. 214.

INDIRECT OUTPUTS

Both alliances perform a number of activities which do not result in accomplishment of the primary goals. The principal indirect function of an alliance is *to prepare* itself to carry out its mission. NATO, which is far ahead of the OAS in this respect, prepares itself by a corporate effort in (1) planning, (2) managing integrated systems, (3) training and maneuvering, (4) and coordinating logistical activities. Let us compare NATO and the OAS in these fields of action.

Planning

Integrated NATO planning starts at the lowest level of international supervision and extends up through the Major Subordinate and Supreme Commanders to culminate in the Military Committee and its international planning directorate. Most products of this activity are classified, but some have, nonetheless, received broad publicity. It is known, for example, that national defense plans are keyed to the NATO strategy, about which there has been continuing argument among the allies. Guidance for the size and composition of national armed forces is taken from the requirements set forth by SACEUR and SACLANT. From the consolidated plan are also derived the outlines for a variety of cooperative efforts like the 200 airfields built under infrastructure. In short, collective NATO planning forms the backdrop for almost everything which the partners do in concert and for much of what the nations do individually.

Planning plays a much less crucial role in the OAS. We have mentioned that the military planning agency, the IADB, is not a formal echelon of the OAS. The limited planning which the OAS does has been devoted to its least likely mission: defense against armed attack from overseas. Through February 1967, apparently, the IADB had formulated no plans for suppressing conflicts between members of combatting subversion within countries.[49]

The focus of IADB planning—that is for defense against external hemispheric armed attack—could be important, particularly in collective measures for protection of shipping and anti-submarine campaigns. Even for the general war role, however, IADB plans do not carry the weight of their NATO counterparts. IADB planners, for example, do not attempt to set force requirements for the individual states or to recommend types of equipment. Their plans are mere recommendations to the countries individually and are never subjected to collective scrutiny or approval. Hence, they entail no commitment.

[49] The quote on page 109 indicates, however, that some such plans are now under development.

Managing Integrated Systems

The NATO international superstructure operates a variety of integrated systems through which it provides services or facilities that would not otherwise be available to many of the partners. In some cases, like the Early Warning network, alliance stewards merely tie the country efforts together to make each component more effective. In other cases, though, NATO has actually built facilities from scratch. Through a complex system of common funding, NATO finances a vast command superstructure, an air defense network, an infrastructure construction program, a communications system and numerous other ventures.[50] The infrastructure program alone has accounted for some 3.5 billion dollars' worth of airfields, pipelines, naval facilities, etc.

The OAS has nothing in the military field to compare with the community systems of NATO.

Training and Maneuvers

NATO has not met with the success which many visualized for it in coordinating the *individual* and *unit* training of the different nations. Still it has been able to establish such institutions as the NATO Defense College and a communications school at Latina, which train officers and technicians in common NATO strategy and procedures.[51] It also operates a huge missile range (NAMFI) on the island of Crete, where crews from most allied nations learn how to fire NIKE, HAWK, and other standard equipment in accordance with NATO operational procedures.

NATO has encountered difficulty in establishing community schools for individuals because of the variety of languages spoken in Europe. This problem would be minimized in Latin America, where some version of Spanish is common to most countries.

The "higher echelon" training, as it is called in NATO, involves the close coordination of large units (often of different services) from neighboring countries. The NATO supervisory structure had developed an imaginative system of maneuvers which not only provides training but also tests unit readiness and evaluates tactical plans. One highly developed portion of the NATO establishment is the Allied Command Europe Mobile Force (AMF), which holds several exercises a year to bring together under simulated combat conditions the battalion-size contingents furnished by five nations.

The OAS operates only the Inter-American Defense College mentioned above. (The United States conducts a large-scale program, of

[50] See *Common Funding in NATO, op. cit.*
[51] See Elliott Vandevanter, "Combined Training in NATO," unpublished paper, for a description of NATO programs for individual, unit and higher echelon training

course, on a bilateral basis to training officers and technicians from Latin America at the School of the Americas.) Several nations have held maneuvers on an *ad hoc* basis, but it is only recently that they have made a practice of even inviting IADB observers.[52]

The Dominican Republic expedition has convinced many that the OAS should establish a permanent inter-American peace force and train it in the use of common procedures. Those who would soften the impact of such a step argue that the units need not be kept in constant assemblage—they need only be "earmarked" for use so that they could prepare in advance.[53] One could scarcely argue against such a proposal on the basis of military efficiency; any operation would proceed more smoothly if units had been selected and notified beforehand, if command arrangements had been formalized, and if logistical provisions had been made in advance. It should be acknowledged, however, that the Dominican Republic operation revealed no serious deficiencies in the spur-of-the-moment provisions made by the participants. In fact, considering the unsettled political situation and the lack of unanimity about what should be done, it appears the expedition was carried out with an amazing absence of confusion.[54] Having weathered this crash experience, expeditionary forces should be able to improve in the next one, if it comes.[55]

While military training per se does not look like an attractive candidate for internationalization, collective effort might be profitably employed in the broad "civic action" phase many visualize in connection with a comprehensive counter-insurgency program. Civic action training involves a variety of engineering, sanitary, and medical courses which are often indistinguishable from civilian education. Community schools operated under a common-funding arrangement associated with the IADB might be sponsored more efficiently under the IADB than under other arrangements for dispensing United States military and economic aid.

Coordinating Logistical Activities

NATO has been involved, with varying success, in a number of collaboration ventures in the logistics field. Much of the experience would not be transferable to Latin America because the European scene pre-

[52] Hanley, *op. cit.*, p. 151.

[53] Robert J. Barrett, "Inter-American Peace Force," *Military Review*, May 1967.

[54] A participant has reported that the Dominican Republic Inter-American Peace Force (IAPF) "demonstrated to the world that soldiers of our hemisphere can work together with no major difficulties." Lt. Col. Frederick C. Turner, "Experiment in Inter-American Peace Keeping," *Army*, June 1967.

[55] The Dominican Republic task force has published a thick volume of recommendations for future organization, equipment and procedures. See Headquarters Inter-American Peace Force, *Activation Plan*, Santo Domingo, D.R., April 18, 1966, unclassified.

sents a much more compact geographical environment. On the other hand, some ventures which have been handicapped in NATO, because of language variations or because of economic and equipment affiliations between cliques of nations, might succeed in Latin America where Spanish is common and where most economies and equipments are United States-oriented.

Logistical experts turn instinctively to spare parts and small items of matériel as a fruitful field for collaboration. Experience with the NATO Maintenance and Supply Organization does not inspire great expectations for Latin America.[56] The prime deficiency is introduced by the fact that an international organization—whose management is subordinate and perhaps beholden to the several national representatives—cannot exert sufficient force to require national components of the system to follow accepted procedures. An independent source of supply, such as the United States Military Assistance Program has been for most of Latin America, can be much more demanding in this regard (even though professional supply men think the United States is too lenient in allowing recipient countries to depart from accepted standards for supply and maintenance).

Thus, the desirability of attempting a common spare parts and supply system in the Western Hemisphere would hinge, as does the training question, on a weighing of cost, efficiency, and morale considerations. An international depot arrangement would undoubtedly be less efficient than the present United States-sponsored system and it would probably cost the United States more (even if Americans only contributed the usual 66 percent for community ventures);[57] but it would probably act as a solidifying influence in the OAS, give more prestige to the international establishment, bring some economic benefits to the nations where the main depot activities would be located, and raise Latin American morale through instilling a sense of independent accomplishment.

In the field of coordinated weapons production, NATO has not achieved the success in consolidating national production efforts that its sponsors initially aspired to. However, over the years nearly a dozen NATO Production and Logistics Organizations—NPLO's as they are called—have been formed with some success.[58] Consortia have produced a number of common weapons under conditions that were more attractive to the purchasers than buying the weapons off the shelf from the original developer. The quantity manufacture of a single model has increased military efficiency through standardization.

[56] *See* Common Funding in NATO, *op. cit.*, pp. 88–91.
[57] Currently, the United States spends annually approximately $70 million on military assistance in Latin America; $55 million for matériel and $15 million for training. Pancake, *op. cit.*, p. 22.
[58] See my RM-4169-PR, *Coordinated Weapons Production in NATO*, The RAND Corporation, Santa Monica, Calif.

The OAS has developed nothing to parallel NATO in this regard. Most weapons used today in Latin America have been supplied by the United States—originally as a form of grant aid but now, increasingly, on a sales basis. For this reason, there has been no demand heretofore on the part of the Latin Americans for any share of the production melon. Nor would there seem to be much future in it, for either North or South Americans, were it not for the desire of the United States to reduce expenditures, to deter a possible arms race, and to prevent incursions by foreign arms manufacturers. A small community program for common production of relatively inexpensive and unsophisticated equipment might help all three aims, but given the hypothesis that community-built weapons generally cost more than nationally manufactured ones, the outlook is not bright.

An Economic Theory
of Alliances

MANCUR OLSON, JR., AND
RICHARD ZECKHAUSER

Introduction   This article outlines a model that attempts to explain the workings of international organizations, and tests this model against the experience of some existing international institutions. Though the model is relevant to any international organization that independent nations establish to further their common interests, this article emphasizes the North Atlantic Treaty Organization, since it involves larger amounts of resources than any other international organization, yet illustrates the model most simply. The United Nations and the provision of foreign aid through the Development Assistance Committee are discussed more briefly.

There are some important respects in which many observers in the United States and in some other countries are disappointed in NATO and other ventures in international cooperation. For one thing, it is often argued that the United States and some of the other larger members are bearing a disproportionate share of the burden of the common defense of the NATO countries, and it is at least true that the smaller members of NATO devote smaller percentages of their incomes to defense than do larger members. There is also some concern about the fact that the NATO alliance has systematically failed to provide the number of divisions that the NATO nations themselves have proclaimed (rightly or wrongly) are necessary or optimal. Similarly, many nations, especially

Reprinted by permission of the publishers from *The Review of Economics and Statistics*, 48, 3 (Cambridge: Harvard University Press, August 1966), pp. 266–279. Copyright, 1966, by the President and Fellows of Harvard College.

smaller nations, have failed to fulfill their quotas for UN contributions with the result that the United States contribution rises to a degree that threatens the independence of the organization. The meager level of total support for the UN and the mean and haphazard state of its finances are also sources of concern.

Some suppose that the apparent disproportion in the support for international undertakings is due largely to an alleged American moral superiority, and that the poverty of international organizations is due to a want of responsibility on the part of some other nations. But before resorting to any such explanations, it would seem necessary to ask whether the different-sized contributions of different countries could be explained in terms of their national interests. Why would it be in the interest of some countries to contribute a larger proportion of their total resources to group undertakings than other countries? The European members of NATO are much nearer the front line than the United States, and they are less able to defend themselves alone. Thus, it might be supposed that they would have an interest in devoting larger proportions of their resources to NATO than does the United States, rather than the smaller proportions that they actually contribute. And why do the NATO nations fail to provide the level of forces that they have themselves described as appropriate, i.e., in their common interest? These questions cannot be answered without developing a logical explanation of how much a nation acting in its national interest will contribute to an international organization.

Any attempt to develop a theory of international organizations must begin with the purposes or functions of these organizations. One purpose that all such organizations must have is that of serving the *common* interests of member states. In the case of NATO, the proclaimed purpose of the alliance is to protect the member nations from aggression by a common enemy. Deterring aggression against any one of the members is supposed to be in the interest of all. The analogy with a nation-state is obvious. Those goods and services, such as defense, that the government provides in the *common* interest of the citizenry, are usually called "public goods." An organization of states allied for defense similarly produces a public good, only in this case the "public"—the members of the organization—are states rather than individuals.

Indeed, almost all kinds of organizations provide public or collective goods. Individual interests normally can best be served by individual action, but when a group of individuals has some common objective or collective goal, then an organization can be useful. Such a common objective is a collective good, since it has one or both of the following properties: (1) if the common goal is achieved, everyone who shares this goal automatically benefits, or, in other words, nonpurchasers cannot feasibly be kept from consuming the good, and (2) if the good is available to any one person in a group, it is or can be made available to the other members of the group at little or no marginal cost.[1] Collective goods are thus the characteristic outputs not only of governments but of organizations in general.[2]

TABLE 1
NATO Statistics: An Empirical Test

Country	GNP 1964 (billions of dollars)	Rank	Defense budget as percentage of GNP	Rank	GNP per capita $	Rank
United States	569.03	1	9.0	1	2933	1
Germany	88.87	2	5.5	6	1579	5
United Kingdom	79.46	3	7.0	3	1471	8
France	73.40	4	6.7	4	1506	6
Italy	43.63	5	4.1	10	855	11
Canada	38.14	6	4.4	8	1981	2
Netherlands	15.00	7	4.9	7	1235	10
Belgium	13.43	8	3.7	12	1429	9
Denmark	7.73	9	3.3	13	1636	3
Turkey	6.69	10	5.8	5	216	14
Norway	5.64	11	3.9	11	1484	7
Greece	4.31	12	4.2	9	507	12
Portugal	2.88	13	7.7	2	316	13
Luxembourg	.53	14	1.7	14	1636	4

Ranks
GNP   1 2 3 4 5 6 7 8 9 10 11 12 13 14
Defense budget as % of GNP   1 6 3 4 10 8 7 12 13 5 11 9 2 14
GNP per capita   1 5 8 6 11 2 10 9 3 14 7 12 13 4

SOURCE: All data are taken from the Institute for Strategic Studies, *The Military Balance 1965–1966* (London, November 1965).

Since the benefits of any action an individual takes to provide a public or organizational good also go to others, individuals acting independently do not have an incentive to provide optimal amounts of such goods. Indeed, when the group interested in a public good is very large, and the share of the total benefit that goes to any single individual is very small, usually no individual has an incentive voluntarily to purchase any of the good, which is why states exact taxes and labor unions de-

[1] See J. G. Head, "Public Goods and Public Policy," *Public Finance*, XVII, 3 (1962), pp. 197–219.
[2] See M. Olson, Jr., *The Logic of Collective Action: Public Goods and the Theory of Groups* (Cambridge: Harvard University Press, 1965), which treats organization of individuals somewhat as this article treats organizations of nation-states.

mand compulsory membership.[3] When—as in any organization repre-senting a limited number of nation-states—the membership of an organi-zation is relatively small, the individual members may have an incentive to make significant sacrifices to obtain the collective good, but they will tend to provide only suboptimal amounts of this good. There will also be a tendency for the "larger" members—those that place a higher absolute value on the public good—to bear a disproportionate share of the bur-den, as the model of alliances developed below will show.

The Model When a nation decides how large a military force to provide in an alliance, it must consider the value it places upon collective defense and the other, nondefense, goods that must be sacrificed to obtain additional military forces. The value each nation in an alliance places upon the alliance collective good vis-à-vis other goods can be shown on a simple indifference map, such as is shown in Figure 1.[4] . . . Defense capability is measured along the hori-zontal axis and valued positively. Defense spending is measured along the vertical axis and valued negatively. The cost curves are assumed to

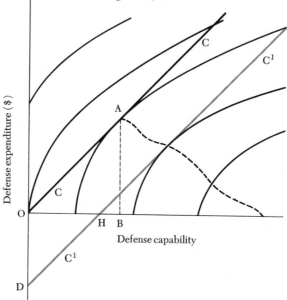

Figure 1. Indifference map.

[3] See M. Olson, Jr., *The Logic of Collective Action: Public Goods and the Theory of Groups,* pp. 5–52.
[4] An indifference curve is a standard tool in economics, used to summarize preference ratios between two goods or alternatives. Moving nearer one axis implies a preference for greater proportions of the good measured on that axis. The point of tangency between an indifference curve and a cost curve indicates the *amount* of each of the two goods that will be bought [Ed.].

be linear for the sake of simplicity. If the nation depicted in Figure 1 were not a part of any alliance, the amount of defense it would obtain (*OB*) could be found by drawing a cost curve coming out of the origin and finding the point (point *A*) where this cost curve is tangent to the "highest" (most southeasterly) indifference curve.

In an alliance, the amount a nation spends on defense will be affected by the amount its allies provide. By moving the cost curve down along the vertical axis beneath the origin we can represent the defense expenditure of allied nations as the distance between the origin and the juncture of the cost curve and the vertical axis. If a nation's allies spend *OD* on defense, and their cost functions are the same as its own, then it receives *OH* of defense without cost. This is directly equivalent to an increase in income of *OD*.[5] The more defense this nation's allies provide, the further the cost contraint moves to the southeast, and the less it spends on defense. By recording all the points of tangency of the total cost curve with the indifference curves, we can obtain this nation's reaction function. The reaction function indicates how much defense this nation will produce for all possible levels of defense expenditure by its allies. The amount of defense that this nation provides will in turn influence the defense output of its allies, whose reaction curves can be determined in the same way.

Figure 2 shows the reaction curves for a two-country model (which can easily be generalized to cover *N* countries). The intersection point of the two reaction curves indicates how much of the alliance good each

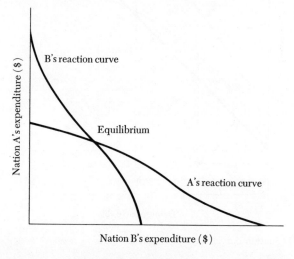

Figure 2. Reaction curves for a two-country model.

[5] Free defense is not, however, the direct equivalent of an increase in income if the nation has already received so much defense that it would like to sell some if that were possible. This is what an ally would want to do if the *CC* curve had shifted so far to the right that it was no longer tangent to any indifference curve. In such a case . . . the nation provides none of the collective good itself.

ally will supply in equilibrium. The two reaction curves need not always intersect. If one nation has a very much larger demand for the alliance good than the other, its reaction curve may lie at every point outside that of the other, in which case it will provide all of the defense. The equilibrium output will then be the same as the isolation output of the country with the largest isolation output. Whether the reaction curves intersect or not, the equilibrium output is necessarily determinate and stable unless defense is an inferior good, in which case there may be a number of equilibria, one or more of which may be unstable.[6]

In equilibrium, the defense expenditures of the two nations are such that the "larger" nation—the one that places the higher absolute value on the alliance good—will bear a *disproportionately* large share of the common burden. It will pay a share of the costs that is larger than its share of the benefits, and thus the distribution of costs will be quite different from that which a system of benefit taxation would bring about.[7]

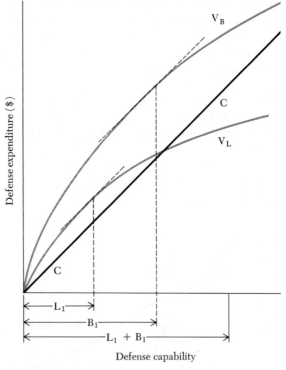

Figure 3. Evaluation curves for two countries.

[6] To see this, suppose that *A* and *B* in Figure 2 trade reaction curves. Then the equilibrium point given by the intersection point will be unstable, and there will be a tendency for one of the nations to provide all the defense. If one nation's reaction curve lies wholly outside that of the other, there will be a unique and stable equilibrium, whether or not defense is an inferior good.

[7] The authors do not advocate benefit taxation, but believe that proportionality of

This becomes obvious when income effects—i.e., the influence that the amount of nondefense goods a nation has already forgone has on its desire to provide additional units of defense—are neglected. This is shown in Figure 3 above, which depicts the evaluation curves of two nations for alliance forces. The larger nation, called Big Atlantis, has the higher, steeper valuation curve, V_B, because it places a higher absolute value on defense than Little Atlantis, which has evaluation curve V_L. The CC curve shows the costs of providing defense capability to each nation, since both, by assumption, have the same costs. In isolation, Big Atlantis would buy B_1 units of defense and Little Atlantis L_1, for at these points their respective valuation curves are parallel to their cost functions. If the two nations continued to provide these outputs in alliance, each would enjoy B_1 plus L_1 units of defense. But then each nation values a marginal unit at less than its marginal cost. Big Atlantis will stop reducing its output of deterrence when the sum applied by the two nations together in B_1. When this amount (or any amount greater than L_1) is available, it is not in Little Atlantis' interest to supply any defense whatever. The two nations are therefore simultaneously in equilibrium *only* when Big Atlantis provides B_1 of defense and Little Atlantis provides no defense whatever.

The disproportionality in the sharing of burdens is less extreme when income effects are taken into account, but it is still important. This can be seen most easily by supposing that Big Atlantis and Little Atlantis are identical in every respect save that Big Atlantis is twice the size of Little Atlantis. Per capita incomes and individual tastes are the same in both countries, but the population and GNP of Big Atlantis are twice that of Little Atlantis. Now imagine also that Big Atlantis is providing twice as much alliance defense as Little Atlantis, as proportionality would require.[8] In equilibrium, the marginal rate of substitution of money for the alliance good (MRS) must equal marginal cost for each of these countries, i.e., $MRS_{Big} = MRS_{Little} = $ marginal cost. But (since each country enjoys the same amount of the collective good) the MRS of Big Atlantis is double that of Little Atlantis, and (since the cost of an additional unit of defense is the same for each country) either Big Atlantis will want more defense or Little Atlantis will want less (or both will be true), and the common burden will come to be shared in a disproportionate way.

benefits and costs provides a useful standard of comparison, particularly in alliances which nations join to further their national interests rather than to bring about any particular distribution of income among member nations. The equilibrium outputs are not consistent with any ordinary conceptions of ability-to-pay either. They would involve a very regressive sharing if the larger nation in an alliance had the lower per capita income.

[8] It could be the case that even in isolation Big Atlantis would buy proportionately more defense than Little Atlantis. This would be the case if a nation's income elasticity of demand for the good were greater than one in the relevant range.

There is one important special case in which there will be no tendency toward disproportionality. That is when the indifference maps of the member nations are such that any perpendicular from the ordinate would intersect all indifference curves at points of equal slope. In this case, when the nation's cost constraint moves to the right as it gets more free defense, it would not reduce its own expenditure on defense. In other words, none of the increase in income that the nation receives in the form of defense is spent on goods other than defense. Defense in this situation is, strictly speaking, a "superior good," a good such that all of any increase in income is used to buy the good.[9]

This special case may sometimes be very important. During periods of all-out war or exceptional insecurity, it is likely that defense is (or is nearly) a superior good, and in such circumstances alliances will not have any tendency toward disproportionate burden sharing. The amount of allied military capability that Great Britain enjoyed in World War II increased from 1941 to 1944 as the United States mobilized, adding more and more strength to the allied side. But the British war effort was maintained, if not increased, during this period.

Although there is then one exception to the rule that alliance burdens are shared disproportionately, there is no equivalent exception to the rule that alliances provide suboptimal amounts of the collective good. The alliance output will always be suboptimal so long as the members of the alliance place a positive value on additional units of defense. This is because each of the alliance members contributes to the point where its *MRS* for the good equals the marginal cost of the good. In other words, the result of independent national maximization in an alli-

Class	Characteristic	Income elasticity of expenditure $= E$
Inferior good	Expenditure on the good decreases or is unchanged as income increases	$E \leqq 0$
Inelastic good	Expenditure on the good increases, but by a smaller percent than income increases	$0 < E < 1$
Elastic good	Expenditure on the good increases by a percentage that is as great or greater than the percentage by which income increases, but by a smaller absolute amount	$1 \leqq E < Y_0/S_0$ [a]
Superior good	Expenditure on the good increases by as much or more than income increases	$E \geqq Y_0/S_0$

[a] S_0 is the expenditure on the good when income is Y_0.

[9] Apparently the literature has neglected goods of this kind, and not made clear that they are simply the logical converse of the much discussed inferior goods. When the phrase "superior good" has been used it has usually been given an unsymmetrical and unclear meaning. We therefore distinguish the following classes of goods, realizing that the category to which a good belongs may depend on the level of income.

ance, when the cost function is linear and the same for all members, is that $MRS_1 = MRS_2 = \ldots MRS_N = MC$. There could be an optimal quantity of the collective good only if the total value which all of the alliance members together placed on an additional unit of the good equalled marginal cost, i.e., only if $MRS_1 + MRS_2 + \ldots MRS_N = MC$. The individual nations in an alliance would have an incentive to keep providing additional alliance forces until the Pareto-optimal level is reached only if there were an arrangement such that the alliance members shared marginal costs in the same proportions in which they shared additional benefits (that is, in the same ratio as their marginal rates of substitution of money for the good).[10] When there is such a marginal cost-sharing scheme, there need be no tendency toward disproportionality in the sharing of burdens.

Qualifications and Elaborations One simplification assumed in the foregoing model was that the costs of defense were constant to scale and the same for all alliance members. Although military forces are composed of diverse types of equipment and manpower, and thus probably vary less both in cost from one country to another and with scale of output than many single products, it is still unlikely that costs are constant and uniform. For some special types of weapon systems there are undoubtedly striking economies of large-scale production, and for conventional ground forces there are probably rising costs as larger proportions of a nation's population are called to arms. Because of this latter tendency, a small country can perhaps get a considerable amount of conventional capability with the first few percentiles of its national income. This tends to keep the military expenditures of small nations in an alliance above the very low level implied by our constant cost assumption. In any event, cross-country variations in marginal costs should not normally alter the basic conclusions deduced from the model. The differences in the amounts which member nations would be willing to pay for marginal units of an alliance good are typically so great that the cost differentials could hardly negate their effect. Even if there were very large differences in marginal costs among nations, there is no reason to assume that national cost functions would vary systematically with the valuation a country places on alliance forces.

A nation's valuation of alliance forces obviously depends not only on its national income but also on other factors. A nation on the enemy's border may value defense more than one some distance away. A nation that has a large area and long frontiers in relation to its resources may

---

[10] A Pareto-optimal solution is defined as a situation such that no individual in the group at issue can be made better off without making someone else worse off. The possibility of dropping below the Pareto-optimal level, as well as of shifting along it, brings a mixture of competition and cooperation to the situation [Ed.].

want a larger army than a compact country. On the other hand, if bomb and missile attacks are the main danger, a crowded country may wish to invest more in defense against attack by air. Similarly, a nation's attitudes or ideologies may partly determine its evaluation of defense. Many observers think that the uniformity and intensity of anticommunism is greater among the NATO countries with the highest per capita incomes, and these also happen to be the largest countries in the alliance. It also seems that many people in small and weak countries, both inside and outside of NATO, tend to be attracted to neutralist or pacifist ideologies. This pattern of attitudes may perhaps be partly explained by our model, for it suggests that small nations, which find that even large sacrifices on their part have little effect on the global balance, would often be attracted to neutral or passive foreign policies, and that large nations which know that their efforts can decisively influence world events in their own interest will continually need to emphasize the urgency of the struggle in which they are engaged. The popularity of pacific ideologies, the frequent adoption of neutralist policies in small and weak countries, and the activist attitudes and policies of the United States and the Soviet Union are at least consistent with our model.[11]

Whatever the reasons for the different evaluations different nations have for military capabilities in an alliance, the model here still applies. If two countries in an alliance had equal national incomes, but one was more concerned about the common enemy for geographic, ideological, historical, or other reasons, the more concerned nation would not only put a higher valuation on the alliance's military capacity, but would bear a share of the total alliance costs that was even greater than its share of the total benefits. The model deals with the general case of differences in the absolute valuation that nations put upon additional units of an alliance good, whether these differences are due to differences in national income or to other reasons.[12]

[11] One factor that might conceivably make small countries outside of an alliance spend little or nothing on defense is that they might think that the maximum force they could raise alone would not be sufficient to defeat any potential enemy, so that there would be no point in having any military forces at all. In an alliance, on the other hand, a small nation might suppose that its forces could provide the margin of victory and therefore increase their defense spending. The kink in the evaluation function that this argument implies is, however, made much less likely by the fact that even a small military force may be quite valuable to a small, unaligned country, for it might increase the costs and risks to an aggressor enough to deter him from attacking a small (and therefore probably not very valuable) country. This seems to be one argument used to support the French nuclear force.

[12] The value which a nation puts upon alliance forces may also vary with alliance policies. An alliance must sometimes choose which of two or more alternative public goods to provide, and one public good may be more valuable to some alliance members and another more valuable to others. The NATO alliance, for example, provides conventional defense as well as nuclear protection, and there have been disagreements about the proper mix between these two goods. In such a case it is

Another assumption in the model developed in the foregoing section was that the military forces in an alliance provide only the collective benefit of alliance security, when in fact they also provide purely national, noncollective benefits to the nations that maintain them. When Portugal mobilizes additional forces to suppress the independence movement in Angola, a national goal unrelated to the purposes of NATO, she may at the same time be increasing the total strength of the alliance. Similarly, allied nations may be suspicious of one another, even as they cooperate in the achievement of common purposes, and may enlarge their military forces because of conceivable future conflicts with each other. In any situation in which the military forces of alliance members provide important noncollective benefits as well as alliance benefits, the degree of suboptimality and the importance of the disproportionality will decrease because the noncollective benefits give the member nations an incentive to maintain larger forces.

This fact leads to the paradoxical conclusion that *a decline in the amity, unity, and community of interest among allies need not necessarily reduce the effectiveness of an alliance*, because the decline in these alliance "virtues" produces a greater ratio of private to collective benefits. This suggests that alliances troubled by suspicions and disagreements may continue to work reasonably well. To be sure, the degree of coordination among the allies will decline, and this will reduce the efficiency of the alliance forces (in a sense leaving them on a poorer production function), but the alliance forces will be larger.

However important the noncollective benefits of alliances may be, there can be little doubt that, above all, alliances produce public goods. It is not easy to think of alliances that provide only private goods, though such alliances are perhaps conceivable. If nations simply trade sites for military bases, no common interests or public goods would necessarily be involved. An alliance might also be set up simply to provide insurance in the sense that two nations without any common purpose or common enemy would agree to defend each other in case of attack, but in which neither knew in advance which would suffer aggression. On the other hand, if these two nations thought (as they presumably would) that the fact of their alliance would make it less profitable for other nations to attack either of them, the alliance would provide a public good

possible that some nations may supply additional forces in return for more influence on alliance policy, whereas other nations may make policy concessions in order to get other members to assume a greater share of alliance costs. Such trade-offs need not change the qualitative conclusions about disproportionate burden sharing. They might simply mean that a nation can bear part of its alliance burden by making policy concessions rather than by providing additional forces. When this happens, though, the allies that obtained the policy they wanted find they value the alliance good more than before, and the opposite is true for those who have relinquished some of their control over alliance policy. This in turn makes the former set of nations provide still more defense and the latter still less.

—a degree of deterrence that could deter an attack on either or both of these nations about as well as it could deter an attack on one alone. There is, moreover, no reason to describe a mere transaction in private goods as an alliance, and the word does not normally appear to be used in that way. A transaction in private goods would be quite as useful between enemies as between "allies," and would normally be completed by a single pair of actions or a single agreement which would not require the continuing consultation, cooperation, and organization characteristic of alliances.

Normally, an additional member can be added to an alliance without substantially subtracting from the amount of defense available to those already in the alliance, and any good that satisfies this criterion is by definition a public good.[13] Suppose two nations of the same size face a common enemy with an army larger than either of them provides by itself. They then form an alliance and maintain a level of military forces larger than either of them had before, but smaller than the sum of their two pre-alliance armies. After alliance both nations enjoy (1) more military security, and (2) lower defense costs, than they had before. This result comes about not only because a military force can often deter attack by a common enemy against an additional nation without a substantial increase in cost, but also because an alliance may make a greater level of security economically feasible and desirable, and the gains from obtaining this extra security can leave both nations better off.

Another defining characteristic that is sufficient (but not necessary) to distinguish a collective good is that the exclusion of those who do not share the cost of the good is impractical or impossible. Typically, once an alliance treaty has been signed, a member nation is legally bound to remain a member for the duration of the treaty. The decisions about how the common burden is to be shared are not, however, usually specified in the alliance treaty. This procedure works to the disadvantage of the larger countries. Often, the smaller and weaker nations gain relatively more from the existence of an alliance than do the larger and stronger powers, and once an alliance treaty has been signed, the larger powers are immediately deprived of their strongest bargaining weapon —the threat that they will not help to defend the recalcitrant smaller powers—in any negotiations about the sharing of the common burden.

---

[13] The number of people defended by a given military force can clearly increase without reducing the security per person. However, additional land area will normally require some additional military forces, if the area previously protected is to have the same degree of security as before, and if actual defensive conflict, rather than deterrence, is at issue. When the additional land area has no common border with the enemy, it can usually be defended without any significant extra cost. The extra cost to NATO of defending Belgium against a Soviet attack, once Germany and France are already defended, is negligible. Even when the extra land does have a common border with an enemy it is not always true that it costs much more to defend it. If the French had believed they had to defend Belgium as well as France in World Wars I and II, they might have fared better.

Even at the time an alliance treaty is negotiated, exclusion may very well not be feasible, since most alliances are implicit in an already existing danger or goal common to some group of states. That common danger or goal gives the nations that share it an incentive tacitly to treat each other as allies, whether or not they have all signed a formal agreement. A nation can only lose from having another nation with whom it shares a common interest succumb to an enemy, for that will strengthen the enemy's side at the expense of the first nation. It may well be that most alliances are never embodied in any formal agreement. Sometimes a nation may have a geopolitical position (e.g., behind an alliance member serving as a buffer state) such that it would be unusually difficult, if not impossible, to deny it the benefits of alliance protection. Then, if it regards alliance membership as a special burden, it may have an incentive to stay out of, or when legally possible to withdraw from, the alliance's formal organization.

This paper also made the simplifying assumption that no alliance member will take into account the reactions other members may have to the size of its alliance contribution. The mutual recognition of oligopolistic interdependence can be profoundly important in small groups of firms, but in the NATO alliance, at least, it seems to have been somewhat less important (except with respect to the infrastructure, which will be considered later). There are at least two important reasons why strategic bargaining interaction is often less important in alliances than in oligopolistic industries. First, alliances are often involved in situations that contain a strong element of irreversibility. Suppose that the United States were to threaten to cut its defense spending to nothing to get its allies to bear larger shares of the NATO burden. The Soviet Union, if it has the characteristics that American policy assumes, would then deprive the United States of its independence, in which case future defense savings would have little relevance. The United States threat would have only a limited credibility in view of the irreversibility of this process. The second factor which limits strategic bargaining interaction among alliance members stems from an important difference between market and nonmarket groups. In an oligopolistic group of firms, any firm knows that its competitors would be better off if it were made bankrupt or otherwise driven out of the industry. Large firms thus sometimes engage in price wars or cutthroat competition to drive out the smaller members of an oligopolistic group. By contrast, nonmarket groups and organizations, such as alliances, usually strive instead for a larger membership, since they provide collective goods the supply of which should increase as the membership increases. Since an ally would typically lose from driving another member out of an alliance, a bargaining threat to that effect may not be credible. This will be especially true if the excluded nation would then fall to the common enemy and (as we argued before) thereby strengthen the enemy at the expense of the alliance.

Even when strategic interaction is important in alliances, the advantage paradoxically still rests in most cases with the smaller nations. There are two reasons for this. First, the large country loses more from withholding an alliance contribution than a small country does, since it values a given amount of alliance force more highly. In other words, it may be deterred by the very importance to itself of its own alliance contribution from carrying out any threat to end that contribution. Second, the large country has relatively less to gain than its small ally from driving a hard bargain. Even if the large nation were successful in the bargaining it would expect only a relatively small addition to the alliance force from the small nation, but when the small nation succeeds in the bargaining it can expect a large addition to the alliance force from the large nation. There is, accordingly, no reason to expect that there is any disparity of bargaining in favor of the larger ally that would negate the tendency toward disproportionality revealed by our model.

Empirical Evidence When other things are equal, the larger a nation is, the higher its valuation of the output of an alliance. Thus, if our model is correct, the larger members of an alliance should, on the average, devote larger percentages of their national incomes to defense than do the smaller nations. This prediction is tested against the recent data on the NATO nations in Table 1. The following specific hypotheses are used to test the model's predictions:

H_1—In an alliance, there will be a significant positive correlation between the size of a member's national income and the percentage of its national income spent on defense. This hypothesis will be tested against:

H_0—There will not be a significant positive correlation between the variables specified in H_1.

Since there is no assurance that the data are parametrically distributed, nonparametrical statistical tests must be used. The Spearman rank correlation coefficient for GNP and *defense budget as a percentage of GNP* is .490. On a one-tailed test this value is significant at the .05 level. We therefore reject the null hypothesis and accept H_1. There is a significant positive correlation indicating that the large nations in NATO bear a disproportionate share of the burden of the common defense. Moreover, this result holds even when the level of per capita income is held constant.

Our model predicts that there are tendencies toward disproportionate burden sharing, not only in military alliances but also in other international organizations, such as the United Nations. The test of this prediction is complicated in the case of the UN by the fact that the organization is supported primarily through assessments levied against individual members. These assessments are determined by a formula constructed by a committee of experts. The model would, however, suggest that the degree to which a member fulfills or oversubscribes its quota would be positively correlated with its size, and thus gives the following hypotheses:

H_2—In a voluntary organization with quota assessments that are not always satisfied, there will be a significant positive correlation between a member's GNP and the percentage of fulfillment or overfulfillment of its quota.

H_0—There will not be a significant positive correlation between the variables in H_2.

The Spearman rank correlation coefficient between 1961 *GNP* and *percentage total UN contributions* in 1961/*normal assessment scale* was .404. This result is significant at the .01 level. We thus accept H_2 and reject H_0, for, as the model predicted, the larger nations in the UN did a better job of living up to their normal assessments. The fact that members may lose prestige and membership rights if they fail to meet their assessments, i.e., that there are distinctly private benefits from contributions to the UN, makes this high correlation more striking.

The foreign aid that the industrialized democracies give to the underdeveloped countries is a collective good to these aid-giving nations, at least to the extent that they all value the development of the less developed areas. On the other hand, individual aid-giving nations often concentrate all of their aid on particular underdeveloped areas, such as past or present colonies, in which they have a special interest. To the extent that different aid-giving nations are interested in different underdeveloped areas, their aid allocations constitute private rather than collective goods. This tends to limit any tendencies toward suboptimality and disproportionality in the provision of foreign aid. We can test for any such disproportionalities with the aid of the following hypotheses:

H_3—Among a group of developed nations there will be a significant positive correlation between foreign aid expenditures as a percentage of national income and the size of the national income.

H_0—There will not be a significant positive correlation between the variables in H_3.

One set of data used to test these hypotheses revealed a correlation between *real national income and total grants and loans to underdeveloped countries as a percentage of national income* in 1960 of .770. This figure is significant at the .01 level. A different set of data for a different year (1962) showed a correlation between *GNP* and *total aid as a percentage of GNP* of .439. With the small sample of only 12 nations, this value falls slightly short of the .05 level of significance (the borderline value is .506). Thus, both sets of data yield correlation coefficients suggesting the expected positive relationship, but in one case the result is clearly statistically significant and in the other case it falls somewhat short of the .05 level of significance. We will take the most conservative course and await further research before finally accepting either H_3 or the null hypothesis. The most reasonable inference at the moment is that there is some tendency toward disproportionate burden sharing, but that the private, or purely national, benefits from foreign aid are probably also very important. This is, moreover, about what might be expected from the fact that the industrialized Western nations express a common interest in the development of the poor nations generally, while at the same time many of these nations individually are interested primarily in particular underdeveloped areas with which they have special relationships.

Our model indicated that when the members of an organization share the costs of marginal units of an alliance good, just as they share in the benefits of additional units of that good, there is no tendency toward disproportionality or suboptimality. In other words, if each ally pays an appropriate percentage of the cost of any additional units of the alliance good, the results are quite different from when each ally pays the full cost of any amount of the alliance good that he provides. The costs of the NATO infrastructure (common supply depots, pipelines, etc.), unlike the costs of providing the main alliance forces, are shared according to percentages worked out in a negotiated agreement. Since each ally pays some percentage of the cost of any addition to the NATO infrastructure, we have here a marginal-cost-sharing arrangement.

Thus, our model suggests that the burdens of the NATO infrastructure should be borne quite differently from the rest of the NATO burden. There are other reasons for expecting that the infrastructure burden would be shared in a different way from the main NATO burdens. For one thing, the infrastructure facilities of NATO are all in continental European countries and ultimately become the property of the host nation. Their construction also brings foreign exchange earnings to these countries, which for the most part are the smaller alliance members. In addition, infrastructure costs are very small in relation to the total burden of common defense, so a small nation may get prestige at a relatively low cost by offering to bear a larger percentage of the infrastructure cost. There are, in short, many private benefits for the smaller alliance members resulting from the infrastructure expenditures. Because of these private benefits, and more important because of the percentage sharing of marginal (and total) costs of the infrastructure, we would predict that the larger members of the alliance would bear a smaller share of the infrastructure burden than of the main alliance burdens.

This prediction suggests that the following hypotheses be tested:

H_4—In an alliance in which the marginal costs of certain activities are *not* shared (but fall instead upon those members who have an incentive to provide additional units of the alliance good by themselves), and in which the marginal costs of other activities are shared (so that each member pays a specified percentage of any costs of these activities), the *ratio* of a member's share of the costs of the activities of the former type to his share of the costs of activities of the latter type will have a significant positive correlation with national income.

H_0—There will be no significant positive correlation between the variables in H_4.

To test these hypotheses we calculated the correlation coefficient between *national income* and *variable T* in Table 2. The Spearman rank correlation coefficient between these variables is .582, which is significant at the .05 level. We therefore reject the null hypothesis and conclude

TABLE 2
NATO Infrastructure

Country	National income 1960 [a] (billions of dollars) (1)	Infrastructure % reconsidered in 1960 [b] (2)	$R = (2)/(1)$ (3)	Military budget 1960 (billions of dollars) (4)	$T = (4)/(2)$ (5)
United States	411.367	36.98	.0899	41.000	1.1087
Germany	51.268	13.77	.2686	2.072	.1504
United Kingdom	57.361	9.88	.1722	4.466	.4520
France	43.468	11.87	.2731	3.311	.2789
Italy	24.950	5.61	.2248	1.076	.1922
Canada	28.178	6.15	.2183	1.680	.2732
Netherlands	9.246	3.51	.3800	.450	.1282
Belgium	8.946	4.39	.4907	.395	.0900
Turkey	4.929	1.75	.3550	.244	.1394
Denmark	4.762	2.63	.5569	.153	.0582
Norway	3.455	2.19	.6338	.168	.0767
Greece	2.684	.87	.3242	.173	.1989
Portugal	2.083	.28	.1344	.093	.3321
Luxembourg	.386	.17	.4404	.007	.0412

Ranks:

(1)	1	3	2	4	6	5	7	8	9	10	11	12	13	14
(3)	14	9	12	8	10	11	5	3	6	2	1	7	13	4
(5)	1	8	2	4	7	5	10	11	9	13	12	6	3	14

[a] United Nations, *Yearbook of National Accounts Statistics* (New York, 1964); and *Balance of Payments Yearbook,* Vol. 15 (Washington: International Monetary Fund, 1964).
[b] Charles Croot, "Coordination in the Sixties," reprinted from *NATO Letter* (August 1960).

that the larger members bear a larger proportion of the costs of the main NATO forces than they do of those NATO activities for which the costs of each unit are shared. The difference between the distribution of infrastructure costs and the distribution of alliance burdens generally is quite striking, as the tests of the following hypotheses indicate:

H_5—In the NATO alliance there is a significant negative correlation between national income and the percentage of national income devoted to infrastructure expenses.

H_0—There is no significant negative correlation between the variables in H_5.

The Spearman rank correlation coefficient between *national income* and *variable R* in Table 2 is –.538, which is significant at the 0.5 level. Thus, not only is it the case that the larger nations pay a smaller share of the infrastructure costs than of other alliance costs; it is also true that there is a significant negative correlation between national income and the percentage of national income devoted to the NATO infrastructure, which is in vivid contrast to the positive correlation that prevails for other NATO burdens. This confirms the prediction that when there are marginal-cost-sharing arrangements, there need no longer be any tendency for the larger nations to bear disproportionately large shares of the costs of international organizations. If it happens at the same time that the smaller nations get greater than average private benefits from their contributions, they may even contribute greater percentages of their national incomes than the larger members.

Conclusions and Recommendations   All of the empirical evidence tended to confirm the model. In the UN there appear to be systematic forces tending to make the small nations fail to meet their quotas and leading larger nations to assume larger shares of the costs. The larger industrialized nations, moreover, seem to bear disproportionate shares of the burden of aid to the less developed countries. In NATO there is again a statistically significant positive correlation between the size of a member's national income and the percentage of its national income devoted to the common defense.

As our model indicated, this is in part because each ally gets only a fraction of the benefits of any collective good that is provided, but each pays the full cost of any additional amounts of the collective good. This means that individual members of an alliance or international organization have an incentive to stop providing the collective good long before the Pareto-optimal output for the group has been provided. This is particularly true of the smaller members, who get smaller shares of the total benefits accruing from the good, and who find that they have little or no incentive to provide additional amounts of the collective good once the larger members have provided the amounts they want for themselves, with the result that the burdens are shared in a disproportionate way. The model indicated two special types of situations in which there need be no such tendency toward disproportionality. First, in cases of all-out war or extreme insecurity defense may be what was strictly defined as a "superior good," in which case a nation's output of a collective good will not be reduced when it receives more of this good from an ally. Second, institutional arrangements such that the members of an organization share marginal costs, just as they share the benefits of each unit of the good, tend to work against disproportionality in burden sharing, and it is a necessary condition of an efficient, Pareto-optimal output that the marginal costs be shared in the same proportions as the benefits of additional units. The NATO nations determine through negotiation what percentages of any infrastructure expenditure each member will pay, and this sharing of marginal costs has led the smaller member to bear a very much larger share of the infrastructure burden than they do of the other NATO burdens. The fact that the model predicts not only the distribution of the principal NATO burdens but also the greatly different distribution of infrastructure costs suggests that the results are, in fact, due to the processes described in the model, rather than to some other cause.

The model's implication that large nations tend to bear disproportionate shares of the burdens of international organization, and the empirical evidence tending to confirm the model, does *not* entail the conclusion that the small nations should be told they "ought" to bear a larger share of the common burdens. No moral conclusions can follow solely from any purely logical model of the kind developed here.[14] Indeed, our analysis suggests that moral suasion is inappropriate, since the different levels of contribution are not due to different moral attitudes, and ineffective, since the less than proportionate contributions of the smaller nations are securely grounded in their national interests (just as the disproportionately large contributions of the larger countries are solidly grounded in their national interests). Thus, American attempts to persuade other nations to bear "fair" shares of the burdens of common ven-

---

[14] We must strongly emphasize that we are *not* here questioning the fairness of the present distribution of the costs of any international undertaking. No statement about what distribution of costs ought to prevail can be made unless some (logically arbitrary) assumption is made about what income redistributions among participating nations would be desirable. Jacques van Ypersele de Strihou, in "Sharing the Burden of Defense Among Allies," an interesting PhD thesis available at Yale University, has shown that, if the British rates of progression are used as a standard of fairness, it appears that the larger European members of NATO pay an unfairly large share of the common costs, that the United States (partly because of its high per capita income) pays about the right amount, and that the smaller NATO nations (because of the same general forces explained in this paper) pay an unfairly small amount.

tures are likely to be divisive and harmful even to American interests in the long run.

The model developed here suggests that the problems of disproportionality and suboptimality in international organizations should be met instead through institutional changes that alter the pattern of incentives. Since suboptimal provision is typical of international organizations, it is possible to design policy changes that would leave everyone better off, and which accordingly may have some chance of adoption. Appropriate marginal-cost-sharing schemes, such as are now used to finance the NATO infrastructure, could solve the problem of suboptimality in international organizations, and might also reduce the degree of disproportionality. Substituting a union for an alliance or international organization would also tend to bring about optimality, for then the unified system as a whole has an incentive to behave in an optimal fashion, and the various parts of the union can be required to contribute the amounts their common interest requires. Even a union of smaller members of NATO, for example, could be helpful, and be in the interest of the United States. Such a union would give the people involved an incentive to contribute more toward the goals they shared with their then more nearly equal partners. Whatever the disadvantages on other grounds of these policy possibilities, they at least have the merit that they help to make the national interests of individual nations more nearly compatible with the efficient attainment of the goals which groups of nations hold in common.

A final implication of our model is that alliances and international organizations, as presently organized, will not work efficiently, or according to any common conception of fairness, however complete the agreement and community of interest among the members. Though there is obviously a point beyond which dissension and divergent purposes will ruin any organization, it is also true that some differences of purpose may improve the working of an alliance, because they increase the private, noncollective benefits from the national contributions to the alliance, and this alleviates the suboptimality and disproportionality. How much smaller would the military forces of the small members of NATO be if they did not have their private fears and quarrels? How much aid would the European nations give if they did not have private interests in the development of their past or present colonies? How much would the smaller nations contribute to the UN if it were not a forum for the expression of their purely national enmities and aspirations? The United States, at least, should perhaps not hope for too much unity in common ventures with other nations. It might prove extremely expensive.

The Role of the United States in NATO

WILLIAM T. R. FOX AND ANNETTE B. FOX

Just as the net advantages of international organization for different members vary, so do the members' perspectives regarding the roles they intend to play in the common enterprise differ. Americans think of the United States as a full member of NATO with all the benefits and responsibilities suggested in the previous chapter. But they do not think of the United States as just another member. Policymakers have at one time or another envisaged at least seven distinctive roles for the United States in furthering the objectives sought through NATO. Each of these seven somewhat overlapping roles has been performed mainly, and a few entirely, by the United States. Each is also without precedent in American peacetime experience.

1. From the beginning, American officials have expectd their country *to make good the deficiencies of the alliance as a whole;* this is the first United States role we shall discuss. What other allies could not or would not provide, the United States would have to contribute, directly in the form of land, sea and air forces or indirectly in the form of military assistance—giving, loaning money for, or selling materials and supplying training and technical help.

Leaders among all the allies expected some form of American military assistance to implement the United States commitment in the North Atlantic Treaty; but at the insistence of Senator Vandenberg and some of

From *NATO and the Range of American Choice,* by William T. R. and Annette B. Fox. Copyright by Columbia University Press, New York, 1967. Pp. 59–76. Reprinted by permission.

his Congressional colleagues, the offer of military aid was conditioned on allied preparation of an integrated plan for mutual defense. Some would have preferred that the aid then be channeled through an alliance organ. Most of it in the first years, however, was granted bilaterally, though in line with multilaterally approved plans. When the various commands were organized and SHAPE was established at the end of 1950, and especially after joint enterprises were started, some of the military "assistance" was actually the American share (the giant one to be sure) in the cost of common undertakings. The United States government expected that American military aid would enable the European allies to increase their contributions of troops and, later, of other essentials. In the earlier years Canada also provided assistance.

At first, aid consisted largely of World War II stocks of equipment given to European allies which were rebuilding their armed forces almost from scratch. Thus Britain, which by 1951 had ceased to need economic assistance under the Marshall Plan, could still receive spare parts for its rearmament effort; similar aid helped to boost the military capacity of the other allies. This was the period when, in the light of the first Soviet atomic bomb test and the heat of the Korean War, American officials were giving budget-making instruction to European allies as to what their defense budget allocations must be if they wished to continue receiving aid.[1] During this period of intense American defense mobilization effort, the United States inaugurated the program of "offshore procurement" which, inter alia, helped the Europeans set up their own productive facilities for military equipment. Purchasing under this program also gave the United States unusual powers in determining allies' foreign economic undertakings, just as the counterpart fund system had provided unprecedented opportunities for participating in other countries' "domestic" affairs.[2] Secretary Dulles denied that aid was ever used as a lever to alter the foreign policy of a recipient.[3] NATO's Annual Review procedure, however, permitted the United States to maintain rather constant pressure on its allies to improve their defense forces in directions which would support strategies and policy objectives approved by the United States while shifting some of the onus for this pressure to an organization in which the allies might come to understand their own needs

[1] See testimony of American aid officials (Milton Katz and Richard Bissell) on efforts to influence European defense budgets [Senate Committee on Foreign Relations, *Hearings, Mutual Assistance Act of 1951*, 82nd Cong., 1st sess. (1951), pp. 61, 63–65, and 180].

[2] As Herman M. Somers said, "Procurement is not merely buying" ["Civil-Military Relations in Mutual Security," *Annals* of the American Academy of Political and Social Science, July, 1953, p. 30]. Cf. also Michael M. Cardozo, *Diplomats in International Cooperation* (Ithaca: Cornell University Press, 1962), pp. 74–75.

[3] It was only for specific purposes sought by the United States [House of Representatives Committee on Foreign Affairs, *Hearings, Mutual Security Act of 1957*, 85th Cong., 1st sess. (1957), p. 535].

and commit themselves to defense programs consonant with those needs.

From the start, American officials insisted in their Congressional appearances that the object of the military aid program was joint protection and that it had no "give-away" aspect whatever. It was, they said, not "foreign," but truly mutual, combined defense. Expenditures for aid to allies' forces gave the United States more defense for the dollar than comparable expenditures for American forces. Secretary Dulles spoke of military assistance as the "foreign component of our own defense structure." Defense officials pointed out that since the security of the United States depended upon allied forces as well as upon its own, the allied forces had to be brought up to American standards, and for this aid was necessary.

The growth of European prosperity and the increasingly variegated threat of the Soviet Union caused changes in the type of aid given to the NATO allies. Economic assistance to them had tapered off by 1955. After 1954 military aid funds were for maintenance, "modern" (nuclear and non-nuclear) weapons available only in the United States and "critical" types of equipment, and training in the use of such weapons and equipment. Eventually, what had at all times been a selective program for individual countries changed from gifts to sales of equipment; only training remained in the "aid" category. Greece and Turkey alone continued to be important recipients of military assistance grants. Methods became more supple. The United States tried pump-priming by cost-sharing projects; it sought to induce European allies to embark on new types of programs and to make a greater contribution to them as American aid diminished. Such projects included the Maintenance and Supply Service, the Anti-Submarine Warfare Research Center, and the Air Defense Technical Center. These, and most especially the Mutual Weapons Development Program, were intended also to bring about the best use of scientific and technical resources in the alliance and to produce compatibility in tactics, weapons systems, and military doctrine. This last objective became increasingly important as the opportunities for standardization afforded in the earlier period by the United States position as the sole supplier of (surplus World War II) equipment lessened. The Mutual Weapons Development Program disappeared from the military aid category in 1964. Its place was taken by aid to allies in jointly financed research and development, but only when the United States was interested in the end product or when another United States program would be helped. The United States also promoted the licensing of American weapons systems and equipment for joint production by a number of manufacturers in the NATO countries. By the 1960's the inflow of payments for military equipment had come to exceed the flow outward in military aid to the NATO allies.[4] The United States had also changed

[4] For the stages in which the United States phased out aid, see David Bendall, "Burden Sharing in NATO," *NATO Letter*, September, 1963, p. 13. He pointed

the emphasis from direct training of allied military personnel to the instruction of allied teachers for allied trainees.

Although military aid to NATO allies, even on this diminished scale, has continued to be the target of determined critics, each administration has found it indispensable. Government officials have variously argued that there was danger, without the remaining projects, of the allies' withdrawing into themselves, that the military aid has encouraged the allies to do things they would not otherwise do, or that United States defense plans depended upon aid. There were few who in their public testimony also pointed out that if an ally knew the United States military really wanted it to have a particular weapon, it could depend on American aid to provide the weapon, with no need for that ally's budget to suffer the cost of supply.[5]

Whatever may have been the case with respect to equipment and training, military leaders in the early 1950's declared and apparently believed that the need for stationing United States military forces in Europe would be temporary. Although these forces were numerically only a minor portion of the total allied forces assigned to NATO, they were much the strongest and were almost literally the backbone of the allied command. As years went by, they continued to be the best-trained and best-equipped forces in Europe and the readiest for any military confrontation.[6]

The United States has filled the breach at sea as well as on land. The United States Sixth Fleet is the major element of NATO's naval

out that the most equitable sharing would still leave the United States the giant contributor. See also House of Representatives Committee on Foreign Affairs, *Hearings, Foreign Assistance Act of 1964*, 88th Cong., 2nd sess. (1964), p. 652; and E. Vandevanter, *Coordinated Weapons Production in NATO* (Santa Monica: The RAND Corporation, 1964), p. 76.

[5] But a RAND member did: Malcolm Hoag in "The Economics of Military Alliance" in Charles J. Hitch and Roland G. McKean *et al.*, *The Economics of Defense in a Nuclear Age* (Cambridge: Harvard University Press, 1960), p. 295. In the 1960's, when the balance of payments problem was being met in several ways, the United States often simply facilitated the recipient ally's obtaining credit assistance commercially.

[6] General Earl Wheeler, Chief of Staff of the Army, described them in February, 1963, as "the finest Army probably that the United States has ever had in peacetime." The only comparable allied force was the Canadian, but it was just one brigade, about a third of a division [House of Representatives Committee on Armed Services, *Hearings, Military Posture and H.R. 2440*, 88th Cong., 1st sess. (1963), p. 767]. What has been said for the provision of United States ground forces in the Central European area can also be said for the American contribution to the Allied Tactical Air Force. For the United States contribution to allied defense, see the annual estimates of the Institute for Strategic Studies, London, *The Military Balance*. For another comment from a European source, on the American contribution, see Forschungsinstitut der Deutschen Gesellschaft für Auswärtige Politik, *Der Stand der europäischen Sicherheit* (Frankfurt am Main: Alfred Metzner Verlag, 1962), pp. 100–01.

strength in the Mediterranean, but it is only to be "assigned" to SA-CEUR in case of war. Naval units belonging to a number of other NATO countries have as a principal task the protection of this fleet.[7] The main portion of NATO's naval strength in the Atlantic, too, is provided by the United States, although here also ships are not permanently assigned to the Supreme Allied Commander Atlantic (SACLANT) in peacetime, but only during joint exercises.

2. The second role Americans have envisaged for the United States in NATO has been *to act as pilot in the strategic planning of the alliance.* He who pays the piper is usually in a position to call the tune (some might say that since the United States has been calling the tune it should pay the piper, or at least the largest share), but there have been other reasons for expecting that this role would be played.[8] In the first years of the alliance American military officers did not want to be committed in advance to any responsibilities which they thought they could not meet.[9] Nor did they consider the possibility that the creation of NATO would alter their planning for American security by requiring them to share responsibility for that planning with others. Whatever the American military views, there were, apart from the British, scarcely any alliance partners capable of significantly sharing in this task at the time. With the increasing importance, after 1954, of the nuclear deterrent in NATO strategy the gap widened between the Americans, who more than ever believed themselves capable of solo piloting of the alliance's strategy, and the others in the alliance. Technological developments were not the only explanation. From the beginning there had been a gap due to the tremendous disparity between American and allied resources and to the Americans' tendency to think of themselves as almost exclusively gifted in knowledge of appropriate strategy because they were "ahead" in some phases.[10] Steps taken to implement American-induced strategy for NATO, particularly those which put main reliance on the strategic deterrent, increased United States dominance in this field. Subsequently, in the 1960's, the United States' stress on mobility increased the likelihood that the country most capable of developing a mobile force would conduct the alliance's strategy. With the new emphasis on the interrelatedness of the several facets of alliance strategy, the United States pressed its European allies for contributions the latter had earlier been

---

[7] F. W. Mulley, *The Politics of Western Defense* (New York: Frederick A. Praeger, 1962), p. 168.

[8] See, for example, Secretary of Defense McNamara's testimony before the House of Representatives Committee on Armed Services, in January, 1963, for an illustration of American reasoning on the responsibilities of the member carrying the giant share [*Hearings, Military Posture and H.R. 2440*, 88th Cong., 1st sess. (1963), p. 297].

[9] See President Truman's description of the view of the Joint Chiefs of Staff, *Memoirs,* vol. II (Garden City: Doubleday and Company, 1956), p. 245.

[10] See Bernard Brodie, "What Price Conventional Capabilities in Europe?" *Reporter,* May 23, 1963, p. 27.

taught to discount in importance, urging these at a time when the allies could no longer be brought by financial inducements to do what they did not believe in. The more the Americans stressed the flexible response, the less credible to their allies appeared United States guarantees regarding the strategic deterrent. During this same period the diversification of the Communist challenge increased the difficulty of maintaining United States dominance in planning NATO's strategy.[11]

3. Closely linked with the first two roles for the United States is the third: *to guide the general policies of NATO*. American initiatives were crucially important both in the adoption of the principle of collective, balanced forces and in the creation of the posts of SACEUR and SACLANT. Influential European officials participated, but the initiative and the insistent pressure came from the United States. Americans also took the lead in persuading the alliance to admit the three new members, the most important of which was Germany, whose rearmament had been an objective of American policy from 1950 onward. When thwarted momentarily by France's setting-up and tearing-down of the EDC, the Americans utilized a device for securing German rearmament that was not of their designing. The British had learned that the way to influence the alliance's policies was to influence the United States, and it was their formula that resolved the impasse created by French rejection of the EDC.[12]

Once a policy was accepted in general by the alliance, bilateral arrangements could be made with the more eager members. Where the United States was not eager and determined, other members' suggestions did not get very far, as in some of the more ambitious proposals to flesh out Article 2 by developing non-military tasks for NATO. For some purposes the other allies have been able to exert counterpressure, however; and the United States has found them more and more recalcitrant as

[11] Cf. Alastair Buchan, *NATO in the 1960's* (New York: Frederick A. Praeger, 1960), p. 17.

[12] Cf. Raymond Aron, *Paix et Guerre* (Paris: Calmann-Lévy, 1962), pp. 438–41, who contrasts the British methods with the French tendency to demonstrate France's power by opposition.

On the admission of Germany see Sir Anthony Eden, *Full Circle* (Boston: Houghton-Mifflin, 1960), esp. pp. 182–83; Laurence W. Martin, "The American Decision to Rearm Germany," in Harold Stein (ed.), *American Civil-Military Decisions* (Birmingham: University of Alabama Press, 1963), pp. 643–65; Truman, *op. cit.*, pp. 253–55; Dean Acheson, *Sketches from Life* (New York: Harper and Brothers, 1959), pp. 25–27; Secretary Dulles' testimony before Senate Committee on Foreign Relations, *Hearings, Mutual Security Act of 1954*, 83rd Cong., 2nd sess. (1954), pp. 3–4; Robert E. Osgood, *NATO: The Entangling Alliance* (Chicago: University of Chicago Press, 1962), pp. 84–87 and 91–98. Recognizing implacable opposition among some allies towards admitting Spain, the United States indirectly coordinated American defense forces in Spain with NATO activities, and American officials regularly visited Spain to brief General Franco after ministerial meetings of the North Atlantic Council.

they have regained confidence in their ability to evaluate American initiatives or withstand the consequences of American displeasure. Seldom, however, have all fourteen joined in active and decisive opposition; many of the smaller members at least have found good reasons for siding with the United States against more powerful states in their immediate vicinity. Highly attractive inducements continue to make American guidance palatable, particularly to the poorer countries of the Mediterranean. In recent years United States officials have talked a great deal about listening to their allies' views, but when they fail to hear a united voice from the other side of the Atlantic, they do not wait long before filling the aching void with their own proposals—to the satisfaction of most of the allies, it should be added.[13] When Americans have suggested that NATO extend the scope of foreign policy coordination to areas outside Europe, however, their guidance has not been accepted.

4. Many important decisions, even within the NATO area, are not for the United States to make; a fourth role for the United States in NATO has been *to induce, energize, and stimulate actions which its allies can only undertake by themselves.* What kinds of actions? First, and foremost, and always, measures to increase the number and improve the quality of the forces the allies devote to collective defense. Quality, because it can be raised by American contributions, has been easier to improve than quantity, which is closely related to the ticklish question of length of military service, a domestic matter in which the Americans can hardly interfere. (Most of the allies have reduced their period of training far below what Americans believe to be the minimum necessary to produce a qualified soldier.) Through NATO the United States has induced research, development, and production programs for military purposes —first in individual countries and later across national boundaries in cooperative undertakings—and has promoted other kinds of cooperative programs, including certain service functions for NATO forces.

Occasionally the United States has sought diplomatic support from its NATO allies for a stand which it was going to take anyway, such as nonrecognition of Red China and the barring of its entrance into the United Nations. Sometimes the United States, instead of trying to stimulate action by its allies, has tried to discourage it, as when Secretary Dulles damped down some of the allies' pressure on the United States to agree to an East-West summit meeting in 1958. Or the government has chosen not to incite action because it wished to avoid similar action itself, as when the architects of the New Look refrained from pressing for increases in either allied or United States conventional forces. On the other hand, the Americans displayed fresh energy in the post-Sputnik era

[13] See, for example, McGeorge Bundy's speech in Copenhagen before the Atlantic Treaty Association, September 27, 1962, quoted in Senate Committee on Foreign Relations, *Problems and Trends in Atlantic Partnership I,* Senate Doc. No. 132, 87th Cong., 2nd sess. (1962), p. 40. Also see Mulley, *op. cit.,* p. 235.

in stimulating cooperative NATO programs, if only to invigorate the lagging European confidence in American technological leadership. Political conditions within NATO countries as well as changes in technology have altered the pressure Americans have exerted for particular programs. Thus they offered strong inducements to gain permission to implant IRBM's on European soil in 1958 but withdrew these same missiles rather quietly in 1963.

What are the means by which the United States has sought to stimulate actions which it wishes its allies to take? For many years the United States could rely on manipulating the military aid program, called by General Norstad the "catalyst." However, the only publicly declared threat to reduce military aid in order to get desired action was the one made when the ratification of the EDC hung in the balance in 1954.

Offers to facilitate the acquisition of desired military equipment, to contribute capital for joint enterprises in military items, and to provide training in the use of "modern" equipment have proved effective incentives to action. Putting up a large share of the necessary funds made possible the installation of the NATO Air Defense Ground Environment System, which helped to unify several national air defense systems under allied command.[14] Training and exchange programs have the special advantage that by reaching key people or individuals who will become leaders, they spread the American viewpoint like ripples on a pond. The heavily subsidized Mutual Weapons Development Program, while useful in other respects did not insure that the end product would be purchased by the member countries, even though a weapon had been designed to meet NATO requirements.

In the American (and also British and Canadian) experience, cost-sharing in the form of a conditional grant-in-aid from a wealthier to a needy government is a familiar voluntary device for getting others to participate. The United States used this method for certain NATO allies in the early 1960's. To achieve the American desire for improved logistics in NATO and at the same time diminish the balance of payments deficit, the United States ceased to subsidize the NATO Maintenance and Supply Organization and persuaded the other members to accept a pro-rata cost-sharing of future programs as well as a greater responsibility for management. It also extended credits for increased purchases of American-made military equipment.[15]

Such methods appear to be more effective than the pep talks by

[14] House of Representatives Committee on Appropriations, *Hearings, Mutual Security Act of 1961*, 86th Cong., 2nd sess. (1961), p. 2564; Vandevanter, *op. cit.*, p. 71; and C. L. Sulzberger in *New York Times*, April 10, 1963. The SHAPE Air Technical Center at first was completely financed by the United States, but after some years was transferred to NATO funding [H. George Franks, "International Team Solving Many Defence Problems," *NATO's Fifteen Nations*, August–September, 1964, p. 84].

[15] House of Representatives Committee on Foreign Affairs, *Hearings, Foreign Assistance Act of 1964*, 88th Cong., 2nd sess. (1964), pp. 93, 508, 510, 638.

leading American officials, which have become almost a ritual since the appointment of General Eisenhower as SACEUR. One limitation to the effectiveness of these lectures in recent years is the loss by most of the European allies of that general sense of urgency in preparing for Soviet aggression which is chronic (or chronically stimulated) in Washington.[16] Warnings have often fallen on deaf ears, especially when the listener targets were France and Portugal, which had other concerns. Since outright criticism would be counterproductive, quiet appeals to reason made by American officials to their opposite numbers either in NATO bodies or their national capitals had to be utilized; such appeals could hope to be only moderately successful. More effective were promises such as that given by President Eisenhower in 1954 during negotiations for Germany's admission into NATO. He assured the allies that the United States would continue to maintain appropriate units of American military forces on the Continent and, in addition, would share information authorized by Congress regarding the military use of the new tactical nuclear weapons.[17]

5. A fifth role for the United States has been *to fill the principal military commands in the alliance.* This does not mean that the NATO commanders who are American take orders from the United States government in their NATO capacity, although several, including SACEUR, also hold American commands. All but the first SACEUR, General Eisenhower, have also been Commander-in-Chief of the United States Forces in Europe. (Their deputies in this latter command seem to have borne the main burdens of it.)

The North Atlantic Council appoints the Supreme Commanders and has always appointed Americans to the SHAPE and Atlantic commands. In anticipation of a vacancy the United States informally sounds out its allies as to a particular officer's acceptability. With foreknowledge of the President's intended nominee, the Council then formally asks him to make a nomination, which it accepts. In addition to SACEUR and SACLANT, the Commander-in-Chief Mediterranean (who is, however, subordinate to SACEUR) has always been an American. In most of the NATO military command structure a commander and his deputy are of different nationalities. Americans have held high positions even where there are no American forces, as in the case of the air commander for Allied Forces Northern Europe, an American serving under a British commander.[18]

[16] For one among many commentaries on such differences in the evaluation of the Soviet danger, see Louis Halle "The Cracked Alliance," *New Republic*, February 23, 1963, pp. 17–20.

[17] "Agreement on Restoration of German Sovereignty and German Association with Western Defense," *Department of State Bulletin*, October 11, 1954, pp. 519–20; "United States Policy Declaration on Western European Union," *ibid.*, March 21, 1955, pp. 464–65.

[18] Testimony of General Norstad, House of Representatives Committee on Foreign Affairs, *Hearings, Mutual Security Act of 1957*, 85th Cong., 1st sess. (1957), p. 540.

Subordinate commands occasionally change as to nationality of the occupant and jurisdiction of the command; but the pattern of nationalities participating in the main commands was set rather early, although not without struggle among the Americans, British, and French and not without considerable scaling down by the Americans of their original demands.[19] American officials were, nevertheless, able to put an enduring print on the military organization, having already begun developing an international staff before SHAPE was established and having then had the dominant voice because there were so few others to oppose them. (Part of the command structure did, however, stem from the work of the Western European Union prior to the organization of NATO.) [20] Successive SHAPE commanders have publicly expressed their sense of double responsibility, to NATO and to the United States government for carrying out their NATO duties. By 1960 some Europeans had become unhappy about the dominating position of SACEUR. On the other hand, Senator Taft's prediction that making an American SACEUR would greatly increase the United States' responsibility toward NATO has been borne out.[21] Since NATO is above all a military alliance, the fact that few Americans are in the civilian secretariat of NATO and that the Secretary General has always been a European does not detract from the importance of Americans in the military command posts.[22]

6. A sixth role assumed by the United States on NATO's behalf has been *to manage the nuclear deterrent for the alliance.* This role, like that of making good NATO's military deficiencies according to the American image of what is essential, is the product less of agreement among the members than of American capabilities and wishes. In the first year this role was natural and one in which the other members concurred; it emerged from the United States' having sole possession of atomic bombs. Even after the Soviet Union had broken the American monopoly, the other members continued to accept American dominance, until the development of missiles. Nor was the United States in the mid-fifties adamant about its monopoly in the alliance. The British having demonstrated their ability to develop and produce nuclear weapons, the Americans were at that time quite ready to acquiesce in their having a minor role in providing NATO's strategic nuclear deterrent.

So long as the European allies did not have to acknowledge how slight was their role in the management of the nuclear deterrent,

[19] Matthew B. Ridgway, *Soldier* (New York: Harper and Brothers, 1956), p. 239; J. D. Warne, *NATO and Its Prospects* (New York: Frederick A. Praeger, 1954), pp. 13–16; Osgood, *op. cit.,* p. 168; William A. Knowlton, "Early Stages in the Organization of SHAPE," *International Organization,* Winter, 1959, pp. 1–18.
[20] Lord Ismay, *NATO: The First Five Years, 1949–1954* (Paris: NATO, n.d.), p. 38.
[21] Senate Committee on Foreign Relations and Committee on Armed Services, *Hearings, Assignment of Ground Forces to Europe,* 82nd Cong., 1st sess. (1951), pp. 623–34.
[22] There are also few Americans in the OAS and SEATO secretariats.

they could accept the fact and feel safe in leaving control with the President of the United States, especially since SACEUR's plans already were very closely coordinated with those of SAC.[23] Yet they could not avoid the fact that an indispensable part of NATO strategy lay outside NATO control, in the hands of American officials. In 1957–1958 discontent grew rapidly; it reached major proportions by the 1960's. In the late 1950's the fear that the Americans might be trigger-happy—demonstrated in mutterings about "no annihilation without representation"—began to be replaced (in part) by the opposite fear. With a growing Soviet missile force capable of delivering thermonuclear bombs to the United States, would the Americans fail to live up to their pledge to use strategic weapons if an attack came in Europe? The Americans, on the other hand, were worrying increasingly about proliferation. An arms control agreement with the Soviet Union, for example, appeared less and less possible the more widespread the proliferation. For this and other reasons the United States did not welcome any further expansion of "the nuclear club" even among their NATO allies.

The United States had already made a solution to the problem of nuclear weapons management more difficult by a course of action, from 1954 to 1958, which had promised short-range benefits to its allies; it succeeded in getting NATO approval for strategy based on the deployment in Europe of tactical nuclear weapons and IRBM's. By such actions and by bilateral agreements for "sharing" technical information on the use of certain nuclear weapons, the Americans had temporarily evaded the critical question of who could "press the button." But the "genie" about which President Kennedy warned in 1963 had already come part of the way out of the bottle some years earlier. Rather suddenly in December, 1960, a lame-duck United States delegation to the NATO ministerial conference responded to European dissatisfactions by offering to earmark Polaris-armed submarines for NATO. The Kennedy administration went further, proposing in 1963 a "mixed-manned" multilateral nuclear force. Since the missiles of the proposed force could not be fired without United States consent, this device did not significantly allay European "credibility anxieties." By 1963 the American government was ready to accept the *principle* that allies should participate in the nuclear strategic planning of NATO. Also, in the same year American officials had begun to provide more technical information to aid allied military strategists in understanding the strategic situation. These moves did not radically change national positions. If others did not wish to be involved in a nuclear war without their consent, neither did the Americans. The Kennedy administration, in fact, tightened up control over some nuclear weapons.[24]

[23] Gardner Patterson and Edgar S. Furniss, Jr., *NATO: A Critical Appraisal* (Princeton: Princeton University Press, 1957), p. 38.
[24] President Kennedy said to the NATO Military Committee, April 11, 1961, that "we propose to see . . . that our military forces operate at all times under con-

7. With respect to "conventional" defense, the United States has assumed a seventh role: *to demonstrate by example what other allies might also profitably do*. Its most important demonstration has been the deployment of approximately six divisions on the central front in Europe, including the best-trained and best-equipped American forces anywhere in the world. From the very beginning of NATO these divisions have had a great psychological impact; they have shown the Europeans that the Americans were with them physically as well as in spirit. Early suggestions from some Congressmen that American numbers should be based on the numbers contributed by the other allies have at no time been accepted by the executive branch. Later temptations to reduce significantly the United States forces in Europe were put aside because American officials feared that this step, instead of inducing the allies to fill the gap, would cause them to lessen their own efforts and have other bad political effects. During and after the Berlin crisis of 1961, the United States expanded its own forces in Germany, partly in the hope of stirring the European allies to follow the American lead. (The allies did expand their forces, but to far less striking a degree.)

The United States has set an example for others to follow in certain aspects of the Mutual Weapons Development Program, in pilot projects such as the NATO Science Program, and in additions to the infrastructure, in this case by financing a new communications system for an early-warning radar network. It has led in expanding the frequency and scope of political consultation in the North Atlantic Council.[25] The greater size of the United States has made the material contribution of all the others in NATO look small, even when all mitigating circum-

tinuous, responsible command and control from the highest authorities all the way downward—and we mean to see that this control is exercised before, during, and after an initiation of hostilities against our forces, and at any level of escalation." In the 1964 presidential campaign a minority view, favoring loosening of American control, was occasionally expressed. Its appearance suggested a difficulty for the United States in managing some of its security problems through NATO.

[25] For example, see General Robert J. Wood's explanation to Representative Morgan that "we have to set the example in saying that we definitely will underwrite our percentage of the cost [of a proposal]" [House of Representatives Committee on Foreign Affairs, *Hearings, Foreign Assistance Act of 1964*, 88th Cong., 2nd sess. (1964), pp. 631–32]. The retiring Deputy Secretary General of NATO said in 1964, ". . . the United States had given in NATO a good example of behavior in arguing their case with their allies, listening to the counter-arguments, coming back with more evidence, their obvious purpose being to be able to persuade or to be persuaded, without ever allowing the discussions to become a dispute" [Guido Colonna di Paliano, "The State of the Alliance," *Atlantic Community Quarterly*, Fall, 1964, p. 405]. See also Secretary General Spaak's speech to the Atlantic Treaty Association September 27, 1958, quoted in Carol E. Baumann, *Political Co-operation in NATO* (Madison: University of Wisconsin, 1960), p. 14. Secretary Rusk stated in April, 1964 that in the previous year the United States "initiated consultation or exchange of information in NATO on approximately thirty issues of importance" ["Mr. Dean Rusk and the Atlantic Alliance," *NATO Letter*, June, 1964, p. 20].

stances are weighed in. (Of course, the United States defense budget, except as a percentage of the American gross national product, could hardly be cited as a model; its level has not been set in order to influence European allies.) The allies were not disposed to follow the American example in embargoing the sale of particular products to various Communist countries. Too frequent exercises in preceding may sometimes be self-defeating because they can stifle important initiatives from the potential emulators.

Problems of Gradually the Americans have been learning
Leadership new attitudes regarding the need for reciprocity and compromise; but the pace is slow because the United States is so powerful a member of the alliance and so energetic a leader. Yet, as Geoffrey Crowther pointed out some years ago, even the leader cannot simply give a lead whenever he feels like it.[26] The United States has been even less willing than other countries to agree to specialize in certain kinds of defense force and to depend more heavily on its allies for certain other kinds; probably this is impossible. As a world leader it cannot leave itself disarmed in any essential component, which rules out some kinds of force specialization which may rationally be expected of other allies. Matériel specialization is another matter; strong economic interests in the United States prevent a more rational distribution of the work load throughout the alliance.[27] We would have a better test of the willingness of the Americans to cooperate if there were more initiatives from the other allies for collective enterprises which include the United States; such initiatives are not often revealed, if they exist. Observers and participants acknowledge that seldom are even a few of the allied governments united in favoring a policy not desired by the Americans.[28] Multilateral undertakings are especially hard to promote where allies prefer their own special arrangements with the leader. It is in the nature of the superpower that is has more to offer each of the others than they have to offer to each other.[29]

Two or three patterns in the United States treatment of its NATO

---

[26] "Reconstruction of an Alliance," *Foreign Affairs*, January, 1957, p. 181. Note relief of allied governments when the new President devoted important speeches to NATO early in February, 1961, after having failed to refer to it specifically in his Inaugural Address [Hanson Baldwin in the *New York Times*, February 5, 1961, and C. L. Sulzberger, *ibid.*, April 17, 1961].

[27] Hoag, *op. cit.*, p. 289.

[28] See C. M. Woodhouse, "Attitudes of NATO Countries Toward the United States," *World Politics*, January, 1958, p. 212. Although this article was written when NATO was less than ten years old, the situation has not since changed so far as unity of European members versus the United States is concerned.

[29] If the other allies were united, their bargaining position vis-à-vis the United States would be much stronger.

allies recur whoever the responsible American officials and whichever the party in power. There are many splendid sermons on how the United States should behave as a genuine partner.[30] Sometimes in the same speech, but more often when caught off guard, the same or officials of equivalent standing reveal an attitude which appears to equate "NATO" alternately with "they" or "American," depending upon the context.

John Foster Dulles, prior to becoming Secretary of State, wrote in January, 1952, that "treaties of alliance and of mutual aid mean little except as they spell out what the people concerned would do anyway."[31] Later he learned to spell out more completely the treaties already in force and the new ones negotiated. On a television program with President Eisenhower in May, 1955, in which the two officials discussed his recent appearance at the North Atlantic Council, Secretary Dulles related how he had explained to the NATO allies that the United States' Asian policy was the same as its policy in Europe and that "the reason we are acting this way in Europe is because we really believe in these things and if we believe in them we are going to act the same way in Asia." "That is a wonderful way to tell them," responded the President.[32]

[30] For example, on retiring from his post as Secretary of State, Dean Acheson said, "We are aware in this country that our European allies are in a true sense of the word partners and that we must work with them and treat them as partners. . . . [O]n their side they see the nature of the effort which they must make to maintain their part of the partnership" [*Department of State Bulletin*, January 26, 1953, p. 130]. Later that year General Gruenther, as SACEUR, had this to say: "Our problem is essentially a task of being the strongest element in the North Atlantic community and still being sufficiently modest and understanding to work well within it. We must be able to work effectively on a partnership basis with a profound respect for views and interests other than our own. The one thing that the European resents —and naturally so—is dictation" ["The Defense of Europe," *ibid.*, November 9, 1953, p. 636]. In presenting the "military posture" of the United States to the House of Representatives Committee on Armed Services in early 1962, Secretary McNamara stated that "if for no other reason than our own self-interest, we must maintain within the NATO alliance the closest kind of cooperation at all levels and in all spheres; we must concert our efforts no matter how great the difficulties. And, indeed, the difficulties or existence of difficulties should not dismay us. After all, we are dealing with sovereign nations whose history extends back far beyond our own, nations with their own particular devotion to . . . freedom. They clearly are entitled to their own views and their views are entitled to the most careful consideration by us [*Hearings, Military Posture*, 87th Cong., 2nd sess. (1962), p. 3166]. Senator Fulbright wrote in 1963: "We must find a way to bring our allies into meaningful participation in the vital decisions relating to war and peace. The crux of the problem is the development of a solid strategic consensus among NATO allies. The development of such a consensus can be approached through a system of allied participation in the planning and shaping of strategic policy, in determining the *conditions* under which the American deterrent will be brought to bear" ["A Community of Free Nations," *Atlantic Community Quarterly*, Summer, 1963, p. 118].

[31] Quoted by Coral Bell, *Negotiation From Strength* (New York: Alfred A. Knopf, 1963), p. 91.

[32] *Department of State Bulletin*, May 30, 1955, p. 872. American perspectives on the role of the United States in SEATO (or in the OAS and the international economic

As the United States became deeply involved in Vietnam, President Johnson and Secretary Rusk began to talk in similar vein.

Some oscillations in American style have come with changing events or complications in the general environment. Thus President Kennedy stated in May, 1962, that "we cannot and do not take any European ally for granted and I hope no one in Europe would take us for granted, either." When such hints failed of their purpose, he was reported on December 31 of that year to have instructed his subordinates that the United States should proceed with what it regarded as the correct course and pay less attention to whether or not that course of action displeased allies.[33] Utterances of national leaders gain widespread public attention; but there can also be pervading, often unconscious, attitudes among lesser officials which do not improve the community spirit within the alliance.[34]

Depending upon one's point of view, one can classify American official manners as "confusing, dictatorial, ruthless, insensitive" or "courteous, tactful, diplomatic." Whichever appellation is given to them, the manners do reveal some special problems of leadership. First, they may spring from the need to appeal to many different groups, both inside and outside the United States, in order to gain consensus for particular policies. Second, they sometimes arise from the mixture of functions of NATO, the symbolic representation of close association and the attention to the hard military realities. Third, and politically most important, they are instances of the dual vocabularies of law and politics, of the difference between the "sovereign equality" of each member of the alliance and the very unequal distribution of power among them. "Partnership," "sharing," "consultation," "balanced," "mutual," and "cooperation" help to make endurable those relationships which are not wholly symmetrical or reciprocal and which are better not publicly described by American officials in the harsher language of power differentials if the alliance is to hold together. The important questions are: do such statements mislead the leaders as to their political functions? At what point do they lead the other allies to brand the Americans as insincere or unworthy of trust?

Lest we assume that the inconsistencies in utterance have been blown up by overzealous journalists, let us note that there have been numerous instances where it was not statements but deeds which revealed heedlessness of the alliance association.

---

organizations) do not, however, seem to us at all comparable with American perspectives on the American role in NATO. This chapter, unlike earlier ones, does not, therefore, have a concluding section comparing NATO and other organizations.

[33] James Reston, *New York Times*, February 7, 1963.

[34] Laurence I. Radway, "Military Behavior in International Organization: NATO's Defense College," in Samuel P. Huntington (ed.), *Changing Patterns of Military Politics* (New York: The Free Press of Glencoe, 1962), p. 106, an essay which examines an early stage in that joint undertaking.

The Warsaw Treaty Organization

RICHARD F. STAAR

The establishment by the Soviet Union of a multilateral military alliance system in Eastern Europe was announced by Moscow as a response to West German membership in NATO. The true reason for the Warsaw Pact which brought this system into being more probably was the desire of the U.S.S.R. to obtain legal justification for stationing its troops in East-Central Europe. The pact was signed in the capital of Poland on May 14, 1955. One day later the Austrian state treaty was signed in Vienna, restoring sovereignty to Austria and obligating Moscow to evacuate its forces from Hungary and Romania within forty days after the latter agreement had gone into effect.[1] The Warsaw Treaty Organization (WTO) also provided an additional legal basis for the continued presence of Soviet troops in Poland and in the so-called German Democratic Republic, although in the latter case such provision was not at all necessary, owing to the absence of a peace treaty.

A U.S.S.R. government declaration at the height of the Hungarian

[1] Boris Meissner (ed.), *Der Warschauer Pakt: Dokumentensammlung* (Cologne, 1962), p. 12. A translation of the Warsaw treaty into English appears in Ruth C. Lawson (ed.), *International Regional Organizations* (New York, 1962), pp. 206–210, reprinted from *United Nations Treaty Series,* CCXIX, Part I, p. 24. The stationing of U.S.S.R. troops in Hungary, Poland, and Romania was based until 1955 on the need to secure lines of communication to Germany.

revolt reaffirmed the right of this presence and added that Soviet forces in Poland had the additional justification of the Potsdam Agreement. This statement claimed that no U.S.S.R. military units existed in any other East European people's democracy—the German Democratic Republic, proclaimed "sovereign" in October 1949, apparently was not considered in this category—and that the Soviet government was ready to discuss the question of its troops abroad with other signatories to the Warsaw Pact.[2]

The subsequently negotiated status-of-forces treaties with Poland (December 1956), East Germany (March 1957), Romania (April 1957), and Hungary (May 1957) all remain in effect today except for the third, which lapsed upon the withdrawal of Soviet troops from Romania in June 1958.[3] These agreements were the first such arrangements to be made known publicly, although secret accords may already have existed. The agreement with East Germany is unique in that it includes a safety clause allowing the U.S.S.R. to interfere if it finds its own security to be endangered. Article 18 of this treaty states:

> In case of a threat to the security of the Soviet forces which are stationed on the territory of the German Democratic Republic [GDR], the High Command of the Soviet forces in the GDR, in appropriate consultation with the GDR Government, and taking into account the actual situation and the measures adopted by GDR state organs, may apply measures for the elimination of such a threat.[4]

This situation has not changed as a result of the bilateral Friendship, Collaboration, and Mutual Assistance Pact signed in 1964 between the two countries.[5]

Apart from the above exception, all the status-of-forces treaties follow a uniform pattern. They deal with the following: [6]

(1) The strength and movement of Soviet forces in the host country.
(2) The jurisdiction over Soviet forces, individual soldiers, members of Soviet military families, and civilian employees while on the territory of the host country.
(3) Soviet control and use of military installations on the territory of the host country.

---

[2] Tass communiqué in *Pravda*, October 31, 1956.
[3] On the withdrawal of Soviet troops from Romania see Günther Wagenlehner, "Die politische Bedeutung des Warschauer Paktes," *Soldat und Technik*, VIII, No. 3 (March 1965), 115.
[4] Meissner, *op. cit.*, p. 128. All status-of-forces treaties are given in German by this source on pp. 117–143.
[5] Text in *Krasnaya zvezda*, June 13, 1964.
[6] Cited by Kazimierz Grzybowski, *The Socialist Commonwealth of Nations* (New Haven, 1964), p. 205.

(4) Jurisdiction of local authorities in civil and criminal matters arising out of, or in conjunction with, the presence of Soviet troops.

(5) Matters subject to the exclusive jurisdiction of Soviet authorities.

(6) Settlement of mutual claims.

The inferior status of the German Democratic Republic can be seen also in certain differences regarding details. For example, the treaties with Poland and Hungary omit the article on the basis of which the GDR guarantees the U.S.S.R. the use of military and nonmilitary facilities, including transport and communications, that were in use on the date the agreement was signed. Further divergencies exist regarding movement of Soviet troops.[7] This can occur in Hungary and Poland only with the consent of the government and by plans made in advance. The GDR agreement provides a general understanding on maneuver areas, but says nothing about troop movements. Again, the treaties with Poland and Hungary require the consent of the governments to changes in the strength of Soviet troops and for the relocation of garrisons, whereas in the GDR only consultation is needed.

The treaty with Hungary is essentially the same as that with Poland, except that the latter is much more elaborate. For example, its Article 5 reads:

> The regulations on entry and exit of Soviet troop units and members of the Soviet armed forces and their families into Poland or from Poland as well as questions concerning types of required documents in connection with their stay on the territory of the People's Republic of Poland will be governed by a special agreement between the contracting parties.[8]

In contrast the Hungarian treaty refers simply to agreement as to the strength of Soviet troops and the places where they will be stationed.

Finally, the treaty with Poland differs from the other two by introducing a statement (Article 15) about a special agreement defining "lines of communication, dates, orders, and compensation conditions for transit of Soviet troops and war material across the territory of the People's Republic of Poland."[9]

A different problem is posed by tiny Albania, which has been outside the bloc since Khrushchev attacked its leadership in October 1961 at the 22d Congress of the CPSU. Although not expelled from the Warsaw Pact, Albania has refused to attend any sessions of its Political Consultative Committee. Since the ouster of Khrushchev, two attempts have been made to bring Albania back into active participation, without success. The Albanian communists in January 1965 rejected an invitation, ex-

---

[7] *Ibid.*
[8] Meissner, *op. cit.*, p. 118.
[9] *Ibid.*, p. 121.

tended by the Polish regime, to attend the seventh meeting of the committee, held in Warsaw later that same month. In January 1966 an invitation from the same source proposed that Tirana send a delegation to a meeting of communist parties from Warsaw Pact and "socialist" countries in Asia to discuss coordination of aid for North Vietnam. The following month the official Albanian news agency published the texts of the short invitation and an extensive refusal.[10]

In September 1965 the CPSU first secretary (since April 1966, secretary general), Leonid I. Brezhnev, informed the party's Central Committee that changes in the military alliance of the pact countries were under consideration:

> With a view to improving the activity of the Warsaw Treaty Organization, it is necessary to establish within the framework of this pact a permanent and operational mechanism for the evaluation of current problems.
>
> The complex international situation forces us to pay special attention to problems of military collaboration with the [other] countries of socialism. A great effort is taking place according to the following plan: standardization of equipment is being implemented, exchange of combat training experience [has been developed] and joint maneuvers are being conducted.[11]

No further information has been forthcoming on this most intriguing subject of a "permanent and operational mechanism." Indeed, the Political Consultative Committee met at Bucharest in July 1966 without mentioning it in any communiqué.

Changes Within the WTO   Initially established as a highly centralized system, the Warsaw Pact has had only three commanding officers to date. The first, Marshal of the Soviet Union Ivan S. Konev, was succeeded in July 1960 by Andrei A. Grechko, who also holds that highest military rank in the Soviet armed forces and is currently minister of Defense. The present WTO commander is Marshal of the Soviet Union Ivan I. Yakubovskii. There have been three chiefs of staff for the WTO Unified Armed Forces Command, all career Soviet officers: Generals of the Army Aleksei I. Antonov, who died in office; Pavel I. Batov, who succeeded Antonov in October 1962; and, since late 1965, Mikhail I. Kazakov.[12] Batov was a

10 Released by the Albanian Telegraphic Agency in Tirana, February 12, 1966.

11 *Krasnaya zvezda*, September 30, 1965. See also Jens Hacker and Alexander Uschakow, *Die Integration Osteuropas 1961 bis 1965* (Cologne, 1966), pp. 67–94, for documents in German on the Warsaw Treaty Organization.

12 Kazakov's appointment was announced by Tass communiqué, November 23, 1965; reported in *Wehrkunde*, XV, No. 1 (January 1966), 51–52.

Khrushchev man who reportedly strove toward a rapid integration of the armed forces of the pact countries along supra-national lines. Kazakov commanded Soviet troops in Hungary for four years after the 1956 rebellion. He has been commanding officer of several U.S.S.R. military districts, most recently at Leningrad. His task may include bringing Eastern Europe into line with the recent Soviet military reorganization.

The Defense ministers of the East European countries are *ex officio* deputy commanding officers of the WTO. (See Table 1.) As can be noted from their appointment dates, relatively little change has occurred in top echelon East European military personnel over the past six to ten years. One reason may be that all of these Defense ministers—with the exception of Lomský, who served as an air force pilot before the Second World War, and possibly Ionita—have had careers as political commissars and not as professional military officers. This probably makes them more reliable in the eyes of the Soviet leadership and, indeed, more dependent upon their Soviet advisers.

TABLE 1

Warsaw Pact, Deputy Commanding Officers, 1967

Name	Rank	Country	Appointed Defense Minister
Spychalski, Marian	Marshal	Poland	November 1956
Lomský, Bohumír	General of the Army	Czechoslovakia	April 1956
Hoffman, Karl Heinz	General of the Army	East Germany	July 1960
Ionita, Ion	Colonel General	Romania	August 1966
Dzhurov, Dobri Marinov	General of the Army	Bulgaria	March 1962
Czinege, Lajos	Colonel General	Hungary	May 1960
Balluku, Beqir	Lieutenant General	Albania	July 1953

SOURCES: Stavro Skendi (ed.), *Albania* (New York, 1956), p. 324. *Krasnaya zvezda,* October 24, 1965. Jens Hacker, "Der Warschauer Pakt," *Das Parlament,* January 13, 1966, p. 23 of Supplement (for names only). *Neue Zürcher Zeitung,* August 31, 1966. *Krasnaya zvezda,* March 1, March 15, April 6, April 30, June 3, and June 24, 1967.

On the other hand, a definite rotation system can be seen in the U.S.S.R. military commands in pact countries where Soviet forces are stationed. The commanders in East Germany, General of the Army P. K. Koshevoi, and Poland, Colonel General G. V. Baklanov, received their appointments in February and September 1965, respectively; in Hungary, Colonel General K. I. Provalov was appointed in October 1962 and is due for a transfer. These men are not permitted to stay abroad for extended tours of duty, perhaps lest they develop an attachment to the local milieu. The fact that there are no Soviet troops on its territory may have allowed Romania in October 1964 unilaterally and "probably against the wishes of the Warsaw Pact command" [13] to reduce basic military service from twenty-four to sixteen months. To some extent, it would seem to follow, centralized control has decreased.

The true functions of the three U.S.S.R. military commanders, unfortunately, are not known. They do represent a symbol of Soviet power in the three countries involved and no longer seem averse to publicity. Their photographs appear from time to time in Soviet military newspapers, as do also articles by them, and their positions are not concealed. The main contact between the Soviet commanding officer and the regime in Poland, Hungary, and East Germany probably would be the Defense minister. Another channel for control purposes almost certainly is provided by the many high-ranking U.S.S.R. military officers who have adopted the citizenship of these countries and still occupy key positions in the several Defense establishments.

STRATEGIC PLANNING

The WTO was at first devised and regarded by the U.S.S.R. as a defensive alliance, the forward area of which would provide a buffer and absorb the anticipated NATO attack. This attitude, however, has undergone a drastic transformation in the course of the qualitative build-up of the East European armed forces. The change can be seen from the scenario implemented during the most recent quadripartite maneuvers in the German Democratic Republic. Pact Commander Marshal Grechko in an interview granted to Tass stated:

> . . . One must above all note the uniform military doctrine of the socialist countries united in the Warsaw Pact. . . . In case of aggression, our armies are ready not to conduct a passive defense but to engage in active military operations, which would be immediately transferred to the territory of the enemy.
> The armies of the Warsaw Pact countries also adhere to a uniform tactic of battleground action. As to armament, it has been standardized to a considerable degree. . . . Consistently, the methods of army training have been almost identical.[14]

The 1965 maneuvers under the code name "October Storm" (during October 16–22) included Soviet, East German, Czechoslovak, and Polish military units among the 10,000 troops involved and allegedly provided substance for the commander's remarks. "Blue" aggressors crossed the GDR border in the southwest and attacked "Red" defending forces.

---

[13] Raymond L. Garthoff, "Die Armeen der Ostblockstaaten," *Osteuropäische Rundschau*, XI, No. 10 (October 1965), 6.
[14] Radio Moscow, February 21, 1966.

Concrete plans for such a NATO blitzkrieg, according to Walter Ulbricht, envisaged a general direction of attack toward

> Eisenach–Erfurt–Karl Marx Stadt [Chemnitz], as far as the upper reaches of the Neisse [River], then swinging north, in order to wrench the GDR out of the socialist camp within 36 to 48 hours. It was argued [by NATO] that if accomplished facts were created so quickly, a world war could be avoided by, as it were, a police action.[15]

During "October Storm," however, the Blue offensive was stopped, and the aggressor "like a cornered beast" decided to risk all and use atomic warheads. Responding "in greater numbers and with more powerful calibers of nuclear weapons," the Red side struck at the firing potential and troops of the aggressor.[16] Nearly 1,000 Polish paratroopers were transported by Antonov-22's (air buses) to the drop zone. Their mission was to capture an airfield near Erfurt and subsequently attack the rear of the enemy force.

Red "defenders" advanced on a strategically important bridge, which had been established by reconnaissance as being intact. "In the very last moment, when Blue forces were retreating already, West German workers disarmed a demolition crew and saved the bridge." [17] These war games took place under General of the Army Koshevoi, commanding the Soviet troops in East Germany. Marshal Grechko and all pact Defense ministers were observers. The same high-ranking officers witnessed Operation "Vltava," held in Czechoslovakia during the latter part of September 1966 with Soviet, East German, Hungarian, and Czechoslovak troops.

Although few details have been released on WTO maneuvers up to 1963, there appears to have occurred then a radical change in conduct of these field exercises to reflect the new Soviet military doctrine which, according to an authoritative spokesman, considers that "in a world war, the possibility of a non-nuclear conflict has become an abstraction." [18]

Following this doctrine, the "Quartet" operation of October 1963 in East Germany, the maneuvers of August 1964 in Bulgaria, "October Storm" of 1965 in East Germany, and the exercises of September 1966 in Czechoslovakia all employed large-scale landings from the air which ei-

[15] Cited over Deutschlandsender (East Berlin), October 31, 1965.

[16] *Neues Deutschland,* October 23, 1965.

[17] Radio Warsaw, October 21, 1965; also reported over Deutschlandsender, October 22, 1965; and in *Neues Deutschland,* October 23, 1965.

    For an analysis of the maneuvers in September 1966 see "Pr." (Colonel Erich Pruck), "Erkenntnisse aus dem Manöver Moldau," *Wehrkunde,* XV, No. 12 (December 1966), 662.

[18] Colonel General Professor N. Lomov (director of instruction, Lenin Academy, Moscow), article on "Influence of Soviet Military Doctrine upon the Development of Military Art," *Kommunist vooruzhënnykh sil,* XLVI, No. 21 (November 1965), 18.

ther introduced or took place simultaneously with attacks by armored and motorized rifle units in division strength.[19] These massed forces, moving at a speed of about a hundred kilometers per day, exploit the element of surprise in order to put out of action NATO troops that have survived the initial nuclear strikes.

That this doctrine is of an offensive nature can be seen clearly in a statement by the GDR first deputy minister of Defense which, in essence, repeats the remarks of Marshal Grechko quoted earlier. Writing in Russian for Soviet military readers, the East German said:

> The national mission of the NVA [GDR National People's Army] is to be prepared and able to . . . destroy the aggressor on his own territory by decisive, offensive action together with [other] brotherly socialist armies and to assist progressive forces in West Germany to liquidate the imperialist system [in that country].[20]

The implementation of the U.S.S.R.'s military doctrine and the role of its East European "allies" in its strategy can be seen in the surface-to-surface missiles now standard equipment for all WTO armies and in the fact that the missiles, capable of carrying nuclear warheads, remain under Soviet control. Missiles and rockets are replacing traditional artillery pieces, of which not a single new model has been produced over the past decade. It would seem likely that heavy mortars and recoilless rifles will also be superseded by tactical nuclear-tipped guided missiles.

DECISION-MAKING

Only eight meetings of the WTO Political Consultative Committee took place between 1956 and 1966, although twenty-two should have been convened during this period on the basis of two per year set forth in the pact statute. Table 2 gives published data on the topics considered in these sessions.[21] The communiqués issued suggest that the committee meetings serve merely as vehicles for bloc propaganda.

Less is known concerning the sessions attended by the first secretaries of the communist parties of Warsaw Pact countries. Only the one held at Moscow during August 3–5, 1961, has been reported publicly. It apparently approved construction of the Berlin Wall by the East German

[19] "L'Adaptation des Forces Terrestres Soviétiques à une Guerre Nucléaire," *Revue de Défense Nationale,* XXI, No. 7 (February 1966), 214–215; "Warschaupakt Manöver Moldau," *Soldat und Technik,* IX, No. 12 (December 1966), 632–633.
[20] Admiral W.[aldemar] Verner, article on "Ten Years of the GDR National People's Army," *Kommunist vooruzhënnykh sil,* XLVII, No. 4 (February 1966), 78.
[21] The eighth session was at Bucharest in July 1966. A communiqué and two declarations appeared in *Krasnaya zvezda,* July 8 and 9, 1966. See also Fritz Ermarth, "Warschauer Pakt vor der Bukarester Konferenz," *Wehrkunde,* XV, No. 7 (July 1966), 336–340.

TABLE 2
Warsaw Pact, Political Consultative Committee Meetings, 1956–1966

Place	Date(s)	Proposals and decisions
Prague	January 27–28, 1956	*Approved:* Statute for Unified Military Command; admission of GDR armed forces; establishment of Standing Commission and Secretariat.
Moscow	May 24, 1958	*Proposed:* Nonaggression pact with NATO; summit meeting. *Approved:* Withdrawal of U.S.S.R. troops from Romania.
Moscow	February 4, 1960	*Proposed:* Atom-free zone and cessation of nuclear tests.
Moscow	March 28–29, 1961	*Proposed:* Universal disarmament.
Moscow	June 7, 1962	*Discussed:* Albanian refusal to cooperate with WTO.
Moscow	July 26, 1963	*Discussed:* Status of pact armed forces and coordination of training.
Warsaw	January 19–20, 1965	*Discussed:* Proposed multilateral nuclear force within NATO and "appropriate countermeasures."
Bucharest	July 4–6, 1966	*Proposed:* Reduction of tensions through military *détente* and a general conference on security in Europe.

SOURCES: U.S. Senate, Committee on Government Operations (89th Cong., 2d sess.), *The Warsaw Pact: Its Role in Soviet Bloc Affairs* (Washington, D.C., 1966), p. 32, for the first seven meetings. *Krasnaya zvezda*, July 8 and 9, 1966, for the eighth meeting.

regime. More important perhaps have been the consultations among Defense ministers of the pact countries at Warsaw in September 1961, at Prague in late January and early February 1962, at Warsaw in February 1963, and at Moscow in May 1966. A special conference of senior commanding personnel including Defense ministers, chiefs of staff, and political indoctrination chiefs met in 1965 for nine days "within the confines of the U.S.S.R. Sub-Carpathian military district," where tactical exercises were held, new types of arms and material demonstrated, and views on different questions of military development exchanged.[22] From time to time, conferences of the deputy ministers of Defense take place, as in a 1965 two-day session in Warsaw which heard Marshal Grechko discuss combat training, military preparedness, and other measures.[23] Unfortunately, no record of debates or decisions is available.

[22] A TASS communiqué, *Krasnaya zvezda*, May 18, 1965, carried the quotation about this conference.

[23] Radio Warsaw, November 23, 1965.

Apart from positions within their own armed forces, no East European military officer heads any top-level WTO organ or command. Of possible subgroupings within the WTO only one, encompassing the Danubian area, has been reported. All troops in this region allegedly are subordinated to a single high command, the *Oberkommando Donau*.[24] Air defense for all of Eastern Europe has been integrated, but here again under a Soviet commander, in 1964 the U.S.S.R. Chief Marshal of Aviation, Vladimir A. Sudets, who directed the equivalent Soviet armed forces branch, the *Voiska PVO Strany*.[25] Although previously a candidate member of the CPSU's Central Committee, he was not reelected to that body by the Twenty-third Congress, in April 1966, and this was followed by his replacement.

Despite the fact that no high position in the WTO is held by any East European, it is probable that at least the Defense ministers (the great majority of whom are Soviet trained) are given the feeling of participation in decision-making. Actually, in certain cases the very opposite is true, where Soviet officers who transferred to satellite armies during and immediately after the war still remain camouflaged in high positions.[26] Some thirty-two former Soviet officers of the rank of general in the Polish army, together with Poland's Defense minister, the former Soviet Marshal Konstantin. K. Rokossovsky, returned to Moscow toward the end of 1956 "with the gratitude of the Polish nation." At least three, however, remain in high positions in Poland. They are Lieutenant General Jerzy Bordziłowski, first deputy minister of Defense and chief inspector of training; Major General Józef Urbanowicz, third deputy minister of Defense and chief of political indoctrination for the armed forces; and Vice Admiral Zdisław Studziński, the navy commander.[27] These three positions are among the more sensitive within the military hierarchy of Poland.

Many of the native-born East European officers have attended military schools in the U.S.S.R., and this may provide them with a common experience if nothing else. Integration of commands obviously requires a single language, and here the chosen language is Russian, knowledge of which is a prerequisite for training in the Soviet Union. Bulgarians,

---

[24] Friedrich Wiener, *Die Armeen der Warschauer-Pakt-Staaten* (Vienna, 1965), p. 11.

[25] Garthoff, *op. cit.*, p. 13. Joint maneuvers with the participation of GDR, Czechoslovak, and Soviet air forces took place over East Germany, possibly to test defenses. *New York Times*, June 14, 1966.

Sudets was replaced by General of the Army P. F. Batitsky. *Krasnaya zvezda*, October 29, 1966.

[26] In Poland, for example, some 17,000 Soviet officers were assigned to that country's armed forces. *Życie i myśl*, No. 10 (October 1964).

[27] Joachim Georg Görlich, "Polens Volksarmee," *Wehrkunde*, XV, No. 5 (May 1966), 256. Bordziłowski is the highest ranking officer below the Defense minister, Marshal Marian Spychalski, who holds four-star rank.

Czechoslovaks, and Poles have found Russian easy to learn because of its similarity to their native tongues. It has proved more difficult for East Germans, Hungarians, and Romanians, whose language groups are not related to the Slavic family. Learning has proceeded rapidly, however, since ignorance of Russian presents an obstacle to obtaining higher command positions within the armed forces of the individual satellite military establishments.[28] Russian expressions have penetrated the military vocabularies of most East European countries.

EXECUTION OF DECISIONS

The WTO Unified Command, which has its headquarters in Moscow, theoretically correlates and orders the execution of decisions reached by the representatives of the deputy commanders (that is, of the bloc countries' Defense ministers) who make up the staff of this command.

Under the unification program, certain national contingents have been earmarked for WTO service. Although these have never been openly specified, it is probable that only elite units are assigned, such as the regiment from the 6th Pomeranian Parachute-Assault Division, stationed near Kraków in Poland, which participated in the operation "October Storm." Its commanding officer, at that time thirty-nine-year-old Colonel Edwin Rozłubirski, was the subject of a biographic sketch which appeared, along with his photograph, in the daily newspaper of the Soviet Defense ministry.[29] The Polish 12th Mechanized Division and a brigade of frontier troops reportedly have been assigned specifically to the WTO. On the other hand, all East German troops are at the disposal of the WTO High Command. This situation has not been changed by the June 1964 Soviet-GDR treaty.

Transfer of Soviet troops from the western parts of the U.S.S.R. to any place in Eastern Europe, other than by air, would be difficult owing to the limited number of interchange points for broad-gauge railroad traffic. These reportedly existed in 1960 at Gerdauen, Brest-Terespol, Przemyśl-Medika, Cop-Zahony, Jassy, and Galati only.[30] In the meanwhile the number of such points must have been increased, with a corresponding expansion in machinery for loading and unloading. Construction of secondary railroad links and transmountain lines has been noted. Traffic management has been centralized through the Council for Mutual Economic Assistance (CMEA).

[28] Hanns von Krannhals, "Leadership Integration in the Warsaw Pact Area," *Military Review*, XLI, No. 5 (May 1961), 47, translated from *Wehrwissenschaftliche Rundschau*, XI, No. 1 (January 1961), 13.
[29] Yezhi Lentsut [Jerzy Lencut], article on "The Commander of Airborne Infantry," *Krasnaya zvezda*, August 21, 1965.
[30] Von Krannhals, *op. cit.*, pp. 50–51.

The CMEA is planning a network of automobile expressways which will link the major cities in Eastern Europe with Moscow and Kiev.[31] The CMEA's Permanent Commission for Transportation has the task of coordinating this ambitious scheme. Another project, just completed, involves the 1,900-mile petroleum pipeline which links the Volga-Ural oil fields with Poland, East Germany, Czechoslovakia, and Hungary. During 1963 and 1964 some 13 million tons of oil went to Eastern Europe through this "Friendship Pipeline," [32] indicating a considerable dependence on the U.S.S.R. in this respect by all WTO members except Romania.

Oil, of course, remains indispensable for moving modern armies, and oil deliveries have facilitated the organization of joint maneuvers, which did not begin until 1961. Credit for this idea has been claimed by the Polish communists:

> Initiated by our side, joint field exercises by the armies of Warsaw Pact countries have become permanent. Our troops, staffs, and commands annually train on land, on sea, and in the air with troops, staffs, and commands from brotherly armies: the Soviet Army, the Czechoslovak People's Army, and the GDR National People's Army. . . .[33]

Actually, these first maneuvers involved only Soviet and East German units. The following spring, the U.S.S.R., Romania, and Hungary conducted joint field exercises.

During the fall of 1963, the code name "Quartet" was assigned to the first set of maneuvers to involve four countries. Tass reported from East Berlin that some 40,000 troops took part, supported by 760 tanks and 350 aircraft, and comprised units from the Soviet Union, Czechoslovakia, the GDR, and Poland.[34] Subsequently it was intimated by the Polish Defense minister that integration and joint command procedures had been improved to the extent that larger formations and more than four countries might participate.

Instead of such a development, however, two separate sets of exercises took place during the following year. One of these included only Soviet and Czechoslovak units. The other brought together Soviet, Romanian, and Bulgarian troops and included the use of paratroopers and the execution of amphibious landings from the Black Sea. Observers representing the other WTO countries could be identified in newspaper pho-

[31] Stefan C. Stolte, "Comecon's Nineteenth Conference," *Bulletin of the Institute for Study of the USSR*, XII, No. 5 (May 1965), p. 21.

[32] *Krasnaya zvezda*, August 11, 1965.

[33] Marshal Marian Spychalski, speech at the Fourth Congress of the Polish communist party, *Trybuna ludu*, June 18, 1964.

[34] *Krasnaya zvezda*, September 15, 1963.

tographs. Soviet marines (*morskaya pekhota*) made a landing on the Bulgarian coast.[35] Unfortunately, few details were released.

It is noteworthy that until the September 1966 operation "Vltava" the Hungarians had never trained with the Czechoslovaks. This may be ascribed not only to the events of 1956, but also to the fact that about a million ethnic Hungarians lived in Czechoslovakia between the wars and many still reside there. Nationality differences make for frictions that could lead to outbreaks during joint field exercises. Except for those in Czechoslovakia and Bulgaria, traditionally the East European populations have always been hostile to the Russians, for good historical reasons. Even so, none of the communist sources mention any Soviet dissatisfaction with the performance of troops of the bloc countries in the course of maneuvers.

Ships of East European countries have been utilized for delivery of military equipment to overseas underdeveloped areas. An instance came to light when the captain of the Bulgarian vessel *Veliko Tirnovo* was fined 5.4 million Lebanese pounds (about 1.75 million United States dollars) in Beirut for smuggling arms. He and six other persons were detained in connection with the discovery of 1,500 automatic rifles in the ship's cargo, concealed in 75 crates. The official Bulgarian news agency argued that: "It is a well-known fact that the carrier is not held responsible for the content of the commodities shipped and declared in the bill of lading," as if the Navibulgare, owning the ship, were not a state-controlled enterprise.[36]

Although the destination of these rifles (possibly intended for the Kurds) was not revealed, it is known that the Bulgarians have been selling weapons to the royalist forces in Yemen since about 1964. Some 25 million dollars in Saudi-Arabian gold reportedly has been paid for these purchases, many of which were channeled through the Bulgarian military attaché in Paris. One such shipment was seized by the French when a chartered transport airplane carrying rifles from Belgium landed at Djibouti in Somaliland.[37] Little information can be found on similar arms shipments during the past decade, although the first known transaction, involving the sale of Czechoslovak weapons to Egypt, occurred as early as 1955. Apart from creating future dependence for spare parts and bringing in foreign exchange, the supplying of arms to insurgents con-

---

[35] Radio Sofia, September 20, 1964. More recently naval and air units of the U.S.S.R., Poland, and East Germany held joint maneuvers for eight days on and over the Baltic Sea. *Krasnaya zvezda,* July 30, 1966.

[36] Radio Sofia, February 2, 1966.

[37] *New York Times,* April 10, 1966; source is Bushrod Howard, registered agent in the United States for the royalists.

Note also the clandestine shipment of Czechoslovak weapons to Cyprus. *Ibid.,* December 16, 1966.

tributes to instability which in turn makes for new communist opportunities to advance the objective of U.S.S.R. control over the underdeveloped countries.

In addition to facilitating the sale of arms clandestinely, military attachés from East European countries also engage in espionage on behalf of the U.S.S.R. Two of these men, Paweł Monat and Władysław Tykociński, defected to the West and have testified about their experiences.[38] After reassignment to Warsaw from abroad, Monat handled reports from all Polish military attachés and forwarded them to Moscow via his office. Tykociński more recently corroborated this fact and disclosed that for a period of time the chief of Polish military intelligence was a Soviet officer.

Another example of espionage is provided by the extensive operations of East European agents in the Federal Republic of Germany. Only the Yugoslav agents no longer may send reports directly to the U.S.S.R., as was their practice until July 1966. During one year more than 1,000 efforts at recruitment of informants was ascertained in West Germany. In

TABLE 3

Espionage in West Germany, 1964

Recruitment efforts		Information targets	
Country of agent	Number	Category	Number
East Germany	860	Military	1,772
U.S.S.R.	39	Political	408
Czechoslovakia	44	Economic	169
Poland	32	Preparatory and support [a]	1,217
Yugoslavia	12	Total	3,566
Hungary	7		
Romania	4		
Unknown	16		
Total	1,014		

SOURCE: Official figures from [West Germany], Bundesamt für Verfassungsschutz, Bundesinnenministerium (Bonn), as cited in *Soldat und Technik*, IX, No. 2 (February 1966), 99.

[a] Activities involving the acquisition of biographic data on possible contacts and other ancillary activities.

consequence, 195 persons were convicted of high treason or treasonable relations by the federal court at Karlsruhe and the appellate tribunals in that country. (See Table 3.)

[38] Paweł Monat, with John Dille, *Spy in the U.S.* (New York, 1962), especially pp. 104–112; U.S. House of Representatives, Committee on Un-American Activities (89th Cong., 2d sess.), *Testimony of Wladyslaw Tykocinski* (Washington, D.C., 1966).

SOVIET FORCES IN EASTERN EUROPE

With the exception of Poland and Czechoslovakia, all the bloc countries have had a so-called Soviet Consultative Group as an element of WTO activity. In 1962 such a Soviet group reportedly operated from the U.S.S.R. embassy in Budapest and thus claimed diplomatic immunity.[39] The rights and privileges of the groups allegedly are concealed in various secret agreements. The effectiveness of the group in Hungary obviously is guaranteed by the presence of U.S.S.R. troops.

The Soviet Consultative Groups function as military advisers. The group in Hungary reportedly controls that country's rear services and armaments industry planning, each headed by a deputy minister of Defense who has as an adviser a Soviet officer with the rank of full colonel. The Defense minister, the deputy ministers, and these highest ranking U.S.S.R. advisers reportedly comprise the "military collegium" in the ministry. The same is said to be true for the general staff. Each section of the latter (operations, intelligence, organization and mobilization, military installations, service regulations, military geography, communications, technology and transportation, air force, anti-air defense, civil defense, training, and logistics) allegedly includes a Soviet staff officer as adviser.[40] To each Weapons Inspectorate—armored and motorized troops, air force, communications troops, artillery, engineers, ABC weapons—there is attached a Soviet colonel or general and two to four other officers as assistants. Similar arrangements allegedly prevail in the military districts and on down into the regimental level. At corps level, one senior Soviet officer is said to control operations and another logistics. It is reported, further, that each of the eleven frontier-guard district commands has a Soviet officer and several aides assigned to it, and that the entire political indoctrination system within the Hungarian armed forces is directed by a high-ranking Soviet officer and six other "advisers." [41]

In Bulgaria, on the other hand, Soviet advisory activities are conducted with considerable restraint. Both the main political administration of the armed forces and the military intelligence section have Soviet "observers." Soviet officers also serve as unit advisers, but mostly at division level, although their network previously extended down into the regiments. Each motorized rifle and armored division allegedly has on its staff a Soviet officer of the rank of lieutenant colonel or major, under whom four or five others function as "instructors." Certain armored regiments and operational squadrons of the Bulgarian air force (possibly

---

[39] Thadaeus Paschta, "Das System der Sowjetischen Militärberater in den Satellitenstaaten," *Wehrkunde*, XI, No. 9 (September 1962), 496, is the source for much of the following information.
[40] *Ibid.*, p. 497.
[41] *Ibid.*, p. 498.

those assigned to the WTO) still have Soviet advisers attached to them.

Among the reasons for these differences between Hungary and Bulgaria would be the 1956 rebellion in Budapest, of which there has been nothing comparable in Sofia. Another probably is Bulgarian national pride. Known as the "Prussians of the Balkans," the people would resent any foreign command exercised openly. A third reason amounts to a corollary of the others. Key positions in the military hierarchy are staffed by natives of Bulgaria who were trained as officers in the U.S.S.R. and resumed their original citizenship upon returning home after the war. These officers have included:

> The former Bulgarian Defense minister, Army General Ivan Mikhailov.
>
> The former chief of the general staff (about 1950–1959), first deputy Defense minister (1959–1962), and head of the Administrative Organs Department (the cover designation for the Military Department) in the communist party's Central Committee (1962–1965), recently ambassador to East Germany, Colonel General Ivan Bachvarov (killed in an airplane crash at Bratislava in 1966).
>
> The former commander of the navy and former Soviet naval officer, now deputy chief of the general staff, Vice Admiral Branimir Ormanov.
>
> The former commandant of the general staff academy, guerrilla fighter subsequently trained as an officer in the U.S.S.R., and now a deputy Defense minister and air force commander, Colonel General Slavcho Trunski.
>
> The current head of the General Political Department (main political administration) in the armed forces, graduate of both the "Frunze" and the general staff academy in the U.S.S.R., and former commander of the Sofia garrison, Lieutenant General Velko Palin.[42]

In Czechoslovakia the Soviet advisers for the most part control industries which produce weapons and war matériel used by the armed forces of the bloc countries. Use of Soviet personnel in training Czechoslovak forces produced an extensive organization called the "Soviet Satellite Coordination Command," which preceded the 1955 military alliance.[43] This organ may still be operative. References have appeared recently to a Soviet colonel general, Aleksandr M. Kushchev, as representing the Joint Military Command of the Warsaw Pact armies at a two-day conference of communist party members within the Defense ministry of Czechoslovakia and at a Liberation Day reception in Prague.[44]

In Poland it was not necessary to establish a Soviet military mission

---

[42] *Ibid.*, p. 499; Radio Sofia, February 15, 1966; U.S. Department of State, Bureau of Intelligence and Research, *Directory of Bulgarian Officials* (Washington, D.C., August 1965), p. 13.

[43] Von Krannhals, *op. cit.*, p. 44.

[44] *Pravda* (Bratislava), May 10, 1966. See also U.S. Department of State, Bureau of Intelligence and Research, *Directory of Soviet Officials* (Washington, D.C., 1966), I, p. B-11, for names of the other WTO representatives in the different East European capitals.

at all. Some 17,000 Soviet officers directed the Polish armed forces after transferring from the Red Army and accepting citizenship in the country to which they had been detailed. Following the change in communist party leadership at Warsaw in October 1956, many of these men returned to the Soviet Union. The function of those who remain consists of observation, giving advice, and serving as liaison officers as well as securing communications with U.S.S.R. troops in Upper Silesia (Poland) and East Germany.[45]

The situation in East Germany need not be discussed, because this area truly reflects the name used for it by the West Germans: the Soviet Occupation Zone. With approximately twenty U.S.S.R. divisions stationed in the GDR, there is no doubt as to who is in control.

In contrast, Romania probably presents a picture of greater independence of the U.S.S.R. than any other bloc country. In October 1964 military service was reduced to sixteen months, and during the summer of 1965 Bucharest reportedly "balked at sending troops out of the country for additional joint activities." [46] The Soviet military mission is said to number only two or three men today [1967], as against fifteen or sixteen as recently as 1964.[47]

Soviet troops are garrisoned in three Warsaw Pact countries. In Poland, there is the Northern Group of Forces, with headquarters at Legnica in Upper Silesia; in Hungary, the Southern Group of Forces, at Tököl near Budapest; and in the GDR, the Group of Soviet Forces in [East] Germany, with headquarters at Wünsdorf near East Berlin. The generally accepted figures for these forces outside the borders of the Soviet Union are respectively two, four, and twenty divisions.[48] The one-to-one ratio of armored to motorized rifle divisions in these Soviet units shows a considerably heavier concentration on the more powerful type than prevails in the indigenous East European forces. (See Table 4.)

In East Germany, the U.S.S.R. troops outnumber those permitted the GDR regime by a ratio of three to one, and in tanks and aircraft the preponderance is even greater. Since 1964, however, the GDR armed forces have been equipped with Frog-4 and Scud-A type ground-to-ground rockets, the latter employing a guided missile. These are being supplied by the U.S.S.R. to East German forces at division levels and are allocated to artillery.[49] These weapons are capable of delivering nuclear

---

[45] I. I. Barits, *Voennaya kharakteristika sovetskikh satellitov* (New York, 1966), chap. vii, no pagination.

[46] Thomas W. Wolfe, *The Evolving Nature of the Warsaw Pact* (Santa Monica, Calif., 1965), p. 20.

[47] The new WTO representative at Bucharest, U.S.S.R. Colonel General G. P. Romanov, is one rank higher than his predecessor. Reuters dispatch, May 18, 1966, cited in RFE report, "Grechko's Man in Bucharest," May 20, 1966.

[48] Institute for Strategic Studies, *The Military Balance 1966–1967* (London, September 1966), p. 2.

[49] *Wehrkunde*, XIV, No. 12 (December 1965), 657. See also Jens Hacker, "Die DDR im Warschauer Pakt," *SBZ Archiv*, XVII, No. 12 (June 1966), 179–182.

TABLE 4
Warsaw Pact, Armed Forces, 1966–1967

Country	Army personnel	Divisions [a]	Tanks	Security Forces personnel	Navy personnel	Naval craft C [b]	D [c]	S [d]	Air Force personnel	Aircraft
Albania	30,000	2	—	12,500	3,000	—	—	4	6,000	100
Bulgaria	125,000	11(3)	2,500	15,000	7,000	—	2	3	24,000	400
Czechoslovakia	175,000	14(4)	3,200	35,000 [e]	—	—	—	—	45,000	750
East Germany	85,000	6(2)	1,800	70,000	17,000	—	4	—	20,000	400
U.S.S.R.	254,900 [f]	20(10)	7,500	—	(80,000) [g]	(4)	(25)	(75)	—	1,100
Hungary	100,000	6(1)	1,000	35,000	—	—	—	—	9,000	150
U.S.S.R.	55,000	4(4)	1,400	—	—	—	—	—	—	350
Poland	185,000	15(5)	3,000	45,000 [e]	15,000	—	3	8	60,000	950
U.S.S.R.	25,000	2(2)	700	—	—	—	—	—	—	350
Romania	175,000	11(1)	1,500	50,000	8,000 (50,000) [h]	(3)	2 (20)	1 (45)	18,000	300
Total	1,209,900	91(32)	21,600	262,500	180,000	7	56	146	182,000	4,850

SOURCE: Institute for Strategic Studies, *The Military Balance 1966–1967* (London, September 1966), pp. 2, 5, 6–8.

[a] Armored divisions, included in total, are indicated in parentheses.

[b] Cruisers.

[c] Destroyers.

[d] Submarines.

[e] Polish security troops were integrated with the regular armed forces and placed under the Defense ministry in July 1965, according to Radio Warsaw, June 30, 1965. The same move took place in Czechoslovakia, effective January 1966, as reported in *Allgemeine Schweizerische Militärzeitschrift*, CXXXII, No. 2 (February 1966), 93.

[f] Includes 4,900 in Berlin.

[g] Figures in parentheses refer to the Soviet Baltic Sea Fleet, estimated allocation.

[h] Soviet Black Sea Fleet, estimated allocation.

warheads over distances up to a hundred miles. It is doubtful that the Soviets would allow the GDR to assume control over such atomic weapons.

According to General Koshevoi, commander of the Soviet forces in East Germany, his troops are in the process of regrouping. Missile and armored units may be increased as other types are reduced. U.S.S.R. antiaircraft defense may be withdrawn completely in the course of gradually transferring this responsibility to the GDR. The main centers of concentration for Soviet troops after reorganization would be the area around Suhl in Thüringen, the province of Brandenburg, and the border territories of the GDR along Czechoslovakia and Poland. Finally, Soviet "instructors" are to be withdrawn from the East German army.[50]

Such regrouping would bring Soviet troops in proximity to Czechoslovakia, where the U.S.S.R. maintains no forces officially and where it is important that the uranium mines at Jachymov, Tepler Hochland, and Przibram be protected, as well as those in adjacent East Germany south of Aue.[51] The output of this strategic raw material goes to the U.S.S.R., in amounts that remain secret. The closer disposition of Soviet troops to Poland would provide for better contact with the two Soviet divisions in Upper Silesia. This would allow for a rapid link-up between forces in the event of another crisis, such as the one in 1956 when Polish troops proved unreliable.

The redeployment of Soviet forces in East Germany may be the result of plans for more flexibility in countering operations, should hostilities break out in Central Europe. The troops formerly were concentrated along the frontier between East and West Germany in several parallel lines from Lübeck in the north to the border with Czechoslovakia at Hof in the south.[52] The new scheme presumably would permit deploying troops in echelons, following an east-west direction, with most of them concentrated along the Oder and Western Neisse rivers.

In Hungary, although indigenous forces number nearly twice those of the U.S.S.R., the latter maintains a preponderance of four to one in armored divisions and more than two to one in aircraft. Besides serving to prevent a repetition of the 1956 rebellion, the Soviet troops ensure delivery of uranium from the Hungarian mines at Fünfkirchen. It should be noted, however, that ground-to-ground missiles were displayed at the April 1965 military parade in Budapest. (The Czechoslovak army's

[50] *Soldat und Technik*, VIII, No. 12 (December 1965), 673. This West German periodical paraphrases Koshevoi's statement but does not provide the original source.
[51] *Československi voenski atlas* (Prague, 1965), as cited in *Wehrkunde*, XIV, No. 11 (November 1965), 599.
[52] Military attachés from the U.S.S.R., Poland, and East Germany heard the Czechoslovak Defense minister, Bohumír Lomský, address a Warsaw Pact anniversary friendship rally and state: "For the first time we have a neighbor to the northwest of us [the GDR] on whom we can look with full confidence." *Rudé právo*, May 14, 1966.

weekly newspaper reported subsequently that all other East European countries except Albania and Yugoslavia have been equipped with these.) [53] In addition, Soviet-built MIG-21 delta-wing fighter intercepters and Ilyushin medium-range bombers flew overhead.

According to the first secretary of the Hungarian communist party, János Kádár, the presence of Soviet troops is in conformity with domestic as well as international law. Early in 1965, speaking to his pseudo-parliament, he declared:

> [The U.S.S.R. armed forces are] an immense help for our people, because if these troops were not here, we would be forced to keep more soldiers under arms at the expense of the living standard, because the fatherland is more important and stronger than the living standard! [Further,] the presence of Soviet troops in Hungary has no internal reason. It depends on the international situation alone. . . . We are not afraid of the withdrawal of Soviet troops, but we do not support any unilateral withdrawal, and this is in the interest of the international political situation. [54]

Kádár suggested "serious talks which do not mean for any side an important shift in the balance of power geographically." No statement has been made since that time which would indicate any change in the above attitude.

Changes in Soviet Control   Penetration by Soviet nationals into the East European military establishments definitely has decreased over the past decade. Whereas, for instance, at one time virtually all high positions in the Polish armed forces were held by former Russian officers newly turned Polish citizens and "fulfilling the duties of Poles," only a few of these can be discerned today.

Although it would be difficult to show where their loyalty lies, the case of Konstantin K. Rokossovsky may be illuminating. He came to Poland in November 1949 as Defense minister and remained exactly seven years. After that, he returned to the U.S.S.R. and resumed his rank as Marshal of the Soviet Union. Apparently not losing any seniority, he was made a deputy Defense minister in Moscow, perhaps in reward for services rendered while on detached duty in Warsaw.

SECRET POLICE IN EASTERN EUROPE

Very little information is available on the secret police of the WTO countries. Close cooperation and perhaps even a superior-subordinate re-

53 *Obrana lidu,* May 7, 1965.
54 Radio Kossuth, February 11, 1965. See also his interview with UPI in *Népszabadság,* August 2, 1966, as translated in *Hungarian Press Survey,* August 18, 1966.

lationship between the secret police establishments of the Soviet Union and a satellite was evident in the arrest of British citizen Greville Wynne by the Soviet and Hungarian security services in Budapest and his subsequent trial with U.S.S.R. Colonel Oleg V. Penkovskiy in Moscow in 1963.[55]

An even more significant and an openly admitted role was played by Soviet secret police during the arrests in April 1965 of plotters against the Bulgarian regime. Communist journalists in Sofia were briefed on the conspiracy, which was "uncovered by Soviet intelligence agents in March."[56] One of the ten men involved, Ivan Todorov-Gorunya, had been a member of the Bulgarian party's Central Committee and chairman of the government's directorate for water economy. He committed suicide. In June the others, five army officers and four civilians, were sentenced to prison terms for high treason by the military tribunal of the Bulgarian Supreme Court.

The first announcement of the plot came on April 22 and only three names were mentioned, those of Todorov-Gorunya, Krastev, and Anev. Had Todorov-Gorunya lived, he would have stood trial as the main defendant, since he was a member of the Central Committee. It is probably more than coincidental that all three belonged to the "Gavril Genov" partisan detachment during the Second World War. At least one more of the plotters, Temkov, also fought in a guerrilla unit. The fact that the majority of those tried were high-ranking military officers on active duty indicated strong army involvement in the conspiracy.

A further case of collaboration between Soviet and East European secret police was divulged in connection with the purge in Yugoslavia of Aleksandar Ranković. His subordinates in the security apparatus, which he had controlled on behalf of the Yugoslav communist party, were accused of having "too close links" with the Soviet secret police.[57] Nothing regarding these charges at the July 1966 plenum of the Yugoslav communist party's Central Committee was made public. It should be recalled, however, that Greville Wynne lost in a Belgrade hotel a notebook which later turned up in Moscow during the 1963 trial of Colonel Penkovskiy.

MILITARY PRODUCTION

As a source of war matériel, the most important geographic area in Eastern Europe is the Czechoslovakia-GDR-Poland industrial triangle. The first two countries encompass a human pool of skilled technicians and are provided with precision equipment and modern scientific research facilities, especially in nuclear physics. That the U.S.S.R. does not permit sophisticated military production can be seen from the decision

[55] Oleg Penkovskiy, *The Penkovskiy Papers* (New York, 1965), pp. 373–375.
[56] *New York Times*, April 21, 1965.
[57] *Ibid.*, July 22, 1966.

taken at the fourteenth CMEA session, in March 1961, which discontinued East German manufacture of four-engine turbo-jet aircraft already in the testing stage.[58]

On the other hand, Eastern Europe is of great value to the U.S.S.R. as a source of uranium in several countries; bauxite for the production of processed aluminium in Czechoslovakia; basic chemicals, rare metals of particular importance for atomic energy programs, and bismuth mined in association with uranium in East Germany; metallic sodium from a Polish Silesian plant for construction of nuclear-powered reactors; cadmium, used in regulating the speed of nuclear reactions, in both Poland and the GDR; molybdenum for the production of crucially important matériel in Bulgaria and Poland; and titanium used in nuclear technology and graphite required for nuclear reactions in Poland.

Party Control Over the Military   Political controls by the local communist parties do not appear to have been altered significantly.

The primary party organizations, however, do comprise a separate hierarchy, with delegates representing the individual military districts at national party congresses. Criteria for admission to the party are the same for officers and enlisted men of the armed forces as for civilians. The trend seems to be toward absorption of the security forces by the regular military establishment, as took place in Poland in 1965 and Czechoslovakia in 1966. This suggests that the ruling communist parties have more confidence in the regular armies.

Apparently, it remains a prerequisite for attainment of the rank of full colonel that an officer be a party member. In the five countries on which data is available, an average of 82.6 percent of regular officers are party members. (See Table 5.) This percentage should not be equated with reliability, which is always difficult to measure.

The only hard figures on defections come from West Germany, and these involve GDR military personnel fleeing west. For example, there are East German battalions of border troops which during 1965 had as many as fifteen successful escape attempts and twenty failures. A total of 1,850 GDR soldiers, including 466 border guards, defected in five years following the building of the Berlin Wall in 1961.[59] The recent Bulgarian military conspiracy, mentioned earlier, would perhaps indicate dissatisfaction with subordination to the U.S.S.R. in that country. Soviet decision-makers probably would not plan to employ jointly Polish and East German, Czechoslovak and Hungarian, or Romanian and Hungarian troops in actual combat, even though combined maneuvers have taken place.

58 *Pravda* (Moscow), March 5, 1961.
59 *Soldat und Technik*, IX, No. 4 (April 1966), 202; *New York Times*, August 3, 1966.

TABLE 5

Membership of Army Officers in Communist Parties, 1963–1966

Country	Percent of total officer personnel	Source
Bulgaria	82	*Krasnaya zvezda,* September 23, 1965.
Czechoslovakia	75	*Krasnaya zvezda,* October 6, 1965.
East Germany	96	[East Germany]. Deutsches Institut für Zeitgeschichte. *Handbuch der Deutschen Demokratischen Republik* (East Berlin, 1964), p. 289.
Hungary	78	*Krasnaya zvezda,* December 3, 1966.
Poland	70	E. Międzyrzecka and J. Klimek (eds.), *Kalendarz robotniczy 1964* (Warsaw, 1963), p. 136.
Romania	90	*Scînteia,* July 24, 1965.
Average	82	

NOTE: Information not available for army officers of Albania.

Changes in Popular Support
In 1959, researchers at the University of Warsaw polled a representative sample of Warsaw inhabitants on their opinion of the profession of the military officer as a career. The standing of the military probably has risen somewhat since then. Compared with the pre-1939 period, however, when officers in the Polish armed forces stood at or near the top of the career scale, at the time of this poll they ranked fourteenth financially, below lathe operators; sixteenth in job security, below accountants; and twenty-first in social prestige, below office supervisors.[60]

No similar investigation is known from the other East European countries, but apart from this limited indication of changed attitudes it seems likely that generally in the bloc countries the lack of any tradition has reduced the attractiveness of a military career among officers and enlisted men alike and has had a deadening effect. Communist propaganda classifies the pre-1939 armies in Eastern Europe as having been either feudal or fascist. The riots in East Germany during June 1953, the Hungarian rebellion in October–November 1956, and the events in Poland at the time of the Hungarian episode, when local forces in each country took up defensive positions against the threat of Soviet troop in-

[60] Adam Sarapata and Włodzimierz Wesołowski, "Evaluation of Occupation by Warsaw Inhabitants," *American Journal of Sociology,* LXVI, No. 6 (May 1961), 583–585.

See also the more recent article by Adam Sarapata, "Social Mobility," *Polish Perspectives,* IX, No. 1 (January 1966), especially table 1, p. 20, regarding prestige of occupations, which also ranks army officers.

tervention, all showed that morale was not high from the communist point of view. It must be remembered, however, that these events took place a decade or more ago.

Future Trends and goals remain difficult to project,
Developments but it is quite clear that the Warsaw Treaty Organization has changed its emphasis radically from defense to offense. This trend most probably will continue, unless Soviet military doctrine itself undergoes a fundamental transformation.

Over the twelve years from 1955 to 1967 the military equipment and the training of WTO forces have developed consistently in one direction: preparation for war in which it is unthinkable to the Soviet High Command that nuclear weapons will not be used. Even the previously avowed intention not to be the first to introduce such arms in a conflict is no longer being repeated. The U.S.S.R. military hierarchy would not knowingly allow an opponent endowed with atomic and hydrogen warheads to apply the element of surprise and to initiate hostilities.

Soviet military doctrine probably anticipates a conflict in Central Europe within the next decade involving a confrontation between the main forces of NATO and the Warsaw Treaty Organization. Beginning with U.S.S.R. strategic nuclear strikes, ground operations would be launched simultaneously by massive armored and motorized rifle divisions in conjunction with airborne units employed on a large scale. These movements at speeds of up to 100 kilometers per day would be supported by tactical nuclear weapons.

The role of WTO members in such a war can be seen in broad outline even today. For example, Soviet conflict managers are making a concentrated effort to woo Turkey away from the Western alliance. In mid-August of 1965 the U.S.S.R. extended the equivalent of 150 million United States dollars in credits for the construction of dams, cement plants, and factories to that country, the first NATO member to accept Soviet economic aid. In February 1966 the Turks announced that they would revise their bilateral agreements, including the status-of-forces treaty, with the United States.

If Turkey and Greece, where a parallel diplomatic offensive is being carried on by Bulgaria, can be neutralized so as to make ineffective their membership in NATO, the Warsaw Treaty Organization could then concentrate on the main enemy: West Germany. Such WTO members as Romania, Bulgaria, and Hungary (not very powerful and not particularly reliable, except for Bulgaria) could be eliminated from Kremlin calculations.

The Warsaw Pact would then base its military plans on East Germany, Poland, and Czechoslovakia as the main allies of the U.S.S.R. The continuous barrage of anti-West German propaganda, especially in Poland and Czechoslovakia, has the obvious purpose of maintaining a war psychosis fed by the fear of a Nazi resurgence and a new *Drang nach Osten.*

Even so, it is doubtful that Polish or Czechoslovak troops would be allowed to operate independently in any conflict. As part of Soviet fronts (groups of armies), they would fight with units on both flanks and in the rear. The performance of the Warsaw Treaty Organization will depend ultimately on the specific military situation. If NATO should be dissolved, WTO forces would march to the Atlantic with little if any opposition.

SEATO

GEORGE MODELSKI

On September 8, 1954, representatives of Australia, France, New Zealand, Pakistan, the Philippines, Thailand, the United Kingdom, and the United States signed the South-East Asia Collective Defense Treaty in Manila. The eight countries thus became members of what was soon described as SEATO. On the same day, and by means of a special protocol, the signatories extended the benefits of the Manila Treaty to three other countries; henceforth, Cambodia, Laos, and South Vietnam became known in SEATO contexts as the Protocol states.

The documents signed at Manila had two crucial features, one military and one political. First of all, they were a device for putting on a more permanent basis the staff consultations that had previously been held by military officers of several countries concerning security in South-East Asia. The treaty served as the framework for the continuation of these contacts and specified the circumstances—"aggression by means of armed attack in the Treaty Area"—in which the plans and programs elaborated in the course of the contacts would assume the form of military operations in support of a signatory or a Protocol state threatened by aggression. It was an alliance extending the shield of military protection to a number of states deemed to require such protection in the Treaty Area (defined as the general area of South-East Asia, including the entire territories of the Asian parties, and the general area of the

From *SEATO* by George Modelski. Copyright by F. W. Cheshire Publishing Pty Ltd. Reprinted by permission.

South-West Pacific south of 21 degrees 30 minutes north latitude, a line that excludes both Hong Kong and Taiwan). Preparations against "aggression by means of armed attack" became a dominant theme of SEATO activities; the prevention of such armed attack, a test of its success.

Just as importantly, however, the Manila Treaty became the expression of a wider political alignment on the part of a number of states concerned with South-East Asia, an alignment formally and explicitly placing them by the side of the United States on matters concerning the security and the political future of this area. For Thailand, Australia, or those Protocol states that accepted the protection offered by the treaty, the Manila Pact represented the choice of a "Western" orientation in international politics, a choice that exposed them to pressures from non-aligned nations and that also had its consequences in the domestic politics of each participating country, since the issues of anti-Americanism and non-alignment became grounds on which opposition could be rallied against the government in office. The Manila arrangements, taken by themselves, did not provide for increased security against internal subversive dangers to the stability of a member country or a protected government, and as the case of Laos demonstrated in 1960–1961, proved to be an insufficiently flexible instrument for dealing with emergencies of this type. But the "Western" alignment they symbolized assured the smaller members of additional American and other aid and support of a variety of types, not the least being increased economic assistance, granted mostly outside the organization framework of SEATO but helping to achieve its purposes and stabilizing the internal situation.

In 1954 the Manila Pact was, nevertheless, only one approach in stabilizing the position in South-East Asia, and in the Indochinese area in particular. The pact underscored the military aspects and expressed the strong American interest in the area; it bore marks of the then vogue for "collective security measures" and the imprint of Secretary Dulles's personal influence. Parallel to it, another series of arrangements was set up in Geneva, involving both negotiations with the Communist powers and the participation of India and, in special roles, that of Britain and France, two members of the Manila Pact. The Geneva truce agreements, signed in July 1954, defined not only the details of the cessation of hostilities in Indochina but also some political arrangements for the future of the area. To the extent that they had afforded the Communist powers the opportunity to register their opposition to the extension of American military influence and military alliances in Indochina, and to the extent that India, Britain, and France gave undertakings on this score, the Geneva approach may be regarded as a tendency contrary to that expressed by SEATO. Yet the two trends were not entirely contradictory, because the treaty in effect represented a one-sided military guarantee of the Geneva settlement, a promise on the part of the three Western great powers that a violation of the armistice lines of 1954 by means of armed attack would be repulsed by force.

The story of SEATO since 1954 has elaborated the themes initiated at Manila, but it has not altered them. The military alliance and guarantee element has remained important and has been strengthened in various ways: through the improved intimacy of contacts between military establishments, through the growing efficiency of military preparations, and through the increased likelihood that the military obligations assumed by treaty members could in fact be honored if the need arose and the political decision were taken. "Aggression by means of armed attack" has not so far occurred, and this part of the treaty therefore remains unimplemented, but American readiness to act, demonstrated on a number of occasions, above all by the landing of United States combat troops in Thailand in May 1962, has been a factor in the international situation and has to a certain extent served to vindicate SEATO purposes.

The political theme of the pro-American and pro-Western alignment has remained the other dominant theme in the organization. For the small member countries and the Protocol states the degree of commitment to the alignment has fluctuated with the internal political situation, the state of the international system, and the benefits accruing from it. . . . But the broad lines of political alignment have remained unchanged since 1954–1955, despite the efforts by the opponents of SEATO to confuse the issues by identifying the organization solely with its military element and by exploiting latent distrust of military activities in order to put obstacles in the way of a pro-American and pro-Western political alignment. The mere existence of SEATO has, however, helped to draw a sharper line between the aligned and the non-aligned states in this part of the world.

Two continuous threads in the story of SEATO have been the recurrent meetings of its Ministerial Council and of its other organs and the work of its permanent organization in Bangkok. The Council has met annually in capital cities of member countries. Although most of the business transacted on these occasions has been routine, the meetings usually had some special features of their own and they illustrate the development of the organization. The first, in Bangkok, laid down the basic framework of future activities. The Karachi Council made headlines for the support it appeared to lend to Pakistani aspirations in Kashmir. The decision to appoint a SEATO Secretary-General was taken in Canberra in 1957. At Manila, the following year, the Pakistanis put in a strong plea for increased economic aid, while Indonesian rebel delegates vainly appealed for recognition. The Wellington meeting authorized the preparations of plans for the defense of Laos. The Washington Council of 1960 met in the shadow of the breakdown of the Paris summit meeting a few weeks previously, and the next meeting (Bangkok, 1961) occurred at the height of the Laos crisis, close to the endangered area and in an atmosphere of rising doubts about SEATO's ability to move at all; it produced the strongest expression to date of collective determination to act in certain contingencies relating to Laos and South Vietnam. The permanent organization, which provides the continuing framework for these activities—a civilian Secretariat-General, the diplomatic meetings of Council Representatives, and the Military Planning Office—has, in the same period, after a slow and hesitant start and from small beginnings, assumed shape and consolidated its operations.

More important developments have taken place outside the organization. Changes in the structure of the international system have tended to raise the influence of the non-aligned states, to increase the authority of the Communist powers, and correspondingly to reduce the freedom of action of the Western great powers and their impact on world events as exercised also through SEATO. China has used such opportunities as have presented themselves to enlarge the domain of her influence in South-East Asia, but in the future may be increasingly handicapped in this respect by her rivalry with the Soviet Union.

The principal issue confronting SEATO in the past few years has been the status of Laos—an issue that apparently cannot be resolved solely by being referred to that organization. The SEATO type of solution is still needed in relation to Laos, and the military guarantee continues to be an indispensable element of a political settlement; but most recently the "Geneva" aspect of the solution had to be reinforced, too. In 1958–1960 it looked for a while as though Laos was firmly in the pro-American alignment, and on terms of some cooperation with SEATO. But a *coup* in August 1960 reversed this trend and subsequent developments brought the chronic state of internal warfare to a new peak at the beginning of 1961. The Royal Government, supported though it has been in the past by lavish aid, has proved incapable of dealing with the Pathet Lao rebel elements allied with the neutralist groups supporting Prince Souvanna Phouma; and a series of international negotiations in Geneva and elsewhere had to be set in motion to determine the future of that country. British and French reluctance to have recourse to SEATO in the Laotian civil war, and Indian preferences, once again pave a way for a Geneva-style settlement. One of the chief issues to be decided in that settlement will be the protection to be afforded Laos by the SEATO Protocol. The Communist powers have demanded the abrogation of this portion of the Manila Treaty as part of establishing neutral status for the country; the Western powers' ability to resist that demand has been a precondition of the continuing vitality of the organization.

Another most important issue for SEATO will continue to be the future of South Vietnam. Since 1958 the government of that country has been under increasing pressure from rebel elements drawing support from North Vietnam; by early 1961 battalion-strength operations were not uncommon and the stability of the political system was in doubt. SEATO as such, it was clear, however, could do little without an "armed attack" from the north; reluctant to decide upon or authorize the stationing of its forces in the country, it had to content itself with issuing declarations of concern and moral support, leaving the center of the stage to the United States. The determination and the resources of that power alone now prevent the disintegration of the South Vietnamese Government.

Since the completion of this volume at the end of 1961, SEATO developments have centered mainly upon Thailand. The most significant of these has been the reinterpretation of conditions under which Thailand may request assistance from its allies; the most spectacular, the stationing of combat units of the United States and of some other SEATO member nations in that country.

Doubts about the reliability of the pledges of aid contained in the Manila Treaty were first aroused in Thailand during the Laotian crises of 1960–1961. Irritation was caused in particular by the hesitancy and the delays in the handling of a seemingly simple procedural request of the Laotian Government for the dispatch of a team of SEATO observers. The stalemating of that request by a minority of SEATO members made the Thai Government apprehensive of the fate which, in a similar emergency, might befall one of its own proposals. All the activities and decisions of SEATO's organs being governed by the rule of unanimity, Thailand's representatives in the organization came out for the "abolition of veto," arguing that no one country and in particular members like France whose responsibilities in South-East Asia were a thing of the past, or even Britain, whose interests were declining, should be in the position to stop the organization from taking positive action. Even though this particular proposal has so far come to naught, the substance of the Thai concern has been met in another way. The joint statement issued during the Thai Foreign Minister's visit to Washington in March 1962 declares that the obligation of the United States to assist Thailand in case of "Communist armed attack" against that country "does not depend upon the prior agreement of all other parties to the Treaty" since "this Treaty obligation is individual as well as collective." In other words, in a possible future crisis the United States would not wait for a unanimous vote of the SEATO Council or Council Representatives before coming to the defense of Thailand in fulfilment of its SEATO obligations. In a public statement the Australian Government associated itself with this interpretation of the treaty obligations.

Occasion soon arose to test these new undertakings. When the collapse of Right-wing government forces in the north threatened to upset the political balance in Laos, gravely adding to the pressures upon Thailand, the United States, acting within the scope of the Manila

Treaty but without first consulting SEATO's organs in Bangkok, sent Marine and Army combat forces to areas bordering the danger zone. In a matter of days, small Australian, British, New Zealand, and Philippine units were on their way to Thailand too. This mid-1962 display of allied solidarity did not produce the much-hoped-for SEATO command; each of the national contingents serves under its own commander under an invitation issued by the Thai Government. Yet the pledges embodied in the Manila Treaty have undoubtedly become more tangible for apprehensive Thai officials for whom the decision to invite foreign troops into the country must have been difficult. Ever since 1954, the Thai Government has been extremely reluctant to see military forces of other SEATO nations established in "bases" on its own territory. It has been the deterioration of the situation in Laos and Vietnam, and fears for the security of the northeast, which induced such an important change of policy.

The events of the first half of 1962 thus vindicated the basic concepts underlying SEATO. They showed that, in case of a threat of aggression, the power of the United States can, and will, be used effectively in defense of the security of Thailand. The American and other forces, legitimately deployed on the mainland of South-East Asia in accordance with the Manila Treaty, now visibly guarantee the existing political order and incidentally also demonstrate that SEATO is not "a paper tiger." Yet if the purposes of SEATO have been validated, the effectiveness of SEATO's organizational arrangements has not been similarly enhanced. The reinterpretation of the Manila Treaty and the manner of the dispatch of troops to Thailand both assigned prime importance to bilateral contacts and cast doubt on the utility of existing consultative organs and planned military command structures. This shift away from multilateralism is no more than the accentuation, under pressure, of strains long inherent in the structure of the organization; it is the necessary consequence of the estrangement of some of its members who no longer feel able to participate fully in the joint enterprise and it is also a process of adjustment to meeting the danger now recognized as the foremost threat to the international security of the area: the danger from internal wars or from so-called wars of national liberation. Unlike wars of aggression, these internal, though foreign-supported, conflicts can only with difficulty be combated by multilateral security organizations of the NATO-SEATO type. Defense against guerrillas must be based foremost upon the soundness of the political system of the affected country and, as shown by the cases of Vietnam and Thailand, is most effectively supplemented through bilateral contacts, benefiting but marginally from international security arrangements.

In the years ahead, both the SEATO and the "Geneva" element of a political settlement in the Indochinese area will remain significant. SEATO stands for the military guarantee of a political order and for the formalization of a pro-American and pro-Western alignment. As long as

military force continues to matter, as long, moreover, as the United
States and the other Western great powers continue to exert influence in
this part of the world, and as long, finally, as small states feel compelled
to invoke that influence to offset the pressures originating from diverse
other sources, the SEATO type of guarantee reinforced by the power of
the United States will act as a deterrent and will continue to be needed
even though the organization itself may have to be refashioned. The
guarantee need not always assume the form of a multilateral organization or even of explicit promises, but experience has shown that both retain their usefulness and have been appreciated by most of the participants in SEATO.

A SEATO-type guarantee of protection does not, however, exhaust
the range of Western and other international action in this area. For a
variety of reasons the Western great powers no longer hold undivided
sway here. China, India, and Japan are closer to it than the Western
powers, and the South-East Asian countries themselves are beginning to
organize. An international settlement of regional affairs cannot be
achieved any longer without the support and cooperation of at least
some, if not all, of these parties. For this reason, the Geneva type of political solution and the participation of non-aligned powers will continue
as key components of international arrangements for the SEATO Area.

        ✻   ✻   ✻   ✻   ✻

For purposes of international relations, contemporary South-East
Asia may be regarded as a subordinate system of the world-wide international system.[1] A sub-system, briefly, is a cluster of small powers: Renais-
sance Italy, East-Central Europe between the two world wars, and pres-
ent-day Latin America are three important examples of this species. In
South-East Asia, the coexistence today of a score of small powers creates
just such a sub-system.[2]

The international problems of South-East Asia, as those of every
sub-system, are inherent, first of all, in the fact that this political arena,
divided as it is among a number of small states, is peculiarly susceptible
to the influence of the great powers.[3] Small states at times seek out the
interest and the protection of great powers; at other times they become
the objects of such interest and the victims of acquisitive designs. All the
world's great powers are interested in South-East Asia: the United States

---

[1] See G. Modelski, "International Relations and Area Studies: The Case of South-
East Asia," *International Relations* (London), ii (1961), iii, 143–155.

[2] As of 1961, Burma, Cambodia, Ceylon, Indonesia, Laos, Malaya, Pakistan, the
Philippines, Thailand, North and South Vietnam, and Singapore, together with the
colonial territories in Borneo, Timor, and New Guinea.

[3] The total population of South-East Asia is 296 million, as compared, for instance,
with 403 million for India and 660 million for mainland China (U.N. *Demographic
Yearbook 1959*).

and the Soviet Union, as much as China, France, India, Japan, and the United Kingdom. But the South-East Asian sub-system consists of countries which, with one exception, are new states and which, although moving toward industrialization, are still underdeveloped. The sub-system itself is new and has not yet had time to consolidate and to produce sentiments of regional solidarity.[4] Its international problems are therefore complicated by difficulties experienced by all newly emergent states and rapidly developing areas.

The Structure of Membership   SEATO is a device whereby three great powers—the United States, Britain, and France—have undertaken to support and protect a number of small states of South-East Asia—Thailand, the Philippines, and Pakistan, together with South Vietnam, Laos, and Cambodia—against the extension of the influence of other great powers, principally Communist China and the Soviet Union. The key to the understanding of SEATO is, therefore, the relationship between the great powers that belong to it and certain members of the South-East Asian sub-system.

The United States is the most important power in SEATO; she is the acknowledged leader of the group and she supplies the power and the initiative without which the alliance would be meaningless. American support for the small states of South-East Asia (in the form of military protection and economic aid) unfolds independently of SEATO. In the framework of American policy the organization has, nevertheless, performed important functions. In 1954–1955 it aroused for the first time widespread American interest in South-East Asia. Previously, interest had been sporadic and, before 1949, except in the Philippines, virtually non-existent. SEATO's formation greatly increased military activities and aid programs and put on a long-term basis America's concern in the sub-system. At present, furthermore, SEATO symbolizes and expresses America's concern for South-East Asian affairs; it gives notice that in appropriate circumstances American power may be exercised in the defense of the small states of South-East Asia.

The two other great powers in SEATO, the United Kingdom and France, played an important part in founding the organization, but have since been increasingly absorbed in the affairs of Europe, have reduced their responsibilities in South-East Asia, and now influence the activities of the alliance more by virtue of their world-wide status as great powers than in respect of their immediate commitments in the area. The scope of British action has greatly declined since the granting of independence to India; the support and reinforcement of British policies now depend on dangerously long lines of communication and to a great extent on the

[4] Most member states attained their independence between 1946 and 1957.

goodwill of India, Australia, and New Zealand. At the time of writing, the United Kingdom was directly responsible only for Singapore and the territories of British Borneo—both of which may soon merge with Malaya to form a Malaysian Federation—and for the Crown Colony of Hong Kong; through the Defense Agreement with the Federation, Britain was also indirectly responsible for the security of Malaya. In the past years, however, the internal situation in Malaya and Singapore had been brought under control with Britain's own resources and without the intervention of outside powers. British and Commonwealth troops now in the area suffice for maintaining internal security; for strategic purposes an aircraft carrier with an atomic strike force is an extension of the independent British nuclear deterrent. Thus, although the Far East is no more than a tertiary theater in the British scheme of operations, ranking after NATO and the Middle East for replacements of personnel and equipment, in the present state of international relations the forces committed to the area adequately perform Britain's greatly reduced responsibilities and create for her a position of independence. Given the predominant role of the United States in SEATO, the most striking characteristic of Britain's approach to it has been caution. She has sought to maintain the *status quo,* to soften declarations and policies likely to arouse Chinese anger or Indian suspicions, and to narrow, rather than to widen, the range of SEATO's commitments and activities.

France quickly lost most of her interest in SEATO soon after 1954 and has not been a happy member of the alliance. In military matters her contribution has been small and of necessity, therefore, she has been a strong advocate of economic and cultural activities.[5] Alone among the alliance members, France went so far as to criticize publicly some of SEATO's military operations. Her Foreign Minister described the 1956 exercise *Firmlink* as "mistaken propaganda" and an unwise and provocative display of strength.[6] President de Gaulle may have found membership in SEATO useful in his quest for greater French influence in the formation of Western policy, but in March 1961 in Bangkok the strongest opposition from within SEATO to a strong Council resolution on Laos came from the French Foreign Minister, and it seemed to be understood that France would not contribute troops if SEATO decided upon military action.

[5] She pushed her views hard and did not shrink on one occasion from taking such an unusual course for an ally as to express regret publicly that "SEATO economic and cultural programs received little support from U.S.A., who now appear to be more interested in bilateral aid with neutral powers." Agence France Presse in *Bangkok Post,* Aug. 27, 1956.
[6] Later that year the semi-official Agence France Presse explained that France supported exercise *Albatross* because "it is not a show of SEATO military strength but a study-exercise . . . ." However, French ships could not take part in it because they were at that time concentrated at Toulon "not to intimidate Egypt in any way but just in case French citizens were endangered" (*ibid.*).

None of the great powers in SEATO is indigenous to the area. The effectiveness of their operations in the sub-system, therefore, depends to an unusual degree on whether South-East Asian states, and the rest of the world, accept such intervention as legitimate. All the three SEATO great powers are "Western," and Western action in this area continues to be accepted as legitimate by a significant number of states, both within and outside SEATO. But some other Asian states, and India in particular, have resented an arrangement symbolizing the continued and exclusive influence in this area of powers whose previous interest towards them was mainly colonial. Association with such a grouping would, they feared, put them once again on an inferior and subordinate footing *vis-à-vis* powers who outclass them in the military sphere in particular. In the absence of prospects that such an inferiority would be compensated by immediate and compelling benefits, they were reluctant to associate with the organization or to accord it their support. With changes now under way in the international society tending to give increased weight to extra-European states, action in South-East Asia under the exclusive direction of the three Western NATO powers has already encountered difficulties and is likely to be increasingly handicapped.

A major determinant of the internal effectiveness of the organization is the degree of cooperation between the three major powers. Whenever they disagree, SEATO is powerless and the separate policies of the three partners in South-East Asia cannot prosper. American and British policies toward Communist China have diverged for at least a decade, with noticeable effect on all SEATO operations. In Laos, in the period since the August *coup* of 1960, great power disagreement reached a new height, immobilized SEATO, and virtually robbed it of its usefulness. British and French policies in that country lent their support and pinned their hopes upon the government of Prince Souvanna Phouma, judging him to be the only person who could reconcile the warring factions in Laos, and France in particular continued to recognize the Prince as Prime Minister after his flight to Phnom Penh in December 1960. Inclined to the belief that Souvanna Phouma was incapable of controlling the situation, the United States withdrew its support of him and gave it to the forces which organized in Savannaket around Prince Boon Oum and General Phoumi Nosavan and formed a new government in January 1961. The consequent split in the front of the three powers confused Western action in Laos. The smaller Asian states began to question the very presence of Britain and France in SEATO. However, the Laotian episode demonstrated that none of the major members of the organization can, singlehanded, control it or influence events in South-East Asia.

The Asian members—Thailand, the Philippines, and Pakistan—are small South-East Asian states that have stood to gain from a direct association with the Western great powers; and, in their turn, they follow the Western lead on most of the great international issues. Their gain may be computed in terms of increased security in response to Chinese and Soviet pressure and a general strengthening of their diplomatic position; their losses, in terms of the increased hostility their governments thereby incur both internally and internationally. The three Indochinese states, South Vietnam, Laos, and Cambodia, have found themselves in a largely similar but, because of their less direct association, a more flexible position; this offers them greater scope for maneuver. Australia and New Zealand, finally, do not belong to South-East Asia proper, but they also fit into the pattern just outlined.[7] A small power with the making of a great nation, Australia in particular is a contributor in her own right to the security of South-East Asia and a "keen" member of the organization.[8] Nonetheless, both Australia and New Zealand are small states amiably dependent upon the great powers for their independent survival.

The Federation of Malaya and the State of Singapore, too, have close links with Britain and Australia in particular but remain outside SEATO. Singapore is the main British base east of Suez from which forces could be deployed in case of a SEATO emergency. The Federation of Malaya has a defense agreement with the United Kingdom, which authorizes, among other things, maintenance of Commonwealth troops and bases. (Under the London agreement of November 1961, Britain would remain free to use her forces in Singapore for carrying out her SEATO obligations even after the establishment of the Malaysian Federation.) But despite its own internal security problems, the close links with Thailand, and the earlier personal inclination of its Prime Minister, Tengku Abdul Rahman, Malaya has declined to enter SEATO.[9] The Tengku's success in promoting the establishment of the Association of South-East Asian States has the effect of by-passing SEATO, replacing it by a purely regional grouping of like-minded states that is without the political liability of a direct and military association with the Western powers (which spells subordination) but that would, nevertheless, maintain links with the principal states of the West.

In North-Eastern Asia there are certain states that cannot be regarded as a part of South-East Asia but that find themselves in the same position as the other small powers associated with SEATO and that could be said to belong, for international purposes, to the South-East Asian sub-system. Nationalist China on Taiwan and South Korea are both small states whose survival depends on the support of the United States

---

[7] See G. Modelski, "Australia and SEATO," *International Organization*, xiv (1960), iii, 429–437.

[8] A mobile Australian Brigade group formed for use in South-East Asia, which could be transported by air to the danger area at short notice, was placed on combat alert in the Laos crisis of 1961, and must be reckoned among SEATO's front-line troops.

[9] *Malay Mail* (Kuala Lumpur), Feb. 17, 1958. By 1960 the Tengku was reported to feel SEATO to be "ineffective, negative, outmoded and under the stigma of Western domination" (A.P. dispatch from Kuala Lumpur, *Manila Chronicle*, Jan. 12, 1960).

in particular. Both Taiwan and South Korea stand exposed to direct pressure from Communist China, to offset which both heavily rely upon American aid. Both have close links with South-East Asia (Taiwan through its efforts to cultivate the overseas Chinese) and have in the past worked for an alliance of anti-communist states in this part of the world. Their initiatives foundered on such political disagreements as that which separates Japan from Korea and on the refusal of most states to be involved in what still is in one sector the continuation of the Chinese civil war.[10] Taipeh "supports" SEATO, has kept up an interest in SEATO operations and in the Asian SEATO members (being active also in supporting the Boon Oum Government in Laos in 1960–1961, for instance, by supplying transport aircraft), and favored military intervention in Laos early in 1961. When SEATO failed to act there, its enthusiasm visibly declined. South Korea, too, sends observers to SEATO operations and dispatches missions to South-East Asian countries. In military matters the policies of South Korea, of Nationalist China, and of SEATO members to the south of them are coordinated through the agency of the United States Pacific Command at Pearl Harbor (which among other things is responsible for the work of United States Military Assistance Groups on Formosa and in Laos, Thailand, and the Philippines). Japan too has recently been under virtually complete American military protection, but although party to a mutual security treaty with the United States she has little desire so far to undertake military responsibilities outside her own territories. After Manila in 1954 Japan declared "moral support" for SEATO,[11] but in the Japan–United States Security Treaty completed in 1960 the two parties undertook no obligations toward South-East Asia. On the contrary, those provisions that express their determination to contribute to the international peace and security are expressly limited to the Far East (defined under questions from the opposition as "the general area north of Philippines, especially the areas immediately surrounding Japan" [12]) and seem designed to avoid an overlap with the SEATO area.

The political problems of the small states that are full members of

---

[10] At one stage in 1954 the United States proposed Nationalist China for membership in SEATO. It could be argued that an alliance designed to contain Communist China was pointless without the two states most strongly opposed to her, but there was little enthusiasm for the proposal; Britain opposed it, and at Manila the area to be protected by SEATO was delimited in such a way as to exclude both Taiwan and Hong Kong from the pact's operation (*New York Times,* July 22, 1951). Britain also opposed the inclusion of South Korea, on the grounds of the unpopularity of its regime.

[11] *The Times* (London), Sept. 10, 1954.

[12] *Japan Times* (Tokyo), Feb. 15, 1960. In January 1961, as the Foreign Ministers of the Philippines, South Korea, Nationalist China, and South Vietnam were meeting in Manila, the Foreign Minister again denied reports that Japan had any intentions of joining a North-East Asia Treaty Organization.

SEATO are thus shared by a number of other powers that for this reason are in various ways associated with SEATO. South Vietnam, Laos and Cambodia, and South Korea and Taiwan, Malaya and Singapore, and in some limited respects Japan, too, are each involved in the network of political and military activities that focuses on Communist China. On occasion and depending on the local situation and the condition of the international system, yet other states evince an interest in SEATO activities. In 1959, for example, Burma and Indonesia dispatched observers to SEATO military exercises in Thailand. As a great power association for the support of certain small nations SEATO thus forms a core around which a variety of activities can be organized without all the participants being full members.

Some SEATO Crises Great power support for small states manifests itself in two ways: continuously, in diplomatic and political contacts, in generous assistance programs, and in the protection afforded by powerful armed forces-in-being; sporadically, in the prompt and unhesitating extension of measures of aid and comfort to a small ally facing an emergency. In South-East Asia the United States and the other Western great powers afford most of their continuing support through bilateral arrangements (such as foreign aid agreements); SEATO has only a symbolic role in these operations. In crises and emergencies, too, the essential backing flows largely through bilateral channels and includes the early and unequivocal reaffirmation of support by the key great powers; SEATO itself, however, has the function of securing an early definition and clear expression of a common outlook and an agreement on joint and separate measures for the common defense.

Like NATO, SEATO has not yet been tested in combat; the need for a trial of forces may never in fact arise. SEATO has, however, been involved in a number of crises, only one of which, the Laotian emergency of 1961, came close to being a real test of strength. A brief analysis of a number of international crises illustrates how SEATO fulfills its functions—the way it helps to mobilize great power support for the states of South-East Asia.

The first occasion on which SEATO support could have been displayed occurred in July 1955, when fighting flared up between Pathet Lao (literally "Land of the Lao") and government forces in northern Laos. Indeed, Thailand tried to bring about a situation in which SEATO members collectively could declare their concern over the situation in that country, and by doing so incidentally also demonstrate the unity of the newly formed organization. Yet as an initiative designed to stir SEATO into public action the Thai attempt failed. It was an ill-considered and ill-prepared move; the Laos Government had not been consulted and duly expressed its annoyance, especially since the fighting had already stopped. Britain, France, and India condemned it on the ground that the International Commission on Laos was fully capable of dealing with the matter. The SEATO representatives discussed Laos but they must have disagreed, because SEATO made no public move, and the demonstration of unity failed to materialize. This first attempt to mobilize SEATO did show, however, the influence of British and French views upon the organization, and imparted an early lesson in the difficulties of bringing the SEATO machinery into action.

Caution was the keynote of SEATO's behavior in the second half of 1956 during frontier incidents involving the occupation of some disputed areas in Burma by Chinese troops. At the beginning of August the Thai Cabinet heard the Minister of Foreign Affairs' report on the incidents and ordered close watch to be kept of developments, but Thailand's Military Adviser to SEATO hastened to emphasize that SEATO would not act on this matter because Burma was outside SEATO's defense area. Next month the Thai Premier defined the Chinese actions as aggression, but the SEATO representatives held a regular meeting and did not discuss the Burmese questions. The Burmese Government evidently decided to use Indian influence for improving its position *vis-à-vis* China; yet SEATO did not cease to be a factor in the diplomatic situation. Burma kept in close touch with Bangkok, and in the midst of the crisis signed a Friendship Treaty with Thailand.[13] Nor was the possibility of SEATO's direct intervention lost either on the Burmese or the Chinese: the Burmese Peace Congress complained, "the border problem [is] being utilized by certain cliques both in Burma and abroad to disrupt the friendship between Burma and China in an attempt to drag Burma into SEATO."[14] Communist China knew that too great a pressure on Burma involved the risk of forcing her into SEATO. SEATO's existence strengthened the hand of the Burmese Government and helped to defend Burma's interests by giving notice that, if the crisis worsened, Burma could call upon the help of the great powers.

During 1957 the Royal Laotian Government arrived at a settlement with the Pathet Lao. SEATO as such had no direct part in this process, but the SEATO great powers maintained continuous contact with the Royal Government and firmly supported it throughout the talks. On February 22, at a crucial stage in the negotiations, Premier Souvanna Phouma asked them for a statement of their policy on Laos. On April 16 the United States, Britain, and France issued identical statements (the Tripartite Note) affirming the interest of the three governments in the independence and unity of Laos and expressing confidence that the political future of the country would not be dictated by the Pathet Lao. Here,

---

[13] *Bangkok Post*, Oct. 15, 1956; the Sino-Burmese agreement was initialed at the beginning of November.
[14] N.C.N.A., Sept. 11, 1956 (*S.C.M.P.* 1370, p. 2).

for the first time, the public support of the three great powers was mobilized in aid of the Laotian Government, albeit outside SEATO.

A more embarrassing test of SEATO came during the Indonesian "Permesta" rebellion of early 1958. It was embarrassing because, in a confused situation, SEATO's help had been requested by a rebel group seeking to overthrow an allegedly Communist-dominated government relying on Soviet arms aid and Chinese political support. It was embarrassing, too, because SEATO had not been created to deal with situations of this kind; the great power support it mobilizes can be effective only through existing governments. The rebels dispatched representatives to Manila at the time of the SEATO Council meeting, requested *de facto* recognition by the SEATO powers, and declared themselves in favor of SEATO's objectives. The Communists, in their turn, made the most of the rebels' declared sympathy for the West and denounced the rebellion as a plot hatched by the SEATO powers. Moscow and Peking made out that SEATO was already giving full aid to the rebels:

> The ringleaders of that clique—Hussein, Simolon, and Sjafruddin— maintain close contacts with Singapore. There, within the framework of SEATO, a special organization has been set up which directs the action of the rebels and separatists. The bulletin of the Indonesian International Press Service says that after talks between the rebels and prominent SEATO representatives in Singapore, SEATO promised help to the rebels on condition that SEATO military bases are set up in Sumatra.[15]

None of this, of course, happened. As will become apparent from the next section, SEATO's framework is not large enough to accommodate such a special organization, which could not possibly have been set up: the unanimous agreement of all members is required before SEATO as such can embark on an action; in February–April 1958 there was not even a slim chance of SEATO unanimity on the Indonesian issue. True, in its early stages the rebellion enjoyed considerable sympathy in Singapore, in the Philippines, and perhaps also in Australia. Nationalist China and some American agencies seem to have been active on its behalf too. The rebellion became the subject of discussion at the Manila Council, during the customary review of the situation in the treaty area. But at no stage was there even majority sentiment for intervention in its favor. The role of SEATO was, again, chiefly negative. Western presence in South-East Asia ensured that the Djakarta Government had to be careful about bringing in Soviet or Chinese aid, the use of which might have called forth public Western supplies for the rebels. The SEATO great powers, in their turn, knew that by aiding the rebels they would invite Communist support for Djakarta. Great power pressures thus balanced each

[15] Moscow Home Service commentary, Mar. 6, 1958 (*S.W.B.* I, 912, p. 23).

other, allowing local influences to take their course; thus demonstrating that the most important feature of SEATO support may be not direct intervention but the offsetting of the pressures of other great powers.[16]

The Quemoy crisis of August–September 1958 found SEATO as unwilling to enter the ring on behalf of Nationalist China on Formosa as it had always been. The United States took a strong stand on an important issue: it refused to bow to a display of strength, even though the islands in dispute seemed intrinsically insignificant. Immediately after the crisis broke, American interest in SEATO soared. Its anniversary, which fell during the crisis, was commemorated by an unprecedented message from President Eisenhower. The Secretary of the Army called at the SEATO headquarters. Secretary Dulles convened a meeting of SEATO ambassadors in Washington and explained the American position to them. Yet SEATO remained silent and withheld support from the American stand. Majority opinion, led by the United Kingdom, Thailand, and New Zealand, refused even the least extension of SEATO's commitments as Communist China embarked on a tougher policy by attacking the Quemoy islands—politically speaking, the weakest among American-supported positions in the Pacific.

Laos re-entered the headlines on New Year's Day 1959 when news came of a North Vietnamese incursion into Laotian territory. Once more Thailand expressed immediate interest, displaying, again, the characteristic anxiety of a small state: would the great powers, then absorbed by the Berlin crisis, spare sufficient attention and resources to this question? SEATO maintained its silence and the immediate crisis blew over, but evidence came to hand that on Laos, at any rate, SEATO would be prepared to move. At the Wellington Council the Military Advisers were authorized to prepare blueprints for dealing with an invasion of Laos.[17]

The flare-up of internal fighting in Laos in the second half of 1959 could therefore hardly have taken SEATO unawares; yet declarations of encouragement or concrete actions were slow in coming. The United

---

[16] By June, when it became obvious that the rebels had not much will to fight and that Djakarta was anxious to restrain the power of the Communist Party, the Western nations decided to throw in their weight behind the official government. This decision was not, however, reached within SEATO; apparently it resulted from consultations within NATO with the participation of Australia and New Zealand (U.P.I. dispatch from London, *Bangkok Post,* June 7, 1958). The NATO framework seems to have been used in order to keep Holland within the discussions; but it appears strange that such an important decision should have been arrived at without the participation of the three Asian SEATO powers.

[17] The SEATO exercise of the preceding year (*Vayabut*) had assumed that neutral Laos would bow to the aggressor's will without a fight. As the exercise "scenario" explained: "Following two weeks of political pressure . . . the tiny country of X . . . conceded to aggressor demands to station troops within her borders . . . military officials took control of the X foreign policy . . ." (Press Release, Office of Information Service, Headquarters Operation *Vayabut,* Don Muang Airfield, Thailand, Apr. 21, 1958).

States lent firm support and, with Thailand's cooperation, sent immediate help, but SEATO hesitated: neither at Bangkok nor in the other capitals was there much eagerness for recourse to SEATO. Pote Sarasin, the Secretary-General, declared these events to be an entirely domestic affair of Laos.

A change occurred at the beginning of September when the Laotian Government found itself under heavy pressure and decided to appeal to the United Nations, alleging aggression by North Vietnamese troops; SEATO's diplomatic wheels then started to move. The Council Representatives met three times in the first eleven days of September. SEATO ambassadors in Washington conferred twice with the Secretary of State. The Laotian Foreign Minister called on Pote Sarasin. The three SEATO great powers took the initiative in the U.N. Security Council and sponsored and rammed through a resolution authorizing the dispatch of a committee of inquiry to Laos. As the United Nations was meeting in New York the Laotian Secretary for Defense announced that the government was considering an appeal to SEATO. The Council Representatives met on September 26 and issued an uncommonly strong statement: "In the event of its becoming necessary to defend the integrity of Laos against outside intervention, SEATO has made preparations so as to be able to act promptly within the framework of the Manila Treaty." [18] Finally, the Foreign Ministers of the SEATO powers held a special meeting to discuss Laos in Washington on September 29.

This display of great power activity (especially the concerted operation in the Security Council) was encouraging for the small countries, although it was the United Nations that held the center of the stage. For Laos it was once again an opportunity of using SEATO for its own purposes: by its "threats" of appeal to SEATO Laos made it easier for India, and even perhaps for the Soviet Union and China, to acquiesce in the withdrawal of the International Commission and in the attempt to establish United Nations competence to deal with the situation. The U.N. Committee which visited Laos failed to find evidence of North Vietnamese aggression and in retrospect SEATO's caution was vindicated. But its reaction seemed to reinforce the view that SEATO's duties were fulfilled after the threat of external attack had been warded off; the real difficulty in Laos, internal insecurity, remained unchanged and was soon to present the organization with an even greater challenge.

LAOS 1960–1961

A crucial test of SEATO's ability to support the government of a small power against Communist pressure occurred in the months between Captain Kong Lee's Vientiane *coup* of August 1960 and the *de facto* truce in the Laotian civil war in May 1961. Up to the battle of

[18] SEATO Press Release No. 214, Sept. 26, 1959.

Vientiane and the formation of the Boon Oum Government in December 1960, the legitimate government of Prince Souvanna Phouma regarded itself as neutralist and had no desire to call upon SEATO. In the absence of an invitation from the government SEATO had little ground for intervening directly in Laos and no intention of doing so. The official view was thus put by Pote Sarasin:

> SEATO will continue to watch carefully the situation in Laos and is sensitive to its responsibilities but under no circumstances will it interfere in the internal affairs of Laos. . . . Neutrality is a thing which we all hope Laos can preserve . . . a country that preserves a neutral policy is satisfactory as far as SEATO is concerned.[19]

He declared SEATO's main object to be "to defend free and independent countries within its responsibility from aggression . . . it must not however be interpreted to be capable of acting like a local police force moving in to settle local conflicts." [20]

The Council Representatives repeatedly discussed the situation as doubts grew about Laos's ability to preserve neutrality, but Thailand almost alone regarded the events in Laos as "alarming," and when anti-Vientiane forces gathered strength in southern Laos gave notice at the Military Advisers' conference (November 1960) that it would use the meeting in order to consult with delegations especially sympathetic to its own viewpoint on measures to be taken with regard to Laos:

> Over and above the decisions arrived at during such a meeting which may be held as the basis of action of each member country, agreement may be sought on several important issues outside the formal sessions. We in Thailand believe in the expediency of this valuable procedure and propose that greater use be made of it.[21]

It may be supposed that the Thai representative was referring to agreements that were about to be reached with the United States delegation on measures to be taken to aid General Phoumi Nosavan in mounting an offensive on Vientiane. A SEATO military meeting thus served as an occasion for concerting views between two member countries upon policies which, to say the least, were disliked by some other members.

In the fighting which followed General Phoumi's offensive the Soviet Union started for the first time to fly in military supplies to the government of Souvanna Phouma; it has continued this aid, which in due course produced a radical alteration in the local power balance, because it claims the Prince, not having resigned, remains the legitimate chief executive of his country. The SEATO Council Representatives took up the question of Soviet arms deliveries but, although they declared for the

---

[19] *Bangkok Post*, Aug. 18, 1960.
[20] *Ibid.*, Sept. 19, 1960.
[21] *Ibid.*, Nov. 16, 1960.

first time that the situation was serious, expressed no more than "concern" at this development.

The position with regard to SEATO changed when a new government headed by Prince Boon Oum established itself in Vientiane and in due course received the constitutional endorsement of the National Assembly and of the King; this government could and might, if necessary, ask for SEATO's aid and protection.

The new government, weak and engaged in a civil war, did in fact immediately declare its support for and expressed a desire to join SEATO as a measure for strengthening its local and international position. At its first meeting the new cabinet adopted as one of its basic aims the policy of entering "all organizations designed to prevent aggression." Some days later Prince Boon Oum, its Premier, was quoted as saying that if necessary Laos would ask for membership in SEATO. But the State Department hastened to declare that the United States, although fully supporting it, would not encourage the new government to apply for SEATO membership, for such a step might appear provocative.[22]

As soon as the Boon Oum Government suffered its first major reverse, and as a means of securing greater international support, it raised a hue and cry about North Vietnamese aggression; on New Year's Eve the headlines read "Seven Vietminh [Short for *Viet Nam Doc Lap Dong Minh Hoi* (League for the Independence of Vietnam), founded in 1941.] battalions attack in Laos." American forces in the Pacific were alerted, Thailand ordered defense preparations, and the United States proposed to the Council Representatives the calling of a special meeting of the SEATO Council, but Britain in particular opposed the idea and Australia assumed a "wait and see" attitude. The meeting expressed the feeling that "every effort should be made to find a solution by peaceful means." [23] The evidence of outside military intervention in force soon proved unconvincing and the opinion prevailed that in the absence of intervention of this type SEATO did not have a *locus standi* in Laos.

Although the Boon Oum Government remained in power in large part by virtue of American and Thai support, SEATO did not afford it much comfort or encouragement. The Philippines and Pakistan were sympathetic, but Britain and France, together with Australia and New Zealand, refused to be drawn to their aid. In the meantime, having suffered severe reverses in their attempt to retain the strategic initiative, Boon Oum and Phoumi Nosavan decided to seek a cease-fire. As the SEATO Council was preparing to hold its regular annual meeting, this time in Bangkok, the military situation had deteriorated so much that Vientiane itself was in imminent danger.

[22] *Bangkok Post,* Dec. 14, 1960; *Thai Daily,* Dec. 23, 1960, in *B.D.N.D.* v, 117, p. 3; *Bangkok Post,* Dec. 22, 1960.
[23] *Phim Thai,* Jan. 4, 1961 in *B.D.N.D.* v, 123, p. 3. SEATO Press Release No. 1, Jan. 4, 1961.

The United States once again rallied to the aid of the threatened government. President Kennedy appealed to the American people, moved new forces to the Pacific and marine helicopter crews into northeast Thailand, and in talks with Prime Minister Macmillan secured a modification of the British attitude. The French remained unconvinced, but after considerable negotiation at the Council meeting agreed to a resolution, the strongest ever passed by a SEATO body, expressing "grave concern" over the continued offensive by "rebel elements." Noting with approval efforts for a cessation of hostilities and for negotiations to achieve "an unaligned and independent Laos," the Council declared in the crucial paragraph five of the resolution:

> If those efforts fail, however, and there continues to be an active military attempt to obtain control of Laos, members of SEATO are prepared, within the terms of the Treaty, to take whatever action may be appropriate in the circumstances.[24]

The resolution may be interpreted as a warning that, pending the results of talks in Laos, in Geneva, and elsewhere, the SEATO powers will not permit a civil war to be decided militarily against the Boon Oum Government, and will not, in effect, allow the armed seizure of main urban centers along the Mekong Valley, including Vientiane and Luang Prabang. The occasion to honor this undertaking threatened to arise a few weeks later when, refusing to accept a cease-fire, the Pathet Lao forces mounted a new offensive and a little later seized a stronghold seventy miles north of Vientiane; SEATO consultations were resumed, and the United States stepped up its military aid and was planning to propose the calling of a "SEATO alert." This might have involved the moving of American and other allied troops to advance areas in northern Thailand, but not the immediate landing of troops in Laos. United States Far East Forces, the Philippines Army, and the Australian Forces were placed on combat alert,[25] and the Chairman of the United States Joint Chiefs of Staff visited Thailand. There is reason to believe that this show of strength induced the Pathet Lao to issue a call for cease-fire on May 3.

After preparing itself for years to defend Thailand, and then Laos, against armed attack on the Korean model, SEATO had to decide whether to intervene in an internal war. Reluctantly it concluded that it had to face such a possibility. Its declared readiness to do so now (1961) guarantees the cease-fire in Laos—and precariously preserves the Boon Oum Government from collapse. It can do little more, yet in years to come internal wars of the Laos type may well prove to be as important

---

[24] *Bangkok Post*, Mar. 29, 1961. The following day the Lao Cabinet "reacted very favorably" to the resolution, but the King is said to have vetoed an immediate request for SEATO aid.
[25] *Ibid.*, Apr. 21, 22, 1961; *Canberra Times*, May 2, 1961; *Japan Times*, May 2, 1961.

as semi-external conflicts in the Korean style. South Vietnam has been experiencing a revival of internal warfare since 1958, greatly intensified at the end of 1960 by the events in Laos. The SEATO Council of March 1961 noted, "with concern," "the efforts of an armed minority, again supported from outside in violation of the Geneva Agreements, to destroy the government of Vietnam," [26] and declared its firm resolve not to acquiesce in any such takeover of that country. American aid for the embattled government was greatly stepped up in the second half of 1961, but here, too, at some late critical stage SEATO may face the awkward decision to intervene in an internal war.

The preceding analysis of the SEATO crises was designed to bring out four points: first, the prime danger area of South-East Asia has so far been its northern rim: Laos, South Vietnam, and to a smaller extent Burma. (Quemoy is outside the Treaty Area, Indonesia faced SEATO with a dilemma it had not been designed to cope with.) Second, in all cases the decisive event at issue had been the actual or potential joint or individual intervention of the Western great powers on behalf of a small state of South-East Asia. Third, such joint intervention as was finally agreed upon took the form of political and diplomatic action, locally, in the world's chancelleries, in the United Nations: no active use has so far been made of outside armed forces; such fighting as occurred was entirely localized. Fourth, although designed to deal with the threat of external attack, SEATO came closest to military intervention in a situation of internal war.

There are grounds for believing that crises of this kind will continue over the next few years. SEATO may yet gain strength and confidence; the non-committed states may learn to live with it, the governments of South-East Asia may consolidate their rule, but the constituent elements of crises will remain the same: the northern rim is still, as it has been for the past seven years, the prime area of weakness that attracts great power influence; Laos, one of the weakest and most underdeveloped countries in the world and unluckily placed on the boundaries of Communist China and North Vietnam, will continue as a trouble spot. South Vietnam, once thought the weakest link in the area defense, has in the first years since SEATO's formation proved more resilient. It will, however, continue to pose grave problems. Furthermore, in future crises the great powers will still have to take the initiative; the United States will have to lead the way, while the role of France—and even of the United Kingdom—though it may ultimately contract, is still important. Western unity on South-East Asian issues can never be lightly presumed; a system of SEATO consultation is one of the ways of maintaining that unity, but in itself it would not be sufficient to achieve that unity. Great

[26] *Bangkok Post*, Mar. 29, 1961.

power initiative may or may not work through SEATO: on issues originating in the Indochinese peninsula SEATO may in some cases prove a suitable instrument, but past crises also show that, if the cooperation of non-committed countries such as India is called for, SEATO may not prove suitable. Thirdly, great power intervention will make itself felt through diplomacy and political action rather than through the active use of Western military units. Although United States armed forces will still be in the Pacific (and may on a number of occasions be alerted for use in South-East Asia as they have been in the past) and British forces will continue in or around Singapore, their function will remain preventative—that of holding the ring and offsetting Chinese and Soviet power.

International war (in most of its forms) thus appears improbable in South-East Asia. A conventional war between major powers, for instance between China and the United States, is becoming increasingly unlikely. A great power thermonuclear war would inevitably engulf the area, but it seems improbable that it should start over a purely South-East Asian issue (such as Laos). Direct Communist Chinese armed aggression against one of the border states, such as Laos, Burma, or Nepal, appears unlikely too. Finally, as long as the area remains free of new Communist states, a limited war on the Korean model can occur solely in relation to North Vietnam and China. Those countries may exert pressure on South Vietnam, and can put a severe strain on Laos, for example, by sending "volunteer" forces in reply to a SEATO or American intervention intended to regain territory occupied by the Pathet Lao, especially territory adjoining North Vietnamese and Chinese borders. Laos is the country in which such a limited war is at present possible, but even here neither side necessarily wants to create a situation in which the engagement of outside forces would be inevitable. Barring this one risk of limited war, it looks as though future South-East Asian crises will follow the pattern of the past few years: the problems to be solved will be principally diplomatic—problems of political subversion and internal war, rather than of external aggression.

The doctrine that SEATO's concern is principally with attack from the outside seems at first to have been firmly upheld in the Laotian crises. The obligations under Article IV (2) of the Manila Treaty "to consult immediately on measures . . . for the common defense" if the "integrity of the territory or the sovereignty or political independence" is threatened "in any way other than by armed attack" have in effect been treated as a dead letter. Rent by internal disagreement, SEATO has been unwilling to become involved in the Laotian civil war; for the same reason it would find it difficult to intervene, for instance, in an internal conflict in South Vietnam or the Philippines, although in the end it would not avoid a commitment if fighting became intense. Armed intervention in an internal war is, of course, no more than a measure of last resort; but no evidence is at hand that effective or imaginative measures to control dangerous internal security situations have been or could be taken through the existing machinery of SEATO. This is a challenging task of political reform, transcending any functions that might be undertaken by an unwieldy international organization.

The Permanent "Guarantor" activities of the kind found in SE-
Organization ATO—great power support for a number of small countries—do not necessarily call for an elaborate institutional framework. The Monroe Doctrine, for instance, served its purpose for decades without any form of organization. The 1950 three-power guarantee of the frontiers of Israel functioned (or failed to function) without special organs. Great power arrangements may in fact work better in this way; such consultation as is required is easily performed through usual diplomatic channels. We have seen, too, how in some of the South-East Asian crises (as during the Laotian settlement of 1957) the great powers acted in unison but outside SEATO, as the result of ordinary diplomatic exchanges. The onus thus seems to rest in the first place on those who argue for institutionalization, but in an important part the issue has already been settled: once it was decided to have a multilateral treaty with the participation of the small states, a treaty, moreover which authorized the formation of a Ministerial Council, the only question was: how much institutionalization?

The past few years have in fact witnessed a steady growth and elaboration of SEATO's permanent machinery and an expansion in its functions. This growth has a number of causes, the most general of them being the complexity of inter-state relations in the modern industrial international system. The member states need permanent organs to handle the flow of information and the profusion of contacts that are a feature of the modern age. The size of membership—eight states—also tends toward the creation of an organization servicing multilateral exchanges. Once set up, an organization grows almost inevitably, assuming duties and discovering functions that were not originally thought to be within its purview. In SEATO two additional tendencies were at work—the influential (and fashionable) example of NATO ("if NATO can have it, why can't we?"), and, most important, the continuous and mounting desire of the small powers for arrangements that afford them opportunities for influencing great power decisions, that make their association with the great powers more nearly equal, and that commit the great powers more firmly to their support. This in fact may be the pattern of future international cooperation between great and small powers—a pattern that assures great power interests and maintains the self-respect of the small nations.

SEATO's permanent organization is made up of three elements: the Secretariat-General, the diplomatic machinery, and the military framework. It was not created all at one stroke; it is the result of an evolutionary process in the course of which the diplomatic consultative organization expanded gradually through the addition of an executive secretariat and the enlargement of functions of the military offices. The process has now advanced to a point where it is possible to speak of the emergence of SEATO as a new international actor, an international personality with its own resources and its own interests, and consequently also with a distinct set of activities.

The striking feature of the permanent organization is the modesty of the resources SEATO commands. Its staff and the Common Budget are remarkably small, particularly by comparison with the large and generously financed United States agencies in this area. (The United States Information Office in Thailand, for instance, has a budget and a staff larger than SEATO's.) Recruitment and staff policies, which tend to limit the growth of SEATO loyalties, and the lack of political support for the organization accentuate the feature. Finally, the smallness of its resources contrasts strikingly with the power attributed to it by those of its critics and opponents who propagate the idea of a vast and scheming *apparatus* that foments rebellions, hatches plots, and stretches its tentacles to every corner of the Treaty Area.

THE SECRETARIAT-GENERAL

The Secretariat-General is the civilian side of the SEATO organization. It has gradually evolved from a purely secretarial body in the Thai Ministry of Foreign Affairs (February 1955–April 1956), through the growth of a number of functional offices loosely coordinated by an Executive Secretary under the general authority of the Council Representatives (April 1956–August 1957), into an autonomous entity that is directed by a Secretary-General of high standing. It operates under the close supervision of the member states' diplomatic missions in Bangkok but is nonetheless, for the first time, physically capable of expressing a SEATO personality.

The first SEATO Secretary-General, Pote Sarasin, took office on September 1, 1957. A former Foreign Minister and interim Prime Minister of Thailand and a respected and influential political figure in his country, Pote Sarasin has added to the stature of SEATO. The Deputy Secretary-General is William Worth, a senior Australian public servant whose energy has already left its mark on the working of the Secretariat-General.

The staff of the Secretariat-General (classified into two categories —"international" and "local"—according to importance of work and method of recruitment) has grown considerably since 1956. As of June 1958 it was slightly larger than the Secretariat-General of CENTO (formerly the Baghdad Pact Organization), but much smaller than NATO's headquarters.[27]

Staff of the SEATO Secretariat-General

	International	Local	Total
1 January 1957	15	39	54
1 January 1958	35	63	98
1 July 1958	40	66	106
1 January 1960	40	88	128
1 January 1961	37	95	132

SOURCE: Information supplied by the Secretariat-General.

The SEATO staff members are international civil servants whose responsibilities are, according to the Staff Regulations promulgated in May 1958 (and modeled after NATO and U.N. Staff Rules), "exclusively international in character." [28] Staff are responsible to, and subject to the authority of, the Secretary-General. They shall not engage in any outside occupation, and on joining the staff they subscribe to the following declaration:

> I solemnly undertake to exercise in all loyalty, discretion and conscience the functions entrusted to me as a member of the staff of the South-East Asia Treaty Organization, to discharge these functions and regulate my conduct solely with the interests of the Organization in view, and not to seek or accept instructions in regard to the performance of my duties from any government or other authority external to the Organization. I will strictly conform to the staff and security rules and regulations now in force in the Organization and to those which may be issued thereafter and will act up to the standards of propriety and efficiency required by the Organization.[29]

With the appointment of a high-ranking Secretary-General, the expansion in staff, and the growth of the concept of a service whose responsibilities are "exclusively international" the organization is now reaching a point where it may start to generate its own *esprit de corps*. Yet despite

[27] CENTO's staff was "about 70" (letter from Deputy Secretary-General, June 19, 1958). NATO's was about 596, including 189 of officer grade, in 1954 (Lord Ismay, *NATO—The First Five Years* (Paris, 1954), p. 62); in April 1957 the officer staff numbered 183.

[28] *NATO's Staff Rules* (revised version issued July 1, 1955), p. 3, stress that the responsibilities of staff are "not national but exclusively international in character."

[29] Information supplied by the Secretariat-General in answer to a questionnaire. The first part of this declaration repeats the NATO formula; the provision of security rules is additional.

lip-service to the international character of the service, and despite the steady consolidation of the Secretariat-General over the past few years, national influences still predominate in recruitment and staff policies, several characteristics of which appear designed to keep within narrow limits the possible growth of SEATO loyalties.

(1) All applicants for posts on the international staff are nominated by member governments; the Secretary-General cannot conduct any direct recruiting. Vacancies are notified to member states six months in advance of the filling of the post; member states are responsible for finding and nominating the candidates, and each puts forward only one nominee. Because of the distances involved there is no means of interviewing candidates. Since mid-1958 appointments for grades I–III (Secretary-General and Deputy Secretary-General, Director and Deputy-Director of Offices) are made by the Council Representatives; for the lower grades they are made by the Secretary-General. But the nomination procedure minimizes opportunities for ensuring the appointment of the best candidate from the point of view of the organization; staff members enter SEATO not only by permission but by virtue of direct support from their own governments.

(2) Some two-thirds of the international staff have been recruited from national public services, most of them seconded for duty with SEATO on leave of absence without pay. Their outlook is molded by the national service which in due course they expect to re-enter, and their careers are unlikely to be greatly influenced by the quality of their performance at SEATO. Because of their background and their future prospects, they are anxious to maintain close links with their home base and with their national embassies at Bangkok. In certain national services—for example, the United States Foreign Service—an officer's work is annually reported upon by his embassy and forms part of his career record; this procedure helps to uphold higher work standards, but it militates against the growth of SEATO loyalties.

(3) Staff contracts are for a fixed term of two or three years only; renewals of contract have so far been few (but have tended to be increasingly frequent in recent years).

(4) Because of this basic rule of short-term contract, even elementary incentives for efficiency and loyalty to the organization do not exist. There are no provisions for a probation period, annual report, salary increments, or promotion prospects. If a promotion were to be made to a higher grade, the candidate would have to be renominated by his own government.

(5) Governments have the power to recall their nationals from the international staff.

Considerations of efficiency alone seem to demand that a nucleus of experienced and permanent staff be built up within the Secretariat-General, especially in those branches of work (political, research) in which intimate acquaintance with the area and the subject matter is a definite advantage. Certainly the policy of governmental nomination and short-term contracts prevents the building up of private empires and helps to keep fresh blood circulating throughout the organization. On health grounds, too, it might be argued that Europeans, at any rate, should not stay longer than two or three years in the climate of Bangkok. But, on the other hand, the current policy leaves too much of the recruitment in the hands of those who are not responsible for the work and maximizes opportunities for political and private pressures. It dissipates the experience built up in the course of the SEATO service and works to the disadvantage of those Asians who come to the organization not highly versed in modern administrative techniques and have to leave soon after acquiring experience of them. Existing staff policies may appear sound to diplomats, who are used to frequent changes of locale and assignment, but they forget that the diplomat, mobile though he may appear, remains throughout within his own organization; assignment to SEATO means entry into a new organization and the readjustment of working habits and political horizons.

Both NATO and CENTO employ officers seconded from national administrations, and invite nominations for some posts, but their Secretaries-General are entitled to conduct direct recruiting, to offer indefinite contracts to the staff, and to hold out prospects of salary increments, promotion, and assistance from provident funds.[30] NATO is already creating a career service; Lord Ismay wrote in 1954: "There will in the course of time be built up a permanent body of international NATO civil servants." [31] The SEATO Secretariat-General is now attaining a size where a career service may well become a necessity, on grounds of both administrative and political efficiency. An international organization limited to a few countries from the same cultural area may be able to maintain a competent and lively staff by drawing upon seconded officers, but institutions comprising states of different cultural histories, political traditions, and educational systems will find it much more difficult to maintain a unity of purpose and build up an *esprit de corps* among their staff. Such institutions call for a career service.[32] SEATO spans countries of completely different cultural background; it includes Western and Asian states, advanced and underdeveloped economies, Christian, Buddhist, and Moslem countries. To bridge the inevitable social and

[30] NATO policy on salary increments has been revised several times; according to the most recent changes (Feb. 26, 1957), most of the officer grades have seven annual increments based on annual reports of satisfactory work; one grade has twelve increments (see NATO, *Staff Rules*).

[31] *NATO—The First Five Years*, p. 64.

[32] A. Loveday uses this argument in his *Reflections on International Administration* (London: Oxford University Press, 1956), p. 41, when he contrasts the recruitment problems facing an organization in one cultural area (the *O.E.E.C.*) with that of an organization cutting across several cultures (the U.N.).

mental differences of its staff SEATO needs a career service. And there is one other consideration. "The more an organization is concerned with international relations or with abstract ideas the greater as a general rule will be its need for career officials with a world outlook." [33] SEATO is first and foremost a political organization; it needs career officers with a broad regional political outlook.

A career service is a way of retaining some of the more experienced SEATO officers and of recruiting young men of exceptional promise, particularly young Asians fresh from university. Direct recruitment of such men by the Secretary-General, combined with carefully planned on-the-job training, could lay the foundations of a permanent SEATO service.

THE DIPLOMATIC MACHINERY

Preliminary negotiation and clarification of national standpoints on all political issues concerning the civil side takes place in the Permanent Working Group. This is a committee of counselors or first secretaries of the seven national missions in Bangkok plus a representative of the Thai Ministry of Foreign Affairs. The Group meets frequently at SEATO headquarters, but for the less important discussions it may be attended by alternates, usually of third secretary rank. The alternates also staff the financial committee, which exercises tight control in budgetary matters.

The Permanent Working Group reports to the Council Representatives. In effect, these are the heads of diplomatic missions of member countries in Bangkok, organized to be convened at short notice but meeting less frequently as more and more of their work is being taken over by the Permanent Working Group and the Secretariat-General. Between meetings of the Council of Foreign Ministers the Council Representatives, nevertheless, remain the supreme policy-making body of the organization; the Secretary-General is no more than their executive agent:

> responsible for the execution and co-ordination, in all Offices of the Secretariat-General, of the policies, programmes and other decisions of the Council and the Council Representatives . . . responsible to the Council when in session and to the Council Representatives at all other times.[34]

The eight Council Representatives and their staffs together constitute the chief political element of the organization,[35] not only by virtue of formal authority but also in terms of personal stature, diplomatic experience,

---

[33] *Ibid.*, pp. 40–41.
[34] Terms of reference of the Secretary-General: information supplied by the Secretariat-General.
[35] Each Council Representative has, in his own embassy, a special staff fully engaged on SEATO affairs. This usually consists of the member and the alternate member of the Permanent Working Group, but some of the embassies have larger SEATO staffs.

and sheer numbers. The Council Representatives are heads of missions of considerable standing, collectively representing a fund of political experience unmatched elsewhere in the organization. Members of the Permanent Working Group, too, are expected to be "of considerable experience" (with alternates of "some experience") and to be fully engaged on SEATO work. The Secretariat-General, by contrast, has no special political division and, apart from the Secretary-General and his Deputy, only a handful of officers of standing and experience comparable with the Permanent Working Group or the Council Representatives.

The influence exercised by the ambassadors and their staff on the day-to-day working of the Secretariat-General is partly a matter of political necessity and partly a matter of historical accident (the Council Representatives were the first operative SEATO organ). Such influence is not a necessary or essential feature of international security organizations. NATO and CENTO, too, have ambassadorial Councils of Permanent Representatives, the majority of whose meetings are devoted to political consultation—in 1956, for example, 66 NATO meetings out of roughly 100 were political. But neither NATO nor CENTO possesses an equivalent of the SEATO Permanent Working Group, a low-level committee that frequently negotiates matters that could be decided by the Secretary-General on his own authority. By contrast, both the NATO and the CENTO Secretariats have their own Political Affairs Divisions which perform most of the functions carried out in SEATO by the Permanent Working Group. In other words, powers elsewhere exercised by the Secretary-General are here allotted to a low-level negotiating body bound by the rule of unanimity. With the appointment of the Secretary-General the power of the Permanent Working Group and even of the Council Representatives has declined—it now meets less frequently and devotes more of its time to matters of political intelligence. The Deputy Secretary-General serves as the chairman of the Group, conducts its discussions, prepares its agenda, and initiates the submission of policy papers; the Secretary-General participates in meetings of the Council Representatives and has on occasions acted as their spokesman. Nevertheless, the tradition of influence on the day-to-day operations of the Secretariat remains.

The other important elements in the SEATO diplomatic machinery are the three expert committees (Committee of Economic Experts, Committee of Security Experts, Committee on Information, Cultural, Education, and Labor Activities) and occasional *ad hoc* committees on special subjects, such as the *Ad Hoc* Committee on Cultural Policy which met in June 1958. The expert committees meet once or twice a year in Bangkok at the SEATO headquarters and report to the Council Representatives. Some thirty-odd delegates attend the average meeting; a large Thai contingent, representatives of Bangkok embassies, but only about a score of medium-level officials from the national capitals. The committees are now beginning to exhibit some continuity in personnel (another element of continuity is provided by the Secretariat-General, which services them), but their effective contribution to SEATO resources and to the increased appreciation of SEATO activities in member countries is still small.

In SEATO's permanent organization all authority flows from the Council of Ministers. The Council meets annually about April (Bangkok, February 1955; Karachi, March 1956; Canberra, March 1957; Manila, March 1958; Wellington, April 1959; Washington, May 1960; Bangkok, March 1961). Under the Manila Treaty, it is so organized as to be able to meet at any time; no such extraordinary meeting has yet occurred, although from time to time, especially during the Laos crisis of 1961, proposals for a meeting were being canvassed; a September 1959 meeting of SEATO Foreign Ministers in Washington was not formally regarded as an extraordinary Council meeting. The Foreign Ministers of member states are members of the Council, but they do not always attend. Australian and New Zealand Foreign Ministers have maintained a steady record of interest in SEATO meetings; the French Foreign Minister, on the other hand, has been to only four of the first eight SEATO ministerial meetings, and the British Foreign Secretary, to five. As SEATO's staunch supporter, Secretary Dulles had by contrast attended every SEATO Council Meeting until 1959. The record of attendance serves as an index of the importance attached to SEATO in member countries.[36]

The Council is authorized to consider matters concerning the implementation of the Treaty and to "provide for consultation with regard to military and any other planning as the situation obtaining in the Treaty area may from time to time require." Some of the consultative functions now devolve upon the Council Representatives and some upon the Secretary-General, but the Council remains the final ratifying body of all SEATO activities and programs. Meeting so infrequently, it cannot effectively control these programs, but its discussions set the tone and create the atmosphere within which SEATO operates.

THE MILITARY FRAMEWORK

The Council of Ministers is also the supreme authority for all military matters coming before the organization; in practice most of its powers in this field are exercised by the half yearly conference of SEATO Military Advisers (customarily attended by the United States Commander-in-Chief, Pacific, the Australian Chief of the General Staff, a British Commander from Singapore, and others).

[36] The attendances by Foreign Ministers and officers of equivalent or higher rank for eight SEATO meetings (1954–1961) were: Australia and New Zealand, eight; Pakistan, Philippines, Thailand, and the United States, seven; the United Kingdom, five; France, four.

Early in the development of the organization the Military Advisers' conferences were supplemented by *ad hoc* meetings of staff planners. The Military Advisers continue to meet and to review military plans and problems, but the more detailed staff planning functions are now carried out in the Military Planning Office, which is in essence a meeting place for delegations of national military planning officers—a conference, in continuous session, of staff planners from branches of the armed forces of member countries concerned with South-East Asia. Somewhat secondarily, project teams of junior planners carry out specific planning tasks.

Combined within the Military Planning Office are a lower-level negotiating element, the Senior Planners' Committee (which roughly parallels the civil diplomatic machinery just discussed) and a more distinctly international body of administrative and junior planning officers (which resembles the Secretariat-General). The basic elements of the civilian administration are thus repeated, in a more primitive form, in the military sector of the organization.

The Office was established on March 1, 1957, in the same Bangkok headquarters building as the Secretariat-General. It consists of a chief (a Filipino, a New Zealander, and an Australian, each a general officer, have already served in that capacity) and deputy chief, eight national senior planners (senior colonels, heads of national military delegations as it were), over a dozen other national planners (colonels or lieutenant-colonels, one or two from each member state), and a military secretariat of six commissioned officers and some clerical staff. The Office is smaller than the civil side of SEATO, the powers of its chiefs more restricted than those of the Secretary-General, and most of its members, unlike the staff of the Secretariat-General, are directly accountable to their national authorities.

The foundation of the Office marked a new stage in the evolution of the SEATO military organization and a distinct advance upon the earlier practice of *ad hoc* meetings in various corners of the Treaty Area. This slow and gradual advance may conceivably continue in some fields: the powers of the chief of the Office have already been increased in procedural and administrative matters; the conference system of military planning may, in the interest of efficiency, be further streamlined; and eventually an entirely international planning staff may be created. The habit of cooperation, which is emerging in Bangkok, may attenuate the nation-centered spirit of each delegation. The deteriorating security situation in Laos and South Vietnam may call for new organizational developments. But the stark facts that have so far limited development of the military machinery are still there: the wide disparity between the military power of the United States and the forces which the other members are capable of mustering in the Treaty Area, the preoccupation with security questions, and the unwillingness to disclose information in a wide forum. The Office constitutes the military core of the organization, but it represents only a small addition to SEATO's operational resources.

Financial resources now available to the SEATO permanent organization amount to just over one million United States dollars per annum. Most of this comes from cash contributions by member states calculated according to a formula, first used in the 1958–1959 budget, by which the United States contributes 25 percent, the United Kingdom 16 percent, Australia and France 13.5 percent each, and the other members 8 percent each of the Common Budget.[37] SEATO's resources are comparable with those of CENTO, but are smaller than NATO's, whose budget alone reached 3,600,000 United States dollars in 1954. The size of SEATO's material resources does not permit substantial programs.

The growth of the permanent organization has been delayed by the reluctance of governments to invest it with powers. Once the United States announced its opposition to a SEATO military command on the model of NATO, it became a matter of indifference to some governments whether the guarantees embodied in the Manila Treaty should be supplemented by a permanent organization. Yet once a headquarters location was agreed upon and the practice of ambassadorial consultation was established in Bangkok, the logic of events imposed the need to set up organs of international administration, even if the process of growth was to be slowed down by governmental disagreement. Two among the member states, the United States and New Zealand (the largest and the smallest of them), were among those willing to see the permanent organization expand. The other governments were, for various reasons, cautious. Britain and France were unprepared to engage more resources in an area in which their national commitments were declining; others still —Thailand, Pakistan, and even Australia—were wary of rashly expanding the powers of an organization of untried value that might yet grow beyond the control of the smaller members. Paradoxically, perhaps, they favored an expansion of SEATO's activities but were reluctant to grant greater powers to the Secretary-General.

Support for the permanent organization (as distinct from support for the alliance as such) seems confined to a narrow section of the member countries' public. Outside Bangkok few people know of the existence of SEATO headquarters; awareness of the organization and its activities is limited mostly to officials who have come into contact with it through their work. Official circles alone (some military leaders, foreign affairs officers, security experts) could be expected to act to promote SEATO purposes within the governmental machine. In the short period since its inception SEATO has not succeeded in establishing much contact outside government circles, though travels by the Secretary-General and his staff and programs such as the various cultural undertakings are now promoting wider knowledge of the organization.

In Bangkok itself SEATO enjoys the hospitality and cordial welcome of the Thai Government; its international staff have been formally accorded diplomatic privileges and are customarily given the usual cour-

[37] Information supplied by the Secretariat-General.

tesies (invitations to official functions, and so forth) by the Foreign Affairs Ministry, the embassies of member states and some other, chiefly West European, diplomatic missions. Its political position is now secure; but when in 1956–1958 the SEATO alliance and the American link were under attack in Thailand, the permanent organization did not escape abuse either. Some of its members became targets of personal attacks.[38] Apart from the member countries in South-East Asia, the organization has so far had few sources of support. It has no permanent contact, for instance, with South-East Asian diplomatic missions in Bangkok, but in the Laotian crises of late 1959 and 1961 Laotian officials found no difficulty in establishing links with the SEATO headquarters, the Foreign Minister conferring with the Secretary-General in one case, and the Laotian Ambassador submitting a request in another.

Staffed by government officials, controlled by diplomatic committees, financed from government contributions, commanding no widespread support outside official circles, the permanent organization necessarily is responsive first and above all to the wishes and demands of member governments as formulated by the respective foreign offices, in so far as they do not offset each other in the process of negotiation. The organization itself has as yet only rudimentary interests of its own.

Within this framework the interests of the United States, the leading and the most important member of the alliance, receive their full share of attention. They are powerfully voiced within the diplomatic machinery and are backed by the substantial contribution the United States makes to SEATO's material and political resources. The American delegation has inspired a number of important SEATO programs, and Americans play a key part in SEATO military activities such as the organization of exercises. But for the United States, too, South-East Asia is merely one among the regions in which foreign policy has to be conducted; United States policy-makers give it only a part of their attention. And here lies the opportunity which the other members have not let pass unexploited; Americans, too, have used it in a far-sighted way. They have, for instance, gone out of their way to leave the actual running of the Secretariat-General and the Military Planning Office in the hands of the other members. (An unwritten rule in Secretariat appointments has been to restrict the number of American representatives. For instance, in July 1958 or in January 1961 only two out of the international staff of about forty were United States citizens.) Nor can the United States carry its proposals without enlisting the active cooperation of other members, such as the United Kingdom or the Asian states.

As the organization is an instrument of member governments, it

---

[38] For instance, the Cultural Officer became the target of a smear campaign in the *Khao Pharb* (issues of March 14, 1958 and following), the purpose of which was to discredit SEATO and its cultural program. Together with several other newspapers suspected of being financed from abroad, the *Khao Pharb* was closed down after Marshal Sarit's second *coup*.

cannot force anything upon unwilling states. As in all cooperative under-takings, members do agree on occasions to steps they would not have ini-tiated and do not welcome enthusiastically; but never can action be taken to which any of them objects strongly.

The Activities of   Two types of international action can be de-
SEATO   scribed as SEATO activities: first, those of
SEATO as an international actor (primarily such activities of the permanent organization as Council meetings or operations of the Bangkok organs); and second, those of member states in their capacity as signatories of the Manila Pact, in support of SEATO's objectives and with the concurrence of all members—activities such as participation in a SEATO exercise, support for a threatened member country or a Protocol state, hospitality for a SEATO event. The distinction is not always sharp, but it is useful for purposes of discussion. (Activities of other kinds, principally member states' foreign-policy operations in the Treaty Area, do not fall within the scope of membership obligations, which are not discussed.)

The dominant note of SEATO's activities is caution, a caution at-tributable to the modesty of its resources, the supremacy of governmen-tal interests within it, and to its sensitivity to criticism from member and non-member countries alike. On occasion, caution has verged on timid-ity.

The permanent organization operates in the three areas in which multilateral action can further the objectives of the alliance: it serves as a center of consultation, performs functions aimed at strengthening the alliance, and carries out multilateral programs for the benefit of member states. In all these fields multilateral action was begun after unilateral or bilateral action proved inadequate. Action is always taken solely through member governments; the organization never deals directly with the public of member states.

CONSULTATION

On South-East Asian issues, political contact between member gov-ernments is maintained on a practically permanent basis by the Bangkok diplomatic machinery. The Permanent Working Group meets several times a week and the Council Representatives at least once a month (forty-eight meetings in 1960; seventeen in 1958; nineteen in 1957; twen-ty-four in 1956). But consultation of only the less important kind takes place within these two groups, which are forums for the confidential ex-change of views and information about developments in the Treaty Area and for the early communication and explanation of national attitudes. The lack of political discussion has been partly a consequence and partly a cause of the excessive attention paid by the Bangkok diplomatic machinery to the day-to-day running of the Secretariat-General. The Permanent Working Group has been preoccupied with administrative details—every ·international staff appointment, for example, has to pass through a process of negotiation governed by the rule of unanimity—and consequently has had less time for political consultation and planning.

Consultation of a higher order, such as discussions with the view to adopting a common standpoint on world issues or negotiations on issues of national policy, does not appear to be part of the work of the SEATO diplomatic machinery. Not even the annual meetings of the Council of Ministers fulfill that function; they are occasions for reviewing the reports of SEATO organs and expressing broad national positions on the political problems of the Treaty Area; little concrete negotiation actually takes place within them.

A typical Council meeting has the following agenda:

    I. Public Opening Session
    II. Election of Chairman
    III. Approval of Agenda
    IV. Exchange of views on matters affecting the Treaty Area
    V. Consideration of the Classified Report
        Recommendations of the Council Representatives and proposals by Member Governments
    VI. Consideration of the Report and Recommendations of the Military Advisers
    VII. Other Business
    VIII. Approval of Communiqué
    IX. Public Closing Session.[39]

Items II, III, VII, and IX are, of course, purely formal, and speeches at the public opening session rarely contain forthright statements of national positions. Most of the real discussion, including heated and frank exchanges on such subjects as economic assistance or attitudes to neutralism, occurs under Item IV. The former Classified Report of the Council Representatives (Item V) has since the 1959 Council been split into two: the Report of the Council Representatives, which contains an agreed collective assessment of developments in the Treaty Area and recommendations for future SEATO activities, programs, and the Budget; and the Report of the Secretary-General, which reviews all aspects of the work of the civilian organization.[40] SEATO Councils conducted much of their business in full plenary sessions, but at the Wellington meeting the

[39] Agenda for the Canberra Council meeting, March 11–13, 1957, *Current Notes on International Affairs* (Canberra), xxviii (Mar. 1957), 235.
[40] Both these reports are classified, but the Secretary-General issues a public report on the work of the organization.

Council adopted the practice of more intimate meetings of ministers accompanied by only one or two advisers. These have yet to prove their worth as opportunities for effective high-level negotiation.

When the Councils are not in session, the Bangkok organization and the normal diplomatic machinery serve as the channels of consultation. A number of reasons have in the past limited the use of the Bangkok organization, an important one being the dearth of serious crises in the Treaty Area since the end of the Indochinese war. On the Formosan offshore crises of 1955 and 1958, the 1957 settlement in Laos, troubles on the Burmese border, and the Indonesian rebellion of 1958, SEATO did not provide the forum for top-level consultation. In the case of Indonesia, members were reluctant to use the machinery even for an exchange of views. Despite the efforts of the Philippines, among others, to secure an agreed SEATO assessment of the matter, no progress of any description was achieved, partly because of basic political disagreement on the best ways of dealing with the problem, and partly because of the limitations of SEATO membership.

Increasing concern over Laos since 1959 has intensified the use of the Bangkok organization and has shown some of its limitations. The Bangkok organization kept in touch with events in Laos and its consultations helped to evolve a SEATO view of the situation. But a conference of ambassadors in a remote post (remote from the great power capitals where the important decisions are made) was not and could not become the venue for high-level discussions. Bangkok may have been somewhat better informed of events on the spot, and if it were not, it should have been; its consultative machinery can conquer its handicap of remoteness from the centers of power and communication only by exploiting its favorable location at the heart of the Treaty Area and by making the SEATO headquarters a regional center for the collation of information and its authoritative interpretation and discussion—authoritative because based on a more intimate acquaintance with regional conditions.

The Laotian crises demonstrated a trend that had been evident for some time: the importance of Washington, London, and Paris as SEATO's key consultative centers.[41] At the beginning of the organization SEATO's regional character was emphasized and efforts were made to locate such activities as Council and Committee meetings, and the headquarters, in the Treaty Area. But the realities of SEATO's power distribution soon asserted themselves as the important decisions continued to be made in the capitals of the great powers, especially in Washington. All

[41] NATO, too, has its personality split between Paris and Washington: although the North Atlantic Council, the Secretariat, and the European Command all have their headquarters in Paris, the three-power (United States, United Kingdom, France) Standing Group "the superior body responsible for the highest strategic guidance . . . to which the NATO Supreme Commanders are responsible" and the Military Committee in Permanent Session both meet in Washington. A Standing Group representative maintains liaison with Paris.

SEATO states maintain excellent communications with the United States and frequently send their most able ambassadors to Washington, so that it is inevitable that a large part of SEATO's business should be transacted there. Thus for certain purposes, especially for securing American support on the one hand and for canvassing American policies on the other, a conference of SEATO ambassadors at Washington is more effective than Bangkok's machinery. In late 1957, for instance, Secretary Dulles reported to SEATO ambassadors the results of the NATO meeting in Paris and asked member nations to recommend means for close liaison between treaty organizations; in the Formosan crisis of 1958 Dulles explained the American position to a similar meeting; during the Laos crisis of 1959 SEATO ambassadors met several times, their continuous consultations culminating in the extraordinary Council meeting of September. Putting these Washington meetings on a permanent basis (and linking them with Bangkok) might conceivably streamline SEATO's consultative procedures more than the establishment of closer liaison with NATO and CENTO. Washington is and will remain the king-pin of alliance systems. But the Laotian crises, in which an important role was played by Britain (as Co-Chairman of the Geneva conference), and by France, also showed that London and Paris remained key consultative centers.

In military consultation the supreme organ is the meeting of Military Advisers, which guides and directs allied military activities. Some of the detailed planning work is still done at meetings of lower level *ad hoc* committees such as in the *Ad Hoc* Military Intelligence Committee which met in November 1957 for the purpose of "revising previous assessments of the military threat to the Treaty Area," [42] or the Committee of Logistics Experts, which meets to discuss problems of moving large formations of troops in the Treaty Area.[43] Most of it, however, is now performed in the Military Planning Office, which is emerging as the most important SEATO center for the preliminary negotiation of agreed military plans. The initial drafts of these plans are prepared by project teams composed of "junior" national planners, one of which might be assigned to study or draw up the program for a military exercise, the comprehensive plan for the defense of a certain area, or the draft terms of reference for a new office or command. The particular project will have been selected from the six-monthly work schedule of some score of tasks approved for the Office by the Military Advisers. The agreed draft is then submitted to the Senior Planners' Committee, who work it over thoroughly and at length, comparing it in particular with national plans providing for a comparable event (without, however, disclosing their contents to their colleagues). Once unanimous agreement is reached, the draft plan or project is forwarded for the approval of the Chief of the

42 SEATO Press Release No. 99, Nov. 27, 1957.
43 *Ibid.*, No. 169, Aug. 17, 1959.

Military Planning Office and is then placed on the agenda of the next meeting of Military Advisers, unless there is need for more urgent action, when the Senior Planner for each country communicates directly with his Military Adviser to secure concurrence of action. After the plan has been approved at all levels, including political, it is incorporated into the planning of the national services. A large part of the military consultative function thus consists of the negotiation, particularly in Bangkok, of agreed contingency plans (and of such related and more technical matters as the logistics, communications, and training they imply). This has been a time-consuming process, registering "steady, rather than spectacular" progress, yet becoming with the passage of time, "more realistic and more effective." [44]

Consultation and coordination of allied action also occurs in the three expert committees. The Economic Experts Committee, hampered by disagreements about SEATO's role in supplying foreign aid, was for a time less successful. It explored in some detail a number of modest though useful projects in fields where the defense effort impinges on the economic system (by creating skilled labor shortages, or requiring special industrial and repair facilities) but has proved unsuitable as a forum for discussing general aid requests. In 1958 the Committee began to study the Communist "economic offensive" in the Treaty Area in order to assist member governments in taking counter-measures; it has since proposed and seen through a number of small-scale technical assistance projects. The Economic Services Office of the Secretariat-General, created at the Karachi Council of 1956 but plagued by frequent changes in personnel, has not so far left its mark on the organization.

The Committee on Information, Cultural, Education, and Labor Activities has been more active, but its work seems to have been restricted to reviewing the work of the SEATO Public and Cultural Relations Programs. It mobilizes and coordinates national support for these programs, and has also had the task of discussing from time to time the character, extent, and effectiveness of Communist propaganda activities in the Treaty Area.

The most interesting of the three appears to be the Committee of Security Experts. Composed of members of national police forces and intelligence services, the Committee meets twice a year to exchange information and to make recommendations to the Council Representatives. Its terms of reference specify that:

> on the intelligence side the Committee shall identify, assess and exchange information on the nature and extent of the threat of Communist subversion, internal and external, to the Treaty Area. There should also be a pooling of experience as to how security forces can best be employed and

[44] From Sir Henry Wells's address to the Bangkok Military Advisers' Meeting, SEATO Press Release No. 77, Sept. 19, 1957.

which measures have been found to be most effective against Communist subversion.

In its advisory capacity, the Committee shall make recommendations regarding fields in which it considers measures are, or are likely to be, necessary to combat Communist subversion. Where appropriate, it should also suggest possible counter-measures for the consideration of the Council Representatives and through them of other organs of SEATO.[45]

The Committee's twice yearly surveys of the internal security situation in the Treaty Area form the background against which agreed recommendations are made for countering subversion. Between sessions the Director of the Security Office in the Secretariat-General serves as liaison officer and ensures continuity in Committee activities and programs. He also acts as a clearing office for the exchange of information and deals with inquiries on subversion problems. His office has not, however, become the center of an inter-country intelligence system for keeping track of spies, agents, and potential saboteurs, such as was reportedly envisaged by Dulles in the formative stage of the SEATO organization.[46]

SEATO's system of consultation for Security Experts is unequal to the task of controlling "subversion" in its broad political sense, either in member countries or elsewhere in the Treaty Area. First, medium-level official committees can hardly deal effectively with matters which in several states are among the most sensitive of political issues. To confess, in an open meeting, to glaring weaknesses in political organization and to agree to having them discussed by a group of several countries without reaping, in exchange, concrete benefits is more than can be expected of most governments. SEATO, moreover, deals only with the Treaty Area; "subversive activities," say in the United States, are outside its scope; hence meetings of the Committee suffer from a basic inequality, for in it the great powers in effect claim to discuss the most intimate affairs of the small states in a large forum. Not surprisingly, the smaller countries have been unwilling to develop this procedure, even on the technical level on which it is most often conducted in SEATO consultations. Discussions of the affairs of other countries not represented in SEATO can be little more than theoretical and cannot fail to annoy, for once again they amount to an assumption of superiority. It would thus seem that "anti-subversion" activities can be undertaken fruitfully either by a strong organization which can offer substantial aid or else as the result of bilateral negotiations in which the inferiority implicit in the procedure is offset by tangible benefits and intimacy of relations. SEATO fits neither of these prescriptions.

---

[45] Information supplied by the Secretariat-General. Note that the terms of reference specify "Communist" subversion.
[46] U.P. dispatch from Washington, *Bangkok Post*, Jan. 6, 1955.

STRENGTHENING THE ALLIANCE

Within the permanent organization, primary responsibility for strengthening the alliance by publicizing SEATO activities belongs to the Public Relations Officer. His job is difficult. The idea of collective security or of defensive alliance with the United States meets with varied degrees of indifference or opposition in member countries and in the Treaty Area. The Public Relations Program must be tailored to fit the needs of audiences in geographically and culturally separate countries, some of which do not have the facilities for using public relations materials. And finally, it is the cardinal (and often frustrating) principle of this work that the message of SEATO and its activities shall be disseminated by member governments in their own territories in the way *they* consider most appropriate.

The Public Relations Officer produces and supplies to member governments a range of publications to explain the SEATO purposes and activities: pamphlets setting out the basic facts about SEATO. "Know your SEATO Partner" leaflets, texts of SEATO annual reports, wallsheets, posters, etc., in English, Thai, Urdu, and Bengali—a total of twenty-four publications in 1957 with a total of over one million copies. He arranges for SEATO events to be filmed and for films to explain SEATO purposes. He prepares radio programs and, following the appointment of a Radio Officer, has expanded the range of radio work. He issues press releases on all SEATO occasions, principally for the Bangkok press but also for distribution in member countries.

There is room for doubt whether materials thus produced for use by member governments are in fact used efficiently. Even if the material were well distributed by the member countries' information services, it is doubtful whether Western-type publicity methods are the most suitable for reaching audiences in underdeveloped countries where information and news spread through personal, "face-to-face," communication networks.

The cultural activities, also, help to strengthen the alliance. The holding of seminars and the award of research fellowships and scholarships increase the awareness of SEATO among member countries and enhance cultural contact among them. But their effect can only be marginal; the most effective instrument for strengthening the alliance is the Secretary-General himself.

The Secretary-General, as it were, personifies SEATO. He is most closely and personally interested in its welfare. In Bangkok he speaks for the organization and is its representative *vis-à-vis* the Thai Government. When traveling in member countries he "sells" new programs to governments, establishes contact with non-governmental bodies, and tries to explain SEATO and its purposes to lukewarm, indifferent, or even hostile audiences. His actions are scrutinized for the light they may throw on SEATO's intentions. He carefully explores ways and means of increasing alliance membership.

Maintaining the unity of the alliance is thus one of the Secretary-General's most important duties, but the entire burden of preserving it does not rest upon his shoulders. Just as important for counteracting the disintegrative processes at work in every alliance is national action, such as the display of respect and attention by national leaders to symbols representing the joint purposes or the forthright and unremitting explanation and advocacy of the common objectives to all sectors of national opinion.

SEATO OPERATIONS

The permanent organization conducts a research service, an "exposure" program, a cultural program, and military planning. The four operations cost approximately 500,000 United States dollars in 1958, but although small in scale they are examples of truly multilateral operations by an alliance organization. In themselves they are not impressive, but they lend some substance to SEATO's regional and international personality.

The Research Services Office of the Secretariat-General, the largest office of the Secretariat, with an international staff of fourteen, receives, collates, and evaluates overt and classified information on current developments in Communist policy and tactics. It works primarily on the basis of overt raw source material such as from radio monitoring, press reading, overt research material, and reports supplied by member governments and such other classified materials "as can be made available to it." Acquisition of material from other than member governments is restricted to publications and other overt materials; [47] hence the Research Services Office is not an intelligence service with facilities for independent collection of covert information.

As a research center the office leaves something to be desired: it works almost entirely on second-hand material gathered not specifically for SEATO purposes, and its staff turnover leaves little opportunity for area or language specialization (but there is now some provision for field research trips). The library, intended as a place of reference on all aspects of Communism and as a repository of information on South-East Asia, has been under-financed.

The materials collected serve as the basis for three types of publication distributed to member governments: the forthnightly *Trends and Highlights* (in 1958 issued in 800 copies); the occasional *Background*

---

[47] Terms of Reference, Research Services Office. Information supplied by the Secretariat-General.

Briefs, and special studies prepared on the request of Council Representatives or of the Security Experts Committee. *Trends and Highlights* regularly describes and analyzes trends in the internal and external activities of the Communist system. It emphasizes events in South-East Asia, in China, India, and Japan (developments in member countries are skipped over very lightly), but scrutinizes policies the world over for the light they might throw on Communist strategy in the Treaty Area. Reports are intended to be useful and practical rather than academic: they do not provide strikingly new information for policy-makers, say, in Washington or London, but should be useful as background information for government officials in the Treaty Area.

Some of the studies undertaken by the Research Services Office supply material to the Public Relations Office for the preparation of pamphlets "exposing" Communist tactics, with the aim of increasing public awareness of the dangers of Communism. One of these pamphlets, *Communist Aims in Education* (1958), for instance, described Communist methods of infiltrating schools and student movements.[48] Material for several exposure pamphlets was provided by the two Seminars on Countering Communist Subversion held under SEATO auspices in the Philippines in November 1957 and in Pakistan in February 1960, occasions on which experts, scholars, and officials from member countries exchanged views on Communist techniques and activities.

The cultural program, like the research service or the exposure program, is an effect a multilaterally conceived and operated aid scheme for the Treaty Area countries. It is also an interesting instance of a rapid expansion of SEATO operations. The original function of the SEATO Cultural Officer was to review bilateral cultural contacts of member countries and to encourage exchanges, particularly among Asian members. But as he found these contacts and exchanges to be practically non-existent he planned, and succeeded in securing support for, a whole series of activities organized and financed by SEATO. One of the first items in the cultural program was the Bangkok (February 1958) "Round Table" discussion by eminent scholars on problems of the impact of technological change on traditional cultures. A feature of this event was the participation of two Indians, a Japanese, and a Vietnamese scholar, in addition to experts from member countries.[49] More continuous in nature have been the Research Fellowship and other programs for nationals of member countries to study and undertake research on some useful and practical problems of interest to South-East Asia. Among the first awards

---

[48] SEATO publications have stressed "the problem of China" and publicized, for example, the hardships of the commune system—see, e.g., the illustrated pamphlet *Life in the Commune,* 1959.

[49] A record of this conference was published as *The South-East Asian Round Table: A Symposium on Traditional Culture and Technological Progress in South-East Asia* (Bangkok: SEATO, 1959).

were grants for research on hydroponics, on corrosion in tropical conditions, and on methods of immunization in underdeveloped countries, and for one-year post-graduate studies by nationals of one Asian country at the university of another Asian member. By the end of 1960 SEATO had awarded forty-four research fellowships, some fifty post-graduate and eighty undergraduate scholarships, and nine SEATO professorships. Following recommendations of the 1958 *Ad Hoc* Committee on Cultural Policy, these programs will be continued for the next few years; conferences have been arranged on problems facing universities in South-East Asia.

The only other centralized operation carried out by the SEATO permanent organization is military planning, here meaning the work of the special project teams previously alluded to in connection with military planning pure and simple (as distinct from later negotiation of these plans in the Senior Planners' Committee). It is the only continuous international operation carried out in the SEATO military field. The planners now also make regular "area familiarization trips" in Thailand to back up their planning work by acquaintance with the terrain. Military plans prepared at the Office are continuously revised in the light of new developments. (The other SEATO military activities with a short-lived international element are the exercises, in the course of which armed forces of various countries are placed under a single command; here are the rudiments of a SEATO command headquarters.)

The prospects of a permanent SEATO command have for long remained poor: the United States was unwilling to tie down a section of its Pacific forces to specific duties in one part only of the "Chinese Front," and the Commonwealth partners preferred not to designate the Far Eastern Strategic Reserve as a SEATO force for fear of political difficulties in Malaya. Nevertheless, the Asian powers' demand for this command, strong in 1954–1955, less prominent since 1956, has once again revived with the toughening of Chinese policies. Laotian developments, too, have for the first time created conditions in which a command may be put in charge of an emergency force intended to control internal security or to combat the intervention, let us say, of North Vietnamese "volunteers." The 1959 Wellington Council meeting reportedly agreed that the establishment of a SEATO command structure should be accepted in principle, and the Military Planning Office was instructed to examine and report upon it. The command has not yet been created, but plans seem to be ready and they could help to speed up action in emergencies. The forces earmarked for use in emergencies (sometimes referred to as a "fire brigade") and for which the command would be responsible do not appear to be stationed close to the danger areas; they are units normally positioned, say, in the Philippines, in Malaya, Okinawa, and Australia, but capable of being transported to a danger spot in a matter of hours or days. Two or three divisions would seem to be the maximum strength of an emergency SEATO force, but they could be speedily reinforced. At

Wellington the Military Planning Office was directed to get from the member states a firm indication of contributions they would supply to such a force.

The setting up of an observer team to watch the situation in Laos for signs of external intervention has been another function the SEATO organization has been asked to assume in past Laotian crises and which it might be called upon to perform on some future occasion. A proposal to dispatch a SEATO observer team to Laos was first made by Thai representatives in September 1959 (although the idea was publicly mentioned for the first time by a Lao official in January of that year). The motivation of the proposal must have been twofold: to find out what is actually taking place in the inaccessible regions where Vietminh troops were alleged to have entered Laos; and to give moral support to the Laotian Government and to find out the nature of the assistance it might require. Nothing came of the proposal, and some of the other member nations and Britain in particular must have argued that the appointment of a U.N. Security Council Sub-Committee obviated the necessity for a separate SEATO mission.

The Thais appear to have proposed the dispatch of a SEATO observer team to Laos once again in the weeks preceding the November 1960 meeting of Military Advisers, but the project seems to have been dropped almost instantly. It became a serious issue, however, when on January 23, 1961, the Lao Ambassador in Bangkok called on the Secretary-General and submitted to him, on an exploratory basis, a tentative appeal for the dispatch of SEATO observers to Laos "to see for themselves the extent of Communist intervention there." The request appeared reasonably plausible; SEATO had proclaimed itself responsible for Laos; members of it disagreed about the state of affairs in the country; a mission might be a way of securing more reliable information and a means of demonstrating support, too.

Aware of the state of feeling within the organization, Pote Sarasin right from the start poured cold water on the proposal, "one of the several approaches" to the problem of Laos. When it came up for discussion at meetings of Council Representatives, only two countries supported it warmly (presumably Thailand and the United States), but Britain and France alone were against it. When a reply was finally sent on February 16, it was understood to be couched in terms unattractive to the Laotian Government; SEATO agreed to appoint observers provided the group was composed of officials of SEATO nations already in Laos. The message was barely dispatched when Pote Sarasin was assuring the press that SEATO observers were not really necessary; the Laotian proposals for a neutral nations' commission would serve the same purpose even better.[50]

---

[50] See *Bangkok Post*, Jan. 25, 27, Feb. 11, 17, 21, 1961.

The offer to appoint an observer mission can, therefore, have been little more than an attempt at saving face in view of mounting criticism of SEATO's ineffectiveness. Given the internal disagreements about Laos, one could not have expected it to act more promptly. But may not these disagreements show that, as at present constituted, SEATO has inherent difficulty in fulfilling its undertakings? A SEATO observer team in Laos could have had a usefulness separate from the functions of, for instance, a United Nations or a neutral countries' commission. It would neither "investigate" nor "mediate"; its purpose would be to assist SEATO organs in reaching agreed decisions and primarily to manifest SEATO's determination to support the country. The delays in deciding upon the dispatch of observers highlighted the absence of this determination and held little encouragement for the future of SEATO operations,[51] and they have since been used as the justification for demanding changes in SEATO's operating procedures. Unanimity has so far been the rule, but, as Thailand and the Philippines have argued, one or two countries should not have the right to veto collective action, especially in procedural matters. They must have pointed out that in the Security Council in 1959 the Soviet Union was ruled out of order when it attempted to veto the procedural resolution on sending an inquiry mission to Laos.

A SEATO command and a SEATO observer team would have been the first real instances of SEATO operations, for the programs so far carried out at SEATO headquarters do not add up to significant proportions. The Secretary-General himself is, of course, a primary source of SEATO operations; he represents SEATO and the Council Representatives, undertakes missions on their behalf, issues press and public statements, and receives requests from non-member nations. During the Laotian crises he has frequently been in touch with Laotian officials. But the powers of his office, his own inclinations, and the weaknesses and the divisions within his organization have prevented him from making of his post what Paul-Henri Spaak did in NATO.

Can SEATO's central operations be expanded? NATO's operations are, of course, wider, but for reasons which are not paralleled in SEATO: they cover, amongst other things, defense production and the building of infrastructure (of airfields, pipelines, etc.), scientific and technical cooperation, and civil emergency planning, but they are grounded in the greater cooperative defense work of NATO's members.

[51] In the Thai view as formulated by the well-informed Theh Chongkhadikij of the *Bangkok Post* (Mar. 25, 1961): "Although a final formula was sufficiently agreed upon to produce a reply to Vientiane with terms and suggestions requiring a response from the Government of the protocol state, the intervening three weeks indicated such divergent views on Laos, despite fundamental agreement on the seriousness of the situation, that there was talk of necessity to make certain revisions in the Treaty. It is felt now that there is no use in revising the Treaty because revision could still not change attitudes, positions and interests of the individual members."

SEATO's joint defense effort is small and for this reason, too, its centralized operations will remain limited.

The scope of SEATO's centralized work cannot be expanded by adding to it economic functions. Economic cooperation in the Treaty Area cannot be based on SEATO's membership. Nor is a politico-military agency a suitable substitute for, or even supplement to, the Colombo Plan or the United Nations' organs. NATO, too, has had to come to terms with the established European economic agencies, the Organization for European Economic Cooperation and the Economic Commission for Europe, and decided against duplicating their functions. Like NATO, SEATO will remain a "functionally specific" organization, limited to guaranteeing, mobilizing, and channeling support to states wishing to utilize it but unsuited to become a multi-purpose international organization in an area as yet politically divided.

The scope of SEATO's activities is, nevertheless, even narrower than that of NATO's, principally because SEATO is less of a cooperative and more of an assistance type of enterprise. In NATO the benefits and the obligations are shared fairly equally. In SEATO the disparity between the great and small powers is sharper and the differentiation greater because none of the three great powers has its own homeland and nerve centers close to South-East Asia. Most of SEATO's concrete operations, therefore, represent a one-way traffic of help to area states and not a two-way cooperative enterprise. To illustrate: post-Sputnik, the United States discovered a new interest in sharing its scientific achievements with its allies, and NATO became an important vehicle of scientific cooperation—the NATO states other than America each making a valuable contribution to the common pool. But although initially American planners thought of extending this arrangement to SEATO, it soon became obvious that this would have been fruitless. The three small Asian states could hardly contribute to American scientific resources, nor did they require greater scientific assistance than they were receiving under existing schemes. As long as the small area states are underdeveloped and militarily and technically weak, and as long as membership is what it now is, the scope of SEATO cooperation will remain small.

NATIONAL OPERATIONS

The most important national operation in implementing the Manila Treaty is armed assistance for a member state threatened with aggression. Fortunately for all, the need for such assistance has not yet arisen, but until war ceases to be a possibility to be reckoned with in world political calculations, states will have to guard against it, in part by seeking refuge in alliances. As long as the threat of war remains, a key component of national operations in support of SEATO will be demonstrations of capacity and willingness to give armed assistance.

In SEATO, member states have been showing this willingness and capacity in several ways. They have refashioned and standardized the training of their armed forces to facilitate their employment in the tropical jungle conditions of mainland South-East Asia and in joint emergency operations of small but mobile striking forces. They have replanned the building of their military facilities to help in the movement of allied armed forces in the Treaty Area. Particular attention has been paid to the construction of airfields, of naval, transport, and telecommunications facilities. They have redrawn national military plans to conform with the general SEATO concept of operations and with its periodic intelligence evaluations. Finally, they have helped each other, bilaterally, to attain these aims (that is, the great powers have assisted the small states in adjusting their military policies).

As tests of capacity and willingness to help, SEATO's military exercises have been peculiarly valuable. They have revealed what each member state intends to contribute to the common defense. They have tested the combat readiness of allied military forces and their ability to cooperate in emergency conditions. They have raised military standards by exposing the armies of the small states to the high quality combat readiness of the units of the great powers. They have shown SEATO to be a living organization. And although at first they have aroused opposition, especially from Indonesia (which officially protested about naval exercises close to its shore), for the display of naval and military power is a traditional method of showing strength, they have by now become a regular and accepted part of Treaty Area activities.

Member states have taken part in three kinds of SEATO exercises. The most important of these have been ground-air exercises in Thailand, each of which was designed to prove and to test the capacity and willingness of the United States and the other allies to aid Thailand in case of an invasion from the north. They have shown progressively higher standards of performance and would facilitate deployment of allied contingents in Thailand.

In March 1961 a command post exercise centered on Udorn, northeast Thailand, assumed a new theme; simulating the air movement of troops to an area of civil disturbances and internal war, exercise *Rajata* in effect acted out problems that would be encountered during an intervention in Laos. Opening the exercise, Marshal Sarit called it "a timely test of our ability to assemble and operate the key SEATO headquarters needed to command and control our ground and air defense forces." [52]

The second group of exercises are combined amphibious operations between United States and other national contingents in the Treaty Area. At first American units have trained only with Filipino forces (as in *Phiblink* [1957], a major amphibious exercise involving sea and landing operations and tactical air support with the simulated use of atomic

[52] *Bangkok Post,* Mar. 10, 1961.

weapons, and *Halang Dagat* [1959], a Filipino-sponsored harbor defense exercise in the Manila Bay to demonstrate the feasibility of a combined SEATO force's taking over the active defense of a harbor against submarines and a surface invasion fleet). But in June 1959, in *Saddle Up*, United States Marines exercised with a British battalion from Malaya on the coast of North Borneo, to show the ability of a "small highly trained and determined SEATO force to act with devastating speed and decision"; [53] and in April–May 1961 six thousand American, British, and Australian troops, accompanied by a task force of sixty ships and one hundred aircraft, staged another amphibious landing exercise on the beaches of North Borneo.

The third group covers naval exercises pure and simple. Designed to ensure Western control of the sea lanes in times of war, they are held annually in the triangle between Singapore, Manila, and Bangkok. They help the United States and Commonwealth navies to train together to standardize naval procedures and to cooperate under emergency conditions. They test defense readiness of allied fleets and convoys against submarine, air, and mine attack.

The SEATO exercises (and, by inference, SEATO military planning) have dealt with Treaty Area military problems pure and simple, but have not touched on such problems as the interdependence of South-East Asia with military developments farther north. The Americans regard:

> the Chinese Communist front . . . as an entirety because if the Chinese Communists engage in open armed aggression this would probably mean that they have decided on general war in Asia. They would then have to take into account the mutual defense treaties of the United States with the Republic of Korea and the Republic of China, and the forces maintained under them. Thus general war would confront the Chinese Communists with tasks at the south, center and north, tasks that would strain their inadequate means of transportation.[54]

This means that because of United States membership of SEATO the other SEATO members can expect Communist Chinese aggression in the south to meet with armed support from Nationalist China and Korea. But the commitment is not reversible, and Chinese action either against Formosa or Korea would not necessarily bring SEATO into action, except in the case of a general war.

In the field of anti-subversion, by contrast, the scope for national activities in implementing the Manila Treaty obligations has been much smaller than was originally suspected. The United States, the United Kingdom, the Philippines, and Australia have helped other states in train-

[53] SEATO Press Release No. 119, June 12, 1959.
[54] Address by J. F. Dulles, Mar. 8, 1955, in Department of State, *The Bangkok Conference of the Manila Powers* (Washington: G.P.O., 1955), p. 5.

ing police officers and intelligence specialists; members have exchanged information about subversive activities. Official and public awareness of Communist techniques may have increased through such measures as seminars on counter-subversion. The occasion of a grand-style SEATO intervention in aid of a government threatened by a Communist revolution, initially thought by observers to be the most likely form of SEATO action in the Treaty Area, has not so far occurred, and SEATO activities have until recently not been planned on such an assumption; but it may occur in relation to Laos, South Vietnam, or other countries whose governments prove incapable of maintaining law and order by their own unaided efforts.

In economic matters, too, national operations in support of SEATO have been modest. Aid to South-East Asian countries increased considerably after the crises of 1953–1954, but none of it has been allotted through SEATO. Australia alone has instituted a small SEATO-label aid project to help strengthen the defense forces of the Asian members with supplies of non-combat materials, such as motor cars and tents, and in training officers. The five other specifically SEATO aid schemes (initiated through the intervention of a SEATO organ, but executed by member governments) have been concerned with technical training and assistance. They are: (1) The Graduate School of Engineering in Bangkok, inaugurated in September 1959—a small project in a specialized field but holding possibilities of expansion into an important center for the training of an engineering-managerial elite for the economic development of South-East Asia. (2) The Skilled Labor Projects aimed at overcoming shortages of skilled labor in the three Asian members, under which vocational training schools, with United States and other help in equipment and personnel, are being converted into general industrial training centers. In 1961 the eighteen new centers in Thailand alone were providing instruction at the annual rate of 3,500 students skilled in metal working, automotive mechanics, electrical engineering, and telecommunications. (3) The United States $400,000 Cholera Research Project agreed upon at Wellington in 1959, involving the establishment of a permanent laboratory in Dacca intended as the principal center for research in cholera and for training investigators and health officers from the countries of the Area. (4) A General Medical Research Project involving the establishment of a laboratory in Bangkok for the study of tropical intestinal diseases in particular. (5) The Rural Development Project, first proposed at Wellington, to be implemented through the setting up of rural development centers in north-east Thailand. A Meteorological Aviation Telecommunication Project is in the planning stage. Large numbers of Asian member nationals receive technical training in the United States, the United Kingdom, France, and Australia; nationals of all member states are encouraged to undertake goodwill tours and to take part in educational exchanges.

All these activities owe their inception to SEATO's "slack period" in 1955–1958, but they are only now gathering momentum. They increase SEATO's prestige and fill a gap not filled by the established aid organizations, but their scope is limited and their effect mostly marginal in relation to kindred national enterprises. SEATO is hardly a cure for all the ills that afflict South-East Asia.

The League of Arab States

ROBERT W. MACDONALD

The Pact of the League of Arab States In preparation for the General Arab Congress envisaged by the Alexandria Protocol, a committee of Arab foreign ministers and other experts met in Cairo during February and March 1945 to draft the constitution of the Arab League. The subject had been a matter for lively debate in the Arab capitals in the fall and early winter following the Alexandria conference. Two days after the approval of the Alexandria Protocol, Nahhas Pasha was relieved of his position as prime minister of Egypt; Egyptian political leaders denounced Nahhas and his followers as traitors and castigated the proposed Arab League as unworkable. The Syrian and Jordanian prime ministers, who had led their delegations to the conference, were also dismissed from their posts. Reaction was particularly violent in Beirut where the Christian Arab community, led by the Maronite patriarch and the Falangists, denounced the Alexandria Protocol as an attack on Lebanese sovereignty. The document which emerged from the preliminary drafting committees, however, generally confirmed the ideas of the Alexandria Protocol.

The General Arab Congress convened in Cairo on March 17 to review the draft pact, and the approved document was signed March 22 by six of the seven founding members: Egypt, Iraq, Lebanon, Syria, Saudi

From *The League of Arab States: A Study in the Dynamics of Regional Organization,* by Robert W. Macdonald (copyright © 1965 by Princeton University Press; Princeton Paperback, 1968). Reprinted by permission of Princeton University Press.

Arabia, and Trans-Jordan. A copy of the Pact was sent to the Imam of Yemen, who signed it on May 10, 1945. Unofficial delegations from Algeria, Libya, Morocco, and Tunisia reportedly requested membership in the League of Arab States during the drafting of the pact, but the final agreement provided that membership was to be restricted to independent Arab states.[1]

The Pact of the League of Arab States is an international treaty signed by the heads of states or representatives of the founding members and duly ratified by the respective member states.[2] The Pact consists of a preamble, twenty numbered articles, and three annexes. In its brevity, the Pact resembles the League of Nations Covenant more than anything else, and some of its phraseology and provisions seem to have been lifted from either the League Covenant or the draft United Nations Charter. A brief analysis of the principal provisions of the Pact will serve as background for the detailed discussion later. Reference points are: (1) purpose and functions, (2) membership and relations between members, and (3) institutional structure.

PURPOSE AND FUNCTIONS

Article 2 of the Pact of the League of Arab States, which amplifies the Preamble, establishes as the purposes of the organization: (1) strengthening relations between member states, (2) coordinating their policies in order to further cooperation and safeguard their independence and sovereignty, and (3) a general concern for the affairs and interests of the Arab countries. In particular, the article provides for "close cooperation" between member states in matters concerning economic and financial affairs, communications, cultural affairs, problems of nationality, social affairs, and health. No mention is made of defense against external attack, coordination of military resources, or uniformity of foreign policy, unlike the Alexandria Protocol, which provided for coordination of foreign policy. The League is, however, to act as a mediator in disputes between members or between a member and a third state according to Article 5. The Pact also provides, in Article 3, for future cooperation with such international bodies as may be formed "in order to guarantee security and peace and regulate economic and social relations." In the vocabulary of functionalism, the primary purpose of the League

---

[1] *al-Ahram* [Cairo], February 18, 1945, reported the foundation of a "Front for the Defense of the Maghreb" in Cairo, under the direction of Sheikh Mohammed el-Khadir Hussein of Tunisia, with the purpose of fostering the entry of the North African Arab countries into the League, *Oriente Moderno*, xxvii (1945), 17.

[2] Ratifications were as follows: Trans-Jordan, March 31, 1945; Iraq, April 1, 1945; Syria, April 3, 1945; Egypt, April 5, 1945; Lebanon, April 7, 1945; Saudi Arabia, April 7; Yemen, May 11. The Pact came into effect on May 11, 1945, fifteen days after Iraq had deposited its ratification with the League's Secretary General in Cairo.

is to foster non-political activities and only incidentally to enter the political arena.

MEMBERSHIP AND RELATIONS BETWEEN MEMBERS

Membership is restricted by Article 1 to independent Arab states; subsequent to the establishment of the League, any such state may apply for membership. Members pledge themselves by Article 8, to respect the sovereignty of other member states and not to take any action "calculated to change established systems of government." Member states which voluntarily elect to form "stronger bonds" than provided by the Pact may do so. Resort to force to settle disputes is, however, prohibited by Article 5. Member states assume an obligation to support the League financially, on a prorated basis to be determined from time to time by the Council. Withdrawal of a member upon one year's notice is permitted, and provisions are made so that errant states may be "separated" from the organization, according to Article 18. The terminology of the Pact leaves little doubt that the League is to be regarded as no more than a device to coordinate the activities of its members and to keep them from quarreling among themselves. The prospect for political unity under the Pact of the League of Arab States is forsworn by its emphasis on preserving the sovereignty and independence of its members.

An interesting feature of the Pact is its provision for future relations with non-members, particularly in the Arab World. Article 2, which establishes the purpose of the League, includes "general concern with the affairs and interests of Arab countries" and not just for the interests of member states. Article 4 permits non-member [Arab] delegations to participate in the work of the technical committees. These provisions are reinforced by Annex 2 to the Pact, "Annex Regarding Cooperation with Countries Which Are Not Members of the Council of the League," which establishes a policy for future cooperation with non-member Arab states. Annex 2 and the other referenced articles of the Pact refer to the expressed desires of the then-dependent Arab areas of Algeria, Libya, Morocco, Palestine, and Tunisia. As a special case, Annex 1 of the Pact provides that Palestine shall be represented on the League Council, by a person to be selected by the Council, until full independence has been achieved. The membership policy is also oriented toward these potentially independent states, since the Pact was originated by all the independent Arab states of the period.

Articles 9 and 17 contain two additional provisions for regulation of relations between member states. Article 9 provides that: "Treaties and agreements already concluded or to be concluded in the future between a member state and another state shall not be binding or restrictive upon other members." Nor shall such treaties become null and void. According to Article 17, all such treaties, including both existing and future treaties between members, must be deposited with the Secretary General. This provision, which resembles that of Article 18 of the Covenant of the League of Nations, is less restrictive than the requirement for unified foreign policy contained in Article 1 of the Alexandria Protocol.

INSTITUTIONAL STRUCTURE

According to the Pact, the principal organs of the Arab League are the Council and the permanent Secretariat. The Pact specifies that the seat of the League is Cairo. Provision was made for future establishment of an "Arab Tribunal of Arbitration," which would work closely with other international bodies on problems of peace and security; this provision has been debated extensively but never implemented. Technical committees, one for each of the functional areas mentioned in Article 2, are provided to assist the League Council. No other organs were provided by the Pact; an Economic Council and a Joint Defense Council, however, were later provided by a special treaty, in 1950.

The organization established by the Pact appears to have combined the principal provisions of the Covenant of the League of Nations and the operating experience of the League's Council. The Arab League Council, unlike that of the League of Nations, comprises all members of the organization. The need for an Assembly such as that of the League of Nations was therefore obviated. On the other hand, the Arab League Pact specifically provides for technical committees to assist the League Council. The League of Nations Council developed the institution of the technical committee over a period of years outside the specific provisions of the Covenant.

The Council is made up of representatives from the member states of the Arab League and meets twice a year, in regular session. Each state has one vote regardless of the number of representatives it sends to the Council.[3] The principal functions of the Council are to supervise the execution of agreements concluded between members, to determine the means by which the League is to cooperate with the United Nations and other international agencies, to mediate disputes between members or between members and non-members, and to coordinate defense measures in the event of attack or threat of aggression. The Council also has internal legislative functions, including the approval of the budget, preparation and approval of administrative regulations for the Council, the technical committees, and the Secretariat, and the regulation of certain personnel matters, including appointment of the Secretary General.

The Secretariat provided by Article 12 consists of a Secretary General, an unspecified number of assistant secretaries, and "an appropriate number of officials." Aside from preparation of the League budget and

[3] See Article 4/6, League Covenant, which provided one vote per country but limited the number of representatives to one.

support of Council meetings, neither organization nor functions of the Secretariat are prescribed by the Pact. The Council is given the responsibility for regulations concerning functions and staff of the Secretariat.

The technical committees are composed of representatives of the member states according to Article 4. Their principal function is to study conditions and to draft agreements on technical cooperation for consideration by the Arab League Council. Representatives of the non-member Arab states may sit on these committees and frequently have. In addition to the six functional committees provided by Article 4, a political committee and a permanent committee on information have been established which directly support the League Council.

The Joint Defense and Economic Cooperation Treaty The original seven members of the League of Arab States completed a supplemental treaty in 1950 officially known as the Joint Defense and Economic Cooperation Treaty Between the States of the Arab League. The treaty, usually known as the Arab Collective Security Pact, was signed by Egypt, Lebanon, Syria, Saudi Arabia, and Yemen on June 17, 1950. Iraq signed on February 2, 1951, and Jordan signed on February 16, 1952. The treaty became effective on August 23, 1952. The treaty is somewhat unique in its juncture of functional and security problems, though the ostensible reason for the treaty was to bring the Arab League in line with the United Nations Charter in matters of collective security. The preamble states that the participating governments desire "to cooperate for the realization of mutual defense and the maintenance of security and peace according to the principles of both the Arab League Pact and the United Nations Charter." The treaty also restates the objectives of the Pact of the League which relate to consolidation of relations between members, maintenance of independence, and development of economic and social welfare. In fact, however, the treaty is based on Article 51 of the UN Charter, as was the defense pact of the Organization of American States.

Relations between members are altered in the 1950 treaty to the extent that, according to Article 10, the contracting parties "undertake to conclude no international agreements which may be contradictory to the provisions of this Treaty." This recalls the earlier attempt, under the terms of the Alexandria Protocol, to secure uniformity of foreign policy. But outside the context of Arab unity, to which this provision is often linked, the provision also resembles that of Article 20 of the Covenant of the League of Nations.[4]

From another point of view, relations between members of the

---

[4] Article 20 of the Covenant states: "The Members of the League [of Nations] . . . solemnly undertake that they will not hereafter enter into any agreements inconsistent with the terms hereof [i.e., the Covenant]."

Arab League have been affected to the extent that only signatories of the 1950 treaty were permitted to join the three new Arab League organs which it established. The League had thirteen members at the end of 1962, but only nine of them had adhered to the treaty. The role of the supplementary organs created by the 1950 treaty has been limited by this provision during most of the intervening period since none of the new members adhered to the treaty until 1961. Although non-adherents could attend meetings as observers, they could not participate officially in the decision-making process. This situation has been particularly embarrassing in the case of the Economic Council.

The new Arab League organs established under the terms of the 1950 treaty were the Joint Defense Council, the Economic Council, and a Permanent Military Commission.

The organization and functions of the Joint Defense Council were established by Article 6. The Council was to comprise the foreign ministers and ministers of defense of the contracting states, or their representatives. It was designed to function under the supervision of the League Council in matters of collective security, including "the use of armed force to repel the aggression and restore security and peace," coordination of available military resources, and the preparation of plans for joint defense.

The Permanent Military Commission, made up of representatives of the general staffs of the contracting states, was charged with drawing up plans for joint defense and, presumably, with effecting the necessary coordination to ensure their implementation. The Commission was supposed to work directly with the Joint Defense Council; its headquarters was established at Cairo. As a concomitant of its military functions, the Military Annex to the treaty provided that the Commission was to submit "proposals for the exploitation of natural, agricultural, industrial, and other resources of all Contracting States in favor of the inter-Arab military effort and joint defense."

The Economic Council was established to coordinate the development of the Arab economies and "generally to organize . . . their economic activities and to conclude the necessary inter-Arab agreements to realize such aims." The Council presumably works under the supervision of the Arab League Council, though this is not specified in the treaty. It is composed of the ministers of economic affairs of the contracting states, or their representatives, and cooperates with the Economic Committee established by Article 4 of the Arab League Pact. In 1960, however, steps were taken to permit representatives of non-contracting Arab states to attend sessions of the Economic Council. In September 1964, all the remaining non-signatories adhered to the Arab Collective Security Treaty as a gesture of Arab brotherhood and thus became full voting members of the Economic Council. By this time, however, the economic aspects of the treaty were rapidly being taken over by the newly organized Council of Economic Union and the projected Arab Common Market.

❀   ❀   ❀   ❀   ❀

Internal Dynamics and Policy Formulation   It has been suggested that crisis situations limit the decision-making processes of the Arab League because they short-circuit established procedures for developing consensus and tend to paralyze the League Council. A corollary to this proposition is that routine problems pass through the decision-making process precisely because they are amenable to unanimous decisions at the League Council level. The purpose of this [section] is to analyze the circumstances that condition the decision-making process of the Arab League and to evaluate their impact on the policies of the organization.

In general terms, the discussion will be concerned with three factors which condition policy formulation: (1) the polarization of power and the formation of blocs within the membership of the Arab League, (2) regional dynamics, and (3) external stimuli. The last two factors will be examined under the general heading of integrative and disintegrative processes, terms that will be explained below. The effects of all three factors will be discussed by reference to actual situations. And, finally, the major operating policies of the Arab League will be discussed in terms of the influence of these factors on League policies.

THE POLARIZATION OF POWER

The rivalry between Iraq and Egypt for leadership of the Arab League has been one of the distinctive factors of the organization since its earliest days. This rivalry has been institutionalized in and through the Arab League in the intervening period and has been a persistent component of the continuum of conflict evident at the League Council level, the level examined in this [section]. The natural outcome of this rivalry has been the development of a balance of power system within the Arab League. In order to understand the internal functioning of the decision-making process, therefore, it is necessary to understand the causes of this relationship and the influence it exerts on policy formulation.

The reasons for the polarization of power within the Arab League are partly objective and partly subjective in nature. Historically, both Iraq and Egypt have been centers of important pre-Islamic civilizations and, later, of great Arab empires. Both countries later passed through pe-

[5] For a provocative discussion of recent inter-Arab relations, see George A. Kirk, *Contemporary Arab Politics* (New York: Praeger, 1961).

riods of British tutelage, developed political consciousness in the years following the First World War and briefly participated in the activities of the League of Nations in the period just prior to the Second World War. While the experience of the two countries have been comparable in quantitative terms, the quality of their experiences has been somewhat different.

Before the arrival of the British in the last quarter of the nineteenth century, Egypt had enjoyed almost 75 years of virtual independence within the loose framework of Ottoman suzerainty. This period had been one of rapid development of commerce and industry, considerable borrowing of Western cultural and political institutions, and the development of a politically conscious elite.

By the First World War, Egypt had experienced the growth of a cultural nationalism which found its origins in the pre-Islamic Egypt of the ancient Pharaohs and developed under the concurrent influence of the Islamic reform movement and of the coordinate Pan-Islamic movement. Inevitably, Egyptian nationalism developed an indigenous character that ran counter to that of the developing Arab nationalism (Pan-Arabism) rooted among Syrian intellectuals of the same period. Even after the First World War, when the British had relaxed their hold on the Egyptian protectorate, Egyptian nationalists had little time for Arab nationalism. Their real concern was with the Nile Valley and the Sudan. Subject to continuous pressure from the British until the end of the Second World War, the major concern of the Egyptians always seemed to be to get rid of the British and get on with their own affairs. Thus, domestic Egyptian politics are characterized by pragmatism; doctrinaire movements affect only the fringes of society.

Iraq, on the other hand, was a backward province of the old Ottoman Empire, meagerly participating in the Arab nationalist movement developing in Syria and Lebanon, and became a political entity only after the defeat of the Turks in 1918, largely as a result of historical accident. Before the First World War, Iraqi adherents to the Arab nationalist movement—many of whom were officers in the Ottoman army—concerned themselves primarily with achieving some form of autonomous Arab state, subordinated to the Ottoman Empire and enjoying a federal status. The projected Arab state was essentially coextensive with the contemporary states of Iraq, Syria, Lebanon, Jordan, and Israel—the area of the so-called Fertile Crescent. The movement was also one of cultural nationalism but, unlike the Egyptian movement, it was oriented to the more illustrious eras of the Arab-Islamic epoch and had no well-defined territorial objectives.[6]

---

[6] Baghdad, the seat of the illustrious Islamic Abbassid dynasty (AD 750–1258), was the center of an Arab empire that rivaled Byzantium and maintained diplomatic relations with Europe. Its wonders are related in the *Tales of a Thousand and One Nights*.

Instead of unity after the defeat of the Turks, the Arabs of the old Ottoman Empire saw the traditional Ottoman administrative units converted to political entities by the French and British and administered as mandates under the League of Nations. Paradoxically, as a semi-independent state, Iraq became a center of Fertile Crescent Arab nationalism after 1920 at the same time that Arab nationalists were licking their wounds over the failure of postwar political unity. And, revived Arab nationalist movements in the Fertile Crescent area have generally been doctrinaire in nature.

Iraq was given virtually complete authority over her internal affairs in 1932 after a few years of political tutelage. And thus one of the most backward provinces of the Ottoman Empire became the first independent modern Arab state. Subjectively, however, the major concern of the Iraqis seemed less to get on with their internal affairs then to maintain their leadership in the Arab nationalist movement. In the balance, Iraq's relatively happy experience with British control was a source of irritation to the Egyptians, especially since the latter had to follow in the Iraqi footsteps on the road to independence.

Thus if the two responses to Anthony Eden's 1941 suggestion of an Arab union were those of Nuri Sa'id (Iraq) and Nahhas Pasha (Egypt), the reasons were quite different. The Egyptians moved largely, if not completely, to head off the proposed union of the Fertile Crescent that would greatly strengthen Iraq vis-à-vis Egypt. That a few Egyptian leaders felt it was time to join the mainstream of the Arab national movement was a secondary consideration.[7] Of more importance was the Egyptian plan to rally Arab opinion behind a pending move to force the British out of Egypt as soon as the Second World War was over.

During the period since the founding of the Arab League, the rivalry between Egypt and Iraq has been demonstrated in a number of concrete situations which form part of the history of the Arab League. The League's policy, assiduously promoted by Egypt, of non-cooperation with the West until Arab national objectives had been realized has frequently found Iraq and Egypt in opposite camps. The controversy over Iraq's participation in the Baghdad Pact is, of course, an outstanding illustration of the differences between the two countries and one which almost wrecked the Arab League. Paradoxically, Egypt, now the leader of the Arab nationalist movement, has persistently opposed the plans for unification of Iraq and Syria (a limited form of Fertile Crescent union)

---

[7] Egyptian leaders who favored the Arab nationalist movement were few but important. Nahhas Pasha reportedly had plans for Egyptian participation in the Arab nationalist movement as early as 1936 but lacked general support. 'Azzam Pasha, the first Secretary General of the Arab League, was a life-long exponent of the idea of Arab unity and one of the best informed Egyptians of his era on the Arab nationalist movement. See T. R. Little, "The Arab League: A Reassessment," *Middle East Journal*, x (1956), 144.

which are periodically proposed to the Arab League Council by both Syrians and Iraqis. Iraq, on the other hand, has generally opposed alleged Egyptian domination of the Arab League and was particularly vehement in the denunciation of the first Secretary General of the League for allegedly exceeding his authority and modeling League policies on those of Egypt, without consulting member states.

It is interesting to note that the disputes between the two countries did not cease with the overthrow of the Iraqi monarchy in 1958, though the Egyptians hastened to sign a mutual defense treaty with the Kassem government a few days after the revolution. Significantly, the Kingdom of Iraq participated in League Council meetings to the end, though annual dues were withheld after 1957. The Republic of Iraq, however, boycotted the League Council between 1959 and 1960 until, in the winter of 1960, Iraq was threatened with expulsion. After Kassem's unsuccessful bid to annex Kuwait, in 1961, Iraq again carried out a partial boycott of League activities and withheld dues amounting to more than $2.5 million.

A balance of power system usually encourages the formation of blocs within the system, and the Arab League is no exception. Table 1 illustrates the shifting nature of the Arab League power blocs, keyed to the two polar powers. These blocs are largely informal and have seldom depended upon military treaty or convention; the spate of bilateral military agreements between Egypt and other members of the League in 1955–1957 was an exception. The North African members of the League have had their own grudges against Egypt at times, but they have not always moved toward Iraq, largely because the radical Kassem government in Iraq coincided with their adherence to the League Pact.

The traditional dynastic rivalry between the Saudi royal house and the Hashemite kings of Jordan and Iraq operated on the League Council at least until the 1956 ouster of Glubb Pasha from Jordan. Subsequent to this time, the Saudis undertook to furnish a major portion of the annual subsidy the British had paid to maintain the Arab Legion. The Saudis also moved closer to friendly relations with Iraq, and away from Egypt, both before and after the 1958 Iraqi revolution; but from 1959 to 1961 the tendency was for improved relations beween the Saudis and the Egyptians. Nasser's support of anti-regime Saudi princes and the Yemeni Republic in 1962, however, reversed the trend and led to a new low in Egyptian-Saudi relations.

Lebanon has tended to remain aloof from both polar powers during most of the period, at times taking the role of mediator between Iraq and Egypt, partly because of the Christian orientation in the early days of the League and, later, because of her opposition to Nasser's bid for leadership of the Arab nationalist movement.

Largely as a result of internal politics during a series of military-supported governments between 1948 and 1955, Syria's course during the

TABLE 1
Bloc Patterns in the Arab League

Year	Alignment		
	Egypt	Neutral	Iraq
1946	Saudi Arabia Syria Yemen Lebanon		Jordan
1950	Saudi Arabia Yemen	Lebanon	Jordan Syria [a]
1955	Saudi Arabia Jordan Yemen Syria	Lebanon Libya	None [b]
1958	Yemen Syria [c]	Lebanon Libya Sudan Jordan Tunisia Morocco	(Morocco and Saudi Arabia) [d]
1960	Yemen Syria Sudan Morocco [f]	Tunisia Lebanon Libya Saudi Arabia Jordan	None [e]
1963	Algeria Kuwait Yemen	Tunisia Morocco Libya Saudi Arabia Sudan Jordan	Syria Lebanon

[a] As of the time Jordan annexed Western Palestine.

[b] Influence of the Baghdad Pact controversy.

[c] Egypt and Syria formed the UAR; Yemen joined the first two as a member of the United Arab States, in a loose federation.

[d] Prior to the Iraqi revolution of 1958, Jordan and Sudan could be listed under the Iraqi bloc. Following the revolution, Morocco and Saudi Arabia were friendly to the Kassem regime because of their opposition to Nasser.

[e] Iraq was threatened with expulsion from the League for its boycott of the League Council and its flirtation with the Soviets.

[f] Morocco drawing closer to Egypt.

period 1945–1958 was an extreme one. In 1945, Syria was the only Arab state willing to sacrifice her sovereignty to the cause of Arab unity, presumably because of the influence of Iraq. By 1955 Syria had moved to the opposite pole by means of a military alliance with Egypt in protest to Iraq's membership in the Baghdad Pact. And, finally, in 1958 Egypt and Syria merged to form the United Arab Republic. Following the breakup of the UAR, in September 1961, Syria tended to resume her traditional oscillation between the two polar powers by improving relations with Iraq.

Jordan, like Syria, has shifted back and forth between the polar powers, attracted first by the pull of the Hashemite ties with Iraq and then (1955–1957) by the support of Nasser's Egypt against continued British control of the country. Jordan's military alliance with Egypt, Syria, and Saudi Arabia in 1957 was transitional, however; in 1958 she moved back into the Iraqi orbit in a loose federal union of the two states. After the Iraqi revolution of 1958, Jordan tended to remain aloof and tried to improve relations with its dynastic enemy, Saudi Arabia. In 1964 Jordan renewed relations with Egypt.

Of the original members of the Arab League, only Yemen has been a consistent supporter of the Egyptians and, even so, she abstained on the 1950 Egyptian-inspired vote to expel Jordan from the League as a result of that country's annexation of the West Bank (eastern Palestine). The newer members of the Arab League (Libya, Sudan, Morocco, and Tunisia) have tended to form a neutralist bloc between Iraq and Egypt, though Tunisia refused to participate in League activities between 1958 and 1961 because of overt differences with Egypt. Kuwait owes its existence to Egypt, in return for its support against Iraq in 1961, but tends toward a neutralist role. Algeria was at least nominally aligned with Egypt in 1963–1964.

The polarization of power and the operation of power blocs within the Arab League has tended to narrow its range of action. On the other hand, it would be wrong to conclude that the polarization of power is the only factor which conditions the decision-making processes of the Arab League. Even in the midst of the most bitter disputes between Iraq and Egypt, there has been substantial agreement on some fundamental Arab League issues between the two states.

Thus, in 1955–1956, when the dispute over Iraq's membership in the Baghdad Pact was threatening to destroy the Arab League, the Iraqis took the initiative in proposing a Joint Arab army, to be maintained by the Arab League, with the mission of defending the borders of Palestine.[8] In April 1956, the Iraqi delegate requested the League Council to direct the almost defunct Military Commission to examine the

[8] Reported by *al-Akhbar* [Cairo], November 17, 1955. Critics argue that Iraq was merely attempting to outmaneuver Egypt, but the effect is that of at least limited consensus.

cases of alleged Israeli aggression against Syria, Jordan, and Egypt with a view to implementing the 1950 Collective Security Pact. Later the same year, after the Egyptian nationalization of the Suez Canal, Iraq reaffirmed her support of Egyptian policy and, when Egypt was attacked by Israel, offered to implement her obligations under the 1950 treaty in the event of further conflict. In August 1959, while Iraq was boycotting the Arab League in protest against alleged Egyptian control of the organization, Iraqi experts met with others from Arab countries to discuss a common Arab League policy on Palestine. And even while he was boycotting the League, Iraq's General Kassem affirmed his country's support of the League's principles, declaring that Iraq "works strenuously for bolstering cultural, economic, and political ties with all Arab states." After the admission of Kuwait to the League in 1961, Iraq continued to implement Council resolutions but boycotted League activities in which Kuwait was represented.

Aside from the fact that polarization is not complete and is far from inflexible, the increasing disengagement of member states from the influence of the two polar powers and the resultant formation of neutral blocs tends to promote mediation. On substantive matters, competition between the two dominant members of the League must take into consideration the positions of member states uncommitted to either member at any given time. It is necessary, therefore, to look beyond the polarization of power in order to understand the operations of the Arab League.

INTEGRATIVE AND DISINTEGRATIVE PROCESSES

Most of the policies, programs, and activities of the Arab League can be classed as "internal" and "external" according to the focus of the issue. About ten general categories suffice to gather together the diverse policies of the Arab League; these are shown in Table 2 based on the Pact and the 1950 Collective Security Treaty or on operating experience.

Even though an effort has been made to pair related issues, the arrangement of activities as "internal" and "external" provides little infor-

TABLE 2
Analysis of Arab League Issues

Internal Issues/Policies	External Issues/Policies
1. Maintenance of state sovereignties	1. Political independence for all Arab peoples
2. Political unification (Arab unity)	2. Afro-Asian solidarity
3. Military cooperation	3. Neutralism
4. Economic and social development	4. Cooperation with the UN
5. Palestine problem	5. Relations with Israel

mation about the operation of the Arab League. If anything, indeed, it provides an erroneous view of the League because the opposed items fit rather neatly together as enumerated. The maintenance of state sovereignties relates well to the policy of political independence for all Arab peoples. Economic and social development and cooperation with the UN seem to complement each other. And the issues of Palestine and Arab relations with Israel are obviously two sides of the same coin. The pairing of military cooperation with neutralism, however, does not provide insight into the failure of the League to achieve military cooperation; nor does the achievement of Afro-Asian solidarity in the face of outright Arab disunity add to understanding the situation.

TABLE 3

Integrative and Disintegrative Processes

Integrative Processes	Disintegrative Processes
Economic and social development	Maintenance of state sovereignties
Collective security	Political unification
Cooperation with the UN	Neutralism
Political independence for all Arab peoples	Palestine problem
Afro-Asian solidarity	
Relations with Israel	

In Table 3 these same issues have been rearranged as *Integrative Processes* and *Disintegrative Processes* on the basis of the historical experience of the Arab League. Using these processes as parameters, a more realistic analysis of the complex workings of the organization can be attempted in an effort to evaluate its successes and failures.

The suggestion has already been made that members of the Arab League, or of any other inter-governmental organization, attempt to realize particularistic goals through the organization and, if necessary, despite the organization. In this context, integrative processes are those which favor consensus on joint policies and collective action toward common objectives: i.e., toward the goals of the organization. Disintegrative processes tend to impede or negate consensus and collective action, largely because particularistic goals conflict with group objectives.

The key question, therefore, becomes that of the relative ability of member states of the Arab League to subordinate particularistic national goals to the common good. The integrative processes listed in Table 3 are generalizations of types of issues on which a large measure of effective consensus between Arab League members exists *a priori*. Disintegrative processes interact with the integrative processes in the course of decision-making and may prevent the realization of objectives which otherwise appear to be of mutual benefit to the entire membership. Furthermore, even the integrative processes are not always mutually reinforcing. On these grounds the policies and procedures of the Arab League cannot be categorized in any such simple manner as that favored by some commentators when they assert that the Arab League is unable to agree on internal issues because of permanent polarization and is, therefore, ineffectual.

It is, of course, true that polarization of power within the membership of the Arab League operates more or less directly to prevent or impede effective action on some issues. The relative positions of Iraq and Egypt on most disintegrative processes have been in complete opposition during most of the life of the League, as illustrated below (plus indicates history of general support and minus general opposition).

	Egypt	*Iraq*
Maintenance of state sovereignties	+	—
Political unification	—	+
Neutralism	+	—
Palestine problem	+	+

But this type of analysis cannot adequately explain the failure to adopt policies, or to implement policies already adopted, from within the field of integrative processes. Only by an analysis of the interaction of the disintegrative processes with the integrative processes, in terms of their influence on the total membership, may a more accurate insight into the internal dynamics of the League be obtained. The following sections show that the polarization of power is not the only villain.

The Palestine Problem and Israel

The question of Arab relations with Israel is, of course, the fundamental issue for the Arab League. It is the issue best known by non-Arab observers and the one on which the organization is most often judged. Far-reaching in its effects, the Arab-Israeli issue interacts with and influences the operation of most of the other integrative and disintegrative processes listed above. The Arab-Israeli problem and its corollary, the "Palestine problem," have already been described as two sides of the same coin, though the first has been termed *integrative* and the other *disintegrative*. A brief review of the Arab positions on these two critical issues, therefore, seems in order.

The establishment of Israel in 1948 was the result of a half century of vigorous Zionist activity dedicated to the establishment of a Jewish state in Palestine. The movement acquired great impetus and marshalled powerful non-Zionist supporters just before and during the Second World War as a result of the infamous German atrocities against Europe's Jewish communities, but its success was not due entirely to these developments. Rather, in the Arab view, Israel was established by force of arms in a prolonged and dramatic struggle that led to the displacement of about two-thirds of the population of Palestine—about 85 percent of the Arab population, or some 650,000 persons—to provide a new refuge for the remnants of Europe's ravished Jewish communities. The Arabs fear further armed encroachments upon Arab territory as a result of Israel's avowed policy to gather in all the remaining Jews of the diaspora.

Arab opposition to the Zionist movement to take over Palestine dates at least from the end of the First World War, but the Arabs proved to be powerless and ineffectual in the face of the overwhelming pressures exerted by the victorious Allies to implement the historic Balfour Declaration through the League of Nations mandate over Palestine. In 1917 the British had bound themselves by the Balfour Declaration to support a movement for a "Jewish national home" in Palestine, a seemingly innocuous objective since the Declaration provided that "nothing shall be done which may prejudice the civil and religious rights of existing non-Jewish communities in Palestine." But, as one astute observer has written, the British administration of the Palestine mandate (1922–1948) "created a situation of irreconcilable discord which was bound to make the exercise of force inevitable." [9]

The Arab League owes its existence to a large extent to joint Arab efforts after the First World War to frustrate the Zionist program for a Jewish national home in an area where only 10 percent of the inhabitants were Jewish. Joint Arab conferences in 1937 and 1938 protested accelerated Jewish immigration and reflected general Arab concern for the future of Palestine. In 1939 the British invitation to the governments of Egypt, Iraq, Trans-Jordan, Saudi Arabia, and Yemen to attend the London Round Table talks on the deteriorating situation in Palestine confirmed the view that any solution to the "Palestine Question" required the approval of all Arab states. After 1942, Nuri Sa'id's "Blue Book" and the other Arab plans and schemes that eventually led to the formation of the Arab League were at least partly motivated by the necessity for a joint Arab solution to the Palestine problem.

After the formation of the Arab League, Arab determination to keep Palestine in the Arab camp was underscored by the special treatment given Palestine in the League Pact, the reservation of a seat on the Arab League Council for a Palestine representative, and the League's strenuous efforts to coordinate joint Arab military action during the Arab-Israeli War of 1948–1949. Despite its failure to prevent the establishment of Israel, the League Council has continued to act as the legal surrogate for all Palestine Arabs, maintaining a seat on the League

[9] H. B. Sharabi, *Government and Politics of the Middle East in the Twentieth Century* (New York: Van Nostrand, 1962), p. 169.

Council for the Palestine representative, sponsoring the "Palestine delegation" to the United Nations, and at least nominally supervising the remaining pieces of Palestine in the Gaza Strip and the "West Bank" region of Jordan.

Arabs consider that the establishment and continued existence of Israel, with the official sanction of the British and Americans, is a fundamental moral issue and a serious affront to Arab sovereignty and the principle of self-determination. They condemn the British for their perfidy and the Americans for political expediency in carrying out policies that led to the Zionist occupation of an "indivisible part of the Arab homeland" and created a "bridgehead of Western imperialism." They refuse to recognize publicly even the *de facto* existence of Israel as a state, and their radios support their claim that the "liberation of Palestine" has become a "sacred Arab cause." They regard the provisional boundaries of Israel as temporary armistice lines, as, indeed, they are under the terms of the 1949 United Nations armistice agreements.

In their efforts to seek redress against the "Zionist occupation of Palestine," the Arab states have generally worked together within the Arab League. In an attempt to rectify the situation, short of a resumption of hostilities, the Arab League has inaugurated a far-reaching economic boycott against Israel, supported Egypt's policy to deny Israel the use of the Suez Canal, refused to cooperate with Israel on any regional undertaking (including boycotts of international meetings attended by Israel), and persistently demanded the implementation of United Nations resolutions affecting Israel and its relations with its Arab neighbors. As a minimum, the Arab position now looks to the United Nations for the rectification of Israel's present boundaries in accordance with the 1947 partition plan, the establishment of an international regime for Jerusalem, and the implementation of a UN resolution that supports the right of the Palestine refugees to elect to return to their former homes or to receive compensation for their lost property and other assets in Israel.

The establishment of Israel has provided the main impetus for the collective security arrangements established by the Arab League. All the original members of the League, including Iraq and Egypt, adhered to the 1950 Arab Collective Security Pact. And, in spite of its subsequent adherence to the ill-fated Baghdad Pact, Iraq repeatedly offered to implement the 1950 agreements in the event that any Arab state was attacked by Israel.[10] In 1964, the formation of a Joint Arab Command under the general terms of the 1950 security pact provided another instance of this consensus on a vital League issue. But most Arabs concede the impracticability of any military move to destroy Israel in the face of

[10] In February 1955, Iraq insisted that her commitment to the Baghdad Pact did not affect her membership in the 1950 Arab Collective Security Pact but, rather, enhanced the Arab position vis-à-vis Israel. See H. Hall, "The Arab League States," *Current History,* xxix (August 1955), 97.

current Western policy, and most observers agree that the Joint Arab Command was designed to be a deterrent force rather than an offensive force aimed at Israel.

The Arab League has not hesitated to take its arguments against recognition of Israel to Afro-Asian bloc conferences, where it also urges the extension of the Arab League boycott. The Arabs have achieved some success with this tactic, particularly since the 1955 Bandung Conference. The Arab League has also exploited its neutralist position to secure military and other assistance from the Communist bloc when the West refused to furnish arms for fear they would be used against Israel. Conversely, of course, Western support of Israel has nudged the Arab League toward a neutralist position and sympathetic relations with the "anti-imperialists" of the Communist bloc and the Afro-Asian bloc. In Arab eyes, the establishment of Israel "represented the final and most dramatic encroachment by the West on Arab society and served to spark the radical postwar revolution in the area which is still going on." [11]

In this situation, several of the integrative processes listed in Table 3 interact and reinforce each other: the Arab League's *relations with Israel* influence the organization's orientation toward *collective security* and its attitude toward *Afro-Asian solidarity*. The League's policy of *cooperation with the UN* is also affected by the Arab-Israeli problem, while the League's policy of *neutralism*—normally a disintegrative process—reinforces other League policies on the question of relations with Israel.

If the Arab League has managed to present a united front in its policy toward Israel, it has usually been less than successful in its attempts to coordinate policy with respect to the vestiges of the Palestine problem. In this context, the "Palestine problem" as it is discussed here refers principally to (1) Arab policies toward the Palestine refugees, (2) attempts to administer a Palestine government in exile, and (3) pressures to dislodge the Israeli bridgehead and restore Palestine to its former Arab inhabitants. The problem is, of course, complicated by the far-reaching effects of the ignominious failure of Arab League policy on Palestine in 1948.

The Arab states most concerned (Jordan, Egypt, Lebanon, and Syria) have refused to resettle the hundreds of thousands of Palestine refugees still living in UNWRA refugee camps in their territories. Criticism of this policy is met by the legal argument that assimilation of the refugees would play into the hands of Israel since the United Nations has supported the Arab demands that the refugees be allowed to return to "Palestine" if they wish to or to be compensated for lost property. (There is also the moral argument that the problem was created by the United Nations—at the urging of the United States and other Western powers—and that the Arab states should not be required to absorb these victims of high policy at the expense of the welfare of their own citi-

[11] Sharabi, *op. cit.*, p. 169.

zens.) However, there is also reason to believe that resettlement is resisted because the refugees are considered, at the least, a potential cause
of political instability. They form a restless force for rapid political change
within the Arab community, often becoming the prey of demagogues and
professional Palestinians who press for radical programs to recover their
lost homeland.

The problem of who shall govern the remnants of Palestine (Gaza
and the "West Bank" of the Jordan River) has never been satisfactorily
solved under the circumstances. An All-Palestine Government was
formed by the Arab League Council in September 1948 and recognized
the following month by all the Arab League members except Jordan.
Composed of the supporters of the Higher Arab Committee, headed by
the controversial former mufti of Jerusalem, Hajj Amin al-Husseini, the
All-Palestine Government has had a tenuous existence. The nominal government was headed by the venerable Ahmad Hilmi until his death in
Beirut in 1963, but it had little to do in recent years. The "West Bank"
was incorporated into the Kingdom of Jordan in 1950, ostensibly in trust
for the Palestinians. Hajj Amin had a falling out with the Egyptians and
moved his apparatus from Cairo to Beirut, while the Egyptians set up an
independent government in Gaza in 1959, also in trust for the Palestinians. The North African Arab leaders were too busy with their own problems to be much concerned.

The problems of reconciling political rivalries and the inability of
the All-Palestine Government to capture the imagination of the Palestinians led the UAR to propose the formation of an ill-defined "Palestine entity" at the September 1959 session of the League Council at Casablanca.
Under study by a committee of five Palestine "experts" (League Secretary General Hassouna, chairman) between 1960 and 1963, the plan was
finally implemented in the spring of 1964 in the era of good feeling that
followed the January 1964 Arab summit conference in Cairo. The death
of Ahmad Hilmi in June 1963 had already broached the problem of a
successor to represent the Palestinians in the League Council. This was
solved in September when the League Council approved the nomination
of Ahmad Shukairy, a one-time Assistant Secretary General and former
Saudi Arabian representative to the United Nations.

Shukairy and his staff worked through the fall and winter of
1963–1964 to draft a "Palestine National Charter" and a constitution for
the so-called "Palestine Liberation organization," meanwhile traveling
extensively for consultations with Arab leaders. This activity was cli-
maxed on May 28, 1964, with the proclamation of the Palestine Liberation Organization at the first significant convocation of Palestine representatives since 1948. The meeting, symbolically convened at Jerusalem,
was opened by Jordan's King Hussein and addressed by League Secretary General Hassouna. Inasmuch as Hussein's grandfather had refused
to recognize the All-Palestine Government of Hajj Amin, this step repre-

sented a giant stride forward in inter-Arab relations. Moreover, delegates of all the Arab states except Saudi Arabia attended. Hajj Amin's Higher Arab Committee, along with several other splinter groups, withheld its cooperation after first denouncing Shukairy and his whole scheme as illegal. Shukairy, nevertheless, promptly cabled the Secretary General of the United Nations that, henceforth, the Palestine Liberation Organization was the official spokesman of the Palestine people.

Much publicity was given in the Arab press to the fact that the emblem of the Palestine Liberation Organization conference bore a huge map of Palestine on which was superimposed the slogan: "We Shall Return!" The oath by some 350 delegates to the congress declared among other things that "Palestine is our homeland . . . repatriation is our goal . . . struggle is our road . . . unity is our guide . . . Palestine is ours . . . and [we] shall accept no substitute homeland. God and history are our witness that we shall sacrifice our blood for your liberation." [12] Nevertheless, the decisions of the conference were largely dedicated to procedural matters: levying token taxes on Palestinians everywhere, setting up executive offices and a nominal governmental structure, providing for a worldwide information campaign, and discussing arrangements for the future election of Palestinian representatives. One potentially explosive issue, the question of constituting a Palestinian armed force, was resolved in favor of training refugees by the new Joint Arab Command and a plan to establish the "Palestine" units within existing national armies, two devices calculated to keep the Palestinians out of trouble. In the final analysis, moreover, the resolutions of the congress required ratification by the Arab League Council, thus keeping the activities of the new organization within an established institutional framework.

Thus the Arabs publicly demonstrated for the second time in 1964 that they did not intend to attack Israel, at least in the foreseeable future. While no Arab will publicly disavow the Arab pledge to recover Palestine, and few will do so privately, the question was obviously being accorded only a relatively low priority. For the Arabs were acutely aware of the military, technological, and economic superiority of Israel and had no desire to experience another humiliating defeat like those of 1948 and 1956, even supposing that the major powers did not intervene.

Beyond the immediate issue of "liberation," a disintegrative factor (maintenance of state sovereignty) comes into play along with an integrative factor (economic development). No Arab leader can afford to agitate the Palestine issue to its ultimate conclusion if he has the slightest fear that he will thereby forfeit his own position of power and possibly even lose a portion of his country in the bargain. Furthermore, it was recognized years before the 1948 disaster that the only possible way for the Arabs to defeat the Zionist encroachment on Palestine was by drastic economic reform. It is, therefore, interesting to note that it was subse-

[12] *The Arab World* [Beirut] (May 29, 1964).

quent to 1948 that Arab writers on the subject of economic reform seemed almost by agreement to turn to the socialist experience as a model for rapid modernization. It is also pertinent to note that the 1950 Arab Collective Security Treaty provided the first mechanism for economic reform, as a concomitant of military reorganization, in a sweeping effort to make efficient use of the economic resources of the area in the future.

The Arab Independence Movement

Despite the League's failure in Palestine in 1948, one of the most successful programs carried out by the Arab League has been that of promoting independence for all Arab peoples. The central League policy of encouraging independent status for dependent Arab areas operates in a field of integrative processes dominated by *Afro-Asian solidarity* and *cooperation with the UN*. The League's subsidiary orientation toward strengthening these two policies permits it to exploit them in favor of regional independence. Meanwhile, the growth of the League's policy of *neutralism* has helped it to interact with the integrative processes in a positive sense. The League states have not shrunk from accepting Soviet bloc assistance with the regional "national liberation movement," but none of the new Arab states has fallen prey to Communist machinations.

While the details of the movement toward independence of Arab states are properly the subject of a separate study, a few principles of action may be deduced here. In the first place, representatives of the North African dependencies were present at Alexandria during the preliminary discussions that led to the Arab League and they participated in the ceremonies by which the League was formally established in March 1945. Annex 2 to the Pact of the League of Arab States, furthermore, provides for cooperation with and assistance to "Arab countries which are not members of the Council" and promises the "safeguarding of their future with all the political means" at the disposal of the League. As early as 1945, League Secretary General 'Azzam told a press conference that formal contacts were to be made between the Arab League and political leaders in North Africa and the Persian Gulf area.[13]

The actual techniques employed by the League, drawn from an analysis of League Council decisions, illustrate a fairly consistent pattern of action:

1. representatives of dependent territories are encouraged to look to the Arab League for encouragement and support of their "national" aspirations, including financial support and participation in League activities and programs;

[13] For an account of the Arab League's role in the independence of Libya, see Majid Khadduri, *Modern Libya* (Baltimore: Johns Hopkins, 1963), pp. 118–20, 224–26, *et passim.*

2. the Arab League makes direct representations to the "imperialist power" (Britain and France), offering in some instances to serve as trustee for the dependent territory until independence has been achieved (e.g., Libya, Tunisia, Persian Gulf sheikhdoms);

3. member states of the Arab League act through established diplomatic channels to bring pressure to bear on the "imperialist power" and/ or to gain sympathy for the Arab cause among other Western powers (e.g., NATO powers were requested in 1959 not to support France in her military campaign in Algeria);

4. member states act through diplomatic channels to win support of the non-Arab members of the Afro-Asian bloc powers to recognize the newly established provisional Algerian government in Cairo;

5. Arab League states' representatives at the United Nations attempt to gain the support of the Afro-Asian bloc, and other powers, in behalf of motions for commissions or investigations by the Security Council and/or the General Assembly into conditions in the dependent Arab territories (the Arab seat on the Trusteeship Council was useful in this respect).

Cooperation among the members of the Arab League has been and continues to be outstanding on the issue of independence for the Arab dependencies. Since 1945, the number of independent Arab states has risen from seven to thirteen. Polarization within the League has not had a noticeably adverse influence on the programs undertaken by the League and, indeed, seems to have acted in quite the opposite way in most cases—with the possible exception of Iraq's obstruction of Kuwait's independence in 1961. Both Iraq and Egypt contributed heavily to the Algerian struggle during a period when the two powers were at each other's throats (1955–1960). Even when Iraq was actively boycotting the League (1959–1962), General Kassem was pointedly receiving delegations of Algerian rebels and signing over to them sums of money which had been voted by the Arab League Council on a pro-rata basis. The focus has now shifted to the Persian Gulf sheikhdoms, however, where UAR and Iraqi national goals may come into open conflict in the future.

Afro-Asian Solidarity

Similar success has been achieved with the programs of Afro-Asian solidarity, which have been supported by all Arab League members and which pre-date the 1955 Bandung Conference. The key integrative processes interacting with *Afro-Asian solidarity* are those of League *cooperation with the UN* and *relations with Israel*. Once again, *neutralism* plays a positive role in determining the League's attitude toward Afro-Asian solidarity.

In this situation, a major impact is on the formation of voting blocs in the UN. The interacting process, *relations with Israel,* is a factor here because of the endeavor of the League to secure the support of the Afro-Asian bloc against Israel, including the extension of the Arab League boycott and non-recognition. The nominal neutralism of a large part of the Afro-Asian bloc operates as a positive factor for the most part and reinforces the Arab League in its dealings with both the East and the West. Conversely, the Arab League has supported the non-Arab states of the Afro-Asian bloc in various undertakings, starting with active support for the Indonesian independence movement in 1946. At various times, for example, the Arab League has attempted to mediate the Kashmir dispute between India and Pakistan, supported Vietnam's independence movement (but not partition), promoted the idea of a mission to the Far East in an effort to keep the Communist Chinese military forces in Korea from crossing the 38th parallel in 1951, and supported independence for Cyprus after 1955. Most of these activities have been in the context of *cooperation with the UN.*

Prior to the Bandung Conference, the League's Secretary General had participated in the New Delhi conference of Afro-Asian nations, in January 1949, and had assisted with the development of a common Afro-Asian policy at several UN sessions.[14] In December 1952, a special Afro-Asian bloc meeting on the situation in North Africa was held in Cairo under Arab League auspices. The non-League participants included India, Indonesia, Afghanistan, Ethiopia, Pakistan, and Iran.[15]

In December 1954, when the League Council approved Arab participation in the Bandung Conference, special emphasis was given to "efforts to put on the conference agenda Arab questions, foremost the Palestine question, along with world problems such as the fight against colonialism and racial discrimination and the regulation of armaments and the use of atomic energy and other problems." The resolution also recommended special efforts "to enlist the support of the sponsors of the Conference . . . for Arab policy."[16] The League Council had earlier recommended that Arab member states "strengthen their diplomatic representation" in the countries of the Afro-Asian bloc. In his report to the League Council on the Bandung Conference, the Secretary General recommended that the Arab League Secretariat in Cairo be made the principal liaison center for Afro-Asian cooperation in the Near East and that the League's permanent office in New York serve the same function at the United Nations.[17]

The polarization of power within the Arab League, however, has

---

[14] Mohammed Abdel Khalek Hassouna, *The First Asian-African Conference, Held at Bandung, Indonesia* (April 18–24, 1955), (Cairo: Imprimerie Misr, SAE, 1955), Chap. 1.

[15] *Middle East Journal,* vii (1953), 203. The conference resolved that the participants should work for a solution to the North African problems through the United Nations.

[16] Hassouna, *op. cit.,* p. 20.

[17] *Ibid.,* p. 174.

affected the development of the League's policies toward Afro-Asian solidarity from time to time. While the Arab League supported the Greek Cypriots at the United Nations after 1955, Iraq's ties to Turkey, within the Baghdad Pact, led her to soft-pedal the issue. When the Arab League member states' delegates at the United Nations voted against Turkey in a General Assembly resolution on the Cyprus issue in 1958, Iraq recalled her UN delegate and formally apologized to the Turkish Government. The incident is inconclusive, but it suggests the incipient development of an Arab League policy independent of the policies of the League's members.

Other Dynamic Processes

Although generally effective programs have emerged from the three situations discussed above, the League's experience with the important questions of economic development, regional collective security, and cooperation with the UN has been somewhat more ambivalent. In particular the interactive processes which influence any program of economic development envisaged by the Arab League minimize hopes for the success of such programs unless some basic approaches are changed.

The integrative processes working toward regional economic integration do not always interact positively. *Cooperation with the UN*, for example, is adversely affected by another integrative process: *relations with Israel*. Moreover, the normally integrative processes are more or less in equilibrium with disintegrative processes.

Formal relations with Israel are prohibited to member states, and the possibility for intra-Arab League development in the areas of trade and industry—not to mention such United States supported proposals as a regional Jordan River Authority—are greatly reduced. At the same time, the attitude toward Israel has precluded full realization of the potential assistance which could be provided by the United Nations. For example, no Middle East Economic Commission has ever been formed. Other things being equal, however, there is considerable scope for concrete action in the area of economic development, including fruitful cooperation with the United Nations and the Specialized Agencies. The realization of concrete projects is blocked to a large degree by the combination of strong disintegrative processes:

a. The question of *maintenance of state sovereignties* is geared to divergent internal economic policies and conditions (commerce and banking in Lebanon versus an autarchic industrial development program in Egypt, for example) which cannot easily be altered, though their external effects could be harmonized.

b. *Political unification* counteracts economic development programs in two ways: (1) anything less than total political unification poses a threat to the continued leadership of Egypt (or other leader) in the economic sense and, (2) premature political unification poses a threat to particularistic economic interests in the unified states. By deviating from its established policy against partial unity in order to "save" Syria in 1958, Egypt inadvertently threatened the economic viability of an otherwise fairly healthy economy. The United Arab Republic broke down when the Egyptians showed a real intent to integrate the economies of the two countries, in July 1961.

   c. The process of *neutralism* is economically and politically disruptive since it threatens established extra-regional commercial ties (e.g., Kuwait and Lebanon to Europe; Algeria, Morocco, and Tunisia to the franc bloc) and eventually extends even to the internal political structures of the affected states. As an illustration of the dependence on ties to the West, both Morocco and Lebanon refused to support a proposed Arab League economic boycott of France during the final phases of the Algerian war.[18]

   The three more or less successful programs carried out by the Arab League are heavily weighted on the side of the integrative processes, while the integrative process of *economic development* has normally formed an equilibrium with other integrative and disintegrative processes. The processes influencing the *collective security* programs of the League are also essentially in equilibrium, and this helps to explain the fact that the collective security mechanism has remained weak and ineffectual. The final integrative process, *cooperation with the UN*, has functioned more freely than either of these two noted above, but the Arab League has never been able to establish the kind of relationships it would like with either the United Nations or its specialized agencies. These three problems, ironically, are considered fundamental to regional organization.

[18] *Middle East Journal*, xiv (1960), 294.

The African States
and the OAU

NORA MC KEON

Africa has earned its share of the headlines the hard way this year—since last autumn *coups d'état* have rocked no less than six states, while the Rhodesian crisis has thrown the whole continent into a turmoil. Although the long-term consequences of these upheavals cannot yet be charted, one immediate effect has been to make life still more difficult for the Organization of African Unity. Since the creation of the Organization, on May 25, 1963, events have proved that the atmosphere of Pan-African amicability which reigned at the Addis Ababa Summit masked a good number of conflicts of interest and differences of opinion. To a certain degree this was to be expected, for Pan-Africanism is a rallying cry whose cohesive qualities are more effective on the emotional than on the practical level. Like many another "ism" in other parts of the world it has proved easier to talk and dream about than to realize, easier to maintain as an aggressive movement, directed against colonial domination, than as a constructive movement, working toward the harmonious cooperation of independent African states.

✻ ✻ ✻ ✻ ✻

Listing the obstacles to African unity is fashionable and, unfortunately, facile. On the level of political theory, despite the compromise reached at Addis Ababa, agreement has not yet been reached on the

From *International Affairs*, 42 (July 1966), pp. 390–409. Copyright by the author. Reprinted by permission of the Oxford University Press.

form which this unity should take. While leaders such as the recently ousted Kwame Nkrumah hold that only a supranational body with extended powers of decision and action can solve Africa's problems and give her voice the weight it deserves in the arena of international affairs, others feel that an all-African organization should concentrate for the moment on economic, technical and cultural cooperation, acting as an arbiter in inter-state conflicts, but leaving the bulk of political initiative to the individual nations. This attitude sometimes stems from a conviction that unity should be built up step by step. Less reasonably, it sometimes reflects the personal competition for leadership which has slowed progress toward unification in areas such as French-speaking West Africa, where Leopold Senghor of Senegal and the Ivory Coast's Houphouet-Boigny long contested the command. The same problem within individual states, personal conflicts between men like Ahomadegbe and Apithy in Dahomey, President Jomo Kenyatta and Vice-President Oginga Odinga in Kenya, and the various personalities of the ex-Belgian Congo, have rendered more difficult the establishment of strong, stable nations which alone can have the self-confidence and the responsibility to form a union and to make it work.

Still in the realm of politics are the inter-state conflicts which oppose states of contrasting ideological complexions or practical interests. The one-party system which the majority of African states have adopted often provides a tempting opportunity to transpose these differences on to the plane of action. In many countries the dominant party is doubled by a party in exile which sets up headquarters in a country whose interests or policies would be furthered by the overthrow of the party in power. The outlawed *Union des Populations du Cameroun,* lodged at Accra until last February's *coup d'état,* and the *Front de la Libération de la Guinée,* based at Abidjan, offer examples of a highly prevalent practice.

Among the most explosive of conflicting interests are boundary disputes. These territorial conflicts are often the legacy of colonial frontiers drawn up without respect for traditional political, cultural, and ethnic divisions. The units which they created are, for the most part, unstable—in some cases ridiculously small, in others combining different and often hostile ethnic strains or unequally endowed regions. Thus, for example, the Ewe tribes are divided among Dahomey, Togo, and Ghana, and Ghana has asserted claims to the territory of Togo.

Finally, the efforts of outside Powers to establish and maintain their influence in the young African nations threaten, despite the proclaimed neutralism of most African countries, to introduce the divisions of the cold war into the African continent. While men such as Tshombe and Houphouet-Boigny have been denounced by some leaders as tools of Western imperialism, others have upbraided countries like Ghana (before the February coup), Tanzania and Algeria for furthering subversion by Chinese Communist agents.

In the domain of economics the obstacles to unity are no less serious. The contrast between rich and poor nations is an impediment which works both ways. On the one hand, Uganda has been wary of projects for an East African Federation because she fears that Nairobi would win the lion's share of commerce and industry at the expense of Kampala. On the other hand, Gabon has shied away from full participation in a Union of Central African Republics to avoid being held back by her poorer neighbors. Another obstacle of an economic nature stems from the low degree of industrialization in most African countries. The external commerce of these predominantly agricultural nations is, for the most part, dependent on a limited range of crops. As a result, the competition is fierce among such resources as the cocoa production of Ghana, Cameroon and the Ivory Coast, or the palm-oil of Nigeria, the ex-Belgian Congo and Dahomey.

A final important consideration is the cultural, ethnic and linguistic multiplicity which has often been cited to refute the very conception of Pan-Africanism. Tribal conflicts are a divisive factor in a large number of countries, including Nigeria, Mauritania, the Sudan, Cameroon, and Chad, and it is significant that, of all the various Pan-African organizations, only the Pan-African Freedom Movement of East and Central Africa (PAFMECA) has been able to adopt an African tongue for its deliberations in preference to a European language.

But if the obstacles to unity are imposing, the arguments in favor of it are strong. The African states are bound together by a similar political and economic position with regard to the rest of the world, and by similar problems of social, cultural, and economic development. Cooperation could offer long-term solutions to those problems by providing an antidote to the fragmentation inherited from the colonial era. It could mean intelligent exploitation of natural resources, broader and rationalized markets, the realization of industrial and agricultural projects for which no single country could raise the necessary capital, sharing of scarce intellectual and scholastic resources, exchange of social and cultural experiences. It could mean more effective action in an area in which consensus is absolute: the struggle to liberate the still dependent territories of the continent. Finally, in the arena of world politics, it could mean that Africa's voice would be listened to, not only on African questions, but also with regard to all the international problems on which African leaders are finding that they have an opinion to express.

✳   ✳   ✳   ✳   ✳

The Pan-African Summit Conference at Addis Ababa in 1963 crowned a series of meetings which had begun with the first Conference of Independent African States in April 1958, and which had been temporarily de-routed by the formation of two rival groups in the course of 1960–1961: the "Brazzaville Group" and the "Casablanca Group." In December 12, 1960, of the ex-French territories (Cameroon, Central African Republic, Chad, Congo-Brazzaville, Dahomey, Gabon, Ivory Coast, Madagascar, Mauritania, Niger, Senegal, and Upper Volta) met at Brazzaville to discuss ways of coordinating their political and economic policies. In September 1961 the Brazzaville states formed the *Union Africaine et Malgache* (UAM), an organization of political collaboration which Ruanda and Togo later joined. Essentially conservative in outlook, the UAM states favored close cooperation with the former metropole and the preservation of the state system bequeathed by the colonial era. Moving to counterpoise the Brazzaville conference, the Heads of State of Ghana, Guinea, Mali, Morocco, and the U.A.R., and the Prime Minister of the Algerian Provisional Government, met at Casablanca in January 1961 and approved a Charter of African Unity. In contrast to the UAM group, the Casablanca states held that the independence of the new African nations would not be complete until ties with the colonial West were cut and "neo-colonial" economic and political influence on the continent liquidated, a view which inclined them to seek their allies in the East. Intervention in the internal affairs of states which catered to the neo-colonial powers was justified in their eyes, and they placed their hopes for the future of Africa in the creation of a supranational organization, a project which the Brazzaville states tended to distrust.[1]

Throughout 1961 and most of 1962 the African political scene was dominated by this split, despite efforts to find a compromise at meetings held in Monrovia and Lagos. Toward the end of 1962, however, the tension between the two groups declined. The independence of Algeria and Mauritania's admission to the UN removed two specific sources of dispute,[2] and the efforts of neutral states like Ethiopia helped to create an atmosphere favorable to reconciliation. At the Addis Ababa Summit meeting a formula for unity was found which won the unanimous approval of the independent African states.

The final draft of the Charter of African Unity, adopted at the close of that meeting, created a flexible organization of cooperation based on certain essential principles: the sovereign equality of all member states, non-interference in the internal affairs of other states, peaceful settlement of all disputes, dedication to the emancipation of the still dependent African territories, and affirmation of a policy of non-alignment with regard to all blocs. Four major institutions were provided for: the

[1] This description does not apply to Morocco, which joined with the radical states largely to win support for her claims to the territory of Mauritania.
[2] The Casablanca states supported the Algerian rebels, while the Brazzaville group, fearful of offending France, hesitated to recognize and work with the revolutionary Provisional Government.

Assembly of Heads of State and Government, the Organization's supreme body; the Council of Ministers, charged with making recommendations to, and implementing the decisions of, the Assembly; the General
Secretariat; and a Commission of Mediation, Conciliation, and Arbitrage,
whose composition and functioning were to be defined in a separate protocol approved by the Assembly of Heads of State and Government.
Technical details of cooperation were to be worked out by five specialized Commissions: Economic and Social, Educational and Cultural,
Health, Sanitation and Nutrition, Defense, and Scientific, Technical and
Research—and a Coordinating Committee would channel aid to liberation movements.

The Addis Ababa Conference thus created the atmosphere, and the
Charter provided the basic tools, for African unity. There was no doubt
that the OAU was, potentially, the most important advance that had yet
been made in the domain of inter-African cooperation. The question that
remained to be answered was whether this potential would be, and
could be, realized. The past three years have not produced a definitive
verdict, but a progress report can be drawn up by reviewing the OAU's
action since its creation; by assessing its success in tackling the problems
which the terms of its charter and the welfare of the continent have
thrown on its shoulders, and by determining whether the African states
have learned to place their faith in the Organization or whether they
have tended to fall back on the smaller groups on which they had previously relied.

*   *   *   *   *

In the months following the Addis Ababa Conference, the OAU set
up shop with no more hitches than were to be expected. The Council of
Ministers held its first meeting at Dakar in August 1963, when it decided
to recommend Addis Ababa as permanent headquarters, but was not
able to agree on the choice of a secretary-general. Two opposing positions were also taken concerning the future of existing regional groups.
Certain countries, notably Guinea, Ghana, Mali, and Nigeria, argued
that such groups should be dissolved and their technical committees integrated into the specialized institutions of the OAU, while the Brazzaville
members of the UAM favored a more gradual evolution.

In October 1963 the Organization underwent its first real test when
an Algerian-Moroccan frontier conflict developed into active hostilities.
An extraordinary session of the Council of Ministers was called at Addis
Ababa from November 15 to 18, and this appointed a committee of arbitration which, in a series of eight meetings, helped to check tension between the two countries. A second extraordinary session was held at
Dar-es-Salaam from February 12 to 14, 1964, at the request of President
Nyerere of Tanganyika, to seek an African alternative to the British
troops which he had been obliged to call in to put down a mutiny of the

Tanganyika Rifles. On this occasion the OAU proved itself capable of finding an acceptable solution to a delicate situation. An agreement was reached providing for the replacement of the British troops by soldiers from African states. The same session was requested, by the Emperor of Ethiopia, to examine the frontier conflict between his country and Somalia. An appeal was launched for a cease-fire, and Kenya and Somalia were requested to settle the quarrel involving the north-eastern zone of Kenya, populated by Somalian tribes.

Little more than a week later, from February 24 to March 1, the Council met at Lagos for its second ordinary session. A major resolution recommended various measures for reinforcing the fight against South African *apartheid*. On the subject of frontier conflicts, the Council congratulated Morocco and Algeria on reaching a provisory accord, and Ethiopia and Somalia were urged to respect the cease-fire. The results of this conference were not entirely satisfactory. On many points the Council simply confirmed decisions already taken at Dar-es-Salaam, while the most important items on the agenda—the definition of a policy of non-alignment, the establishment of a permanent commission of conciliation, and a Ghanaian proposal for the creation of an African High Command—were passed on to the Assembly of Heads of State.

From July 17 to 21, 1964, the 33 African Heads of State met at Cairo for their first ordinary session, after a preparatory meeting of the Council of Ministers from which Tshombe, who had become Prime Minister of the Congo on July 10, was excluded. Two specific administrative decisions were reached: Diallo Telli, a Guinean, was elected secretary-general over the candidate proposed by the UAM states, and the choice of Addis Ababa as permanent headquarters was confirmed. The meeting reached a compromise concerning regional groups, recognizing that such organizations, so long as they confined themselves to technical and economic goals, could be a valuable step toward continental unity. The Assembly approved a protocol of conciliation, and also a resolution in which member states agreed to respect the borders inherited from the colonial epoch. In an effort to intensify the fight for liberation, contributions to the Freedom Fund administered by the Coordinating Committee were made mandatory and a special department for South Africa was prescribed.

The balance of the OAU's first year and a half of activity was fairly even. The Organization had had some success in facing and initiating solutions to a number of pressing problems. Delicate administrative questions such as the choice of a secretary-general and the role of regional groups had been settled. The Organization had prevented one explosive frontier dispute from degenerating into armed conflict and had been instrumental in settling another, and it had instituted permanent machinery for mediation. The Tanganyikan incident had offered a concrete example of how African cooperation could help to render the continent more independent of the former colonial Powers.

In other areas progress was less tangible. The OAU's efforts to harmonize the foreign policies of the African states, and to create a common African view and voice, had met with indifferent results. Generally speaking, Africa had adopted a policy of non-alignment with regard to the cold war—a position dictated both by a desire to prevent the continent from becoming involved in the quarrels of others and by a conviction that the status of neutralism has a dignity far above that of a member of one or the other camp. Yet "non-alignment" is an ambiguous term which each leader can interpret as he pleases, and, until a consensus has been reached as to its content, it threatens to be more divisive than unifying. The OAU has not succeeded in establishing such a consensus. As noted above, the second ordinary session of the Council of Ministers failed to agree on a definition of non-alignment and passed the question on to the Assembly of Heads of State, which neglected it completely. The problem is, of course, not merely one of semantics, and in recent months the attitudes of some states *vis-à-vis* the cold war have injected a heightened note of tension into inter-African affairs.

Another sore spot was the question of unifying nationalist movements in the still dependent territories and offering them effective aid. This task, delicate in itself, is complicated by the fact that internal divisions in the liberation movement of a particular territory are often reinforced by antagonistic independent states which offer aid to rival freedom groups.[3] Under these circumstances, the efforts of the Coordinating Committee to conciliate warring factions met with small success. Conflicts in these domains foreshadowed the divisions which were to plague the OAU in the coming months, but for the moment the enthusiasm of the member states for their newly launched organization, and their sincere desire to make it work, helped to smooth over differences of opinion.

* * * * *

The termination of the relatively idyllic period represented by the Organization's first 18 months of life was partly the fault of circumstances. The OAU was unfortunate enough to be hit with a series of problems that would have shaken even an older, more solidly based organization: the Congo question, the problem of inter-state subversion, the Rhodesian crisis, and the epidemic of *coups d'état* in West Africa.

[3] With regard to Angola, for example, the moderate states support the government in exile (GRAE) of Roberto Holden, while the radical countries favor the more leftist Union of the Populations of Angola (UPA), headed by Agostino Neto. The situation is similar in Portuguese Guinea, where the African Party of Independence of Guinea and the Cape Verde Islands (PAIGCV) dispute the scene with the Front for the Fight for National Independence of Guinea (FLING). Here the situation is complicated by the fact that Portuguese Guinea, a tiny territory sandwiched in between Guinea and Senegal, would in all probability fuse with one of her neighbors when it attains independence. The Guinean Government supports the PAIGCV, while Dakar shelters the more moderate FLING.

The efficacy of OAU action, and the faith which its member states placed in it, began its downward spiral in the summer of 1964, with the eruption of the Congo crisis. The OAU had worked in disputes where only two countries were involved and the united pressure of the other members could be brought to bear on them; it had worked in cases such as that of Tanganyika, where all that was involved was finding practical means of arriving at an end on which all agreed. But the Congo question offered far less favorable terrain for negotiation. The crisis was not a unique and isolated problem. The situation in the Congo represented an exaggerated symbol of what could occur in many other regions, where different races and disparate regions were pasted together to form vulnerable political units. The object-lesson aspect of the question, the presence of a nation torn by civil war at the very center of the continent; of a regime headed by a leader who was considered as controversial by a good number of African states; of an army led by white mercenaries; of a focal point for foreign intervention—these factors combined to create an extremely explosive situation. It was a difficult test for the fledgling organization, and in facing it the OAU proved powerless to create and enforce harmony when a significant number of its members were in basic disagreement.

The Organization was first called upon to examine the Congo situation at an extraordinary session of the Council of Ministers held at Addis Ababa from September 5 to 10, 1964. The situation at that point was already drastic—on July 23, Gaston Soumialot had announced the formation of a Provisional Government of the National Committee of Liberation and on August 5 the rebels had won control of Stanleyville. The conference, attended by Tshombe in person, adopted a six-point resolution urging the Congolese Government to stop employing mercenary soldiers and to work for national reconciliation, appealing to foreign powers to cease intervention in the internal affairs of the Congo, and requesting all OAU members to refrain from action which might aggravate the situation. An ad hoc committee was set up [4] and was charged with working for a suspension of hostilities and for a restoration of normal relations between the Congo and her neighbors.

On November 24, in a joint American-Belgian operation, parachutists were dropped into rebel-held Stanleyville. The Stanleyville incident served to harden the lines of division which had already become evident between African states which supported the rebels and those who favored the central government. The UAR and Algeria offered the rebels material and moral aid. The Sudan, after a change of regime, became a sanctuary for rebel activity, and Congo-Brazzaville and Uganda allowed the "liberation movement" soldiers to infiltrate into Congo-Leopoldville across their frontiers. In addition, a number of states, including Ghana,

[4] This committee was comprised of Ethiopia, Nigeria, Guinea, the U.A.R., Somalia, Ghana, Upper Volta, Kenya, and Cameroon and was presided over by Kenyatta.

Guinea, Mali, Morocco, and Tunisia, declared themselves against Tshombe. On the other hand, the French-speaking states maintained a neutral silence for a period of time, although two leaders, Presidents Tsiranana of Madagascar and Houphouet-Boigny of the Ivory Coast, later began to call for a condemnation of the rebel movement. The ad hoc committee was unable to stem this growing controversy.

From February 26 to March 9, 1965, the Council of Ministers met at Nairobi for its fourth ordinary session. The Congo question was, of course, at the center of its preoccupations. The basic document under study was the final report of the ad hoc committee. This report, while "reaffirming its faith in the resolutions of the conference of Addis Ababa," which had seemed to support the central government, recommended that negotiations be opened with the rebel leaders, a step which Tshombe consistently refused to take. Starting from this basis, the debates were enlivened by the arrival of Tshombe himself, who denounced the ad hoc committee's report and persuaded the Council to reject, in a vote in which 14 states abstained, a Sudanese proposal demanding that the representatives of the rebel movement be heard. A split among the delegations soon made itself felt, and neither Tshombe's advocates nor his opponents were able to command a majority. Two resolutions proposing that white mercenaries be replaced with African troops failed to win the required majority, and the Council finally decided to shelve rather than to resolve the deadlock by passing the question on to the Assembly of Heads of State. This abdication on the part of the Council perpetuated an open sore in inter-African relations and left the OAU open to accusations of *impuissance*. The Congo crisis, focusing and magnifying the conflict between moderate and radical states, had split Africa down the middle, and the Organization had been unable to heal the gap.

The initiative was thus handed back to the individual countries and, implicitly, to the groups of states which had confronted each other in pre-OAU Africa. In fact, the first months of 1965 saw the re-consolidation of these groups. The names were different, the specific issues referred to had changed, but the basic divergence of outlook and ideology which had separated the Brazzaville states from the Casablanca group were still at the bottom of the split, and its divisive implications were as great in 1965 as they had been in 1962.

One of the first straws in the wind was the reactivation of the *Conseil de l'Entente*. This loose union, formed in May 1959 by the Ivory Coast, Niger, Dahomey, and Upper Volta, is led by Houphouet-Boigny, who, since his break with the French Communist Party in 1950–1951, has consistently favored close collaboration with the West on the international scene and maintenance of the status quo on the African continent. In the first month of 1965 it was announced that Togo was to join the Council. Speeches by the leaders of the union revealed one major preoccupation which underlay their renascent activity: the threat of what the

President of Niger called "the siege of Africa by Chinese communism." Niger, in particular, had been the object, in October 1964, of attacks by Sawaba commandos allegedly trained and furnished by the Chinese, through the intermediary of Ghana. The *Conseil's* overtures to Togo were directed toward setting up a *"cordon sanitaire"* around the offending neighbor.

On a larger scale, Houphouet-Boigny advocated a re-creation of the former *Union Africaine et Malgache,* which, in April 1964, bowing to the majority sentiment of the OAU, had been transformed into the *Union Africaine et Malgache de Coopération Economique* (UAMCE), a purely economic and cultural group.[5] Houphouet-Boigny's position, however, was not accepted unanimously by the members of the UAMCE. Some feared that an organization of French-speaking states with political overtones would menace the action of the OAU, while Senegal remained faithful to the format of the UAMCE in the hope of persuading Guinea and Mali, her partners in the exploitation of the Senegal River, to rejoin the group of the former French West African states.

✳   ✳   ✳   ✳   ✳

These were the basic positions at the start of a conference held at Nouakchott, Mauritania, from February 10 to 12, 1965, to lay down the institutional bases of the UAMCE, which had existed only on paper since the signing of its charter. In addition to differences of opinion concerning the form which the new organization should take, the participants were divided on two important questions. On the Congo, although the majority regarded Tshombe as the head of the legal Congolese Government, the group was far from unanimous as to the type and degree of support to offer him, and certain states, like Congo-Brazzaville and Dahomey, were openly hostile to him. The divergence was still clearer concerning Communist China. The Entente states had denounced Chinese penetration, and their position was shared by Madagascar's President Tsiranana, an ardent anti-Communist, and by other states, such as Gabon, which have had to deal with serious internal tensions. At the other end of the spectrum, Congo-Brazzaville and the Central African Republic had recently inaugurated a policy of close cooperation with Peking, while Senegal had recognized the Communist government in 1964.

Given these differences, only a flexible compromise could win the unanimous consent of the participants. Concerning the Congo, the 13 states agreed to support the "legal government," without mentioning Tshombe by name. This approbation, however mild, was a windfall for Tshombe, who, for the first time, could claim that his regime had won

---

[5] The four states of the Entente, disapproving the change, had refused to sign the new charter.

support on the African continent. On the question of Communist subversion, the compromise was reflected in a denunciation which referred only to Ghana, and not to Communist China. The 13 states represented at the conference thus associated themselves with the anti-Ghanaian campaign already launched by the *Conseil de l'Entente*. Such events as the attempted assassination of the President of Niger on April 13, 1965, by a member of the Sawaba party, allegedly trained in Ghana, only served to reinforce their solidarity on this point.

The compromise on the type of cooperation to be instituted among the French-speaking states took the form of a new organization, the *Organisation Commune Africaine et Malgache* (OCAM), which mediates between the partisans of a political union and those of purely economic and cultural collaboration. According to the final *communiqué*, the OCAM is "an African group whose goal, in the context of the OAU, is to reinforce cooperation and solidarity among the African and Malagasy states, in order to accelerate their development in the political, economic, social, technical and cultural domains." However, it is difficult to identify any sphere in which a group of this sort can operate without threatening the harmony of the OAU. In his inaugural speech, President Ould Daddah of Mauritania, elected acting head of the new organization, declared that "our future organization, whatever it may be, cannot be a regional group, since the Malagasy and the Mauritanian Republics, to mention only these two, are at the antipodes. This future organization should rather be a sort of intermediary between the OAU and the economic regional groups in which many of our countries participate." The OCAM is thus situated in a sort of diplomatic no-man's land, justified neither by specific technical and economic aims nor by the goal of cooperation on a continental level.

This lack of a well-defined purpose permitted the OCAM's most vigorous faction, the *Conseil de l'Entente*, to use the new organization as a vehicle for its own policies. In the months following the Nouakchott meeting, the *Conseil* largely succeeded in associating the OCAM with its campaign to isolate Ghana, and to integrate Tshombe's Congo into the "club" of French-speaking states. On May 23, a special meeting of the OCAM, held at Abidjan on the Ivory Coast's initiative, welcomed Congo-Leopoldville as a member of the organization. This event was engineered before the OAU had worked out an "all-African" attitude toward Tshombe's regime, and so had a tremendously controversial impact.

The Nouakchott meeting and its implications could hardly pass unnoticed by the states of the former Casablanca group. Mali, Guinea, Ghana, and Algeria regarded the OCAM as a reincarnation of the UAM. The OCAM's pledge to support the "legal" Congolese Government conflicted with these states' *penchant* for the rebel cause. Finally, the group was concerned by the anti-Ghanaian campaign opened up by the Entente states and underwritten by the final *communiqué* of the Nouak-chott conference. With these considerations in mind, the Heads of State of Algeria, Mali, Guinea, and Ghana met at Bamako on March 14, 1965. The talks were continued by three of the leaders, Modibo Keita, Ben Bella, and Kwame Nkrumah, at Conakry the following day. On his return to Algiers on March 17, Ben Bella declared, "We have had the possibility at Bamako and at Conakry of establishing a common position against the imperialist- and colonialist-inspired maneuvers which are becoming manifest in Africa." The Algerian President spoke in terms of a union of the four states, to be realized in the near future, which would be dedicated to "reinforcing the unity of the OAU." This union, however, failed to materialize—both because the former Casablanca states seemed anxious not to complicate the OAU's position and because they had their own practical interests which precluded siding with Ghana in an open break with the rest of the French-speaking countries.[6] The radical states, nonetheless, did not abandon their opposition to the OCAM nor their condemnation of Tshombe.

By the end of April the exchange of insults and accusations had grown so bitter that Nigeria, seconded by Liberia and Ethiopia, requested an extraordinary session of the Council of Ministers of the OAU. This session met at Lagos from June 10 to 13 to mediate in the quarrel between Ghana and the Entente states, which had announced their intention of boycotting the next Assembly of Heads of State, to be held at Accra, if the Ghanaian Government refused to expel the political exiles it sheltered. The meeting was not highly illuminating. The Entente foreign ministers produced dossiers accusing Ghana of supporting subversive groups, particularly the outlawed Sawaba Party (Niger) and the Sanwi tribal opposition group (Ivory Coast), while the Ghanaian Foreign Minister categorically denied all charges. The conference unanimously passed a seven-point resolution asking all members to attend the summit and to do everything possible to make it a success, noting Ghana's promise to clear the country of "undesirables" before the meeting's opening date and recommending that the problem of refugees and subversion be examined at the scheduled summit meeting at Accra.

Despite Nkrumah's efforts to placate his neighbors,[7] the Entente states reiterated, on October 19, their decision to boycott the Assembly. They were joined by Togo, Gabon, Chad, and Madagascar, while nine other states sent only ministerial delegations. The Assembly of Heads of

---

[6] Mali and Guinea, for example, are members of the *Union des états riverains du fleuve Sénégal*, which also includes Senegal and Mauritania.

[7] At Nkrumah's request a meeting was arranged with Houphouet-Boigny, Hamani (Niger), and Yameogo (Upper Volta) at Bamako on October 13. At the end of the closed-door discussions, Nkrumah agreed to ban not only political refugees but their families as well, and a large number of exiles were in fact expelled before the conference opened.

State thus opened on October 21 with one serious count against it: the absence of the presidents of half its member states.[8]

Secretary-General Diallo Telli chalked up a second black mark in a report which he presented at the meeting. The OAU, he announced, was nearly $2.5 million in debt. Twenty-four nations had failed to pay all their dues, and participation in the meetings of specialized committees had been scandalously spotty. With the financial health of the Organization uncertain and the allegiance of some of its members in doubt, the summit was obviously not able to accomplish much on a concrete plane. The Congo question was taboo—President Kasavubu had agreed to attend only on the condition that the internal problems of his country would not be discussed. The question of political refugees and subversion was aired in a frank and excited debate, and the conference unanimously passed two resolutions, engaging the participants to refrain from subversive activity and from press and radio campaigns directed against another state and to encourage political refugees to return to their own countries. The fact, however, that the very states which had pushed for a firm resolution on subversion were boycotting the meeting cast a shadow over even this accomplishment.

One final problem occupied the Assembly's attention, one which was to monopolize African affairs in the months to come—the threat of a unilateral declaration of independence by Ian Smith's white Rhodesian government. Although Nkrumah's assurance in his opening address that "the OAU will take whatever steps are necessary" drew an emotional response, the resolution voted on October 22 was moderate in tone. The Assembly did not consider a motion passed by the preparatory meeting of foreign ministers, recommending that an OAU peace-keeping contingent be set up, and a proposal to impose economic sanctions against Rhodesia was defeated as unrealistic. The final resolution placed the greatest responsibility on Great Britain, urged to use force to prevent a unilateral declaration of independence, and on the UN.

❋   ❋   ❋   ❋

Three weeks later, on November 11, Rhodesia declared her independence and the threat became an open crisis. OAU members were unanimous in condemning Rhodesia's move, but while some states felt that all initiative should be left to Great Britain, others spoke in terms of African military preparations and called for an OAU conference. At the UN, where they immediately set up a sub-group for action against Rho-

[8] Nineteen countries were represented by their Head of State or Prime Minister: Algeria, Guinea, Somalia, Zambia, Congo-Leopoldville, Congo-Brazzaville, Gambia, Sierra-Leone, Liberia, Tanzania, Cameroon, U.A.R., Nigeria, Ethiopia, Malawi, Mauritania, Mali, Ghana, and Sudan. Nine were represented by ministerial delegations: Burundi, the Central African Republic, Kenya, Libya, Morocco, Ruanda, Senegal, Tunisia, and Uganda.

desia, the African states ran into the difficulties which traditionally hamper their diplomatic offensives in that organization: on November 9, the General Assembly, where the Afro-Asian group is by far the largest caucus, urged Britain to use all means, including force, to stem the revolt; but in the Security Council the Africans were unable to push through a resolution invoking Chapter VII of the Charter, which calls for military measures in the event that other efforts fail to resolve a situation endangering world peace.

The OAU itself got down to business at an extraordinary meeting of the Council of Ministers held at Addis Ababa on December 3. Here the radicals won the day, and the resolution adopted by the conference was strong enough to satisfy the most die-hard opponent of the Smith regime. The African states announced that if the revolt had not been crushed by December 15, they would declare war on Rhodesia, cut all economic exchanges and communications and, finally, break off diplomatic relations with Britain. Although this last measure was voted unanimously,[9] it was the crux of the internal divisions that were to develop in the course of the month. On the eve of the deadline, Sir Abubakar Balewa, the Nigerian Prime Minister, in a move to preserve the Commonwealth from the disintegration that the diplomatic rupture would entail, launched a proposal for a Commonwealth meeting at Lagos to discuss the Rhodesian crisis. In all, only 10 states carried out the terms of the December 3 resolution, and the split clearly delineated the radical and moderate camps.[10] Much the same lines of division were evident on December 16, when nine states ignored an African walkout on Prime Minister Wilson's speech at the UN, organized by the Guinean and Tanzanian delegates.[11]

The split in the African ranks continued throughout the month of January.[12] Proposals to hold another extraordinary session of the Council of Ministers met with protests on the part of the states which had broken off relations with Great Britain. As Congo-Brazzaville's President Massemba-Debat put it: [13]

> The Rhodesian problem has been studied sufficiently and was the object of unanimous decisions at Accra and at Addis Ababa. By calling a new "summit" Africa would show that it doesn't know what it wants. Before

[9] Gambia was the only state absent from the conference.
[10] The 10 states which severed relations with Great Britain were: Guinea, Tanzania, Ghana, U.A.R., Mali, Mauritania, Congo-Brazzaville, Sudan, Algeria, and Somalia.
[11] The delegates from the Central African Republic, Liberia, Togo, Ivory Coast, Dahomey, Upper Volta, Gabon, Malawi, and Malagasy stayed in their seats.
[12] The Lagos Commonwealth meeting, although it succeeded in agreeing on a final resolution, had little effect on the state of the OAU since only a fraction of the African countries are members of the Commonwealth, and of these the two most radical, Ghana and Tanzania, refused to attend the conference.
[13] In a telegram addressed to Diallo Telli at the end of December.

seeking new decisions, it would be best to apply courageously those that have already been pronounced.

The question of reconstituting unanimity on the Rhodesian question was thus postponed until the sixth ordinary meeting of the Council of Ministers, scheduled to be held at Addis Ababa on February 28. But by the time this conference took place, the situation had been further complicated by a factor which operated to upset the balance of radical and moderate states: the series of *coups d'état* in West Africa.

✿   ✿   ✿   ✿   ✿

The epidemic of military takeovers first broke out in Congo-Leopoldville, where General Mobutu ousted President Kasavubu on November 25. In the following months it spread to Dahomey, where General Soglo took over on December 22, to the Central African Republic, where Colonel Bokassa deposed President David Dacko in the night of December 31–January 1, to Upper Volta, where the army ousted President Yameogo on January 4, to Nigeria, where a confusing coup left the country in the hands of General Ironsi on January 15, and, finally, to Ghana, where the seemingly impregnable Nkrumah was overthrown on February 24. Although each coup was undoubtedly largely determined by economic and social conditions particular to the country involved, in at least four cases—Congo-Leopoldville, Dahomey, Central African Republic, and Ghana—the army was also motivated by a distrust of the government's more or less pro-Communist tendencies and by a desire to step up cooperation with the former colonial power.[14] On the all-African scale, the most significant result of the military takeovers was thus to strengthen the moderate camp at the expense of the radicals and, in the immediate future, to scuttle any chances the OAU conference had of drawing the two groups together in united opposition to Rhodesia.

Meeting at Addis Ababa four days after the Ghana coup, the foreign ministers tried unsuccessfully to come to an agreement on the seat-

----

[14] In the case of the Congo, President Kasavubu had been leaning on anti-West backers in his effort to discredit Tshombe, and Minister of the Interior, Nendaka, had just announced a decision to exclude Belgian officers from the Congolese army. In Dahomey two of the first measures proclaimed by Colonel Soglo's government were the intention of forming closer ties with France and the suspension of diplomatic relations with Communist China. In the Central African Republic relations with Communist China were broken off less than a week after the coup, following the discovery of an alleged Chinese plot to build up a "revolutionary army" within the country. In Ghana, the standard-bearer of the African socialist states, the shift in allegiance was most dramatic. Chinese, Russian, and East German technical advisers were expelled and the size of the Communist diplomatic missions enormously reduced. On the other hand, relations with Britain were re-established on March 5, and an American offer of aid, which had been refused to the Nkrumah regime, was announced on April 4.

ing of the delegation sent by the new military government of Ghana. The eventual decision to recognize the delegation, compounded by a resolution on Rhodesia which practically annulled the December 3 decision to break relations with Britain, was too much for the radical states. One by one, Mali, Guinea, Tanzania, the U.A.R., Algeria, Kenya, Somalia, and Congo-Brazzaville walked out of the session, and Mauritania and Sudan joined them in refusing to take part in the final vote.

The failure of the OAU to establish a consensus on Rhodesia has clearly hampered African efforts to work for a swift overthrow of the Smith regime. United in their opposition to the white Rhodesian government, the African states have wasted their strength and tried their tempers in quarrels over details, such as the rupture with Great Britain and aid to nationalist movements.[15] The views and actions of an organization which can muster only two-thirds of its members in favor of a final resolution on Rhodesia obviously have less weight than if they were backed unanimously by the entire group, and the unorthodox stalling procedures in which the African states indulged at the UN in April [16] were hardly likely to improve their reputation with the "Great Powers" whose collaboration is essential in the anti-Rhodesian campaign. Although in the last week of April the African delegates to the UN stepped up their diplomatic activity, it was clear that, unless the OAU managed to patch up its internal quarrels, its contribution to the fight against Rhodesia would be less significant, and above all less coherent, than could have been expected. The crisis, which had been expected to work as a cohesive factor, had magnified the division between radicals and moderates and dramatized the weak points of the OAU.

*   *   *   *   *

The OAU's difficulties are thus due in large measure to the division of its members into two camps, and their inability or unwillingness to resolve their differences within the framework of the Organization. The spell of relative calm in inter-African affairs following the creation of the OAU seemed to indicate that both radicals and moderates had come to accept the fact that a state-in-the-making cannot afford too flamboyant a

---

[15] An Algerian proposal to "intensify the organization . . . of the nationalists in Rhodesia with a view to launching armed action within the country and to recognize the ZAPU as the only liberation movement in Rhodesia" was rejected at the February meeting in favor of a more general and moderately worded resolution.

[16] While a majority of the Security Council supported Britain's call for an emergency meeting on April 7, to approve British use of force to stop the tanker *Joanna V* from unloading oil at Beira (and actually staged a "sit-in" in the conference room), the Council's president for the month, Mali's Moussa Leo Keita, refused to convene the meeting until April 9, in the hopes of achieving unanimous African support for a broader application of Chapter VII of the Charter. In the end the two moderate African members of the Security Council, Uganda and Nigeria, rallied to the British proposal, while Mali abstained.

foreign policy, and that they had tended to abandon their original extreme positions. The events of the past months demonstrate, however, that the calm was only a lull, and that neither of the two groups has modified its basic outlook to any significant degree. The Entente's anti-Ghanaian campaign underlined not only the four states' legitimate concern with their neighbor's policy of sheltering "subversive" elements, but also a basic difference in opinion, only superficially veiled by vague terms, such as "African socialism," as to the scope and the goals of the African "revolution." In their support of the Congolese rebels the radical states showed that they are still ready to intervene when an occasion arises to strike a blow against "neo-colonialism" and "Western imperialism." On the other side of the fence, the ex-French states' approbation of Tshombe was just another episode in this group's traditional defense of the status quo. The creation of the OCAM has qualified their acceptance of the Pan-African cause in the form of the OAU and has re-emphasized the gap between the French- and English-speaking states.[17] The question of relations with the former colonial power and with the "colonialist" powers in general, a strictly *tiers monde* factor in the alignment of radical and moderate camps, is just as explosive as ever. The radical states were unanimous in condemning the West African *coups d'état* as transparent imperialist maneuvers,[18] while in the bitter Entente-Guinea exchange which exploded after the Ghanaian upset, Sekou Touré adopted as his own Nkrumah's invectives against the Entente's alleged collaboration with the neo-colonialists—a charge which Houphouet-Boigny's threat to call in France if Guinea got nasty was hardly calculated to belie.[19]

[17] These tendencies were reinforced at a meeting held at Tananarive from January 12–18, 1965, to initial the charter of the new organization. Described by the Foreign Minister of Dahomey as "no different from that of the UAM" the charter marked the victory of the partisans of political collaboration. The conference also declared itself in favor of the idea of a "Commonwealth *à la française*" (proposed by Bourguiba and Senghor), a project which Sekou Touré has denounced as a maneuver by "the agents of division who wish to weaken, if not liquidate the OAU."

[18] To quote a sampling of radical declarations: Modibo Keita (February 20): "Imperialism has decided to set up puppets in Africa after having sowed permanent instability and disorders all over, in order to perpetuate their exploitation." Political Bureau of the MNR, ruling party of the Congo-Brazzaville (February 26): The overthrow of Nkrumah was the result of "imperialist intrigues." Sekou Touré (February 27): "Let us consider ourselves in a state of war. . . . It is in Guinea that we will stop the criminal hand of imperialism that is strangling Africa."

[19] It must be kept in mind, however, that the same sort of divisions which threaten the OAU operate at the level of the sub-group as well. The OCAM is hardly more homogeneous than the OAU itself. It, too, has its more "moderate" and its more "radical" members, and it is even more likely to break up over an issue like the Congo or Chinese penetration in the measure that it does not enjoy the prestige and the ideological foundation of the larger organization. Three countries, in fact, Mauritania, Cameroon, and Congo-Brazzaville, refused to attend the Abidjan conference which granted the Congo-Leopoldville membership and committed the

These divisions have inevitably been reflected at the level of the OAU. There is no reason why the constitution of pressure groups should necessarily bode ill for the Organization. In a certain sense, the existence of lobbies is a sign of a healthy institution, for they indicate a general belief that the organization is worth pushing in one direction or another. But the danger lies in the fact that only a flourishing organism can support the action of pressure groups without being split by them, and only responsible lobbies can sense where pressure stops and bullying begins. In the months preceding the Accra conference of October 1965 the moderate French-speaking states took the initiative, with the clear intention of dragging the rest of the OAU with them. As the President of Chad remarked after the Nouakchott meeting: "The OCAM has an important role to play within the OAU for the resolution of the Congo problem. If need be, the OCAM will impose its views in order to bring an end to the Congolese crisis." The irresponsibility of their position was most dramatically evident in their decision to boycott the Accra conference, where one of the very problems on which they had been campaigning vociferously—the question of inter-state subversion—came up for comprehensive discussion. At the December 3 meeting at Addis Ababa the radicals ran out in front, and succeeded in pushing through a resolution on Rhodesia which two-thirds of the members who voted it refused to carry out. By the end of February the balance had swung to the moderate camp, and it was the radicals who walked out of a meeting they could not control rather than abide by the majority decision. Such attitudes are danger signals, for they indicate that, in the event that discreet pressure fails, the "lobbies" are tempted to jeopardize the existence of the OAU rather than abandon their claims. The play of extremes in a none too sturdy institutional framework results not in a golden mean, but in confusion and paralysis, and the OAU thus becomes a sort of diplomatic tautology—an organization which works only when harmony already exists rather than a force creating, or at least favoring, good relations among its members.

Another disquieting tendency is the Council of Ministers' habit of shelving major decisions and passing them on to the Assembly of Heads of State, a practice which threatens to turn the OAU into a façade, rather than an active instrument, of cooperation. Required to meet in ordinary session at least twice each year, and in extraordinary session on the approval of two-thirds of its members, the Council was conceived to provide a permanent safety-valve for the tensions which are bound to arise among new states still seeking their equilibrium. Its abdication on a

OCAM to an active anti-Communist, anti-Ghanaian campaign, and on July 6, 1965, Mauritania withdrew from the organization. On the other side of the fence, the radicals seem just as unlikely to create a cohesive sub-group. Although a meeting grouping Nkrumah, Touré, Keita, and various Sudanese ministers was held at Bamako after the Ghanaian coup, neither Touré's proposal to organize the revolutionary wing of the OAU nor his project to invade Ghana have met with any official support from his radical colleagues.

number of important occasions marks a failure to make the Organization work on a day-to-day basis, and a reliance instead on diplomatic maneuvering among individual leaders of separate states. The problem is not particular to the African states, as many of the UN crises demonstrate, but this is a negative comfort at best. In order to build a truly viable organization, there must be cooperation at all levels, and the member states must agree to delegate enough of their sovereignty to ensure that the OAU's decisions, those of the Council of Ministers and the various committees no less than those of the Assembly of Heads of State, carry the weight of authority.

The OAU undoubtedly bit off more than it could chew at the 1963 Pan-African summit. It proclaimed the institutional realization of African unity when all that existed was a general belief in the necessity of inter-African cooperation. It set out to construct this unity immediately in all possible spheres and on all levels. The result was, on the one hand, a sense of disillusionment when the African states realized that unity is not something only to be proclaimed, but something to be worked for, with all the give and take, renunciation and compromise that are involved in making 36 voices speak as one. On the other hand, the outcome was a multiplication of meetings which half the states failed to attend, and a financial crisis caused by irregularity in the payment of dues. On the administrative level, at least, the OAU has proved its ability to learn from past mistakes. The budget adopted by the sixth ordinary session of the Council of Ministers marked a drastic reduction over past years: $1,700,000 as opposed to $4,500,000. This measure of economy was made possible by a simplification of the Organization's top-heavy structures. In the political domain as well, the African states must learn to limit their sights and define their objectives more realistically. Both factions must learn that the OAU will serve their interests better if they regard it not as a prize to be conquered or rejected, but as an institutional framework for the harmonization of contrasting positions; that while within the OAU they might run the risk of being overruled on occasion by the other camp, outside the OAU they have little prospect of resolving the differences which nourish the existence of these two camps, nor of solving the economic, political and social problems which Africa as a whole, both radicals and moderates, are facing.

PART IV

ALLIANCE DISINTEGRATION

Sino-Soviet Military Relations, 1945-1966

RAYMOND L. GARTHOFF

The Soviet Union and Communist China are both drawn together and divided by ideology, national interest, military alliance, and political collaboration. The military is only one strand in a complex pattern of relationships. Military frictions have aggravated the serious rift between the two powers; even more significantly, the military has been the victim of political and ideological conflicts.

Chinese Communist–Soviet military relations have passed through four more or less equal periods. First is the background period from the Soviet occupation of Manchuria in August, 1945, through the Chinese Civil War, to the establishment of Communist rule in Mainland China and the signing of the Sino-Soviet treaty of alliance in February, 1950. The second period can be traced from that date through the Korean War until late 1954, following the visit of Khrushchev and Bulganin to Peking. Their subsequent succession to power in Moscow in February, 1955, marks the beginning of a period of growing but strained cooperation. The current period began in mid-1960 with the sudden cut-off of Soviet military and other assistance. This phase has been distinguished by the virtual absence of military relations in any form. Each of these periods is sufficiently distinctive, and sufficiently significant, to merit close attention.

The full story of Soviet relations with the Chinese Communists during the postwar phase of the Chinese Civil War is not yet clear, but the features relevant to the present inquiry are known. Stalin cautiously reinsured Soviet influence by his "correct" diplomatic dealings with the Nationalist Government, while he gave some assistance to the Communists. The Soviet policy of double-dealing may be explained by Stalin's uncertainty as to the outcome of the Civil War, but it is also entirely possible that he wanted China to remain divided for a long period, and therefore chose to aid both sides in different ways.

During the critical years from 1945 through 1948, Soviet assistance to China was limited. Military assistance consisted in allowing the Chinese Communists to gain strategic footholds and to acquire captured Japanese ordnance in Manchuria; political assistance was initially given to the Nationalist Government by the 1945 Treaty of Friendship, which clearly recognized it as the government of all China; and economic "assistance" was limited to stripping Manchuria of its industrial assets at the expense of both Chinese rivals. The Soviet looting of Manchurian "reparations" is inconsistent with the contention that the Russians handed Manchuria over to the Chinese Communists so that they could have a base to defeat the Nationalists. If that were the case, why destroy the major part of the great Mukden arsenals which could have given the Chinese Communists the wherewithal to fight? Finally, there is evidence that, in 1945 and 1946, Stalin urged the Chinese Communists to form a coalition with the Nationalists.[1] Mao did not do so, not only because he may have been more aware of the opportunities than Stalin, but because his one objective was to seize complete power and build a strong Communist China. The Soviet objective was to win concessions and influence for the U.S.S.R. from a weak China, and to keep China weak through a nominal Nationalist role in which the Russians had powerful leverage through the Communists (and through other elements such as dissidents in Sinkiang, and various war lords).

The Russians, therefore, permitted the Chinese Communist Eighth Route Army to enter Manchuria, harassed (but did not prevent) the arrival of Chinese Nationalist troops, and allowed the Communists to "seize" captured Japanese military equipment and supplies in raids on lightly "guarded" stocks. In all, the Russians captured from the Japanese about 300,000 rifles, nearly 5,000 machine guns, 1,226 artillery pieces, 369 tanks, and 925 aircraft. Much of the artillery and small arms, and some of the tanks and aircraft, were then acquired by the Chinese Communist forces in the spring of 1946. This equipment included their first tanks and combat aircraft in the whole Civil War. The Russians also released the ex-Manchukuo Army personnel, a number of whom were recruited by the Communists. The Russians withdrew from Manchuria in May, 1946, leaving the Chinese Nationalists in nominal control—but the Com-

---

[1] For example, Stalin informed Yugoslav Party leaders that he had advised the Chinese Communists to enter a coalition government. See Vladimir Dedijer, *Tito* (New York, 1953), p. 322.

munists in effective control of the northeastern two-thirds of the region.[2]

There is no evidence of further Soviet military assistance to the Chinese Communists during the four years of Civil War. The Chinese Communist forces were equipped with a conglomeration of United States and Japanese-produced weapons, most of them captured from the Nationalist forces. Chinese Communist claims for *gross* capture during the whole period from mid-1946 to 1950 were 3,160,000 rifles, 320,000 machine guns, 55,000 artillery pieces, 622 tanks and 389 armored cars, 189 military aircraft, and 200 small warships.[3] Assuming these figures are correct, it is evident that the Russians permitted the Chinese Communists to seize only small amounts of tanks and aircraft in Manchuria. The Chinese Nationalists took much larger quantities of captured Japanese ordnance in 1945–1946 than the Russians did—twice as many rifles, six times as many machine guns, and ten times as many artillery pieces.[4] The items the Communists seized from the Nationalists, including the United States matériel originally supplied to the Nationalist armies, and not Soviet-supplied weapons, provided the Chinese Communist forces with the implements for winning the Civil War.

By the end of the Civil War in 1950, the People's Liberation Army (as it had been renamed in 1946) was a poorly equipped and ill-balanced infantry force of about 5 million men (many from the Nationalist or war-lord armies) formed loosely into four "field armies" with a total of 215 "divisions." [5] Air, naval, armored, and technical units were few and miscellaneous. When, in 1949, the retreating Nationalists stood their ground at Quemoy, the Chinese Communists were not even able to take that modestly defended offshore island.

A Treaty of Friendship, Alliance, and Mutual Assistance between the U.S.S.R. and the C.P.R. was signed in Moscow on February 14, 1950. An economic development loan of $300 million from the Soviet Union was included in the agreements.[6] Protocols for military assistance were not known or published, but it is clear that arrangements were made for the Soviet Union to supply matériel and training. Under these arrangements, a Soviet military mission was established in Peking and an estimated 3,000 Soviet military advisers were sent to China.[7] Some Chinese

---

[2] These data are taken largely from Lieutenant Colonel Robert Rigg, *Red China's Fighting Hordes* (Harrisburg, Pa., 1952), pp. 100, 248, 251, 277, and 297. See also Max Beloff, *Soviet Policy in the Far East, 1944–1951* (New York, 1953), pp. 20–64; F. F. Liu, *A Military History of Modern China, 1924–1949* (Princeton, N.J., 1956), pp. 227–29; and General L. M. Chassin, *La Conquête de la Chine par Mao Tse-tung* (Paris, 1952), *passim*.

[3] Rigg, *op. cit.*, p. 255.

[4] *Ibid.*, p. 276.

[5] See Harold C. Hinton, "Communist China's Military Posture," *Current History*, September, 1962, pp. 150–51.

[6] The full texts of the treaty and associated agreements are given in Appendix B.

[7] This estimated figure is given by Rigg, *op. cit.*, p. 302.

military men may also have been sent to the U.S.S.R. for specialized training.[8] Hundreds of obsolescent Soviet La-9 and La-11 piston fighters and Tu-2 twin piston-engine light bombers appeared in China. Thus, a program of military aid was begun.

In his exhaustive analysis of Chinese policy on the eve of the Korean War, Dr. Allen Whiting finds no signs of Chinese Communist participation in planning that conflict, nor, until the summer of 1950, any preparation for possible participation in it.[9] The Russians alone had been involved in building up the North Korean Army and in unleashing it. However, the unexpected United States intervention in support of the defenders, and the unexpected United States success in crushing the North Korean forces (autumn, 1950), led to what General MacArthur termed, with some justice, "an entirely new war." The Chinese entered the contest.

The Sino-Soviet military relationship also entered a new phase, for the Chinese had to be entrusted with waging a war begun without them. It is likely that the Russians had been planning that the Chinese acquire jet fighters—apart from the Korean War. But under the exigencies of the war, MIG fighters appeared in Manchuria in late October, and entered combat against United States aircraft along the Yalu on November 1, 1950.[10] By December, 1951, the Chinese Communists had about 700 MIG-15 fighters and 200 Tu-2 piston light bombers, mostly concentrated in North China, and claimed a total air strength of 2,480 aircraft of all types.[11] By 1952, they had Il-28 jet light bombers, though these were not used in combat.[12] Later, at about the end of the war, a token number of Tu-4's (B-29-type piston medium bombers) were transferred to Communist China.

Military expenditures represented 48 percent of the Chinese budget by 1951.[13] The Soviet military-aid program became and remained extensive, but it also was expensive. The Chinese were compelled to *purchase* all this matériel, and they incurred heavy debts in the process. From 1950 to 1957, the value of such aid approximated $2 billion, of which perhaps half was covered by Soviet credits.[14] Even school children were canvassed for funds to be spent on Soviet tanks and aircraft in 1953.[15] Early in 1957, during a period of relative freedom of expression in

---

[8] Rigg (*op. cit.*, p. 321) notes that the Russians unofficially provided training to some Chinese Communist airmen in the U.S.S.R. in 1947–49. If true, this is the one exception to nonassistance from 1946 to 1950.

[9] Allen S. Whiting, *China Crosses the Yalu* (New York, 1960), pp. iv–v *et passim.*

[10] *Ibid.*, p. 135.

[11] Rigg, *op. cit.*, pp. 323–24.

[12] The piston light bombers were used in combat but once; a flight of ten sent down the North Korean coast was intercepted by U.S. jet fighters, and nine were destroyed.

[13] Rigg, "Red Army in Retreat," *Current History*, January, 1957, p. 3.

[14] Allen S. Whiting, " 'Contradictions' in the Moscow-Peking Axis," *Journal of Politics*, February, 1958, pp. 127–61.

[15] Rigg, *Current History*, January, 1957, p. 3.

China, General Lung Yun, a former dissident Nationalist, but then a member of the Revolutionary Military Committee of the C.P.R. and a vice-chairman of the National Defense Committee, publicly declared that it was "totally unfair for the People's Republic of China to bear all the expenses of the Korean War." [16] He noted that the United States had forgiven Allied debts in World Wars I and II, while the Soviet Union had not. Finally, he recalled that the Soviet Army had dismantled and taken away Manchurian industry in 1946.

Finally, in 1965, the Chinese Communists succeeded in repaying in full the heavy debt imposed by the Soviet Union for military assistance in the Korean War.

Soviet assistance was essential to China; the Chinese had no choice but to accept Soviet terms. Modernization and mechanization of the Chinese military establishment required production, logistics, and communications systems that would have been impossible to obtain otherwise.

While building Chinese military power, Stalin kept it fully dependent on the Soviet Union. Weapons were supplied, but not assistance in creating military production. China was held on a short leash: The MIG's and Ilyushins, and the few obsolescent Soviet submarines and destroyers, would need to be replaced in a few years, and their replacement could come only from the U.S.S.R. The Russians could not directly prevent the Chinese Communists from building their own military industry, but they could withhold their assistance while arguing that it was more economical to buy Soviet-produced weapons. And, by saddling them with outlays as heavy as they could bear, the Russians further held back the Chinese from building an independent military establishment.

Stalin used the occasion of the Korean War to sell more modern weapons to China; he also pressed the Chinese in other ways. In September, 1952, he forced a modification of the 1950 Treaty extending indefinitely the Soviet occupation of Port Arthur on the Yellow Sea by deferring withdrawal until after a Japanese peace treaty was signed.[17]

The death of Stalin profoundly—though not immediately—affected Sino-Soviet relations. Soviet and Chinese interests converged in finishing the Korean War, but beyond this, both countries recognized the need for redefining their relationship. Accordingly, a high-level Soviet delegation visited Peking in October, 1954.

Symbolically, it was important that the review of Sino-Soviet relations took place in Peking rather than in Moscow. Khrushchev, Bulganin, Mikoyan, and Shvernik headed the delegation, reflecting the combined political, Party, economic, and military interests involved. Agreements were signed on October 11, 1954. One reversed the Stalin *diktat* of only

[16] *Hsinhua,* June 18, 1957. See Greg MacGregor, "Peiping General Criticizes Soviet on Seized Plants," *The New York Times,* June 24, 1957.
[17] See the text in Appendix B [of *Sino-Soviet Military Relations* by Raymond L. Garthoff].

two years earlier; the U.S.S.R. agreed to withdraw from Port Arthur by May 31, 1955, and to turn over the Soviet installations there without compensation. A scientific-technical agreement was also signed. The provision of the 1950 Treaty for joint exploitation of uranium resources in Sinkiang was revoked,[18] with full control reverting to China on January 1, 1955. No new military agreements were announced or, apparently, reached.

In May, 1955, the Chinese Communist Minister of Defense, Marshal P'eng Teh-huai, was invited to the ceremony founding the Warsaw Pact, and then spent June in Moscow in discussions with Soviet military representatives. But China did not become a member of the Warsaw Pact.

In 1955, the Russians withdrew from Port Arthur as promised, leaving the aircraft belonging to their units there to extend the impression of generosity. An additional agreement on cooperation in the peaceful applications of atomic energy was reached in 1955. The following year, China joined other Communist states in entering the cooperative "socialist" nonmilitary atomic research center at Dubna near Moscow (where the Russians, incidentally, could siphon off the work of the best East European and Chinese nuclear physicists). Chinese specialists at Dubna were finally all withdrawn in 1965.

The flow of Soviet modern weapons diminished during the late 1950's, not because the Russians decided to choke it off but because the short-term air force and naval strength levels had been reached. In retrospect, it seems clear that the Chinese demand that modern defense industry be built up in China was gaining acceptance. Progress had been made by the Chinese in conventional basic land armaments such as small arms and artillery; but now, with Soviet help, a beginning was also made in the partial construction and assembly of jet fighters, complete construction of light piston aircraft, and construction of tanks, submarines, and small patrol craft. By September, 1956, the first jet fighters of Chinese "manufacture" were flown—with some fanfare.[19] By the end of the 1950's, the Chinese Communist Air Force had hundreds of MIG-17's and some MIG-19's, as well as many older MIG-15's.

The Chinese Communist Army, by the late 1950's, had been substantially modernized into a force of reasonably well-equipped light infantry divisions.[20] Soviet training activities had been largely completed and phased out in the mid- and late-1950's, and the military mission in Peking turned to problems of production facilities in more modern armaments and to coordination of military activities.

It should be noted that, throughout both the Stalin and post-Stalin periods, there has been no indication of coordinated training exercises or

[18] George A. Modelski, *Atomic Energy in the Communist Bloc* (Melbourne, 1959), pp. 181–95.
[19] Rigg, *Current History*, January, 1957, p. 5.
[20] *Ibid.*, p. 3.

maneuvers between the Soviet and Chinese Communist armies, navies, or air forces. Apart from the very limited direct Soviet support to the Chinese during the Korean War, there has been no real coordination of their military operations or training. In the Far East, there has been no bilateral equivalent of the Warsaw Pact to integrate air defenses and naval operations. Why? Political factors must have put a damper on the exercising of alliance privileges that would bring such military benefit. Political charges between the Soviet and Chinese Communist parties later revealed that a Soviet-proposed joint naval command in the Pacific foundered because of Chinese refusal to accept a subordinate role.[21] Chinese sensitivity over equality of roles probably also was responsible for failure to integrate an air defense system.

Ultimately, the growing political estrangement between the Russian and Chinese Communists more sharply affected military relationships, but, even when the political surface was placid and harmonious, there were severe limits on the nature and extent of military relationships.

During the period after 1954, there were important developments in military doctrine in the Soviet Union and Communist China. Both countries belatedly recognized the implications of nuclear war, though the implications for each were very different. The Russians had to adjust their concepts to weapons they had or were acquiring, while the Chinese military leaders were faced with the frustration of recognizing the decisive importance of weapons they did not possess.

In 1955, a number of Chinese military men began to stress the importance of nuclear weapons and of new military technology in general, and to state specifically that China needed and would acquire "a sufficient quantity of the most modern matériel to arm the Chinese People's Liberation Army." [22] However, some military leaders (especially in the General Staff) placed most emphasis on the immediate need for modern weapons, while those in the Ministry of Defense (and the political officers) continued to emphasize the basic political-morale factors of a people's army, in the Maoist tradition.[23] This divergence was in part over doctrine and in part over policy: Should Communist China acquire her own nuclear weapons or rely on the Soviet Union? By either approach, China would depend heavily on the U.S.S.R.—either for Soviet nuclear protection and support, or for Soviet assistance in developing Chinese capabilities.[24] In 1955, also, the Russians began to assist in the

[21] See Edward Crankshaw, "Sino-Soviet Rift Held Very Deep," *Washington Post*, February 12, 1961.

[22] Marshal Yeh Chien-ying, *NCNA* (New China News Agency release), Peking, July 27, 1955.

[23] See the detailed account of the 1954–57 debate in Alice L. Hsieh, *Communist China's Strategy in the Nuclear Era* (New York, 1962), pp. 15–75.

[24] *Ibid.*, pp. 72–75.

development of a modern Chinese military industry and a nonmilitary nuclear program.

On October 15, 1957, an important agreement with respect to "new technology for national defense" was concluded between the U.S.S.R. and Communist China. This agreement was secret, and was disclosed by the Chinese only in 1963, in protest over alleged Soviet perfidy in unilaterally "tearing it up" in June, 1959.[25] The Russians have not explicitly discussed the agreement, but they have implicitly acknowledged its existence by criticizing the Chinese for revealing joint defense secrets. The precise terms of the agreement are still not known, but it is likely that they were vague and general. The Chinese disclosure of the agreement did not specify its content, but stated that, in June, 1959, the Russians "tore up the agreement, *and* refused to supply a sample atomic bomb and technical data concerning its manufacture"; they did not state the supply of a sample nuclear weapon and technical data was promised in the agreement, which is extremely unlikely, but they imply that liberal interpretation of the spirit of the agreement *should* have extended to supply detailed data on nuclear weapons. It is clear that the Soviet leaders in the latter half of the 1950's were torn between wishing to improve relations with China and seeking to prevent Chinese acquisition of nuclear and other advanced weapons. As a consequence of these opposing motivations, their policies were not fully consistent. The Russians refused to assist in nuclear-weapon technology, but they did assist the Chinese in building a major gaseous diffusion facility for production of fissionable materials (U-235) useful for weapons as well as for other purposes. Thus, they assisted the Chinese Communist nuclear program until 1960—but reluctantly and incompletely.

On the fortieth anniversary of the Russian Revolution, November, 1957, Mao Tse-tung and a delegation of Chinese military leaders visited Moscow. The successful Soviet testing of an ICBM and launching of the first artificial earth satellite encouraged the Chinese almost more than it did the Russians, but it also underlined the gap between Chinese and Soviet capabilities. Later indications suggest that Mao sought a greater role for China in the Communist camp, and that he may have requested nuclear weapons for China and other far-reaching concrete actions not specified in the new agreement.[26] Among Mao's colleagues visiting Moscow were the Minister of Defense, Marshal P'eng Teh-huai, and the two leading Army "modernizers," Marshal Yeh Chien-ying and General Su Yu, the Chief of the General Staff.[27] Presumably, the military mission

25 See *Hsinhua*, August 15, 1963, and September 1, 1963, and *Hung Ch'i* (*Red Flag*) and *Jen-min Jih-pao* (*People's Daily*), September 6, 1963.
26 See Hsieh, *Communist China's Strategy*, pp. 76–109; and Hsieh, "China, Russia and the Bomb," *The New Leader*, October 17, 1960.
27 *Ibid.* See also Donald S. Zagoria, *The Sino-Soviet Conflict, 1956–1961* (Princeton, N.J., 1962), pp. 169–71.

was concerned with implementing the October agreement. It is, however, possible that additional assistance on nuclear weapons was requested—and denied. It is thus possible that the nuclear issue became associated with the ideological-political disagreements over the 1957 multi-Party declaration.

During the period from late 1957 until mid-1960, the Russians continued to aid the Chinese in developing their own missiles and aircraft, and probably in working toward construction of their own fissionable materials production. But it is quite clear that, at some point between November, 1957, and May, 1958, the Russians disclosed the "strings" that they placed on any disposition of nuclear warheads: Soviet control in a joint enterprise. The Chinese have since declared that: "In 1958 the leadership of the CPSU put forward unreasonable demands designed to bring China under Soviet military control. These unreasonable demands were rightly and firmly rejected by the Chinese Government." [28] The Russian proposals were for a joint Sino-Soviet naval command in the Far East, for more closely integrated air defenses, and possibly also concerned deployments of offensive Soviet nuclear weapons systems. The Secretary General of the Sino-Japanese Friendship Association, Chang An-po, has said that these Soviet proposals were made in April, 1958.[29]

At some point (or points) between October, 1957, and June, 1959, the Chinese pressed to get actual nuclear weapons. The Russians themselves have acknowledged that they refused even to consider Chinese requests for nuclear weapons. As Radio Moscow has stated: "The Chinese leaders have been at great pains to obtain possession of nuclear weapons. They strenuously tried—this is no secret—to get the Soviet Union to give them the atomic bomb. The CPSU and the Soviet Government naturally could not consider this, since it might have led to the most serious consequences." [30]

As the facts of nuclear-missile warfare, and the implications of Soviet refusal to provide nuclear weapons to China, sank more deeply into the Chinese consciousness in 1958, significant policy disputes led to new decisions. During the spring and summer of 1958, a debate over military doctrine erupted. The unreconstructed "modernizers" who stressed the urgent need for nuclear weapons and other advanced military technology were pitted against the "conservatives" who stressed the importance of the basic political factors and massive military manpower and relied on eventual Chinese development of its own weapons needs.

As early as January, Marshal P'eng declared that the Chinese must "on the basis of *our national* industrialization systematically arm our army with new technical equipment. In the light of *our* industrial capac-

---

[28] *Hung Ch'i* and *Jen-min Jih-pao*, September 6, 1965.
[29] BBC monitoring, cited in *China Quarterly*, April–June, 1964, p. 238.
[30] Radio Moscow, July 10, 1964.

ity, we can do so only gradually." [31] In May, Foreign Minister Marshal Ch'en Yi remarked in an interview that "At the moment China does not own atomic weapons, but we shall have them in the future." [32] And also in May, Air Force General Liu Ya-lou emphasized the need first to press priority economic build-up of the country, and then, on that basis, "*China's* working class and scientists will certainly be able to make the most up-to-date aircraft and atomic bombs in the not distant future." [33]

This new line combined the importance of nuclear weapons with a major *Chinese* effort to design and construct them (Chinese scientists, as well as workers and engineers, were referred to). But, faced with the Soviet refusal to supply nuclear weapons, the new line did not last long. It placed too much emphasis on the need for early Chinese acquisition of nuclear weapons—an impossibility, despite vigorous efforts. Doctrinal confusion over balancing the decisive importance of something that they did not have with assertions of *current* Chinese strength was too great. The military leaders may also have pressed Mao too hard. For these reasons, a major conference called by the Military Committee of the Party's Central Committee met from May 27 until July 22—two whole months of debate. Party leaders (including Mao) addressed the conference, which reportedly was attended by a thousand Chinese military officers. By the end of July, a new line had been adopted. Marshal Chu Teh spoke on July 31 of "defects" resulting from "tendencies toward an exclusive military viewpoint." [34] He said that the Chinese should study Soviet military experience, but by a "selective and creative" approach. The *Liberation Army Daily* on the next day explained that "a very few comrades" had "one-sidedly stressed the role of atomic weapons and modern military technology, and neglected the role of man." [35] Also on August 1, Marshal Ho Lung warned in *People's Daily* against relying on "outside aid" in solving China's military problems.[36] Yu Chao-li, in *Red Flag* on August 16, quoted Mao that "the atomic bomb is a paper tiger," a theme quickly picked up by others.[37] Finally, on September 6, 1958, the Central Committee of the Party adopted a resolution to mobilize the entire male population into a "people's militia," a development explicitly tied to Mao Tse-tung's "strategic thinking on the people's war." [38] In October, General Su Yu was removed as Chief of the General Staff.

The Chinese thus were forced gradually to build up advanced

---

31 Hsieh, *Communist China's Strategy in the Nuclear Era*, pp. 109–10.
32 *Ibid.*, pp. 106–8.
33 *Ibid.*, p. 112. See also Zagoria, *op. cit.*, p. 192.
34 Hsieh, *op. cit.*, pp. 114 and 116. For discussion of the conference, see also Zagoria, *op. cit.*, pp. 189–94.
35 Hsieh, *op. cit.*, p. 116.
36 Zagoria, *op. cit.*, p. 193.
37 Yu Chao-li, in *Hung Ch'i*, August 16, 1958. See also *Liberation Army Daily*, October 24, 1958, and *Jen-min Jih-pao*, November 12, 1958.
38 *Hung Ch'i*, October 16, 1958.

weapons capabilities with minimal Soviet assistance, while playing down the significance of these weapons that they did not yet have. There were ample signs of undercurrents of military dissatisfaction with this solution.[39]

The impotence of the Chinese, and Soviet refusal to back them in any risky situation of Chinese interest, was evident in the Quemoy crisis of August–September, 1958.[40] It is not clear to what extent the Russians approved Chinese plans to stir up a crisis in the Taiwan Straits by heavy artillery bombardment of Quemoy. Khrushchev met Mao in Peking at the end of July, 1958, probably to discuss both the recent Middle Eastern crisis and the Chinese plans with respect to Quemoy. In meeting the Middle Eastern crisis, which had been touched off by the revolution in Iraq on July 13, Khrushchev veered from one line to another, and the Chinese were probably troubled by his shift from bellicosity to proposing either a meeting of the U.N. Security Council or of the Big Five (with India)—both of which could have involved settlement of an Asian crisis with Communist China conspicuously absent, and either the Republic of China or India involved. Thus, by the time of Mao's meeting with Khrushchev, the Chinese leaders had doubts about the consistency of Soviet support.

Subsequent Soviet action in the course of the Quemoy crisis was hardly reassuring. Only when the Russians were sure that the Chinese would enter negotiations and not press the confrontation to the extent of a direct challenge to the United States did Khrushchev, on September 7, give a public pledge of Soviet assistance, and then only if China itself were attacked by the United States. Thus the Soviets attempted to deter the United States from expanding the crisis, but also failed to lend real support to Mao's offensive move against the offshore islands.

At the time of Khrushchev's meeting with Mao, Marshals Malinovsky and P'eng Teh-huai were also present. Soon thereafter, "leaks" in Warsaw allegedly disclosed Soviet-Chinese accords on increased economic and military assistance. These reports suggested that the Russians had even agreed to supply the Chinese with nuclear warheads.[41] On the basis of later information, it is clear that nuclear warheads were neither promised nor supplied, and neither the Russians nor the Chinese have ever referred to such an agreement.

During 1958 and 1959, the Chinese continued to stress their determination to get nuclear weapons. At first, in 1958, the Chinese supported

---

[39] See A. Kashin, "Chinese Military Doctrine," *Bulletin of the Institute for the Study of the USSR*, Munich, November, 1960, pp. 39–44.

[40] See discussion in Chapter 7; and see Hsieh, *Communist China's Strategy*, pp. 119–36.

[41] A. M. Rosenthal, "Warsaw Reports Soviet-China Pact," *The New York Times*, August 7, 1958, and "Soviet Atom Arms To Go To Peiping, Warsaw Learns," *The New York Times*, August 18, 1958.

the idea of a nuclear-free zone in the Far East, but when Khrushchev proposed this in a speech on January 27, 1959, Chinese reaction was cool.[42] Rather, the Chinese seized an East German statement of January 26, that, if West Germany got nuclear missiles, they too would "request" them from *their* allies. The Chinese (alone of the other Communist states) commented this would be "not only fully justified, but also necessary." [43] On January 21, 1960, the National People's Congress passed a resolution stressing that China would not be bound by any disarmament agreement except with its express consent, and that it would accept no disarmament agreement unless it had participated in its negotiation. The Russians were not being trusted to look out for Chinese politico-military interests.

Two startling developments in over-all Sino-Soviet relations occurred in mid-1959. From April 24 to June 13, 1959, Minister of Defense P'eng Teh-huai visited Eastern Europe, and was in Albania at the time of Khrushchev's visit. Marshal P'eng had not been one of the ardent "modernizers" in the mid-1950's, but he was well aware of the crucial importance of modern weapons. If he again asked for increased Soviet assistance, there is no evidence that he achieved anything. (In June, W. Averell Harriman was told by Khrushchev that the Soviet Union had sent missiles—he did not say with nuclear warheads—to protect Communist China against Taiwan, but this may have been an overstatement.) [44]

Suddenly, on September 17, 1959, the dismissal of Marshal P'eng Teh-huai and four vice-ministers was announced. P'eng was charged with heading an "anti-Party group." And, indeed, he had directly challenged Mao at the Lushan Central Committee plenum in August, 1959.[45] Moreover, P'eng had apparently written a letter to the Soviet Communist Party attacking Chinese Communist policies. (In an unpublished speech at Bucharest in June, 1960, Khrushchev criticized the Chinese Communist removal of P'eng for having communicated his views to the CPSU.) [46] P'eng may have been disturbed that the growing breach with the U.S.S.R. jeopardized Soviet arms aid. Meanwhile, another sign of the growing estrangement between the two Communist powers was the rehabilitation, in April, 1959, of former General Lung Yun who, in 1957, had openly criticized Soviet military assistance.[47]

Details are not known of the Russians' alleged repudiation of the 1957 agreement on June 20, 1959, and of their refusal to supply data on nuclear weapons technology. Perhaps Chinese Defense Minister P'eng

[42] See Hsieh, *Communist China's Strategy,* pp. 103–9 and 155–61.
[43] Editorial, *Jen-min Jih-pao,* February 4, 1959.
[44] Hsieh, *Communist China's Strategy,* p. 164.
[45] David A. Charles, "The Dismissal of Marshal P'eng Teh-huai," *The China Quarterly,* October–December, 1961, pp. 63 ff.
[46] *Ibid.,* pp. 64–65 and 74–75.
[47] See Ronald Farquhar, "China Posts Go to 18 Rightists," *Washington Post,* April 18, 1959.

Teh-huai had requested such aid during his visit to Moscow, and a Soviet reply on June 20 canceled the 1957 arrangements. If so, the Russians may have contributed to P'eng's downfall on his return to China. Be that as it may, such a Soviet move in June, 1959, fits both the trend of the deteriorating relationship between the two countries and the pattern of *détente* being built between the U.S.S.R. and the United States at that time.

The deterioration of Sino-Soviet relations over the next year was rapid, and finally erupted in April, 1960, with the publication by the Chinese of an ideological attack on the Russians. In July and August, 1960, the Russians withdrew their 1,300 economic and military advisers and technicians. This action was drastic, sudden, and virtually complete.

Since the sudden virtual cessation of Soviet military and economic assistance, there has been almost no Sino-Soviet military relationship. The effects, even in the short run, have been significant for the Chinese. Continued, though declining, Soviet export of petroleum products to China has been the chief form of indirect aid. On the other hand, clashes on the Sinkiang border have been reported in recent years.

After 1960, the Chinese Communist armed forces actually *decreased* in net capability. In the few years immediately ahead, the Chinese will undoubtedly develop their own capacity to build jet fighters, defensive surface-to-air missiles, radar, small warships, and short-range rockets. It is also to be expected that they will develop their nuclear devices into deliverable bombs and warheads, and will probably develop medium-range missiles. But all these developments were seriously delayed and are still hindered by the sharp slow-down of Soviet military and economic assistance of mid-1960, its complete cessation by 1963, and declining over-all trade since that time. For several years, the Chinese had to postpone their production of jet fighters and submarines; also postponed have been whatever plans they may have had for producing jet medium bombers. The numbers, and still more the proficiency, of the air forces have declined from attrition of matériel and from shortage of fuel for proficiency training. The ground forces have been much less affected, but they, too, are short of modern heavy ordnance.

At present, the Chinese Communist Army numbers about 2.5 million men, with about 110 infantry, about 4 armored, and about 2 airborne, divisions.[48] The Air Forces total about 2,300 aircraft of all types, including about 2,000 combat aircraft, mainly jet fighters (mostly older model MIG-15's and MIG-17's, with several hundred MIG-19's and from 25 to 35 MIG-21's), and about 275 Il-28 jet light bombers. Apart from about a dozen Tu-4 piston medium bombers, not new when given to the

[48] See the Institute for Strategic Studies, *The Military Balance, 1965–66* (London, 1965), pp. 9–10; *The Military Balance, 1964–65* (London, 1964), pp. 8–10; and *The Communist Bloc and the Western Alliances: The Military Balance, 1962–1963* (London, 1962), p. 8, and the same serial for 1963–64 (1963), pp. 9–10.

Chinese in the mid-1950's, and one or two Tu-16 medium jet bombers, the Chinese have no long-range air forces.[49] The Navy has 4 destroyers, 4 destroyer escorts, about 30 conventional attack submarines, and a modest number of patrol craft. By the end of 1965, the Chinese were probably beginning to produce jet fighter aircraft and submarines, including one missile-launching submarine (though not yet equipped with missiles).[50] Within a few years, the Chinese will probably have a small operational capability with 1,000 n.m. range MRBM's.[51]

The end of Soviet aid—apart from its material effects on the Chinese—placed the military alliance commitment in question. Soviet spokesman S. Titarenko, in a celebrated article in August, 1960, mentioned China directly in regard to the economic and military vulnerability of a socialist state that had strayed outside the socialist camp, was "isolated," and no longer engaged in "mutual cooperation." By the same token, he implied that Soviet support to China in case of war was conditional.[52] Marshal Malinovsky, in January, 1962, noted that Soviet strength would protect only "those socialist states *friendly* to us"—a very blunt warning indeed.[53] *Pravda*, in January, 1963 bitterly remarked that "those who criticized the U.S.S.R." for the Cuban missile venture could not hold off the imperialists without the U.S.S.R.[54]

The Soviet Government statement of September 21, 1963, carried further the earlier indications of a more careful and controlled Soviet interpretation of alliance commitments to China. On the one hand, the statement nullifies any Chinese Communist requirement for nuclear weapons of its own by pledging the protection of the Soviet nuclear deterrent to the whole socialist camp; but on the other hand, it criticizes Chinese Communist pursuit of "special aims and interests" which go *beyond* the legitimate interests of the socialist camp and "which *cannot* be supported by the military power of the socialist camp." [55] Thus, it made

---

[49] See Clare Hollingsworth, "China Soon to be Nuclear Power," *Manchester Guardian Weekly*, October 1, 1961; *China News* (Taiwan), July 10, 1962; Richard Frykland, "Chinese Reds Believed Building MiG Fighters," Washington *Evening Star*, December 31, 1964; Seymour Topping, "New Jet Fighters Detected in China," *The New York Times*, December 30, 1964; and Richard Frykland, "Joint Chiefs Minimize China's Military Power," Washington *Evening Star*, March 18, 1966. See also references cited in Note 48.

[50] See references cited in Note 49; and see "Missile Submarine in Red China's Navy," *The New York Times*, November 14, 1965.

[51] See Frykland, Washington *Evening Star*, March 18, 1966, citing Secretary of Defense Robert S. McNamara.

[52] See Zagoria, *op. cit.*, pp. 335–36.

[53] Marshal R. Malinovsky, *Tass*, January 24, 1962.

Malinovsky's restrictive statement about protecting socialist states "friendly" to the Soviet Union has been repeated on various occasions since, including Marshal Malinovsky's address to the Twenty-third Congress of the CPSU (*Krasnaya zvezda*, [*Red Star*], April 2, 1966).

[54] Editorial, *Pravda*, January 7, 1963.

[55] *Pravda*, September 21 and 22, 1963.

clear that Soviet alliance commitments do *not* extend to such situations and that Moscow will make the ultimate decision on what it regards as the legitimate interests of China (or Cuba, or any other socialist state), and, therefore, on its own course of action if China becomes embroiled with the United States.

The Chinese, in turn, have had to recognize (as Li Fu-Ch'un put it —coincidentally on the same day Titarenko's article was published in August, 1960) that China must "mainly rely on our own efforts" in the future.[56] And again, when Malinovsky was threatening the Chinese in 1962, Marshal Ch'en Yi was saying that all the Chinese problems including "*national* defense" could be solved by self-reliance.[57]

Unfettered by considerations of the Chinese reaction, the Russians opened new military assistance programs with more modern armament to Indonesia and the Middle East. Thanks to the U.S.S.R., Indonesia had a cruiser, Tu-16 jet medium bombers, and air-defense and short-range missiles by the mid-1960's, while the Chinese did not. Tu-16's were also provided to several other neutrals. In a move particularly galling to the Chinese, the Russians promised to provide India with a factory to produce MIG-21's. The Russians have more recently tried, with some success, to bribe the North Koreans toward their side in the dispute within the Communist Bloc with modern military aid. (Both the U.S.S.R. and China signed separate military defense pacts with North Korea in July, 1961.) Some Chinese military men may hanker for military cooperation with the U.S.S.R., but they probably exert no influence on the political controversy.

One or two paramount features of the decline in Sino-Soviet military relations may help in understanding, if not in predicting, future developments.

As the Soviet Union became increasingly concerned with avoiding risks of a nuclear war, and saw advantage in cultivating a *détente* with the United States, the Chinese Communists became increasingly assertive in urging more active confrontation of the imperialists.

The Russians have not wished to lessen fundamental Chinese dependence on the U.S.S.R., to give the Chinese Communists a fulcrum for bargaining power vis-à-vis the Russians, to raise Chinese prestige in the Communist movement or the world at large, or to increase the risks they themselves would run if the Chinese had capabilities that might tempt them to risk a conflict with the West. The Russians recognize the dilemma they would then face of supporting China at unacceptable costs to the Soviet Union, or of seeing Communist China destroyed at irreparable cost to Communism. Intensifying these concerns is the Chinese Communist pressure for stronger support of revolutionary activity by Communists elsewhere, as well as for more vigorous support of immediate

[56] Li Fu-Ch'un, *Hung Ch'i,* August 16, 1960.
[57] Ch'en Yi, *NCNA,* January 5, 1962.

Chinese aims. The Soviets define their policy in terms of their own interests.

Consequently, it is not surprising that in pursuing *their* objectives the Chinese have been dissatisfied with Soviet policy. The Russians may want a nuclear-free zone in the Far East to disarm both the United States and Communist China; the Chinese are unwilling to give up their aspirations to nuclear great-power status, even if their "security" were otherwise ensured. The Soviet efforts in the mid-1950's to give up the most imperialistic of Stalin's extortions vis-à-vis China, such as the Port Arthur base, were not sufficient; neither was the grudging support given from 1958 to mid-1960 to the production of aircraft and the creation of Chinese missiles.

Lobbying *within* the opposing countries is another point of interest in respect to the present and future. Chinese leaders, by indirection discussing Soviet internal affairs, made a fairly open bid to the Soviet *military* to oppose Khrushchev. In his interview with foreign reporters on October 28, 1963, Foreign Minister Ch'en Yi stated: ". . . the CPSU, the Soviet people, *and the Red Army* will not readily give up their friendship toward China," despite the Khrushchev policies.[58] With equal pointedness, the Chinese, on November 19, 1963, declared that, while the Red Army remains "a great force safeguarding world peace . . . Khrushchev's whole set of military theories runs completely counter to Marxist-Leninist teachings on war and the army. To follow his wrong theories will necessarily involve disintegrating the Army." [59] The situation has not basically changed since Khrushchev's ouster. Similarly, the Russians have continued to bid indirectly for the support of the Chinese Communist military leaders by such flattering references as the following: ". . . the mass heroism of its fighters and commanders turned the People's Liberation Army into an integral factor of victory of the Chinese Revolution." [60]

The broader political causes of the Sino-Soviet dispute, and the widening split since 1959, have intensified further military disassociation from the never-intimate relationship of the 1950's. These developments burden and delay, but do not completely foreclose, Chinese military modernization. The course of Sino-Soviet military relations will depend upon the political relations of the two powers.

If the conflict continues to deepen, and either side feels vitally threatened by the other, even the possibility of Sino-Soviet military hostilities cannot be entirely excluded from the consideration of both parties. The release of secret Chinese Communist People's Liberation Army

[58] See *Kyodo*, Tokyo, October 28, 1963 (evening edition), and "Peking Foresees a Delay of Years on Atomic Bomb," *The New York Times*, October 29, 1963.
[59] *Jen-min Jih-pao*, November 19, 1963.
[60] "Internationalism is the Source of Victory in Revolutionary Struggle," editorial, *Pravda*, October 1, 1965.

papers by the United States Department of State has disclosed a Military Affairs Committee directive of early 1961 on the need to preserve security of the Southwest and *Northwest* (i.e., Sino-Soviet) frontiers of China.[61] On the tenth anniversary of the founding of the Sinkiang Uighur Autonomous Region, the official report of the Chinese National Committee, and the concomitant press accounts, stressed that the peoples of Sinkiang "completely smashed the large-scale subversive activities and sabotage carried out by the Khrushchev revisionist group." [62] Vice-Premier (and former Marshal) Ho Lung stated more specifically: "In 1962, the people in the Sinkiang-Uighur Autonomous Region resolutely smashed the subversion and destruction frenziedly carried out by the Khrushchev revisionist clique in Sinkiang . . . and safeguarded the northwest frontier of the motherland." [63]

There have been reports since 1963 of tightening of the Soviet frontier defenses, and of strengthening of both Army and Border Guard units along the Sino-Soviet frontiers. Soviet military exercises in the Far East have involved mock repulse of a Chinese attack into the Maritime Province.[64] In early 1966, the Central Committee of the CPSU, in a secret letter sent to all Party organizations in the Soviet Union and to all fraternal Communist Parties, stated that the Chinese (Communist) Government was spreading false allegations "that the Soviet Union unlawfully holds Chinese territory in the Far East," and that "the Chinese side is provoking border conflicts. Such conflicts have again increased in recent months." [65] In a statement by Foreign Minister Ch'en Yi, the Chinese replied to the effect that the Russians have carried out "unbridled subversive activities in China's border areas. . . . They have deployed their troops on the Sino-Soviet border and carried out continual military maneuvers on the border, which presupposes China as the enemy." [66]

The same secret CPSU letter also raised two other new politico-military issues. One arises from the polemical dispute over whether the Soviet Union is giving sufficient assistance to the Democratic Republic of Vietnam (North Vietnam). After asserting that "military aid is being ren-

[61] *Kung Tso T'ung Hsün (Work Correspondence)*, Peking, February 1, 1961.

[62] CPPCC National Committee Message to the People's Council of the Sinkiang-Uighur Autonomous Region, Radio Peking, NCNA, September 29, 1965; and "Great Triumph for the Policy of National Solidarity of the Party," *Jen-min Jih-pao*, September 30, 1965.

[63] Speech by Vice Premier Ho Lung in Urumchi, Radio Peking, September 30, 1965.

[64] Victor Zorza, *The Guardian*, London, October 9, 1964.

[65] Excerpts From a Secret CPSU Letter to All Party Organizations in the Soviet Union and to All Fraternal Communist Parties, in *Die Welt (The World)*, Hamburg, March 21, 1966. The authenticity of the Letter as published in *Die Welt* has not been challenged.

[66] Official English-language *Press Release* by the Chinese Communist Embassy in Stockholm of Ch'en Yi interview with the Danish News Agency, May 24, 1966.

dered to the extent that the Vietnamese leadership itself considers necessary," despite the fact that the Chinese refuse to permit Soviet aircraft transporting weapons to overfly China, and have raised obstacles to rail shipment, the Russians conclude that: "There is every reason to assert that it is one of the goals of the policy of the Chinese leadership on the Vietnamese question to originate a military conflict between the U.S.S.R. and the United States. They want a clash between the U.S.S.R. and the United States in order that they may, as they themselves say, 'sit on the mountain and watch the battle of the tigers.' " [67] Finally, as though that were not enough, the Soviet leaders' letter also states: "The C.P.R. leadership ever more obstinately propagates the thesis of potential military clashes between China and the Soviet Union." [68] As an example, the letter cites Chinese Foreign Minister Ch'en Yi's reference at his press conference on September 29, 1965, to "a possible 'coordination' of Soviet actions in north China with an aggressive war by the United States against the C.P.R."; it termed this charge "utterly false." [69]

Complete reconciliation, with broad and deep alliance ties in all aspects of military preparation and planning—which would go far beyond anything achieved in the 1950's—seems as remote and unlikely as open conflict. The outlook is for a continuation of relative mutual military isolation, politico-military rivalry and indirect conflict, and, at best, conditional alliance commitments.

[67] In *Die Welt,* March 21, 1966.
[68] *Ibid.*
[69] *Ibid.*

Reflections on Empires

WILLIAM H. RIKER

Three main propositions about political coalitions have been developed from the model of n-person games:

1. *The size principle.* This is the assertion that, with complete and perfect information, winning coalitions tend toward the minimal winning size.
2. *The strategic principle.* This is the assertion that, in systems or bodies in which the size principle is operative, participants in the final stages of coalition-formation should and do move toward a minimal winning coalition.
3. *The disequilibrium principle.* This is the assertion that, in systems or bodies where the size and strategic principles are operative, the systems or bodies are themselves unstable. That is, they contain forces leading toward decision regardless of stakes and hence toward the elimination of participants.

The first principle was deduced from the model, and the latter two were deduced both from the model and the first principle. Some empirical evidence was offered from the size principle, though of course it needs much more detailed verification from less partial hands than mine before it can be generally accepted. Insofar as the size principle is verified, however, its two corollaries are somewhat verified also.

In one sense it is proper to end at this point, for the theory from the model has now been carried as far as I am at present prepared to carry it. Nevertheless, the model was constructed in order to study the real world and, because of that purpose, it seems appropriate to conclude by inquiring further into the significance of the principles for reality. Assuming, then, that the three principles are validly deduced and either verified or verifiable empirically, what do they imply about the state of world politics?

The Decline of A speculation which has frequently entranced
Empires historians and sociologists with a broad view
of their studies is the dynamics of the decline
of empires and great coalitions. Few scholars have wondered greatly about the rise of empires, for this phenomenon is readily explicable in terms of the rational desire to win and the energy and aggressiveness of particular politicians. But the opposite occurrence, the atrophy of bureaucracies and the dismemberment of viable social systems, has no readily apparent explanation—or at least no readily apparent explanation that men are willing to accept. Just as men generally have often been unwilling to accept the obvious physiological explanation of the death of individual persons and have disguised the unpalatable fact with a variety of probably delusive theories, so scholars have been reluctant to accept simple explanations of the death of societies. Thus, in the last three centuries, scholars have produced a plethora of contrived explanations of the decline of empires. Some have explained the events in terms of a (usually mystical) dissipation of the will to win (e.g., Gibbon, Spengler, Toynbee). Others have explained them in terms of some (equally mystical) death and rebirth process in disguised and probably unconscious analogy to animal life (e.g., Hegel and Marx). Still others, especially those in the Christian tradition, have explained in terms of unresolved conflicts in the human psyche (e.g., Niebuhr) or more simply still in terms of divine retribution and testing (e.g., Berdyaev). None of these have, however, explained in terms of ordinary social processes that are observable on a less grand scale than in the decline of empires.[1] [Our]

[1] I have elsewhere criticized the method of such theorizing about history on the ground that the gross events studied (e.g., the decline of empires) are too unprecise to be generalized about by some sort of inductive process (Riker, "Events and Situations," *Journal of Philosophy,* **54,** 57–70). The criticism here, however, is of a substantive rather than methodological nature, for I am asserting that the content of such theories is unrelated to ordinary social processes. Still, the two criticisms are related in the sense that exclusive preoccupation with the grand question of the rise and decline of empires, a question far too complex to approach *de novo,* leads writers to overlook the relevance of considerations apparent in lesser events to the grand questions they are trying to answer. The approach to these questions undertaken here avoids, I hope, both pitfalls. By starting from a simple model for simple events it

model, however, suggests interpretations of the decline of empires in terms analogous in their simplicity and lack of mysticism to the explanation of death as a physiological event.

Two processes have special relevance for the explanation of the decline of empires and great coalitions. One is the size principle itself and the other is the tendency for leaders to miscalculate side-payments and to pay more for winning than winning is "objectively" worth. By reason of the size principle, leaders with the certain assurance of winning may actually expel some "minor" members whose interests conflict with the interests of some "major" members of the coalition. Even without expulsions, however, such leaders may reduce the size of their coalition simply by neglecting the interests of some members until the neglected ones defect to the other side. By such processes of expulsion and neglect, world-dominating empires can be expected to pare off their excess weight, even to the point at which they are barely capable of winning. At this point the danger of overpayment for victory becomes great indeed. Assuming that an opposing coalition or empire exists and that the ejected or defecting ex-members of winning coalitions join this opponent, then the size principle guarantees the existence of a formidable opponent for the winner. And if such an opponent exists, then it is imperative for the winner to keep on winning. In such circumstances, each decision reallocates relative weights and serves as a harbinger of the eventual outcome. When a previous winner loses on one decision, however minor, the very loss strengthens its opponent and, furthermore, renders the opponent more likely to succeed on future decisions. In this sense the whole of the future of a winning coalition or dominant empire may appear to be—and may actually be—at stake on each decision. This is the setting for overpayment. Decisions with a negligible objective worth are by the positional considerations rendered very important. Thus the expenditure of great amounts of working and fixed capital may appear to be justified even on decisions that cannot possibly result in any substantial repayment to capital resources. Repeated victory on such trivial decisions dissipates the winner's resources until it becomes incapable of winning.

At the end of the nineteenth century there were four world-dominating empires, England, France, Austria-Hungary, and Germany, whose leadership of the world was expressed not only in the force of arms but also in the creativity of scientific and humanistic culture. Today all four have been dismembered; their arms are negligible; and their intellectual creativity is overshadowed by people in other nations. All four are still rather well off financially—better off, for example, than most of their former dependencies. But relative to the rest of the world, they have lost place even in this respect. The decline of Germany and Austria-Hungary

avoids basing generalizations on wholly ambiguous events. At the same time, the extension of the principles from simple events to complex ones permits an explanation of history in terms of ordinary social processes.

is explicable enough by the fact that they lost two major decisions involving dismemberment as a penalty for loss. The decline of England and France, however, is not so easily explained. Were not these the winners? Should not their empires have flourished in victory? But they did not flourish. One can only conclude that, in the exigencies of conflict, they paid more for winning than winning was objectively worth. In the decadence of these nations, in the fact that even their cultural and intellectual leadership has passed to other peoples, one can see the results of overpayment. This is not to say that either of these winners might reasonably have acted other than they did, for the loss they would have sustained as losers would undoubtedly have been far greater than the loss they actually sustained. But, nevertheless, in the very act of winning they lost most of what had made their leadership worthwhile.

It would be tedious and unrewarding to examine here all instances of notable declines of empires. But the interested reader may, if he chooses, carry through such an examination for himself. If he does so, he will find that the decline of every one of Toynbee's twenty-three past civilizations, as well as the decline of empires within the four existent ones, is fully explicable in terms of the size principle and overpayment to allies and followers, especially by means of military expenditures on Pyrrhic victories. In short, one can explain all declines of empires in terms of bad management rather than in terms of such mystical categories as a loss of will or a drive toward death or divine intervention. Bad management may, of course, be an inherent and inescapable feature of the political system, but it is an ordinary process within the system, not some mystical force outside it.

The Place of Since 1945 at least consciously and since 1941
The United States in retrospective consciousness, the United
in the World States has been the leader of a world-dominating coalition. It has been challenged, of course, by the Soviet Union, but at least as late as 1957 the challenger acknowledged a subordinate position for itself. In the course of an interview on July 24, 1957, in which Prime Minister Khrushchev was advocating a greater degree of exchange of persons between the United States and the U.S.S.R., he spoke quite incidentally of the power relationships between the two countries, calling his own nation "the second greatest power in the world." Considering the incidental and accidental nature of the utterance, this statement probably represented his actual intuitive judgment at the time.[2] Whether the subsequent Soviet success in the technology of

[2] For the sake of conveying the full flavor of the judgment a larger quotation from the interview follows:

Even Soviet cooks are not allowed in the United States because the United States is afraid they will shake the foundations of its way of life! I met a farmer

rockets and missiles has altered his judgment, one cannot say. Yet the tone of his remarks during his visit to the United States in 1960 (e.g., his references to passing the United States in the next decade) indicate, I believe, that he still holds his pre-Sputnik opinion. If the main opponent of United States leadership regards the United States as its superior to be emulated, there can be little doubt, I believe, that this country has, at least from 1945 to 1957 and probably still today, been the leader of a world-dominating coalition.

American citizens have on the whole been loath to recognize and accept this national role. The prevailing isolationist sentiment among politicians of all persuasions during the 1920's and 1930's effectively prevented our assumption of the role of world leader in that period, although probably this role was ours for the asking even then. Still today, in the face of the objective fact of our leadership, we are isolationists enough in sentiment to try to close our eyes to our real position. Our national reluctance to play the role of world leader in Korea—a reluctance demonstrated by Eisenhower's overwhelming victory in 1952—was undoubtedly a reflection of this isolationist temper. In short, most Americans would prefer that their government be a follower rather than a leader so that, freed from the responsibilities of leadership, the citizens can go quietly about their business.

This political isolationism has been socially intertwined with a kind of cultural timidity and deference. Despite our cultural chauvinism on a

by the name of Garston who is a specialist on the hybridization of corn. He was very nice and wanted to invite a group of agronomists to the United States. They were refused entry by your government and when he went to champion their entry he had no luck. How can we improve prospects for peace when we can't even discuss corn.

Question [Mr. Jerome Davis]: We had an exchange of farmers recently, didn't we?

Answer: Yes, but only once, then it stopped. We would like to maintain the exchange. We favor an exchange of engineers since we have ideas of engineering even as you do.

The idea of not letting people into our respective countries is stupid or foolish. I don't know if such words are polite and I don't want to insult but I think so anyway. When people respect or accept a certain idea or system, that depends on their will but you can't ignore the fact that Bulgaria, Romania, Albania, China, one third of Germany, North Vietnam and Poland exist. When we set up our system we didn't ask Dulles. You hate Communism and we Capitalism but that's not important. We have done wonders in our country and you envy us because *we are the second greatest power in the world* and will, through Communism, soon be the first. We must subdue passion and subordinate it into commonsense. Some politicians are blinded by hate and, like a bull seeing red, they leap forth blindly. Let us exchange scientific information and cooperate with each other.

Report of the American European Seminar on the USSR Including their Interview with Khrushchev in the Kremlin (West Haven, Conn., Promoting Enduring Peace, Inc., no date, presumably 1957), p. 18, emphasis added.

popular level—a chauvinism that may well have had its roots in a repressed sense of inferiority—our intellectuals have generally been accustomed to defer to the taste and intellectual standards of Europeans. We have sent our best students to study painting in France, philosophy in England, medicine in Austria, chemistry in Germany, music in Italy, and mathematics all over Europe. Such action was objectively justified up to the time of the First World War, for indeed the world centers of learning were in European cities. Since then, and especially since the Second World War, the export of students has been justifiable only on political or sentimental grounds—not on intellectual grounds, especially since the cream of European scholarship has gradually migrated to the United States. But despite the change, the export of students continues—a kind of intellectual deference that expresses our deep-felt hesitation about the role of world leadership, even on the intellectual level.

As a consequence of our isolationism and our reluctance to lead or to acknowledge leadership even in areas of action quite peripheral to politics, we have been quite unable to formulate a political position appropriate to our role. While many of our international difficulties of the past score of years have been an inescapable function of circumstances beyond our control, part of our difficulty does stem, it seems to me, from our reluctance to recognize the role we actually now play. Hence, one of the first steps toward the construction of an adequate posture in world affairs is the self-recognition of our leadership. The next step is to discover the content and possibilities for action in this role.

The Conditions of Leadership

Probably the essential fact about the role of leader in a world-dominating coalition is that the actor who once occupies this role cannot resign from it without unpleasant consequences. Many Americans, harking back to a joyful and carefree golden age of national adolescence in the nineteenth century, would perhaps prefer to resign from the role rather than accept its incessant crises, its worrisome calculations, and its perpetual sense of high stakes on a hair trigger. But such sentimental preference for resignation—which is probably the main emotion driving such diverse groups as peace-marchers and McCarthyites, both of whom prefer domestic conflict to combating the external enemy—is almost invariably expressed in ignorance or scorn of the actual consequences of resignation. In order to demonstrate, therefore, how fully committed we are to (some would say "trapped in") the role of leadership, let us consider some of the putative consequences of resigning from the role.

Most Americans fancy that their commanding position has been achieved without forceful mistreatment of other peoples. Compared with other empires of the past, compared even with so liberal and guilt-stricken an empire as the British, American leadership has been milder still. But mild as it has probably been, it does not follow that our dependents have felt kindly toward us. The discovery that Castro expresses the deep hostility of the Cuban—and indeed the Latin American—middle class toward the United States, has been a shock to many North Americans. But we have used force, mostly economic, but occasionally military, to control Latin America. It should be no surprise, therefore, that the persons so controlled have regarded the controller as a tyrant. To the degree that some dependent nations have regarded our leadership as tyrannical, we can expect retribution if we relinquish the leadership role. Initially such retribution might be no more than the seizure of our investment in Latin America and a restriction of trade. (This may or may not be negligible: About one-third of our income from foreign investments and about one-third of our imports originate there. About one-fifth of our exports are destined for there. If one assumes that foreign trade has a multiplier effect, then this loss alone might have serious repercussions on our economy.) But in the course of time surely the effects of the loss of leadership would be greater than this. It is not too fanciful to suggest that the ultimate effects would even include a reopening of the territorial settlement after the Mexican War.

Our leadership elsewhere in the world has involved less use of force than in Latin America and hence the loss of the role would doubtless involve less retribution. But political loss would surely involve also the loss of many commercial advantages and a drastic reduction in foreign trade. It would be an interesting enterprise in economic prediction to calculate the effect of these potential losses on our gross national product. Although I cannot make such a calculation in detail, a reasonable guess seems to me that we would return initially to about the level of our pre-leadership position, adjusted for the loss of income from Latin America. This would mean an average family income about like that of the early 1930's. Eventually, of course, one would expect the income to slide much lower.

Entirely apart from economic losses, which would undoubtedly be very great were the United States to abandon its leadership, other potential losses seem to me to be greater still. As a function of our leadership we have developed a really large intellectual class, perhaps the largest the world has seen. The mathematicians, physicists, biologists, psychologists, and social scientists necessary to maintain our military position vis-à-vis the Soviet Union are a remarkable collection just now beginning to establish an intellectual tradition which holds great promise of creativity. American intellectual life was once dominated by a kind of utilitarianism or pragmatism that produced much of immediate value but little new knowledge in the absolute sense. The postwar generation of intellectuals is, however, gradually overcoming the pragmatism of its ancestors and hence stands on the threshold of magnificent intellectual achievements. Should the United States abandon its role of leadership, most of this class would no longer be necessary and indeed too expensive to support. The loss of leadership would then mean also a heavy sacrifice of potential intellectual creativity.

It can be expected also that the loss of leadership—even though in our present imaginary examination it would occur by voluntary resignation—would, very probably, also involve a loss of self-confidence in all other areas of life, as well as the intellectual. American self-confidence, which often unfortunately appears to be brashness to other peoples, is, in my opinion, one of the most attractive of our national traits of character. Its replacement with either a chastened humility or a querulous debility would, I believe, be an incalculable personal loss.

Finally, resignation of leadership would involve the systematic betrayal of many peoples who have believed in us. A foretaste of what might happen can be observed in the results of the abortive Hungarian revolution of 1956. That revolution, which was partly predicated on an expectation of American aid, resulted in the slaughter of a large number of people, especially of idealistic and trusting adolescents. They did not understand that the foreign policy of "liberation" was announced by Secretary Dulles mostly for domestic consumption as an incident for the struggle for votes in the era of McCarthyism. Nor did they realize that Radio Free Europe, again inspired by McCarthyism, represented purely the private opinion of persons who would doubtless have liked to make American policy but in fact did not. The United States was culpable, of course, to the degree that it did not indicate that the slogan of "liberation" did not mean what it might appear to mean and that Radio Free Europe did not represent the United States. But to how much greater a degree would it be culpable if it abandoned the smaller nations of NATO, CENTO, and SEATO to Soviet imperialism after binding them into formal defensive alliances. The guilt of betrayal would be almost insurmountable.

In short, the loss of or resignation from leadership would involve, at the very least, unpleasant consequences for economic life, for intellectual creativity, for national character, and for the national conscience. The isolationists of the last generation may well have been wiser than they knew in seeking to avoid the leader's role. But once we are in it, we cannot abandon it without substantial sacrifice. This is indeed a larger sacrifice than most citizens are, I believe, willing to make. Hence, we probably cannot voluntarily abandon our position of leadership. This is the first and essential fact about our present occupancy of the leader's role.

The Present Balance of Coalitions in World Politics In 1945 the United States stood at what has turned out to be the apex of its world leadership. Its previous enemies—Germany, Italy, and Japan—had been reduced to insignificance and the way was prepared to bring them back into the world society under the aegis of American leadership. Its most immediate allies —England, France, and China—were so crippled by the war that they had no choice but to look to the United States for leadership. Most of Latin America, while perhaps covertly hostile to the United States (and, in the case of the Peronist Argentine, openly hostile), was nonetheless willing to accept American leadership in affairs outside the hemisphere. The only conceivable threat to world leadership by the United States lay in the Soviet Union, which, somewhat like the United States, had been physically strengthened by its very participation in the war. Yet the Soviet Union could not then defend itself against nuclear weapons so that it too had reason to accept American leadership.

Five years later, however, American hegemony was a thing entirely of the past. The United States was opposed by a fairly strong minority coalition which could check many American actions and might even reasonably aspire to defeat it. How did this change come about?

In 1945 and for a few years thereafter, the United States had an opportunity to consolidate its position as world leader and to impose, perhaps, an imperial order on the whole world. There were some among us, indeed, who urged that we do so (e.g., Henry Luce, whose notion of the American century apparently meant an imperial *pax Americana*). But with characteristic reluctance to lead, with characteristic hesitation to tell other people what to do, the United States chose not to maintain the commanding position. (Although it is doubtless immodest for an American to say so, there stands no finer tribute to the essential modesty of the American character than the fact that, during the brief period of our exclusive possession of atomic weapons, the nation as a whole rejected as preposterous the temptation to establish world empire. It does not, I think, detract seriously from the humaneness of this decision that we subsequently executed the traitors Rosenberg who were in some part responsible for removing this temptation from our consciousness.)

Having chosen not to maintain indefinitely the status quo of 1945, something which could have been done only by the imposition of world empire, the United States necessarily also condemned itself to a long (?) period of attrition in which, by the operation of the size principle, the scope of its leadership would be reduced. Since it refused the imperial technique (the only feasible technique) of preventing change and since it was in an almost world-dominating position, its decision to allow change meant that most change that might occur would be to its disadvantage.

This is, of course, what happened. First, without serious opposition the Soviet Union was allowed to solidify its influence in all those nations whose territory it physically occupied in 1945. Presumably the ejection of the Red Army from those places was a task beyond our energy. That is to say, having accepted the international world not as something to govern but as something in which to play an *n*-person (probably zero-sum) game, the United States decided that the allegiance of Poland, Hungary, Bulgaria, Romania, Czechoslovakia, Eastern Germany, and Yugoslavia was not worth expending energy for, inasmuch as it could control the main things it desired to control without them. Put another way, the United States decided to rehabilitate Western Europe, but not to go to the expense and trouble of rehabilitating Eastern Europe. Very shortly thereafter, however, the United States decided to expend considerable energy in preventing further Soviet expansion in Greece and Turkey, an action which doubtless informed Tito that when Yugoslavia defected from the Soviet bloc it could count on sympathy from the United States. In Eastern Europe, then, the United States, after initially losing those Soviet satellites which it had initially expected to return to their prewar status of independence, successfully contained its opponent and even weaned partially away one of its opponent's hitherto wholly dependent allies. Almost all American energy was spent on maintaining this portion of its coalition, however. Consequently, elsewhere in the world its opponent was able to make serious inroads on the American coalition.

In concentrating on the rehabilitation of its European allies, the United States in effect decided that it would not pay very much to keep China, which perhaps seemed relatively worthless in military potential and indeed would have been an extremely expensive ally to maintain. It seems fairly clear also that the Soviet Union devoted relatively little energy to winning China, but when, suddenly, the Chinese Communists were successful, naturally, the Soviet Union expended considerable energy in helping them consolidate their power. The important point is that here the size principle operated in terms of American policymakers' judgments of where to spend their working capital on side-payments. Having chosen Europe and the Near East, the United States allowed its relatively unsupported ally in the Far East, beset with internal strife, to be taken over by the other side. At the time most Americans did not even regard China as a serious loss.

While the United States chose to expend considerable energy on maintaining its European alliance, it made no effort to maintain its allies' empires. Indeed, for ideological reasons, it usually approved the dismemberment of them, doubtless hoping that if it covertly aided the revolutionaries, they would as leaders of free governments ally themselves with the United States. Unfortunately for the United States, however, it has not always turned out that way. To ally with the United States has often meant that the ex-colonies ally with the ex-colonial powers and this has

often been an unpalatable contract. Furthermore, each of the new participants in world affairs (whether ex-colonies or hitherto neglected states)
has been the object of courtship by the opposing coalition. In selected instances it has bid the price of alliance up to the point that the United
States has believed it not worthwhile, either in terms of the price itself or
in terms of internal strains within the coalition led by the United States.
Thus, in the case of Egypt, the price has become much military equipment, much purchasing of cotton, and perhaps the financing of the
Aswan Dam. But military subsidies are not only costly; they are also
deeply offensive to Israel, one of our few firm allies in the Near East. As
for cotton, we already have too much of it. And the Aswan Dam is not
only extremely expensive and a doubtful financial risk, but also is opposed by the Sudan, which might well turn out to be as valuable an ally
as Egypt. And so, in accordance with the size principle, we have not
paid for an ally which is not, at the moment at least, necessary for winning interim decisions. Similar considerations have led us to bid only
half-heartedly for Afghanistan, which the Soviet Union has successfully
integrated into its own economy. Not only is Afghanistan hard to defend,
directly exposed as it is to the Soviet Union, but also to arm it is offensive to our firm ally, Pakistan. Furthermore, Afghanistan's oil, which
presently the West does not need, is with little expense exported to the
Soviet Union, while to export it to the West would require a very large
capital investment. And so we have in effect allowed the Soviet Union to
integrate the Afghan economy with its own.

In other areas, where substantial economic or military penetration
has not been feasible for either side, the curious phenomenon of neutralism has appeared. By judicious management of the neutralist position,
numerous Asian and African governments have been able to wring some
side-payments from each coalition for temporary support (as on a vote in
the United Nations) without firmly committing themselves to either side.
In a sense, both Africa south of the Sahara and many states of north Africa and the Near East have managed to avoid both coalitions, thus reducing the significance of each, and to deploy their mobile diplomacy to
their own greatest advantage.

Thus, in accordance with the size principle, the coalition led by the
United States has been whittled down in size fairly continuously since
the end of the Second World War. Where once it controlled most of the
world, it now has certain control only of Western Europe, the Americas,
some of the maritime portions of Eastern Asia and scattered portions of
the Near East. Its opponent controls Eastern Europe and two-thirds of
Asia. The remainder of the world is in balance between them, although it
appears that the United States has at the moment closer ties with India
and other Southeast Asian neutrals (except Indonesia) and with most of
the new states of Africa than does the Soviet Union.

A question of great import for the future of the West is whether or not this gradual whittling down of Western strength in accordance with the size principle is a now completed process. I do not believe that it is, for it seems to me that the West is still sufficiently confident of its winning strength to allow further losses of allies. The occurrences in Cuba are instructive in this respect. While the Cuban revolution was probably home-grown, still the revolutionaries have turned to the Soviet Union for protection. If the Soviet Union has not yet gained a firm ally, the United States has lost one. Will the United States attempt to regain it? To regain probably means fostering and financing another revolution, as we seem to have done on a much smaller scale in Guatemala. Whether or not we will pay such a relatively high price remains to be seen. If we do not, then we can, I assume, expect further such defections, even in the Americas. And outside the Americas further defections seem more likely still, especially if we should fail to maintain the status quo in Laos. The rest of the Indo-Chinese peninsula as well as Thailand and Burma seem likely candidates for defection. And if they should go, Indonesia, already aggressively neutral, may well prefer to plump openly for the other side. So it seems likely that the Soviet Union will continue to gain allies, both neutrals and former allies of the West, until in the world's opinion the two great coalitions are roughly equal in size.

In the journalism of the West the dominant interpretation of the events in the world society during the last fifteen years is that of an aggressive imperial power (i.e., the Soviet Union) constantly upsetting the status quo. In this theory, the main propulsion of change is the evil motive of the Communist leaders. In the interpretation offered here, on the other hand, a rational (rather than evil) motive is ascribed to the leaders of both sides. The changes in the relative strength of coalitions is viewed as a normal political process. In both theories, the Soviet Union is interpreted as aggressive while the Western bloc is seen as a defender of the status quo. The difference between the theories is that, from the journalistic theory, one might infer that, were Communists to be replaced by liberals or democrats or aristocrats or kings, the aggression would cease. In the interpretation offered here, however, the aggression is a function of the total situation and would not be affected by a change of Eastern rulers except perhaps that kings might be less efficient aggressors than Communists.

Politics in an Age   The fifteen years since the Second World War
of Maneuver   may well be called the Age of Equalization. This is the period in which, in accordance with the size principle, the Western coalition has diminished and the Communist one expanded. How long this age may be expected to continue is not entirely clear. The United States has lost much power relative to the Soviet Union, which suggests that the age may be nearly over; but

since the two coalitions do not yet seem to be roughly equal, one can expect the equalization process to continue for an indefinite time.

It is possible, however, to suggest a standard by which one may know when the Age of Equalization has come to an end. The standard is an inference from the United States policy of "containment." The basic form of the political problem for the United States in the Age of Equalization has been to determine what final coalition to seek to hold. While few, if any, policymakers in the United States have had a broad enough view of the political process to realize that this was what they were doing, still in building the NATO, CENTO, and SEATO alliances, they were in effect deciding where to draw the line of their future coalition, what to attempt to retain, and what to abandon. In the period in which both the policy of containment (which, though the policymakers ordinarily did not realize it, contained both the United States and the Soviet Union) and the actual alliances were constructed, the main kind of political event was border warfare, or what the Communists euphemistically call "wars of national liberation." Such warfare was in effect a probe by the Communist alliance to find weak spots in the Western coalition (i.e., allies the West would not pay or fight to hold on to). The Korean action was the main instance of such border warfare, but the guerrilla wars in Vietnam, Laos, Burma, Iran, and Greece, as well as the political strikes in Italy and France, were also instances of the same kind of border probing. The number of places where such probing may now continue is limited. A probe is worthwhile only if it is reasonably close to the borders of the Soviet bloc so that the guerrillas et al., can be adequately supplied. Since the West has now made firm alliances and commitments over most of the border territories, the occasion for border warfare has substantially disappeared. Of course, the probing is still going on in various parts of the Indo-Chinese peninsula and the position of India, especially Kashmir, is perhaps vague enough to occasion some probing. Further, the exact position of Afghanistan and Finland and even Sweden is somewhat ambiguous, although the United States acts as if it expects the first two to be absorbed ultimately into a Soviet alliance. Still, unless the Communists reopen border warfare in places in which it has been effectively settled, there are not very many places left for probing. When the few remaining ambiguities of border territory have been clarified, the Age of Equalization will be over.

At that point the character of world politics will change rather abruptly. We will pass from the Age of Equalization to the Age of Maneuver. And there will then be an entirely different tone to world politics.

The main features of the Age of Maneuver will, I submit, be the following:

1. The price asked by neutrals or marginal members for their allegiance to one side or the other will rise steadily.

2. The tone of politics will become more intense in the sense that each decision will seem to involve the entire future of each coalition.

3. As a result of the previous effect, the danger of general warfare will increase.

4. Finally, as a result of all three previous effects, the two main opposing powers will exhaust their resources in maintaining their alliances and other nations will come to the fore as world leaders.

Let us examine each of these effects in some detail.

The price asked by neutrals can hardly fail to rise as the border territories are worked into a tight set of alliances. That is, a reduction in the supply of neutrals will raise their individual prices, probably to the point that, for each side, the total bill for allegiance will be considerably greater than it is now. Up to the present time this rise in the price of side-payments has been obscured by the systematic dismemberment of the colonial holdings of the United States, Italy, Britain, France, the Netherlands, and Belgium. Only the Portuguese empire remains for dismemberment, something which (judging from the events in Goa and the Congo) can be expected to occur fairly soon. In effect, there has been a constant increase in the supply of neutrals over the last fifteen years. But now the source of neutrals in the system is about exhausted. From now on the supply may be expected to contract gradually as some neutrals are firmly drawn into one orbit or the other. Entirely apart from this kind of restriction on supply is another and essentially independent restriction, namely, the prospective tendency of ex-colonial nations to federate with each other. The boundaries of most of the new nations of Africa, the Near East, and Southeast Asia were drawn originally by the colonial powers for administrative or military convenience. No effort was made to ensure the viability of any particular colony inasmuch as viability was felt to be a feature not of the parts but of the colonial system as a whole. As a result, when, as often happened, the empires were dismembered in accord with the colonial boundaries, many new states were not large enough to develop either military or economic strength. Undoubtedly this result was intended by the colonial powers, for it permits a kind of sub rosa economic imperialism to flourish long after the political imperialism ostensibly ends. But in the long run the economic disadvantages for the too small states of Africa and the Near East and Southeast Asia will probably be unsupportable. If so, then consolidation will occur on the pattern of the Canadian absorption of Newfoundland. In this way also, then, the supply of neutrals will probably contract.

On the other hand, the supply of neutrals may well be increased by occasional flurries of Titoism. The process can be visualized thus: Dependent members of each alliance, resentful of the fact that their foreign policies are actually made in either Washington or Moscow, and resentful also of the fact that the pattern of their domestic lives is deeply influenced by the foreign-made foreign policy, may declare themselves neutral. Often such declarations will fail (as in Hungary or Guatemala, for example); but often they will succeed (as in Yugoslavia or, provisionally at least, Cuba). As the possession of the technology of nuclear warfare spreads, such defections may well become more frequent. Thus, in the last few years, France, gaining confidence with each Saharan explosion and resenting more and more rabidly the part played by the United States in the dismemberment of the French empire, has become a less and less reliable member of NATO and the Western alliance generally. It is not too fanciful to suggest that France may neutralize itself, not by means of a Communist revolt—the French Communist party seems to be decreasingly effective—but rather by an independent rapprochement with the Soviet Union, a rapprochement reminiscent of numerous Franco-Russian treaties of friendship over the past several hundred years.

Titoist defections of this sort can, however, hardly be expected to occur frequently or in large numbers. Hence, the supply of neutrals may be expected to decline.

Along with the prospective decline in the supply of neutrals, an effect which alone will raise their price, an entirely independent force will probably operate on the demand for allies in such fashion as to raise the price from the demand side. If, as I shall try to show in subsequent paragraphs, the tone of world politics becomes more intense in the Age of Maneuver than it has been in the Age of Equalization, then allies will be more desperately needed than they are now. If the fate of world leaders is believed to hang on every decision, however minor, then allies must be acquired at any price in order to assure victory.

Anticipating, then, a shorter supply of prospective new allies and a greater demand for those available, one can also anticipate that the price will go up. In an auction in which the ultimate outcome determines life or death, it is unreasonable to suppose that there will be table stakes. Hence, one can further anticipate that the total bill for allies will also increase for both sides. Not only will they have to continue to maintain the allegiance of already attracted ex-neutrals, but also they will have to pay inflated prices for new ones. In the United States there has been much resentment (which seems to me to have grown in recent years) of the large expenditure on allies in the Age of Equalization. If, as I suggest, the expenditures already made will appear minute in comparison with those needed in the Age of Maneuver, one of the great political problems of the Western alliance will be the persuasion of its own citizens to pay the necessary costs of leadership. Indeed, it may well be that a failure of the United States and Western Europe to solve that elementary problem within a democratic framework will result in either the abandonment of democracy or a total defeat for the West.

The second previously listed feature of the Age of Maneuver is a putative intensification of the tone of politics. It may seem to some who have lived through the recurrent crises of the Cold War in the Age of Equalization that the sense of crisis cannot be deepened. Yet, I suggest, exactly such deepening will occur. In the similar phases of equalization and maneuver in American politics of the last century and three-quarters the atmosphere of politics has been much more heated in ages of maneuver than in ages of equalization. The ages of maneuver have been those in which the two parties are approximately equal in voting strength, namely, the late 1790's, the 1840's, the late 1870's and the 1880's, the late 1930's and early 1940's and, possibly the period we are entering now. Assuming that the participation of a large proportion of eligible voters is evidence of an intensity of emotion in politics, then the ages of maneuver are also the ages of greatest intensity of emotion. The proportion of eligible voters participating was at a high point for a generation on either side in the Presidential elections of 1840, 1888, and 1940. While we have no adequate record of voting in the 1790's, it seems likely from scattered evidence that the turnout in the election of 1800 was exceptionally high for its era. Even without the evidence from the amount of voting, however, there is much evidence that political life in the ages of maneuver was more vituperative than at other times. And excessive vituperation seems to me evidence of intensity of emotion. In the age of Jefferson the pattern of extreme vituperation was established by such journalists as Freneau, Bache, and Cobbett. It was revived in Jackson's day by Isaac Hill, Duff Green, and Nicholas Biddle. In the 1870's and 1880's one kind of vituperation was so common it acquired a special name, "waving the bloody shirt." And those who remember the late 1930's know well the vituperative emotions aroused by Franklin Roosevelt.

And so, arguing from the analogy of the ages of maneuver in American politics, I suggest that the coming Age of Maneuver in world politics will generate its own new levels of intensity of emotion. Nor, on reflection, is this surprising. If each side has a chance to win on even the interim decisions, then the energy that each side puts into trying to win will probably be much greater than the energy either has put into decisions likely to be won by the much weightier side. And the mutual expenditure of energy will undoubtedly generate intense emotion.

The third feature of the Age of Maneuver is that, owing to the increase of tension, the danger of general war becomes much greater. As emotions become more intense on each decision, as, increasingly, both sides believe that every decision, however trivial objectively, determines the pattern of the future, then the temptation to deploy all resources on a particular decision is seductive indeed. In previous ages, when the technology of warfare was simpler, governments could succumb to this temptation without serious consequences to the species. The total wars both of antiquity and modern times have been total only in the sense of involving all governments. But the total war of the forthcoming Age of Maneuver will involve, if it occurs, every complex living thing. Out of fear of this prospect reasonable men on both sides have sought for some way to control atomic weapons. But, unfortunately, safety for the species cannot be obtained by as simple an expedient as arms control. The dilemma is this: If men know about nuclear weapons and if they believe that their entire future is at stake, then they may use them regardless of all the elaborate plans for nuclear disarmament and the like. Hence, no matter how much reasonable men may wish to avoid the obliteration of mammals, they still may do so. If a government comes to believe that it may use nuclear weapons without totally destructive retaliation, then in the prospective tension of the Age of Maneuver, when emotions will probably run so much higher than they do now, the temptation to use these weapons may be irresistible. If the belief is correct that complete retaliation is impossible, then the species may survive; but if the belief is false (as it may well be), then the species will be obliterated—and probably not in as pleasantly romantic a fashion as depicted by Nevil Shute.

This is the main horror of the forthcoming Age of Maneuver. But there is another horror, not nearly so terrifying to all mankind, but unpleasant enough for people in the United States and the Soviet Union. This lesser horror is the prospect of systematic overpayment of allies or, alternatively, mutual self-destruction so that at the end of the age both nations are thoroughly enfeebled. If and when this comes about—and it is the fourth listed feature of politics in the Age of Maneuver—the United States and the Soviet Union will have been reduced to dismembered followers and other more vigorous peoples will take up the leadership of the world.

This lesser horror for the citizens of the two world-dominating nations is almost certain to come about. Assuming that the tone of world politics becomes increasingly intense and that the price of the allegiance of neutrals becomes greatly inflated, then both leading nations will feel compelled to pay the anticipated high prices for allies. Entirely apart from side-payments to allies, both the major powers will be required to continue to expend vast sums on armaments. Even if they can come to an agreement to restrict the production of nuclear weapons and even if they can agree on a practical and efficient system of inspection to enforce the agreement, they will still need to spend large amounts of money on both the technology of space travel and conventional military devices. Bases on natural or artificial satellites will unquestionably be of great military significance throughout the Age of Maneuver. It does not seem fanciful to suppose, should the emotions of this age concentrate competition on a race for space, that both nations might spend a quarter of their national income in the competition. And all this without reference to nuclear weapons. On a more mundane level, military equipment of the conventional sort will continue to be necessary in large quantities in order to fight such occasional limited wars as may arise and in order to keep one's allies properly awed. A curious phenomenon: One of the chief kinds of side-payments presently desired by neutrals and marginal allies is a supply of conventional arms. In most instances these are desired in order to awe or even to fight another neutral. But as the supply of them increases, each of the two main powers must increase its own supply simply in order to police those whom it has armed. And, of course, rapid technological change and obsolescence of conventional weapons is a necessary part of offering acceptable side-payments. So the supply of conventional weapons alone can be expected to be inordinately expensive.

Even if no wars occur, therefore, allies and armaments will undoubtedly be a heavy drain on the resources of both leading powers. Their dependents, freed to some degree from these costs, may then be expected to grow rich and powerful at the expense of their leaders. If wars occur, either limited or total, it is, of course, the two leading powers that must bear the greater portion of the expense both in money and men. The leaders have most at stake and hence will be expected to stand most of the cost. And this will, in the long run, also favor the marginal allies at the expense of the leaders.

In the beginning of this chapter the fall of empires was attributed both to the size principle and to systematic overestimation by leaders of the objective value of decisions. In the Age of Equalization, it is the size principle that contributes most to the decline, but in the Age of Maneuver it will doubtless be the overpayment of followers and the excessive expenditure of energy on the maintenance of leadership. The end-product of both processes in both ages is, of course, the decline of the leaders. And that is what the United States and the Soviet Union have to look forward to toward the end of the Age of Maneuver.

Strategy in the
Age of Maneuver

In the Age of Maneuver, for both the United States and the Soviet Union, the main strategic goal—albeit perhaps a goal unrecognized by one or both governments—is the prolongation of the age for the greatest possible duration. Inasmuch as the end of this age is likely also to be the end of the leadership of both powers, it is in the objective interests of both to forestall the end.

For the achievement of this goal, there are several obvious strategic policies.

First and foremost, each ought to take every possible precaution to avoid nuclear war or even total war without nuclear weapons. If either such war occurs, neither of the leading powers can possibly be the winner, even though the wars are zero-sum. The winner will, of course, win the power that the loser loses. But soon after the war is over, it will appear that marginal members of both sides are stronger than the original leaders. I do not know how such wars are to be avoided, except by the conscious intention of both powers. Indeed, both must recognize that they are playing not only a zero-sum game against each other but also are playing a sub rosa zero-sum game in which they are allies against the rest of the world. The main challenge to the diplomacy of both powers is to keep the other forever cognizant of the sub rosa game even when the tensions of the Age of Maneuver are at their most intense. Like parliamentary leaders who at heart have greater sympathy with the leaders of the parliamentary opposition than they have with their own back benchers, these two powers can only at their deepest peril forget that leadership itself is as much a value as winning.

In order to remember this point, both governments need institutional reminders. This is the chief role that the United Nations can play. Since the beginning of the Korean conflict the U.N. General Assembly has been something of a covert American agent. But with the projection into it of African neutrals, it seems likely that the U.N. as a whole will revert to its intended function as a world parliament. As such it may be able to transmute military hostilities into verbal ones. If it is able to do so, then it may be a genuine institutional damper on the war-inducing tensions of the Age of Maneuver. Every institutional change that strengthens the U.N.—e.g., giving it responsibilities for, initially, controlling nuclear testing; giving it, subsequently, responsibility for arms control; giving it, ultimately, some of the powers of a genuine world government—will increase its effectiveness as a damper. Hence, it is in the best interests of both the United States and the Soviet Union now to strengthen the U.N. in preparation for the Age of Maneuver. Of course, in many daily ways, a strengthened U.N. appears to be a threat to both powers, especially when it is strengthened somewhat at the expense of one of them, as occurred in 1950 and as will occur when Red China gets its seat on the Security Council. But daily threats are, I think, less significant than the ultimate potentiality of this institution to dampen the tensions that may induce military action. Hence, it seems to me strategically correct, from the point of view of prolonging the Age of Maneuver, to strengthen the U.N. as much as possible.

A second obvious and basic strategy for the Age of Maneuver is to control in some way the prices paid for allies. If the free market price is allowed to prevail, it will, as I have earlier suggested, be extraordinarily high. There is no reason, however, why clever men cannot rig these prices just as prices of all other commodities have in one way or another been controlled to advantage. The Soviet Union has made most of its conquests in the Age of Equalization at a remarkably low price, that is, by infusing home-grown guerrillas with the Communist ideology and perhaps by supplying a rather small quantity of equipment for guerrilla warfare. It has been able to do this in so-called underdeveloped societies because the statist technique of modernization and industrialization, invented by Lenin and demonstrated to be practicable for a rural society by Stalin, has proved extraordinarily attractive to the intelligentsia of underdeveloped societies. By contrast, the liberal ideology of the West, which depends for its economic effectiveness on the existence of a large class of literate and cosmopolitan entrepreneurs, has seemed economically irrelevant in places where most of the people are illiterate peasants or tribesmen. On the other hand, the United States has retained some of its most secure allies at little cost simply because it was the main exponent of the liberal ideology of freedom. Freedom may be a somewhat defective ideal, for it is difficult to imagine the commitment the human psyche craves directed at so instrumental and morally empty a goal as freedom. Yet for those who do not have a bit of it, freedom can become an absolute. Those who remember a past tyranny have rejoicingly identified with the American standard of freedom, simply because it is freedom and regardless of its economic significance. Thus in two contrasting ways during the Age of Equalization the two main antagonists have bought allies with ideology, which costs very little. Doubtless they will continue to be able to do so.

But as the possibilities of the neutralist role are more thoroughly grasped and exploited, it may well happen that ideology is not enough to hold even thoroughly convinced allies. In the case of Yugoslavia, for example, neither devotion to Marxism nor gratitude for Soviet assistance were sufficient to maintain the alliance in the face of Stalinist tyranny. It seems likely that such Titoist behavior will be more common in the future than in the past and will involve defections from both sides. And it is at this point that the problem of price control becomes most pressing.

For the United States, presumably the leader of the leading coalition and presumably desirous of maintaining its lead, this poses an extraordinarily important strategic problem. Will it meet the price that neutrals and marginal and recalcitrant members of its coalition demand? If it meets every price asked, it may well squander its resources. So the strategic problem will necessarily be the establishment of a policy for dealing with high prices. Control of prices is, it seems to me, possible on the basis of a fine sense of necessity. In a world in which ultimate victory or defeat is controlled by the possession of nuclear warheads in intercontinental missiles, the allegiance of recalcitrant allies is neither desirable nor negotiable. Those allies attracted by our ideology—which, I believe, is more attractive than the Communist one to nations on what Rostow has called the "take-off" level of development—and those attracted by a simple fear of Soviet imperialism should of course be welcomed. But those who must be coerced or heavily bribed need not be paid for at all, especially if they find the Soviet ideology deeply unpalatable (e.g., Spain). All this calls for very delicate calculations. The United States must pay heavily, but not too heavily.

In making these calculations, the most important consideration, it seems to me, is that the United States not be mesmerized by the need to maintain a weightier alliance than, the Soviet Union. Let us suppose—what is not essentially unreasonable—that to win a nuclear or non-nuclear total war a leader must have a coalition comprising two-thirds the weight of the world. If so, the consistent maintenance of an alliance of considerably over half but somewhat less than two-thirds the weight of the world is overly expensive. Yet this is precisely what the United States is now doing. Without endangering its position it could allow the Soviet alliance to grow to a weight greater than half. Indeed, such action, if gradually and consciously but secretly taken, would tend to prolong the Age of Maneuver and at the same time to increase the costs of leadership for the Soviet Union while reducing them for the United States. This is, however, a difficult policy to follow and one requiring both delicacy and political maturity on the part of both government and citizenry. A democracy bedeviled by a McCarthyite demagoguery, for example, would probably be entirely unable to follow such a policy and would, therefore, be expected to exhaust itself in overpayments quite quickly. But if the American democracy can learn to transcend demagoguery of this and other sorts, it may actually be able to follow such a policy for a long period of years.

If it can establish a policy involving relatively little overpayment and if it can avoid great wars, then the Age of Maneuver may be prolonged indefinitely.

APPENDIXES

Selected Bibliography
Treaty Abstracts
Brief Chronologies
Organization Charts
Military Forces

appendix I

Selected Bibliography

NATO

The literature on NATO is voluminous. This organization is certainly the most analyzed and researched of contemporary alliances. Most of the work concentrates on the alliance's political-military features. The early period is comprehensively covered by Robert Endicott Osgood in *NATO: The Entangling Alliance* (Chicago: University of Chicago Press, 1962). Later discussions include Henry A. Kissinger, *The Troubled Partnership: A Reappraisal of the Atlantic Alliance* (Garden City, N.Y.: Doubleday, 1966); William T. R. Fox and Annette B. Fox, *NATO and the Range of American Choice* (New York: Columbia University Press, 1967); and Francis A. Beer, *Integration and Disintegration in NATO: Processes of Alliance Cohesion and Prospects for Atlantic Community* (Columbus: Ohio State University Press, 1969).

A particularly sharp focus on the interrelationship between political consultation and crisis in NATO is provided by Alastair Buchan, *Crisis Management: The New Diplomacy* (Boulogne-sur-Seine: The Atlantic Institute, 1966). Research on other alliance sectors is scattered and not always easily available. Three works of note are Robert Rhodes James, *Standardization and Common Production of Weapons in NATO* (London: Institute for Strategic Studies, 1967); and Brig. Gen. E. Vandevanter, Jr., *Coordinated Weapons Production in NATO: A Study of Alliance Processes*, RM-4169-PR, and *Common Funding in NATO*, RM-5282-PR (Santa Monica, Calif.: The RAND Corporation, 1964 and 1967).

Two accounts of international leadership during NATO's early years are Lord Ismay, *NATO: 1949–1954* (Utrecht: Bosch, 1954), and Robert S. Jordan, *The NATO International Staff/Secretariat, 1952/57: A Study in International Administration* (New York: Oxford, 1967). Dirk Stikker also provides valuable information in *Men of Responsibility: A Memoir* (New York: Harper & Row, 1966).

An official and detailed exposition of NATO's institutional structure appears in *NATO: Facts about the North Atlantic Treaty Organization* (Brussels: NATO Information Service, 1969). Additional bibliographical references may be found *inter alia* in *NATO Bibliography* (Brussels: NATO, 1963) and Conference on the Atlantic Community, *An Introductory Bibliography* (Leiden: Sythoff, 1961). Finally, a listing of studies currently in process is contained in the semiannual publication *Atlantic Studies* (Boulogne-sur-Seine: The Atlantic Institute).

WEU

Excellent material on many aspects of Atlantic and European relations and on the Western European Union is contained in the extensive series of publications by the WEU Assembly. Early studies of the WEU include: Jacques Benoist, *L'Union de L'Europe Occidentale* (Paris: Pedone, 1955); Chatham House Study Group, *Britain in Western Europe, WEU and the Atlantic Alliance* (London: Royal Institute of International Affairs, 1956); and Ralph G. Hawtrey, *Western European Union: Implications for the United Kingdom* (London: Royal Institute of International Affairs, 1949). See also Paul Borcier, *The Political Role of the Assembly of WEU* (Strasbourg: WEU, 1963); Ernst B. Haas and Peter H. Merkl, "Parliamentarians Against Ministers: The Case of Western European Union," *International Organization,* 14 (Winter, 1960), 39–59; and Noel Salter, "WEU—The Role of the Assembly 1954–1963," *International Affairs,* 40 (January, 1964), 34–36.

ANGLO-AMERICAN AND FRANCO-GERMAN RELATIONS

The Anglo-American relationship is examined in Bruce M. Russett, *Community and Contention: Britain and America in the Twentieth Century* (Cambridge, Mass.: MIT Press, 1963); Coral Bell, *The Debatable Alliance: An Essay in Anglo-American Relations* (London: Oxford, 1964); and Raymond Dawson and Richard Rosecrance, "Theory and Reality in the Anglo-American Alliance," *World Politics,* 19 (October, 1966), 21–51. Alfred Grosser discusses the Franco-German alliance in *French Foreign Policy Under de Gaulle* (Boston: Little, Brown, 1965), as does F. Roy Willis in *France, Germany and the New Europe, 1945–1967* (London: Oxford, 1968).

OAS

Two excellent analyses that concentrate on the political-military activities of the OAS are Jerome Slater, *The OAS and United States For-*

eign Policy (Columbus: Ohio State University Press, 1967), and Inis L. Claude, Jr., "The OAS, the UN, and the United States," *International Conciliation*, No. 547 (March, 1964). Slater discusses at length the role of the OAS as an "anti-communist alliance" and an "anti-dictatorial alliance" as well as considering the OAS in terms of the larger international system and as a collective security system in its own right. Claude closely interweaves the strands of regional and global security.

There are a number of general works that deal with the OAS, including: Committee on Foreign Relations, U.S. Senate, *U.S.-Latin American Relations*, Part 3, *The Organization of American States*, 86th Cong., 1st Sess. (December 24, 1959). Gordon Connell-Smith, *The Inter-American System* (London: Oxford, 1966); John C. Dreier, *The Organization of American States and the Hemisphere Crisis* (New York: Harper & Row, 1962); Charles G. Fenwick, *The Organization of American States: The Inter-American Regional System* (Washington, D.C.: Kaufmann Printing, 1963); Robert W. Gregg, ed., *International Organization in the Western Hemisphere* (Syracuse, N.Y.: Syracuse University Press, 1968); William Manger, *Pan-America in Crisis: The Future of the OAS* (Washington, D.C.: Public Affairs Press, 1961); J. Lloyd Mecham, *The United States and Inter-American Security, 1889–1960* (Austin: University of Texas Press, 1961); O. Carlos Stoetzer, *The Organization of American States: An Introduction* (New York: Praeger, 1966); and Ann Van Wynen and A. J. Thomas, Jr., *The Organization of American States* (Dallas: Southern Methodist University Press, 1963).

Slater presents an excellent selected bibliography. In addition to the articles he lists, political-military affairs are discussed in: Gordon Connell-Smith, "The OAS and the Dominican Crisis," *The World Today*, 21 (June, 1965), 229–235; C. G. Fenwick, "The Dominican Republic: Intervention or Collective Self-Defense," *American Journal of International Law*, 60 (January, 1966); Charles O. Lerche, Jr., "Development of Rules Relating to Peacekeeping by the Organization of American States," *Proceedings of the American Society of International Law, 59th Annual Meeting*, April 22–24, 1965; John N. Plank, "The Caribbean: Intervention, When and How," *Foreign Affairs*, 44 (October, 1965), 37–48; Robert D. Tomasek, "The Chilean-Bolivian Lauca River Dispute and the OAS," *Journal of Inter-American Studies*, 9 (July 19, 1967), 351–366; Arthur P. Whitaker, "Cuba's Intervention in Venezuela: A Test of the OAS," *Orbis*, 8 (Fall, 1964), 511–536; and Larman C. Wilson, "The Monroe Doctrine, Cold War Anachronism: Cuba and the Dominican Republic," *Journal of Politics*, 28 (May, 1966), 322–346.

Discussions of provisions for structural change include: John C. Dreier, "New Wine and Old Bottles: The Changing Inter-American System," *International Organization*, 22 (Spring, 1968), 477–493; William Manger, "Reform of the OAS," *Journal of Inter-American Studies*, 10 (January, 1968), 1–14; and A. H. Robertson, "Revision of the Charter of the Organization of American States," *The International and Comparative Law Quarterly*, 17, Pt. 2 (April, 1968), 346–367.

SEATO

A great deal has been written about security problems in Asia, especially with regard to Southeast Asia, but little of this material focuses directly on SEATO. Although no longer completely up-to-date, the most comprehensive work is George A. Modelski, ed., *SEATO: Six Studies* (Melbourne: Cheshire, 1962). Ram Tirath's *U.S. Octopus in Asia* (Ghaziabad, India: National Publications, 1964) is interesting because of its heavy bias against SEATO.

Books on SEATO's founding and early history include: Ralph K. Braibanti, *International Implications of the Manila Pact* (New York: American Institute of Pacific Relations, 1957); *Collective Defense in South East Asia: The Manila Treaty and Its Implications* (London: Royal Institute of International Affairs, 1956); R. K. Karanjia, *Seato, Security or Menace* (Bombay: Blitz Publications, 1956); and Roger M. Smith, *The Philippines and the Southeast Asia Treaty Organization* (Ithaca, N.Y.: Cornell University Southeast Asia Program, 1959).

A number of more general studies give space to SEATO. In Amry Vandenbosch and Richard Butwell, *The Changing Face of Southeast Asia* (Lexington: University of Kentucky Press, 1966), there is a select bibliography of writings about the area. For other works discussing SEATO see: Oliver E. Clubb, Jr., *The United States and the Sino-Soviet Bloc in Southeast Asia* (Washington, D.C.: Brookings, 1962); Brian Crozier, *South-East Asia in Turmoil* (Baltimore: Penguin, 1965); Russell H. Fifield, *Southeast Asia in United States Policy* (New York: Praeger, 1963); C. Hartley Grattan, *The United States and the Southwest Pacific* (Cambridge: Harvard University Press, 1961); Fred Greene, *U.S. Policy and the Security of Asia* (New York: McGraw-Hill, 1968); D. E. Kennedy, *The Security of Southern Asia* (New York: Praeger, 1965); and Donald E. Nuechterlein, *Thailand and the Struggle for Southeast Asia* (Ithaca, N.Y.: Cornell University Press, 1965).

Relevant articles include: M. Brecher, "International Relations and Asian Studies: The Subordinate State System of Southern Asia," *World Politics*, 15 (January, 1963), 213–235; M. Caldwell, "Non-Alignment in South East Asia," in John W. Burton, ed., *Nonalignment* (New York: Heinemann, 1967), pp. 38–55; B. K. Gordon, "Problems of Regional Cooperation in Southeast Asia," *World Politics*, 16 (January, 1964), 222–253; Paul Hasluck, "Viet-Nam and SEATO," *Current Notes on International Affairs*, 37 (May, 1966), 257–260; Peter Lyon, "SEATO in Perspective," in *The Yearbook of World Affairs*, 1965 (London: Stevens, 1965), 113–136, and "Substitutes for SEATO?" *International Journal*, 24 (Winter, 1968–1969), 35–46; August C. Miller, Jr., "SEATO—Segment of Collective Security," *U.S. Naval Institute Proceedings*, 86 (February,

1960), 50–62; Ronald C. Nairn, "SEATO: A Critique," *Pacific Affairs,* 41 (Spring, 1968), 5–18; and Frank N. Trager, "The United States, SEATO, and the Defense of Southeast Asia: A Forward Look," *United Asia,* 17 (July–August, 1965), 278–286.

ANZUS

Material on ANZUS is skimpier than that on SEATO. A detailed analysis, together with a bibliography, is provided by J. G. Starke, *The Anzus Treaty Alliance* (Carlton: Melbourne University Press, 1965). Other discussions can be found in R. G. Casey, *Friends and Neighbors: Australia and the World* (Melbourne: Cheshire, 1954); Dean E. McHenry and Richard N. Rosecrance, "The 'Exclusion' of the United Kingdom from the ANZUS Pact," *International Organization,* 13 (Summer, 1958), 320–329; and Norman J. Padelford, "Collective Security in the Pacific: Nine Years of the ANZUS Pact," *U.S. Naval Institute Proceedings,* 86 (September, 1960), 38–48.

UNITED STATES AND ASIA

A number of articles emphasize related aspects of American arrangements in Asia. See especially: David P. Mozingo, "Containment in Asia Reconsidered," *World Politics,* 19 (April, 1967), 361–377; Carl F. Salans, "U.S. Alliances in the Pacific," *U.S. Naval Institute Proceedings,* 92 (July, 1966), 62–71; Mohammed Ayub Khan, "The Pakistan-American Alliance, Stresses and Strains," *Foreign Affairs,* 42 (January, 1964), 195–209; George J. Lerski, "The Pakistan-American Alliance: A Reevaluation of the Past Decade," *Asian Survey,* 7 (May, 1968), 400–432; Douglas H. Mendel, Jr., "Japan Reviews Her American Alliance," *Public Opinion Quarterly,* 30 (Spring, 1966), 1–18; and Akio Watanabe, "The Okinawa Conflict and the U.S.-Japan Alliance," *Australian Outlook,* 20 (April, 1966), 36–42.

THE COMMONWEALTH AND ASIA

Concerning other security relationships in Asia, Alastair Buchan deals with "Commonwealth Military Relations" in W. B. Hamilton, Kenneth Robinson, and C. D. W. Goodwin, eds., *A Decade of the Commonwealth* (Durham, N.C.: Duke University Press, 1966). T. B. Millar analyzes *Australia's Defense* (Carlton: Melbourne University Press, 1965) and provides a select bibliography of previous work on this subject. See also: Coral Bell, "Asian Crisis and Australian Security," *The World Today,* 23 (February, 1967), 80–88; Norman Harper, "A Changing Commonwealth in a Chaotic World," *Australian Outlook,* 19 (April, 1965), 20–34; Shane Paltridge, "Australia and the Defense of Southeast Asia," *Foreign Affairs,* 44 (October, 1965), 49–61; Trevor R. Reese, "Keeping Calm About the Commonwealth," *International Affairs,* 41 (July, 1965), 451–462; A. D. Robinson, "Some Aspects of Future Australian-New Zealand Defense Cooperation," *Australian Outlook,* 20 (April, 1966), 66–72; Amry and Mary Bell Vandenbosch, *Australia Faces Southeast Asia* (Lexington: University of Kentucky Press, 1967); and Maurice Zinkin, "The Commonwealth and Britain East of Suez," *International Affairs,* 42 (April, 1966), 207–218.

THE MIDDLE EAST

CENTO and the League of Arab States are the two major Middle Eastern alliances. The two are substantially different. CENTO represents a link in the worldwide chain of Western regional security arrangements, while the League of Arab States owes its origin in part to the anti-colonial sentiments of politically important Middle Eastern leaders. In spite of an impressive number of official CENTO studies in English, there is no prominent independent analysis of the mechanisms of the alliance itself. Nevertheless, John C. Campbell provides an overview of security politics in *Defense of the Middle East* (New York: Harper & Row, 1960) and *The Middle East in the Muted Cold War* (Denver: University of Denver Monograph Series in World Affairs, 1964–1965).

The Arab League is the focus of the selection in the text taken from Robert W. Macdonald, *The League of Arab States: A Study in the Dynamics of Regional Organization* (Princeton: Princeton University Press, 1965). The book itself includes a select bibliography. Works not listed there that discuss the Arab League include: M. F. Anabtawi, *Arab Unity in Terms of Law* (The Hague: Martinus Nijhoff, 1963); E. C. Flowers, Jr., *The Arab League in Perspective* (Charleston: The Citadel, 1961); and George Lenczowski, *The Middle East in World Affairs* (Ithaca, N.Y.: Cornell University Press, 1962).

For details of inter-Arab conflicts after the Arab-Israeli war of 1967, see George Lenczowski, "Arab Bloc Realignments," *Current History,* 53 (December, 1967), 346–351, and D. C. Watt, "The Arab Summit Conference and After," *The World Today,* 23 (October, 1967), 443–450.

AFRICA

The Organization of African Unity is probably the most important African organization with alliance aspects. Studies that examine the OAU include: Ali A. Mazrui, *Towards a Pax Africana: A Study of Ideology and Ambition* (Chicago: University of Chicago Press, 1967); Immanuel Wallerstein, *Africa: The Politics of Unity* (New York: Random House, 1967); and I. W. Zartman, *International Relations in the New Africa* (Englewood Cliffs, N.J.: Prentice-Hall, 1966). For a selected bibliography on "Africa and International Organization," see Norman J. Padelford and Rupert Emerson, eds., *Africa and World Order* (New York: Praeger, 1963).

In shorter pieces the legal foundations of the OAU are discussed by Boutros Boutros-Ghali, "The Addis Ababa Charter," *International*

Conciliation, No. 546 (January, 1964), and T. O. Elias, "The Charter of the Organization of African Unity," *American Journal of International Law*, 59 (April, 1965), 243–267. An interesting report on OAU activities appears in R. Nagel and R. Rathbone, "The OAU at Kinshasa," *The World Today*, 23 (November, 1967), 473–483.

Articles emphasizing the political-military affairs of the OAU include: Dennis Austin and Ronald Nagel, "The Organization of African Unity," *The World Today*, 22 (December, 1966), 520–528; Catherine Hoskyns, "Trends and Developments in the Organization of African Unity," *The Yearbook of World Affairs* (London: Stevens, 1967), 164–179; John Markakis, "The Organization of African Unity: A Progress Report," *The Journal of Modern African Studies*, 4 (October, 1966), 135–154; Norman J. Padelford, "The Organization of African Unity," *International Organization*, 18 (Summer, 1964), 521–542; Arhold Rivkin, "The Organization of African Unity," *Current History*, 48 (April, 1965), 193–200; Immanuel Wallerstein, "The Early Years of the OAU; The Search for Organizational Preeminence," *International Organization*, 20 (Autumn, 1966), 774–787; and I. William Zartman, "Africa as a Subordinate State System in International Relations," *International Organization*, 21 (Fall, 1967), 545–564. Analyses of particular peacekeeping cases are Patricia Berko Wild, "The Organization of African Unity and the Algerian-Moroccan Border Conflict: A Study of New Machinery for Peacekeeping and for the Peaceful Settlement of Disputes among African States," *International Organization*, 20 (Winter, 1966), 18–36, and Saadia Touval, "The Organization of African Unity and African Borders," *International Organization*, 21 (Winter, 1967), 102–127.

EASTERN EUROPE

Collections of significant documents on both Eastern European and Sino-Soviet relations are presented in Alexander Dallin, ed., *Diversity in International Communism: Documentary Record, 1961–1963* (New York: Columbia University Press, 1963), and Robert H. McNeal, ed., *International Relations among Communists* (Englewood Cliffs, N.J.: Prentice-Hall, 1967). An extensive bibliography, focusing on the Soviet Union, is found in Thomas T. Hammond, *Soviet Foreign Relations and World Communism* (Princeton: Princeton University Press, 1965).

Detailed treatments of the Warsaw Treaty Organization are: Committee on Government Operations, Subcommittee on National Security and International Operations, U.S. Senate, *The Warsaw Pact: Its Role in Soviet Bloc Affairs*, 89th Cong. 2d Sess. (1967); Kasimierz Grzybowski, *The Socialist Commonwealth of Nations: Organizations and Institutions* (New Haven: Yale University Press, 1964), Ch. 5; Andrzej Korbonski, "The Warsaw Pact," *International Conciliation*, No. 573 (May, 1969); Robin Alison Remington, *The Changing Soviet Perception of the Warsaw Pact* (Cambridge, Mass.: MIT Center for International Studies,

1967); and Thomas W. Wolfe, "The Warsaw Pact in Evolution," in Kurt London, ed., *Eastern Europe in Transition* (Baltimore: Johns Hopkins Press, 1966).

Broader discussions of relations between the Warsaw Pact nations also appear in Adam Bromke, ed., *The Communist States at the Crossroads: Between Moscow and Peking* (New York: Praeger, 1965); Adam Bromke and Philip E. Uren, *The Communist States and the West* (New York: Praeger, 1967); J. F. Brown, *The New Eastern Europe* (New York: Praeger, 1966); Zbigniew K. Brzezinski, *The Soviet Bloc: Unity and Conflict* (Cambridge: Harvard University Press, 1967); Stephen Fischer Galati, ed., *Eastern Europe in the Sixties* (New York: Praeger, 1963); Raymond L. Garthoff, *Soviet Military Policy* (New York: Praeger, 1966); William E. Griffith, ed., *Communism in Europe*, 2 Vols. (Cambridge, Mass.: MIT Press, 1964 and 1966); Ghita Ionescu, *The Breakup of the Soviet Empire in Eastern Europe* (Baltimore: Penguin, 1965), and *The Politics of the European Communist States* (New York: Praeger, 1967); George A. Modelski, *The Communist International System* (Princeton, N.J.: Center of International Studies, 1960); Roger Pethyridge, ed., *The Development of the Communist Bloc* (Boston: Heath, 1965); and H. Gordon Skilling, ed., *Communism National and International: Eastern Europe After Stalin* (Toronto: University of Toronto Press, 1969).

Articles that focus on cohesion in the Warsaw Pact in particular and among its members in general are: Walter C. Clemens, Jr., "The Future of the Warsaw Pact," *Orbis*, 11 (Winter, 1968), 996–1033; Raymond L. Garthoff, "The Military Establishment," *East Europe*, 14 (September, 1965), 2–16; Michael P. Gehlen, "The Integrative Process in East Europe: A Theoretical Framework," *Journal of Politics*, 30 (February, 1968), 90–113; Patricia Haigh, "Reflections on the Warsaw Pact," *The World Today*, 24 (April, 1968), 166–172; E. Hinterhoff, "The Czechoslovak Crisis and the Warsaw Pact," *NATO's Fifteen Nations*, 13 (October–November, 1968), 26–31; P. Terry Hopmann, "International Conflict and Cohesion in the Communist System," *International Studies Quarterly*, 11 (September, 1967), 212–236; and Bela K. Kiraly, "Why the Soviets Need the Warsaw Pact," *East Europe*, 18 (April, 1969), 8–18.

SINO-SOVIET RELATIONS

A significant number of works have dealt with Sino-Soviet relationships. In addition to many of the broader treatments of Communist relations that have been cited under Eastern Europe, see especially: A. Doak Barnett, *Communist China and Asia: Challenge to American Policy* (New York: Random House, 1960); David Floyd, *Mao Against Khrushchev: A Short History of the Sino-Soviet Conflict* (New York: Praeger, 1963); Raymond L. Garthoff, ed., *Sino-Soviet Military Relations* (New York: Praeger, 1966); John Gittings, ed., *Survey of the Sino-Soviet*

Dispute (London: Oxford, 1968); William E. Griffith, ed., *Sino-Soviet Relations: 1964–1965* (Cambridge, Mass.: MIT Press, 1967) and *The Sino-Soviet Rift* (Cambridge, Mass.: MIT Press, 1964); Morton H. Halperin, ed., *Sino-Soviet Relations and Arms Control* (Cambridge, Mass.: MIT Press, 1967); Harold Hinton, *Communist China in World Politics* (Boston: Houghton Mifflin, 1966); Geoffrey F. Hudson, ed., *The Sino-Soviet Dispute* (New York: Praeger, 1961); Kurt London, *Unity and Contradiction* (New York: Praeger, 1962); Richard Lowenthal, *World Communism: The Disintegration of a Secular Faith* (New York: Oxford, 1964); Clement J. Zablocki, *Sino-Soviet Rivalry* (New York: Praeger, 1966); and Donald S. Zagoria, *The Sino-Soviet Conflict, 1956–1961* (Princeton: Princeton University Press, 1962).

Shorter discussions include: A. Kashin, "The Geopolitical Aspect of the Sino-Soviet Conflict," *Bulletin for the Institute for the Study of the USSR,* 13 (January, 1966), 37–49; Thomas W. Robinson, "A National Interest Analysis of Sino-Soviet Relations," *International Studies Quarterly,* 11 (June, 1967), 135–175; and Thomas W. Wolfe, *The Soviet Union and the Sino-Soviet Dispute,* P-3203 (Santa Monica: The RAND Corporation, 1965).

ALLIANCE AGGREGATION AND THE ONSET OF WAR

General references for the study of alliance aggregation and the onset of war are: Theodore Abel, "The Element of Decision in the Pattern of War," *American Sociological Review,* 6 (December, 1941), 853–859; Claude Berge, *The Theory of Graphs* (London: Methuen, 1962); Gaston Bodart, *Losses of Life in Modern Wars* (Oxford: Clarendon, 1916); Robert N. Burr, "The Balance of Power in Nineteenth Century South America: An Exploratory Essay," *Hispanic American Historical Review,* 25 (February, 1955), 37–60; Inis L. Claude, Jr., *Power and International Relations* (New York: Random House, 1962); James Coleman, *Introduction to Mathematical Sociology* (New York: Free Press, 1964); Frank H. Denton, "Some Irregularities in International Conflict, 1820–1949," *Background,* 9, No. 4 (1966), 283–296; Karl W. Deutsch and J. David Singer, "Multipolar Power Systems and International Stability," *World Politics,* 16 (April, 1964), 390–406; S. Dumas and K. O. Vedel-Peterson, *Losses of Life Caused by War* (Oxford: Clarendon, 1923); Harry Eckstein, ed., *Internal War: Basic Problems and Approaches* (New York: Free Press, 1963); Richard Falk, "International Jurisdiction: Horizontal and Vertical Conceptions of Legal Order," *Temple Law Quarterly,* 32 (1959); Claude Flament, *Applications of Graph Theory to Group Structure* (Englewood Cliffs, N.J.: Prentice-Hall, 1963); Frederick H. Gareau, *The Balance of Power and Nuclear Deterrence: A Book of Readings* (Boston: Houghton Mifflin, 1962); Edward V. Gulick, *Europe's Classical Balance of Power* (Ithaca, N.Y.: Cornell University Press, 1955); Ernst B. Haas, "The Balance of Power: Prescription, Concept, or Propaganda," *World Politics,* 5 (1953), 442–477; Frank Harary, "A Structural Analysis of the Situation in the Middle East," *Journal of Conflict Resolution,* 5, No. 2 (1961), 167–178; Reginald Hargreaves, *The Enemy at the Gate: A Book of Famous Sieges, Their Causes, Their Progress, and Their Consequences* (Harrisburg, Pa.: Stackpole, 1948); Ole R. Holsti, Richard A. Brody and Robert C. North, *Theory and Measurement of Interstate Relations: An Application of Automated Content Analysis* (Stanford, Calif.: 1964, mimeo); William J. Horvath and Caxton C. Foster," Stochastic Models of War Alliances," *Journal of Conflict Resolution,* 7, No. 2 (1963), 110–116; Frank L. Klingberg, *Historical Study of War Casualties* (Washington, D.C.: War Department, 1945); William L. Langer, *European Alliances and Alignments, 1871–1890* (New York: Knopf, 1931); George Liska, *Nations in Alliance: The Limits of Interdependence* (Baltimore: Johns Hopkins Press, 1962); George Modelski, *The International Relations of Internal War* (Princeton, N.J.: Center of International Studies, 1961); W. E. Moore, "Predicting Discontinuities in Social Change," *American Sociological Review,* 29 (June, 1964), 331–338; Hans J. Morgenthau, *Politics Among Nations* (New York: Knopf, 1956); Anatol Rapoport, "Mathematical Models of Social Interaction," in R. Duncan Luce, Robert Bush and Eugene Galanter, eds., *Handbook of Mathematical Psychology,* Vol. 2 (New York: John Wiley, 1963), 494–579; Anatol Rapoport and W. J. Horvath, "A Study of a Large Sociogram," *Behavioral Science,* 6 (October, 1961), 279–291; Lewis F. Richardson, *Arms and Insecurity* and *Statistics of Deadly Quarrels* (Chicago: Quadrangle, 1960); Richard Rosecrance, *Action and Reaction in World Politics* (Boston: Little, Brown, 1962); James N. Rosenau, *International Aspects of Civil Strife* (Princeton, N.J.: Princeton University Press, 1964); J. David Singer and Melvin Small, "The Composition and Status Ordering of the International System, 1815–1940," *World Politics,* 18 (January, 1966), 236–282; "Formal Alliances, 1815–1939: A Quantitative Description," *Journal of Peace Research,* 3 (1966), 1–32; *International War, 1815–1965: A Statistical Handbook* (forthcoming); Paul A. Smoker, "Fear in the Arms Race: A Mathematical Study," *Journal of Peace Research,* 1 (1964), 55–63; Pitrim A. Sorokin, *Social and Cultural Dynamics,* Vol. 3 (New York: American Book, 1937); Boris T. Urlanis, *Volny i Narodonaselenie Evropy (Wars and the Population of Europe)* (Moscow: Government Publishing House, 1960); Kenneth N. Waltz, "The Stability of a Bipolar World, *Daedalus,* 93 (1964), 881–909; Herbert K. Weiss, "Stochastic Models for the Duration and Magnitude of a 'Deadly Quarrel,'" *Operations Research,* 11 (January–February, 1963), 101–121; Quincy Wright, *A Study of War,* 2 vols. (Chicago: University of Chicago Press, 1942); Dina A. Zinnes, "Testing a Balance of Power Theory," (Bloomington, Ind.: Indiana University, 1966, mimeo).

appendix II

Brief Chronologies

1948   Czechoslovakian coup.
      Berlin blockade.
1949   The North Atlantic Treaty is signed in Washington.
1950   South Korea is attacked.
      General Dwight D. Eisenhower is appointed Supreme Allied Commander in Europe.
1951   The North Atlantic Council becomes the sole ministerial body of NATO.
      The member countries sign an agreement on the status of their forces.
      Inauguration of the NATO Defense College in Paris.
1952   Greece and Turkey accede to the North Atlantic Treaty.
      At the Lisbon meeting the Council reorganizes the structure of the Alliance with permanent headquarters in Paris.
1954   The Paris Agreements are signed and the Federal Republic of Germany is invited to join NATO.
1955   First conference of NATO parliamentarians in Paris.
      The Council decides at a ministerial meeting to equip the Atlantic forces with atomic weapons.
1956   Hungary (Soviet intervention).
      Suez Canal (Anglo-French-Israeli intervention).

---

[1] Adapted from *NATO Handbook* (Brussels: NATO, 1967), pp. 32–33.

The Council approves the Report of the Committee of Three on non-military cooperation.

1957   Soviet Sputnik launched.

December meeting in Paris of the heads of government of the NATO countries.

1958   Khrushchev's Berlin proposals.

1961   Berlin Wall is erected.

The Soviet Union resumes nuclear testing.

1962   Cuban missile crisis.

Nassau meeting (Kennedy-Macmillan).

1965   The Council decides at a ministerial meeting to create a Special Committee of NATO Defense Ministers to study nuclear problems.

1966   President Charles de Gaulle announces in an *aide-mémoire* that France intends to withdraw from the military organization of NATO.

The Council, meeting in ministerial session in Brussels, decides to transfer NATO's European Military Headquarters as well as the Defense College from French territory. It also decides to abolish the Standing Group and to establish an integrated International Military Staff responsible to the Military Committee.

The Defense Planning Committee decides to move the Military Committee from Washington to Brussels.

Ministers, in session at Paris, establish two Nuclear Planning committees and decide to build a new permanent political headquarters at Brussels. France does not associate herself with the military decisions.

1967   The new SHAPE Headquarters are opened at Casteau in Belgium.

The inauguration in Brussels of the new headquarters of the North Atlantic Council, the Military Committee, and the International Secretariat.

ORGANIZATION OF AMERICAN STATES [2]

1947   Inter-American Treaty of Reciprocal Assistance (Rio Treaty) is signed.

1948   OAS Charter is drawn up.

American Declaration of the Rights and Duties of Man.

1950   OAS Program of Technical Cooperation is inaugurated.

1956   Presidents of the American republics meet in Panama City.

1960   Act of Bogotá sets forth measures for social improvement and economic development.

1961   Charter of Punta del Este launches the Alliance for Progress.

1962   OAS excludes the Castro government of Cuba.

[2] For additional information on OAS activities in support of the Rio Treaty, see pp. 94–96 above.

1965–1966 First OAS Inter-American Peace Force helps to end civil warfare in the Dominican Republic.
1967 Delegates sign the Protocol of Amendment to the Charter of the Organization of American States, revising the organization's institutions.

Barbados, Trinidad, and Tobago are admitted to membership.

SOUTHEAST ASIA

1951 United States-Philippines Defense Treaty.

ANZUS Pact.

Japanese-United States Peace Treaty and United States-Japanese Mutual Security Agreement.
1953 United States-Korean Defense Treaty.
1954 Geneva Conference on Korea and Indochina opens.

Fall of Dien Bien Phu.

Pakistan-United States Mutual Defense Assistance Agreement.

Truce agreements for Vietnam, Cambodia, and Laos are signed at Geneva.

SEATO is formed.

United States-Republic of China Defense Treaty.
1955 First meeting of SEATO Council of Ministers in Bangkok.
1957 Pote Sarasin (Thailand) is appointed first SEATO Secretary General.
1958 Communist China begins concentrated shelling of Quemoy.
1959 United States signs bilaterial defense agreements with Pakistan, Iran, and Turkey.

Laos requests United States assistance against North Vietnamese troops.
1961 The United Kingdom and the Soviet Union (co-chairmen of Geneva Conference) call for cease fire in Laos.

Cease fire is arranged in Laos.

Geneva Conference of 1961 on Laos opens.
1962 United States Military Command in Vietnam is established.

Thailand announces boycott of SEATO because of alleged United States favoritism to Cambodia in the Thailand-Cambodia dispute over a temple on their borders. Boycott ends on July 19.

Geneva Conference guarantees Laos neutrality, and Laos is removed from any protection by SEATO.
1964 The United States bombs North Vietnamese bases.

China explodes its first atomic bomb.
1965 President Lyndon Johnson's speech asking Congress for $1 billion for Southeast Asia regional development. The first installment of $89 million is approved June 14.

SEATO Operation Seahorse; France withdraws from the exercise.

Cambodia breaks off relations with the United States.

France withdraws its delegation from SEATO Military Planning Staff.

1967 Pakistan boycotts semiannual meeting of SEATO Military Advisers.

1968 Prime Minister Harold Wilson reports that Great Britain will withdraw all military forces east of Suez by the end of 1971.

Foreign Minister Husain of Pakistan, in a speech to the Pakistani National Assembly, reports that Pakistan is progressively disengaging itself from SEATO.

MIDDLE EAST

1944 Alexandria Protocol.

1945 Pact of the League of Arab States.

1950 Joint Defense and Economic Cooperation Treaty between the states of the Arab League is signed by Egypt, Lebanon, Saudi Arabia, Syria, and Yemen.

1951 Iraq signs Joint Defense and Economic Cooperation Treaty.

1952 Jordan signs Joint Defense and Economic Cooperation Treaty.

1953 Economic Council of Arab States is established.

1955 Pact of Mutual Cooperation is signed by Iran, Iraq, Pakistan, Turkey, and the United Kingdom.

1956 Suez crisis.

1958 Baghdad Pact headquarters is moved from Baghdad to Ankara.

1959 Bilateral Agreements of Cooperation between the United States and Iran, Pakistan, and Turkey.

Iraq withdraws from the Baghdad Pact, which is subsequently renamed the Central Treaty Organization.

1964 Summit Conference at Alexandria. Remainder of the Arab League states sign the Joint Defense and Economic Cooperation Treaty.

Arab "Common Market" Agreement is signed.

1967 Arab-Israeli War.

ORGANIZATION OF AFRICAN UNITY

1963 OAU Charter is agreed upon by representatives of thirty African states at Addis Ababa.

Special session of Council of Ministers to discuss Morocco-Algeria border dispute.

1964 Burundi appeals to OAU and UN to intervene in Rwanda-Burundi dispute; no direct action is taken by OAU.

Somalia-Ethiopia and Somalia-Kenya boundary disputes are noted by OAU; bilateral settlement is made outside OAU.

Special meeting of Council of Ministers approves "temporary" use of British troops to restore order after mutiny in Tanzanian army.

OAU meeting discusses use of French paratroops to restore

President Leon Mba after coup in Gabon, but no resolution is proposed. A Commission is created to "look into" the Rwanda refugee problem.

First ordinary session of OAU Assembly meets in Cairo. Headquarters site and Secretary General are chosen. Little interest is shown in Kwame Nkrumah's proposal for "union government for Africa."

Special session of Council of Ministers is called to discuss the worsening Congo crisis; disagreement divides OAU members.

Council of Ministers holds meeting at Addis Ababa and creates ad hoc commission to seek solution to Congo crisis.

Commission asserts that Congo crisis is being prolonged by foreign intervention and decides to send delegation to talk to President Lyndon Johnson in United States.

Belgian paratroops, conveyed in United States planes, land in Stanleyville, scatter CNL (rebel) forces, and turn over control to Leopoldville government forces. Action causes split among OAU members.

Special session of Council of Ministers held at the United Nations in New York; after heated debate a weak resolution is passed that "deplored recent events in Congo."

1965   Council of Ministers meets in Nairobi. OCAM group criticizes OAU Secretariat for taking too active role in Congo crisis; proposal of Defense Commission to create African peace force (national contingents are available to OAU) is disapproved.

Special session of Council of Ministers meets in Lagos to consider accusations by OCAM group that Ghana is aiding subversion in neighboring countries. Attempt to reconcile two rival liberation factions in Rhodesia is unsuccessful.

Regular meeting of Council of Ministers is held in Accra; some members of OCAM (entente) boycott meeting. Joseph Kasavubu attends on promise that OAU will not discuss Congo issue. The Secretary General reports organization has $2.5 million deficit (twenty-four nations failed to pay dues). African Liberation Committee (ALC) is criticized.

Unilateral declaration of independence by Rhodesia.

Special session of Council of Ministers is called to discuss Rhodesian problem. Failure to agree upon which faction to support causes split among OAU members.

1966   Seven nations walk out of Council of Ministers meeting in dispute over recognition of delegation from Ghana. Council fails to agree on size and use of OAU budget.

Assembly is also unable to agree on budget.

Council approves budget for ALC. Toure shuns conference. Lesotho and Botswana are admitted as new members.

1967   Council of Ministers meets in Cairo.

       Biafra attempts to break away from Nigeria; members of OAU are divided on stand to take.

       Assembly meets at Kinshasa and adopts pruned budget. Disagreement exists over OAU role concerning Nigeria, and attitude toward full-scale war between Arab states and Israel; creation of Committee of Military Advisers.

1968   Council of Ministers meets in Algeria.

       U Thant attends Assembly meeting and expresses opinion that OAU is most appropriate instrument for promoting peace in Nigeria. Nigeria insists on closed session to discuss war. Mauritius and Swaziland are admitted.

COMMUNIST WORLD

1949   The Soviet Union protests against formation of NATO.

       The People's Republic of China is proclaimed in Peking.

       The Soviet Union accredits its diplomatic mission in the "Soviet Occupied Zone" of Germany to full embassy status in the German Democratic Republic (GDR).

1950   Sino-Soviet Treaty of Alliance.

       Korean War begins.

1953   Riots in East Germany.

1954   Molotov draft of a collective security treaty for Europe.

       Soviet note asks admission of the Soviet Union to NATO.

       Agreements allowing German rearmament are drawn up; they are ratified April, 1955.

       NATO announces military reequipment of Germany.

1955   Warsaw Treaty signed in Warsaw.

       Austrian State Treaty is signed in Vienna obligating Moscow to evacuate its forces from Hungary and Rumania ninety days after signing.

1956   East German law establishes the National People's Army and the Ministry of Defense.

       Change in Polish party leadership.

       Hungarian rebellion is suppressed by Soviet army.

       Status of Forces Treaty: Soviet Union-Poland.

1957   Status of Forces Treaty: Soviet Union-East Germany.

       Status of Forces Treaty: Soviet Union-Rumania.

       Status of Forces Treaty: Soviet Union-Hungary.

1958   Soviet troops are withdrawn from Rumania. Status of Forces pact between Soviet Union and Rumania lapses.

       Concentrated shelling of Quemoy begins.

1961   Fourteenth COMECON session discontinues East German manufacture of four-engine turbo-jet fighter aircraft already in testing stage.

Berlin Wall is erected.

First publicly announced consultation of defense ministers of Warsaw Pact countries is held in Warsaw.

First joint maneuvers of several Warsaw Pact countries.

1964 Friendship, Collaboration, and Mutual Assistance Pact is signed between Soviet Union and East Germany.

Rumania reduces basic military service from twenty-four to sixteen months.

China explodes its first atomic bomb.

1965 Turkey becomes the first NATO member to accept Soviet economic aid—$150 million in credits.

1968 The Soviet Union intervenes militarily in Czechoslovakia.

appendix III
Treaty Abstracts

SOURCE: Committee on Foreign Affairs, U.S. House of Representatives, *Collective Defense Treaties*, 90th Cong., 1st Sess. (1967), pp. 5–14.

NORTH ATLANTIC TREATY ORGANIZATION (NATO)

Belgium, Canada, Denmark, Federal Republic of Germany, France, Greece, Iceland, Italy, Luxembourg, the Netherlands, Norway, Portugal, Turkey, the United Kingdom, and the United States.

The French government withdrew its forces committed to NATO commands and its personnel assigned to the staffs of those commands effective July 1, 1966, and has denounced the Paris Protocol on the Status of International Military Headquarters of August 28, 1952, effective March 31, 1967. In a preliminary *aide-mémoire*, delivered to its NATO allies on March 11, 1966, the French government made the following statement (in translation):

"This . . . does not by any means lead the French government to call into question the treaty signed at Washington on April 4, 1949. In other words, barring events in the coming years that might come to alter fundamentally the relations between the East and the West, it does not intend to avail itself, in 1969, of the provisions of Article 13 of the treaty and considers that the Alliance must continue as long as it appears necessary."

COLLECTIVE DEFENSE

"The Parties agree that an armed attack against one or more of them in Europe or North America shall be considered an attack against them all; and consequently they agree that, if such an armed attack occurs, each of them, in exercise of the right of individual or collective self-defense recognized by Article 51 of the Charter of the United Nations, will assist the Party or Parties so attacked by taking forthwith, individually and in concert with the other Parties, such action as it deems necessary, including the use of armed force, to restore and maintain the security of the North Atlantic area.

"Any such armed attack and all measures taken as a result thereof shall immediately be reported to the Security Council. Such measures shall be terminated when the Security Council has taken the measures necessary to restore and maintain international peace and security." (Article 5)

TREATY AREA

". . . an armed attack on one or more of the Parties is deemed to include an armed attack—

"(i) on the territory of any of the Parties in Europe or North America, on the Algerian Departments of France, on the territory of Turkey or on the islands under the jurisdiction of any of the Parties in the North Atlantic area north of the Tropic of Cancer;

"(ii) on the forces, vessels or aircraft of any of the Parties, when in or over these territories or any other area in Europe in which occupation forces of any of the Parties were stationed on the date when the Treaty entered into force or the Mediterranean Sea or the North Atlantic area north of the Tropic of Cancer." (Article 6, as modified by Article 2 of the protocol on the accession of Greece and Turkey.)

The *only outlying areas covered* are the islands in the North Atlantic area, the Aleutian Islands, and the islands of the Canadian Arctic. Alaska, as a part of the territory of the United States in North America, is covered. Greenland, as part of the Kingdom of Denmark, and the Bahamas and Bermuda as "islands under the jurisdiction of any of the parties in the North Atlantic area north of the Tropic of Cancer" are likewise covered by that Treaty.

The three Algerian departments of France were an integral part of metropolitan France under its constitution at the time that the North Atlantic Treaty was signed. However, Algeria became independent on July 3, 1962, and on January 16, 1963, the Council of NATO noted that insofar as the former Algerian departments of France are concerned, the relevant clauses of the North Atlantic Treaty had become inapplicable as of July 3, 1962.

The area, originally including the western part of the Mediterranean as well as the North Sea and most of the Gulf of Mexico, was broadened by the protocol on the accession of Greece and Turkey to include the forces, vessels, and aircraft of the parties in the eastern Mediterranean.

Also, the area was redefined by this protocol so that, if in the future occupation forces in Europe of any of the parties ceased to be occupation forces, e.g., in Germany, but were still on European soil, they would still be covered by the treaty in the event of an attack.

INTER-AMERICAN TREATY OF RECIPROCAL ASSISTANCE
(RIO TREATY)

PARTIES

Argentina, Barbados, Bolivia, Brazil, Chile, Colombia, Costa Rica, Cuba,[1] the Dominican Republic, Ecuador, El Salvador, Guatemala, Haiti, Honduras, Mexico, Nicaragua, Panama, Paraguay, Peru, Trinidad, Tobago, the United States, Uruguay, and Venezuela.

COLLECTIVE DEFENSE

"1. The High Contracting Parties agree that an armed attack by any State against an American State shall be considered as an attack against all the American States and, consequently, each one of the said Contracting Parties undertakes to assist in meeting the attack in the exercise of the inherent right of individual or collective self-defense recognized by Article 51 of the Charter of the United Nations.

"2. On the request of the State or States directly attacked and until the decision of the Organ of Consultation of the Inter-American System, each one of the Contracting Parties may determine the immediate measures which it may individually take in fulfillment of the obligation contained in the preceding paragraph and in accordance with the principle of continental solidarity. The Organ of Consultation shall meet without delay for the purpose of examining those measures and agreeing upon the measures of a collective character that should be taken.

"3. The provisions of this Article shall be applied in case of any armed attack which takes place within the region described in Article 4 or within the territory of an American State. When the attack takes place outside of the said areas, the provisions of Article 6 shall be applied.

"4. Measures of self-defense provided for under this Article may be taken until the Security Council of the United Nations has taken the measures necessary to maintain international peace and security." (Article 3)

✲ ✲ ✲ ✲ ✲

"If the inviolability or the integrity of the territory or the sovereignty or political independence of any American State should be affected by an aggression which is not an armed attack or by an extra-continental or intra-continental conflict, or by any other fact or situation that might

---

[1] The Organization of American States Foreign Ministers voted at Punta del Este (Jan. 22–31, 1962) to exclude "the present Government of Cuba" from participation in the Inter-American System.

endanger the peace of America, the Organ of Consultation shall meet immediately in order to agree on the measures which must be taken in case of aggression to assist the victim of the aggression or, in any case, the measures which should be taken for the common defense and for the maintenance of the peace and security of the Continent." (Article 6)

✼   ✼   ✼   ✼   ✼

"For the purposes of this Treaty, the measures on which the Organ of Consultation may agree will comprise one or more of the following: recall of chiefs of diplomatic missions; breaking of diplomatic relations; breaking of consular relations; partial or complete interruption of economic relations or of rail, sea, air, postal, telegraphic, telephonic, and radiotelephonic or radiotelegraphic communications; and use of armed force." (Article 8)

✼   ✼   ✼   ✼   ✼

"In addition to other acts which the Organ of Consultation may characterize as aggression, the following shall be considered as such:
"a. Unprovoked armed attack by a State against the territory, the people, or the land, sea or air forces of another State;
"b. Invasion, by the armed forces of a State, of the territory of an American State, through the trespassing of boundaries demarcated in accordance with a treaty, judicial decision, or arbitral award, or, in the absence of frontiers thus demarcated, invasion affecting a region which is under the effective jurisdiction of another State." (Article 9)

✼   ✼   ✼   ✼   ✼

"Decisions which require the application of the measures specified in Article 8 shall be binding upon all the Signatory States which have ratified this Treaty, with the sole exception that no State shall be required to use armed force without its consent." (Article 20)

TREATY AREA
"The region to which this Treaty refers is bounded as follows: beginning at the North Pole; thence due south to a point 74 degrees north latitude, 10 degrees west longitude; thence by a rhumb line to a point 47 degrees 30 minutes north latitude, 50 degrees west longitude; thence by a rhumb line to a point 35 degrees north latitude, 60 degrees west longitude; thence due south to a point in 20 degrees north latitude; thence by a rhumb line to a point 5 degrees north latitude, 24 degrees west longitude; thence due south to the South Pole; thence due north to a point 30 degrees south latitude, 90 degrees west longitude; thence by a rhumb line to a point on the Equator at 97 degrees west longitude; thence by a rhumb line to a point 15 degrees north latitude, 120 degrees west longi-

tude; thence by a rhumb line to a point 50 degrees north latitude, 170 degrees east longitude; thence due north to a point in 54 degrees north latitude; thence by a rhumb line to a point 65 degrees 30 minutes north latitude, 168 degrees 58 minutes 5 seconds west longitude; thence due north to the North Pole." (Article 4)

This description includes more than the land area of the parties to the treaty; it embraces both North and South America, including Canada, Greenland, the Arctic and Antarctic regions of the continents, as well as all the area lying between. In addition, the newly independent states of Jamaica, Trinidad and Tobago, Guyana, and Barbados fall within the defined region.

In addition to the region as defined, the treaty states that measures to be taken in the event of an armed attack thereon shall be applied if the armed attack is "within the territory of an American State" (par. 3, Art. 3). This includes more than the continental territory of the United States and of the other American states. It includes the State of Hawaii as well as the Island of Guam and any other possessions abroad, since they all constitute a part of the "territory of an American State." Canada, while not a signatory state, is included in the term "American State." Furthermore, if the armed attack is directed against an American State and takes place within the region described, it need not be against the territory of an American State but could take place anywhere within the region and might be against the land, sea, or air forces of such American State.

Honduras, at the time of the signing of the treaty, made a formal reservation concerning the boundary between itself and Nicaragua, which was included in the treaty. Guatemala, when it deposited its ratification, also made a formal reservation concerning the sovereignty of Belize (British Honduras); and upon Guatemala's declaration that the reservation did not intend to constitute any alteration of the treaty and that it was disposed to act within the limits of international agreements which it had accepted, the contracting states accepted the reservation.

In addition, Ecuador and Nicaragua included a statement and reservation, respectively, in their instruments of ratification; and as part of the Final Act of the Rio Conference where this treaty was drawn, Argentina, Guatemala, Mexico, and Chile made formal statements on historic rights and claims to areas within the treaty area. The United States also made the following formal statement there:

"With reference to the reservations made by other Delegations concerning territories located within the region defined in the Treaty, their boundaries, and questions of sovereignty over them, the Delegation of the United States of America wishes to record its position that the Treaty of Rio de Janeiro has no effect upon the sovereignty, national or international status of any of the territories included in the region defined in Article 4 of the Treaty."

SOUTHEAST ASIA COLLECTIVE DEFENSE TREATY
(SEATO)

PARTIES

Australia, France, New Zealand, Pakistan, the Republic of the Philippines, Thailand, the United Kingdom, and the United States. By a protocol signed on the same date as the treaty, the states of Cambodia, Laos, and Vietnam were designated for the purposes of Article IV, quoted below. Subsequently, Cambodia has indicated disinterest in the protection of the Southeast Asia Treaty. The Royal Government of Laos, in the Geneva Declaration on the Neutrality of Laos, signed July 23, 1962, declared that it will not "recognize the protection of any alliance or military coalition including SEATO" and the United States and other nations agreed to "respect the wish of the Kingdom of Laos not to recognize the protection of any alliance or military coalition, including SEATO."

COLLECTIVE DEFENSE

"1. Each Party recognizes that aggression by means of armed attack in the treaty area against any of the Parties or against any State or territory which the Parties by unanimous agreement may hereafter designate, would endanger its own peace and safety, and agrees that it will in that event act to meet the common danger in accordance with its constitutional processes. Measures taken under this paragraph shall be immediately reported to the Security Council of the United Nations.

"2. If, in the opinion of any of the Parties, the inviolability or the integrity of the territory or the sovereignty or political independence of any Party in the treaty area or of any other State or territory to which the provisions of paragraph 1 of this Article from time to time apply is threatened in any way other than by armed attack or is affected or threatened by any fact or situation which might endanger the peace of the area, the Parties shall consult immediately in order to agree on the measures which should be taken for the common defense.

"3. It is understood that no action on the territory of any State designated by unanimous agreement under paragraph 1 of this Article or on any territory so designated shall be taken except at the invitation or with the consent of the government concerned." (Article IV)

UNDERSTANDING OF THE UNITED STATES OF AMERICA
(INCLUDED IN THE TREATY)

"The United States of America in executing the present Treaty does so with the understanding that its recognition of the effect of aggression and armed attack and its agreement with reference thereto in Article IV, paragraph 1, apply only to communist aggression but affirms that in the event of other aggression or armed attack it will consult under the provisions of Article IV, paragraph 2."

TREATY AREA

"As used in this Treaty, the 'treaty area' is the general area of Southeast Asia, including also the entire territories of the Asian Parties, and the general area of the Southwest Pacific not including the Pacific area north of 21 degrees 30 minutes north latitude. The Parties may, by unanimous agreement, amend this Article to include within the treaty area the territory of any State acceding to this Treaty . . . or otherwise to change the treaty area." (Article VIII)

The basic area involved comprises Pakistan; Thailand; Laos, the free territory of Vietnam and Cambodia (by protocol); Malaysia; Australia and New Zealand; and the Philippines. (See above, under "Parties," concerning the present status of Cambodia and Laos.) Although the United Kingdom is a party, Hong Kong is excluded because of the limiting clause—"not including the Pacific area north of 21 degrees 30 minutes north latitude"—a line running north of the Philippines.

SECURITY TREATY BETWEEN AUSTRALIA, NEW ZEALAND, AND THE UNITED STATES (ANZUS)

PARTIES

Australia, New Zealand, and the United States.

COLLECTIVE DEFENSE

"Each Party recognizes that an armed attack in the Pacific Area on any of the Parties would be dangerous to its own peace and safety and declares that it would act to meet the common danger in accordance with its constitutional processes.

"Any such armed attack and all measures taken as a result thereof shall be immediately reported to the Security Council of the United Nations. Such measures shall be terminated when the Security Council has taken the measures necessary to restore and maintain international peace and security." (Article IV)

TREATY AREA

". . . an armed attack on any of the Parties is deemed to include an armed attack on the metropolitan territory of any of the Parties, or on the island territories under its jurisdiction in the Pacific or on its armed forces, public vessels or aircraft in the Pacific." (Article V)

PACT OF MUTUAL COOPERATION (BAGHDAD PACT, SUBSEQUENTLY REDESIGNATED CENTRAL TREATY ORGANIZATION [CENTO])

PARTIES

Iran, Pakistan, Turkey, and the United Kingdom. In addition, the United States actively participates on the basis of Bilateral Agreements of Cooperation that it signed with Iran, Pakistan, and Turkey in 1959.

COLLECTIVE DEFENSE

"Consistent with Article 51 of the United Nations Charter the High Contracting Parties will cooperate for their security and defense." (Article 1, Baghdad Pact)

"The members of the Baghdad Pact . . . conclude that the need which called the Pact into being is greater than ever. These members declare their determination to maintain their collective security and to resist aggression, direct or indirect. . . .

"Similarly, the United States, in the interest of world peace, and pursuant to existing Congressional authorization, agrees to cooperate with the nations making this Declaration for their security and defense, and will promptly enter into agreements designed to give effect to this cooperation. (Articles 1 and 4, Declaration Respecting the Baghdad Pact Between the United States of America and Iran, Pakistan, Turkey, and the United Kingdom)

"In case of aggression against Pakistan, the Government of the United States of America, in accordance with the Constitution of the United States of America, will take such appropriate action, including the use of armed forces, as may be mutually agreed upon and as is envisaged in the Joint Resolution to Promote Peace and Stability in the Middle East, in order to assist the Government of Pakistan at its request." (Article 1, Agreement of Cooperation Between the Government of the United States of America and the Government of Pakistan March 5, 1959. Two additional identical agreements were entered into between the United States and Iran and Turkey on the same date.)

JOINT DEFENSE AND ECONOMIC COOPERATION TREATY BETWEEN THE STATES OF THE ARAB LEAGUE

PARTIES

Algeria, Iraq, Jordan, Kuwait, Lebanon, Libya, Morocco, Saudi Arabia, Sudan, Syria, Tunisia, the United Arab Republic, and Yemen.

COLLECTIVE DEFENSE

"The Contracting States consider any (act of) armed aggression made against any one or more of them or their armed forces, to be directed against them all. Therefore, in accordance with the right of self-defense, individually and collectively, they undertake to go without delay to the aid of the State or States against which such an act of aggression is made, and immediately to take, individually and collectively, all steps available, including the use of armed force, to repel the aggression and restore security and peace. In conformity with Article 6 of the Arab League Pact and Article 51 of the United Nations Charter, the Arab League Council and the UN Security Council shall be notified of such act of aggression and the means and procedure taken to check it." (Article 2)

CHARTER OF THE ORGANIZATION OF AFRICAN UNITY (OAU)

PARTIES

Algeria, Botswana, Burundi, Cameroun, Central African Republic, Chad, Congo (Brazzaville), Congo (Leopoldville), Dahomey, Ethiopia, Equatorial Guinea, Gabon, Gambia, Ghana, Guinea, Ivory Coast, Kenya, Lesotho, Liberia, Libya, Madagascar, Malawi, Mali, Mauritania, Mauritius, Morocco, Niger, Nigeria, Rwanda, Senegal, Sierra Leone, Somalia, Sudan, Swaziland, Tanzania, Togo, Tunisia, Uganda, the United Arab Republic, the United Republic of Tanzania, Upper Volta, and Zambia.

COLLECTIVE DEFENSE

The charter is not so explicit as others concerning provisions for collective defense. Nevertheless, Article II states that: "1. The Organization shall have the following purposes: a. to promote the unity and solidarity of the African States . . . ; c. to defend their sovereignty, their territorial integrity and independence; d. to eradicate all forms of colonialism from Africa . . . 2. To these ends, the Member States shall coordinate and harmonize their general policies, especially in the following fields . . . ; f. cooperation for defense and security."

TREATY OF FRIENDSHIP, COOPERATION, AND MUTUAL ASSISTANCE (WARSAW PACT)

PARTIES

Albania, Bulgaria, Czechoslovakia, the German Democratic Republic, Hungary, Poland, Rumania, and the Union of Soviet Socialist Republics.

COLLECTIVE DEFENSE

"In the event of armed attack in Europe on one or more of the Parties to the Treaty by any state or group of states, each of the Parties to the Treaty, in the exercise of its right to individual or collective self-defense in accordance with Article 51 of the Charter of the United Nations Organization, shall immediately, either individually or in agreement with other Parties to the Treaty, come to the assistance of the state or states attacked with all such means as it deems necessary, including armed force. The Parties to the Treaty shall immediately consult concerning the necessary measures to be taken by them jointly in order to restore and maintain international peace and security.

"Measures taken on the basis of this Article shall be reported to the Security Council in conformity with the provisions of the Charter of the United Nations Organization. These measures shall be discontinued immediately the Security Council adopts the necessary measures to restore and maintain international peace and security." (Article 4)

TREATY OF FRIENDSHIP, ALLIANCE, AND MUTUAL ASSISTANCE (*SINO-SOVIET TREATY OF 1950*)

PARTIES

The People's Republic of China and the Union of Soviet Socialist Republics.

COLLECTIVE DEFENSE

"The Central People's Government of the People's Republic of China and the Presidium of the Supreme Soviet of the Union of Soviet Socialist Republics:

"Fully determined jointly to prevent, by strengthening friendship and cooperation between the People's Republic of China and the Union of Soviet Socialist Republics, the revival of Japanese imperialism and the resumption of aggression on the part of Japan or any other state that may collaborate in any way with Japan in acts of aggression;

"Imbued with the desire to consolidate lasting peace and universal security in the Far East and throughout the world in conformity with the aims and principles of the United Nations;

"Profoundly convinced that the consolidation of good neighborly relations and friendship between the People's Republic of China and the Union of Soviet Socialist Republics meets the vital interest of the peoples of China and the Soviet Union;

"Resolved toward this end to conclude the present Treaty and have appointed as their plenipotentiary representatives:

"Chou En-lai, Premier of the Government Administration Council and Minister of Foreign Affairs, acting for the Central People's Government of the People's Republic of China; and Andrei Yanauryevich Vyshinsky, Minister of Foreign Affairs of the U.S.S.R., acting for the Presidium of the Supreme Soviet of the Union of Soviet Socialist Republics.

"Both plenipotentiary representatives having communicated their full powers, and found them in good and due form, have agreed upon the following:

"ARTICLE I: Both High Contracting Parties undertake jointly to adopt all necessary measures at their disposal for the purpose of preventing the resumption of aggression and violation of peace on the part of Japan or any other state that may collaborate with Japan directly or indirectly in acts of aggression. In the event of one of the High Contracting Parties being attacked by Japan or any state allied with her, and thus being involved in a state of war, the other High Contracting Party shall immediately render military and other assistance by all means at its disposal.

"The High Contracting Parties also declare their readiness to participate in a spirit of sincere cooperation in all international actions aimed at ensuring peace and security throughout the world, and to contribute their full share to the earliest implementation of these tasks.

"ARTICLE II: Both High Contracting Parties undertake in a spirit of mutual agreement to bring about the earliest conclusion of a peace treaty with Japan, jointly with the other powers which were allies in the Second World War.

"ARTICLE III: Both High Contracting Parties undertake not to conclude any alliance directed against the other High Contracting Party, and not to take part in any coalition or in any actions or measures directed against the other High Contracting Party.

"ARTICLE IV: Both High Contracting Parties will consult with each other in regard to all important international problems affecting the common interests of China and the Soviet Union, being guided by the interests of consolidating peace and universal security.

"ARTICLE V: Both High Contracting Parties undertake, in a spirit of friendship and cooperation and in conformity with the principles of equality, mutual benefit, mutual respect for national sovereignty and territorial integrity, and noninterference in the internal affairs of the other High Contracting Party, to develop and consolidate economic and cultural ties between China and the Soviet Union, to render the other all possible economic assistance, and to carry out necessary economic cooperation.

"ARTICLE VI: The present Treaty shall come into force immediately after its ratification; the exchange of instruments of ratification shall take place in Peking.[1]

"The present Treaty shall be valid for thirty years. If neither of the High Contracting Parties gives notice a year before the expiration of this term of its intention to denounce the Treaty, it shall remain in force for another five years and shall be further extended in compliance with this provision.

"Done in Moscow on February 14, 1950, in two copies, each in the Chinese and Russian languages, both texts being equally valid."

[1] The treaty was separately but simultaneously ratified by both governments on April 11, 1950; the instruments of ratification were exchanged in Peking on September 30, 1950.

appendix IV
Organization Charts

SOURCES

NATO Handbook (Brussels: NATO, 1968), pp. 20, 21.

The Organization of American States (Washington, D.C.: Pan American Union, 1968), pp. iv, v, 20, 21.

The Story of SEATO (Bangkok: SEATO, undated), pp. 10, 11.

CENTO (Ankara: CENTO, undated), pp. 52, 53.

Robert W. Macdonald, *The League of Arab States* (Princeton: Princeton University Press, 1965, p. 47.

Boutros Boutros-Ghali, "The Addis Ababa Charter," *International Conciliation*, 546 (January, 1964), 24.

Committee on Government Operations, Subcommittee on National Security and International Operations, U.S. Senate, *The Warsaw Pact: Its Role in Soviet Bloc Affairs*, 89th Cong. 2d Sess. (1967), p. 9.

NORTH ATLANTIC TREATY ORGANIZATION

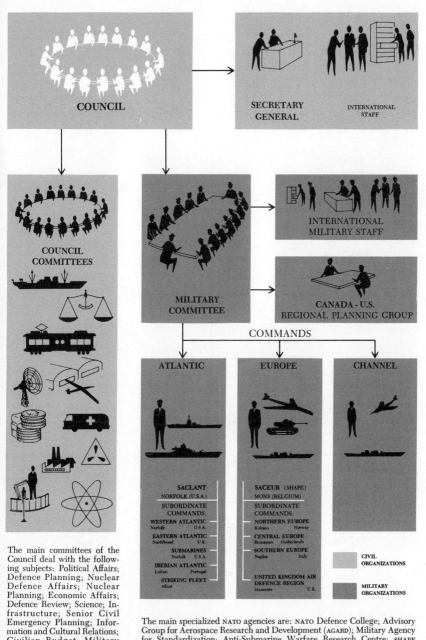

COUNCIL

SECRETARY GENERAL

INTERNATIONAL STAFF

COUNCIL COMMITTEES

MILITARY COMMITTEE

INTERNATIONAL MILITARY STAFF

CANADA - U.S. REGIONAL PLANNING GROUP

COMMANDS

ATLANTIC

EUROPE

CHANNEL

SACLANT
NORFOLK (U.S.A.)
SUBORDINATE COMMANDS:
WESTERN ATLANTIC
Norfolk   U.S.A.
EASTERN ATLANTIC
Northwood   U.K.
SUBMARINES
Norfolk   U.S.A.
IBERIAN ATLANTIC
Lisbon   Portugal
STRIKING FLEET
Afloat

SACEUR (SHAPE)
MONS (BELGIUM)
SUBORDINATE COMMANDS:
NORTHERN EUROPE
Kolsaas   Norway
CENTRAL EUROPE
Brunssum   Netherlands
SOUTHERN EUROPE
Naples   Italy
UNITED KINGDOM AIR DEFENCE REGION
Stanmore   U.K.

CIVIL ORGANIZATIONS

MILITARY ORGANIZATIONS

The main committees of the Council deal with the following subjects: Political Affairs; Defence Planning; Nuclear Defence Affairs; Nuclear Planning; Economic Affairs; Defence Review; Science; Infrastructure; Senior Civil Emergency Planning; Information and Cultural Relations; Civilian Budget; Military Budget; European Airspace Co-ordination; NATO Pipelines; etc.

The main specialized NATO agencies are: NATO Defence College; Advisory Group for Aerospace Research and Development (AGARD); Military Agency for Standardization; Anti-Submarine Warfare Research Centre; SHAPE Technical Centre; Allied Communications Agencies; Central Europe Operating Agency for Pipelines; NATO Air Defence Ground Environment Organization (NADGE); NATO Maintenance and Supply Agency; etc.

ORGANIZATION OF AMERICAN STATES

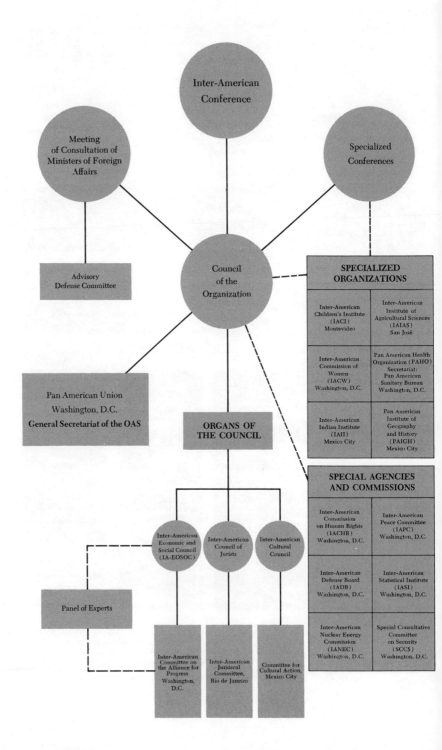

ORGANIZATION OF AMERICAN STATES

(The OAS as it will be when the "Protocol of Buenos Aires" is in effect.)

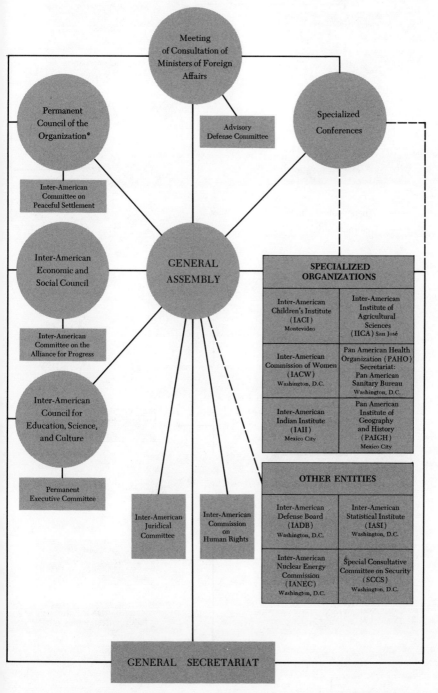

* Acts as the Preparatory Committee of the General Assembly unless the General Assembly should decide otherwise. October 1967.

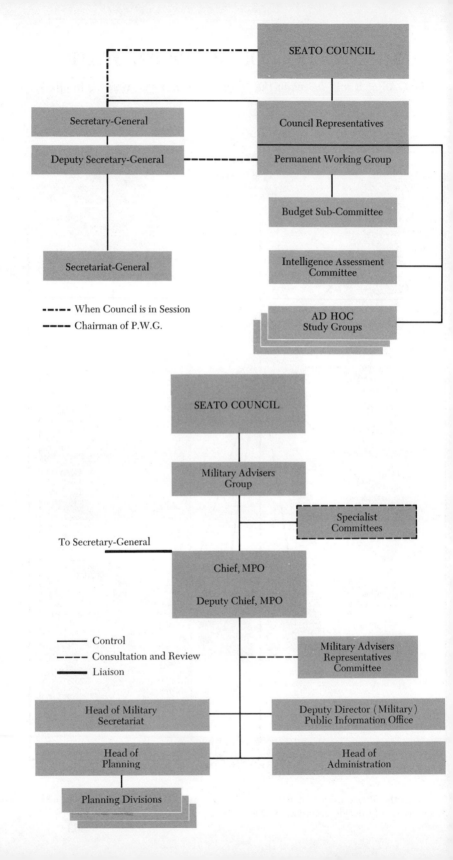

SEATO COUNCIL

Secretary-General

Deputy Secretary-General

Council Representatives

Permanent Working Group

Budget Sub-Committee

Intelligence Assessment Committee

Secretariat-General

AD HOC Study Groups

- - - - When Council is in Session
- - - - Chairman of P.W.G.

SEATO COUNCIL

Military Advisers Group

Specialist Committees

To Secretary-General

Chief, MPO

Deputy Chief, MPO

——— Control
- - - - Consultation and Review
——— Liaison

Military Advisers Representatives Committee

Head of Military Secretariat

Deputy Director (Military) Public Information Office

Head of Planning

Head of Administration

Planning Divisions

CENTRAL TREATY ORGANIZATION*

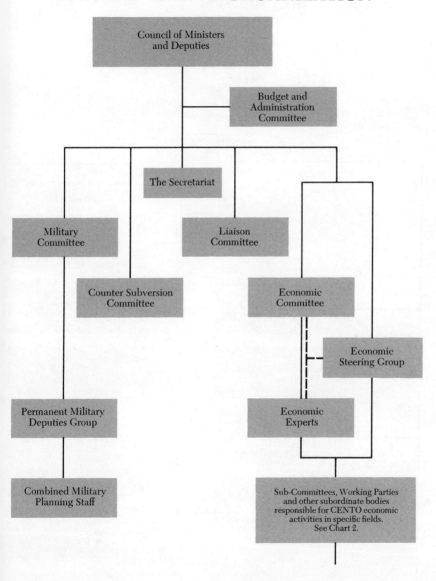

Council of Ministers and Deputies

Budget and Administration Committee

The Secretariat

Military Committee

Liaison Committee

Counter Subversion Committee

Economic Committee

Economic Steering Group

Permanent Military Deputies Group

Economic Experts

Combined Military Planning Staff

Sub-Committees, Working Parties and other subordinate bodies responsible for CENTO economic activities in specific fields. See Chart 2.

* Chart 1.

CENTRAL TREATY ORGANIZATION*

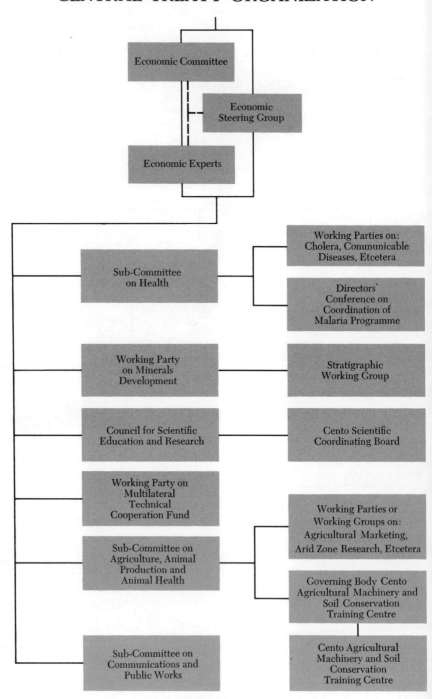

* Chart 2.

366

THE ARAB LEAGUE

COUNCIL OF THE LEAGUE OF ARAB STATES[a]

Composition: Delegations of member states, one vote per member state; permanent delegations/delegates.
Functions: Principal decision-making body of League.
Voting Rule: Unanimity required except as specified by League Pact.
Meetings: Two regular meetings each year, March and October; special meetings on request.

ECONOMIC COUNCIL[b]

Composition: Ministers of Economic Affairs from states adhering to 1950 Collective Security Treaty.
Function: Coordinate economic development programs & mobilize resources for regional security actions.
Voting Rule: Simple majority.
Meetings: Annual.

JOINT DEFENSE COUNCIL[b]

Composition: Ministers of Defense & Foreign Affairs from states adhering to 1950 Security Treaty.
Function: Coordinate Arab security affairs. Permanent Mil. Commission provides continuity.
Voting Rule: 2/3 majority.
Meetings: Annual; special sessions on request of one member state.

PERMANENT COMMITTEES[a]

Composition: Delegates of member states of Arab League plus observers from non-member states.
Function: Coordinate programs in areas of responsibility, prepare draft programs & recommendations for League Council.

Voting: Simple majority.
Meetings: Annual; interim actions coordinated by Secretariat Dept. concerned.

GENERAL SECRETARIAT[a]

Composition: Secretary General, Assistant Secretaries General, Departmental staffs, Special Agencies and Offices.
Function: Administration of League affairs; execution of decisions of League Councils and other organs.

[a] Provided by League Pact   [b] Added by Security Treaty of 1950

THE ORGANIZATION OF AFRICAN UNITY

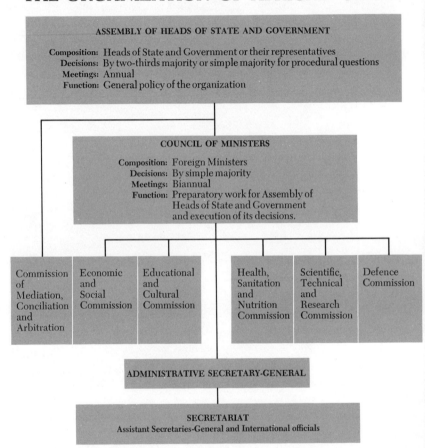

ASSEMBLY OF HEADS OF STATE AND GOVERNMENT

Composition: Heads of State and Government or their representatives
Decisions: By two-thirds majority or simple majority for procedural questions
Meetings: Annual
Function: General policy of the organization

COUNCIL OF MINISTERS

Composition: Foreign Ministers
Decisions: By simple majority
Meetings: Biannual
Function: Preparatory work for Assembly of Heads of State and Government and execution of its decisions.

| Commission of Mediation, Conciliation and Arbitration | Economic and Social Commission | Educational and Cultural Commission | Health, Sanitation and Nutrition Commission | Scientific, Technical and Research Commission | Defence Commission |

ADMINISTRATIVE SECRETARY-GENERAL

SECRETARIAT
Assistant Secretaries-General and International officials

THE WARSAW PACT:
WARSAW PACT STRUCTURE

POLITICAL CONSULTATIVE COMMITTEE
1. 1st Secretaries of Communist parties
2. Heads of Government and their assistants
3. Ministers of Foreign Affairs
4. Ministers of Defense or Armed Forces

PERMANENT COMMISSION
(Composition unknown; deals with recommendations concerning foreign policy questions)

JOINT SECRETARIAT
(Representatives of member states)

JOINT ARMED FORCES COMMAND
1. Commander-in-Chief
2. Ministers of Defense or other military leaders — Deputies — Commanders-in-Chief
3. General Staff

appendix V
Military Forces

SOURCES: The Institute for Strategic Studies, *The Military Balance* (London: Institute for Strategic Studies, 1962–1968), and *The Statesman's Yearbook* edited by S. H. Steinberg (New York: St. Martin's Press, 1962–1969).

MILITARY FORCE LEVELS, 1962-1968
(in thousands of men)

		Army	Air Force	Navy
ALBANIA	1962	25	1.5	3
	1963	25	7.2	2.8
	1964	30	5	2.8
	1965	30	5	3
	1966	30	6	3
	1967	30	5	3
	1968	30	5	3
ALGERIA	1965	60		
	1966	45		
	1967	45	2	1
	1968	55	2	1.5
ARGENTINA	1962		.3	22
	1963	75	.3	22
	1964	75	.3	33.8
	1965	80	.3	33.8
	1966		.3	33.8
	1967		15	33.8

AUSTRALIA	1962	21.6	16	11.1
	1963	22.7	16	12
	1964	23.4	16.1	12.5
	1965	37.5	17.7	14
	1966	34.6	19.5	15
	1967	43.3	20.5	16.5
	1968	45.4	21.7	17.2
AUSTRIA	1968	45	5	
BELGIUM	1962	85	20	5
	1963	85	19	5
	1964	85	20	5
	1965	83.5	19	4.5
	1966	83.5	19	4.5
	1967	76.4	20.9	4.7
	1968	75	20	4.0
BOLIVIA	1966	13.5	1.8	
	1967	20	1.5	
BOTSWANA	1966	.7		
	1967	.7		
BRAZIL	1962	200	30	42.7
	1963	200	30	42.7
	1964	200	30	42.7
	1965	200	30	42.7
	1966	120	30	53
	1967	120	30	53
BRITAIN	1962	170	145	100
	1963	189	138	96
	1964	190	134	100
	1965	208	132	100
	1966	218.2	122.2	97.2
	1967	215	120	94.3
	1968	210	121	96
BULGARIA	1962	100	15	5
	1963	110	20	5
	1964	125	20	5
	1965	125	20	7
	1966	125	24	7
	1967	125	22	7
	1968	125	22	6
BURMA	1968	125.0	6.5	6.0
BURUNDI	1963	1		
	1964	1		
	1965	1		

	1966	1		
	1967	1		
CAMBODIA	1963	27		1.1
	1964	27.3	1	1.3
	1965	28.5	1.5	1.4
	1966	34	2.5	1.5
	1967	34	2.5	1.4
	1968	45	2.5	1.5
CAMEROUN	1963	1.4		
	1964	1.4		
	1965	1.4		
	1966	3	.3	.2
	1967	3	.3	.2
CANADA	1962	50	52.5	21.7
	1963	50	52	22
	1964	49	50.6	20.7
	1965	49	50.6	20.7
	1966	44	45	18.1
	1967	42	44	17
	1968	41.5	43.5	16.6
CENT AF REP	1966	.5	.1	
	1967	.5	.1	
CHAD	1966	.7	.2	
	1967	.7	.2	
CHILE	1962	21.5	8	17
	1963	21.5	8	13.8
	1964	21.5	8	13.8
	1965	21.5		15
	1966	38	8	15
	1967	38	8	15
[1] CHINA	1962	2000	90	
	1963	2250	90	136
	1964	2250	90	136
	1965	2250	100	136
	1966	2250	100	136
	1967	2500	100	136
	1968	2500	120	141
COLOMBIA	1962	13.5		7.8
	1963	13.5		7.8
	1964	13.5		7.8
	1965	13.5		7.8
	1966	50		8
	1967	50	6	8

[1] People's Republic of China.

CONGO (B)	1966	1.4	.2	.2
	1967	1.4	.2	.2
CONGO (L)	1963	37		
	1964	37		
	1965	37		
	1966	30		
	1967	30	.2	
COSTA RICA	1962	1.2		
	1963	1.2		
	1964	1.2		
	1965	1.2		
	1966	1.2		
	1967	1.2		
CUBA	1962	80		
	1963	90		
	1964	90		
	1965	90	20	6
	1966	90	25	6
	1967	90	25	6
	1968	175	12	7
CZECHOSLOVAKIA	1962	150	35	
	1963	150	35	
	1964	200	35	
	1965	200	35	
	1966	175	45	
	1967	175	50	
	1968	175	50	
DAHOMEY	1966	1.7	.1	
	1967	1.7	.1	
DENMARK	1962	32	7.5	7
	1963	33.6	8.4	7
	1964	34	10	8
	1965	33	10	8
	1966	30	12.6	7.2
	1967	28	10.3	7.2
	1968	28	10.3	7.2
DOMINICAN REP	1962	12	3.5	3.5
	1963	12	3.5	3.5
	1964	12	3.5	3.5
	1965	12	3.5	3.8
	1966	12	3.5	4
	1967	12	3.5	4
EAST GERMANY	1962	65	9	11

	1963	90	15	11
	1964	80	15	15
	1965	80	15	17
	1966	85	20	17
	1967	85	25	17
	1968	85	25	16
ECUADOR	1962			3.7
	1963			3.7
	1964			3.7
	1965			3.7
	1966			4
	1967		3.5	4
EL SALVADOR	1966	4.5		
	1967	4.5		
ETHIOPIA	1963	28		
	1964	28		.7
	1965	28		.9
	1966	40	2.1	1.1
	1967	40	2.1	1.2
FINLAND	1968	31.4	3.0	2.0
FRANCE	1962	500	137	68
	1963	430	125	76
	1964	415	125	72.5
	1965	350	122.5	72.5
	1966	338	113	84
	1967	340	108	72
	1968	328	108	69
GABON	1966	.6		
	1967	.6	.1	
WEST GERMANY	1962	245	83	25
	1963	256	92	28
	1964	274	92	30
	1965	278	97	35
	1966	307	100	33
	1967	325	102	33
	1968	326	98	32
GHANA	1963	7		
	1964	7.5		
	1965	7		
	1966	14	1	1
	1967	14	1	1
GREECE	1962	120	22	17
	1963	120	22	19

	Year			
	1964	120	23	19
	1965	119	23.5	17.5
	1966	118	23	18
	1967	118	23	17
	1968	118	23	20
GUATEMALA	1962	7.5		
	1963	7.5		
	1964	7.5		
	1965	7.5		
	1966	7.5		
	1967	7.5	1	
GUINEA	1963	2		
	1964	2		
	1965	2		
	1966	4.8		
	1967	4.8		
HAITI	1962	5.2	.2	.3
	1963	5.2	.2	.3
	1964	5.2	.2	.3
	1965	4.9	.2	.3
	1966	4.9	.2	.3
	1967	4.9	.2	.3
HONDURAS	1962	2.5		
	1963	2.5		
	1964	2.5		
	1965	2.5		
	1966	2.5		
	1967	2.5	1.2	
HUNGARY	1962	75	5.5	
	1963	90	9	
	1964	95	9	
	1965	100	9	
	1966	100	9	
	1967	95	7	
	1968	95	7	
INDIA	1963	550	18	16
	1964	825	28	16
	1965	825	28	16
	1966	807	55	17
	1967	900	60	17
	1968	950	58	25
INDONESIA	1963	200	20	26
	1964	200	57	35

	1965	200	22	40
	1966	290	22	40
	1967	290	22	40
	1968	275	25	40
IRAN	1962	208	7.5	1
	1963	200	7	1
	1964	200	7	1
	1965	164	10	6
	1966	164	10	6
	1967	164	10	6
	1968	200	15	6
IRAQ	1967	70	10	2
	1968	70	10	2
ISRAEL	1964		14	
	1965	60	8	3
	1966	60	8	3
	1967	60	8	3
	1968	29	8	3
ITALY	1962	370	60	40
	1963	380	60	40
	1964	380	60	40
	1965	292	60	38
	1966	270	66	40
	1967	310	66	40
	1968	265	60	40
IVORY COAST	1966	3.5	.3	
	1967	3.5	.3	
JAPAN	1962	171.5	39	24.5
	1963	171.5	44	34
	1964	171.5	39	35
	1965	172	39	35
	1966	171.5	39.5	35
	1967	171.5	39.5	35
	1968	174	40	36
JORDAN	1967	30	1.8	.3
	1968	53	1.8	.3
KENYA	1967	4.2		
2 LAOS	1964	50		
	1965	50		
	1966	58	1.0	.5
	1967	65	1.5	.5
	1968	60	1.5	.4
LEBANON	1963	10	.6	.2

[2] Laos, central government.

	1964	10	.6	.2
	1965	10	.6	
	1966	12	.6	.2
	1967	10	.6	.2
LESOTHO	1966	.8		
LIBERIA	1965	5		
	1966	6		
	1967	5	.2	.1
LIBYA	1963	5		
	1964	5		
	1965	5		
	1966	6		
	1967	6		
LUXEMBOURG	1962	5.5		
	1963	5.5		
	1964	5.5		
	1965	5.5		
	1966	1.5		
	1967	.8		
	1968	.6		
MALAGASY REP	1966	3.5	.4	
	1967	3.5	.4	
MALAWI	1965	1.5		
	1966	.9		
	1967	1.1		
MALAYSIA	1964	19		2.1
	1965	25	1.5	2.1
	1966	26	2	2.1
	1967	27.6	2.6	3
	1968	28	3	2.8
MALI	1967	3.5		
MAURITANIA	1966	.5	.1	
	1967	.5	.1	
MAURITIUS	1963	1.4		.1
	1964	1.5		.1
	1965	1.5		.1
	1966	1.7		.1
MEXICO	1962		3.6	6.2
	1963	51	3.6	6.2
	1964	51	5	
	1965	51	5	11
	1966	51	5	11.1
	1967	51	5	11

MONGOLIA	1967	17	.5	
	1968	17	.5	
MOROCCO	1962	40		
	1963	40		
	1964	40		
	1965	20		
	1966	42		
	1967	42	2	.8
	1968	50	3	1
NETHERLANDS	1962	98	20	23
	1963	98	21	22
	1964	80	21.5	22
	1965	92	21.5	22
	1966	85	23	21.3
	1967	85	24	21
	1968	83.5	23.5	21.5
NEW ZEALAND	1962	4.9	4.4	2.9
	1963	5	4.1	2.9
	1964	5.6	4.0	2.9
	1965	5.4	4.5	3
	1966	5.6	4.4	2.9
	1967	5.6	4.3	2.9
	1968	5.8	4.5	2.9
NICARAGUA	1962	5.4		
	1963	5.4		
	1964	5.4		
	1965	5.4		
	1966	5.4		
	1967	5.4	1.5	
NIGER	1966	1.1	.1	
	1967	1.1	.1	
NIGERIA	1963	7		.9
	1964	7		.9
	1965	7		.9
	1966	9		.9
	1967	9	2	1.3
NORTH KOREA	1963	280	30	
	1964	325	20	7
	1965	325	20	8.8
	1966	340	20	8
	1967	340	20	8
	1968	345	30	9
NORTH VIETNAM	1964	250		2.5

	1965	240		2.5
	1966	250	3.5	2.7
	1967	410	4.5	3.5
	1968	440	4.5	2.5
NORWAY	1962	18	10	5.5
	1963	18	10	8
	1964	18	10	9
	1965	16	8.8	7.4
	1966	17	9	8
	1967	18	9	8
	1968	19	9	7
PAKISTAN	1962	230	15	7.7
	1963	230	15	7.7
	1964	230	20	7.7
	1965	180		
	1966	250	20	8.3
	1967	300	14	9
	1968	300	15	9
PANAMA	1962	3.4		
	1963	3.4		
	1964	3.4		
	1965		3.9	
	1966		3.9	
	1967		4.7	
PARAGUAY	1965			1.9
	1966			1.9
	1967		.8	1.9
PERU	1962	30		6.6
	1963	30		6.6
	1964	30		7.2
	1965	30		7.2
	1966	35.5		7.2
	1967	35.5	9	7.2
PHILIPPINES	1962	22	6.3	4
	1963	20	6	4
	1964	25.5	9.5	6.5
	1965	25.5	7	4
	1966	25.5	7.0	5.0
	1967	17	8	5.0
	1968	15.5	9	5.5
POLAND	1962	200	45	12
	1963	200	45	12
	1964	215	45	12

	1965	215	45	17
	1966	185	60	15
	1967	185	70	15
	1968	185	70	19
PORTUGAL	1962	58	12.5	9.8
	1963	94	12.5	11.2
	1964	94	14	14.5
	1965	134	13.5	14.5
	1966	134	13.5	14.5
	1967	120	13.5	15
	1968	150	17.5	15
RUMANIA	1962	200	15	7
	1963	200	20	7
	1964	200	15	7
	1965	175	15	8
	1966	175	18	8
	1967	150	15	8
	1968	150	15	8
RWANDA	1963	1		
	1964	1		
	1965	2.5		
	1966	2.5		
	1967	2.5		
SAUDI ARABIA	1967	30	5	1
	1968	30	5	1
SENEGAL	1966	5	.3	
	1967	5	.3	
SIERRA LEONE	1963	2.3		
	1964	2.3		
	1966	1.3		
	1967	1.3		
SINGAPORE	1967	2		
	1968	4.5		
SOMALI REP	1963	5		
	1964	5		
	1965	5		
	1966	10		
	1967	10	1.5	.1
SOUTH AFRICA	1965	19	4	3.5
	1966	16.2	3	3
	1968	28	7.7	2.5
SOUTH KOREA	1962	570	15	17
	1963	570	15	42

	1964	560	15	44
	1965	550	20	44
	1966	500	25	46•6
	1967	540	25	47
	1968	550	23	47
SOUTH VIETNAM	1963	200		10
	1964	210	20	15•4
	1965	280	10	15•4
	1966	275	14	15
	1967	285	16	24
	1968	370	16	24
SOVIET UNION	1962	2500	600	500
	1963	2300	500	500
	1964	2200	510	460
	1965	2000	510	450
	1966	2000	500	465
	1967	2000	505	465
	1968	2000	505	465
SPAIN	1965	248	38	44
	1966	212	37	42
	1967	200	35	40
	1968	225	38	42
SUDAN	1962	5		
	1963	5		
	1964	5		
	1965	16		
	1966	17		
	1967	17•5	•4	•5
SWAZILAND	1963	•4		
	1964	•4		
	1965	•6		
SWEDEN	1963	55	13	12
	1964	55	13•0	12
	1965	62	23•7	19•1
	1966	47	23•7	11•5
	1968	50	24	11.6
SWITZERLAND	1963	16•5	12	
	1964	35•5	12	
	1965	35•5	6•6	
	1966	1	5	
	1968	1	7	
SYRIA	1967	50	9	1•5
	1968	50	9	1•5

TAIWAN	1962	400	110	62
	1963	400	82	62
	1964	400	82	62
	1965	380	82	62
	1966	400	82	62
	1967	400	85	62
	1968	372	85	71
TANZANIA	1965		.4	
	1966	1.7	.4	
	1967	1.7	.4	
THAILAND	1962	90	22	22
	1963	90	22	22
	1964	50	13	21.5
	1965	85	20	26.5
	1966	85	20	21
	1967	85	20	21
	1968	95	25	22
TOGO	1966	1.2		
	1967	1.5		
TUNISIA	1957	6		
	1958	6		
	1960	20		
	1965	15		
	1966	17		
	1967	16	.5	.5
TURKEY	1962	400	20	35
	1963	400	20	32
	1964	400	43	37
	1965	360	45	37
	1966	360	53	37
	1967	390	53	37
	1968	425	50	39
UAR	1964	100	20	10
	1965	150	13	11
	1966	160	15	11
	1967	140	15	11
	1968	180	15	12
UGANDA	1966	5.7		
	1967	5.7		
UNITED STATES	1962	1080	885	850
	1963	975	865	855
	1964	972	840	858.5
	1965	963	829	867

	1966	1200	887.3	1006.6
	1967	1470	900	1030
	1968	1535	900	1065
UPPER VOLTA	1966	1.2		
	1967	1.2		
URUGUAY	1962			1.9
	1963			1.9
	1964			1.9
	1965			1.9
	1966	12		1.9
	1967	12		
VENEZUELA	1962	15		5.7
	1963	15		5.7
	1964	15		5.7
	1965	15		5.7
	1966	18	3.5	5.7
	1967	18	9	5.7
YUGOSLAVIA	1963	250	24	30
	1964	230	20	27
	1965	200	20	27
	1966	220	20	24
	1968	180	20	20
ZAMBIA	1964	6.2		
	1965	2.2	.3	
	1966	3	.3	
	1967	3	.3	